OXFORD MODERN LANGUAGES
AND LITERATURE MONOGRAPHS

THE
HISTORICAL EPIC
IN FRANCE

1500–1700

BY

DAVID MASKELL

OXFORD UNIVERSITY PRESS
1973

Oxford University Press, Ely House, London W.1

GLASGOW NEW YORK TORONTO MELBOURNE WELLINGTON
CAPE TOWN IBADAN NAIROBI DAR ES SALAAM LUSAKA ADDIS ABABA
DELHI BOMBAY CALCUTTA MADRAS KARACHI LAHORE DACCA
KUALA LUMPUR SINGAPORE HONG KONG TOKYO

ISBN 0 19 815525 5

ⓒ OXFORD UNIVERSITY PRESS 1973

Reproduced and printed by photolithography and bound in
Great Britain at The Pitman Press, Bath

TYPESETTING BY LINOCOMP LTD.
CHURCH STREET, MARCHAM, BERKS

PREFACE

SOME subjects require no apology: fashion renders them
acceptable. Epic poetry in France in the sixteenth and seventeenth centuries is not such a subject. The usual reaction to
Ronsard's *Franciade*, or to the epics of Chapelain, Desmarets,
or Scudéry, is dismay. Like other unfashionable literary works,
these epics have become the targets for the same repetitive
judgements, handed on from critic to critic. Whenever the literary history of this period is written, the epics appear like unwelcome guests at a banquet, and, like unwelcome guests, once
their presence is acknowledged, they receive no further attention. To remedy this is the purpose of this book.

A hundred years ago Duchesne surveyed the general field of
seventeenth-century epic; thirty years later, Toinet's copious
bibliography of epic poetry was confined to the same century;
Dr. Sayce's tudy of the Biblical epic, though it contains a
chapter on the sixteenth century, also deals mainly with the
later period. No one has yet studied the historical epic in both
the sixteenth and seventeenth centuries: in attempting the
task, I am conscious of my debt to the bibliographical
researches and literary studies of many earlier scholars.

My first chapter distinguishes different kinds of epic, and
offers a brief chronological survey of the historical epics
treated in this book. In the remaining chapters or Part I, I have
been guided by the poets themselves, who, in their prefaces,
invite us to consider the epic genre from a theoretical point of
view, invite us to look back to the models they emulate, invite
us to reflect on the history they recount. Chapter II therefore,
deals with the theory of epic—very briefly, since much has
been written on it elsewhere. Chapter III deals with the epic
models, and Chapter IV with the historical sources which the
poets drew on. I have compared the respective roles of the epic
poet and the historian, since this was a topic close to the poets'
hearts.

These epics were meant to be read from beginning to end.
In Part II I have tried to give an impression of what it is like
to do so. Each epic is considered on its own merits, and its

peculiar characteristics emphasized. The heroic epics, being the most numerous, occupy Chapters IV to X; the method of arrangement here is a compromise between chronological order of composition, and grouping according to subject-matter Romanesque and annalistic epic are discussed in Chapters XI and XII.

The epic poets also invite comparison with each other; this I have tried to do in Part III. Epic themes, the structure of epic, the use of topoi, and the style of epic, are the subjects of the last three chapters. Epic has many facets: I have tried to look at it from many points of view.

For assistance during my researches I should like to thank the librarians and staff of the British Museum, Bodleian Library, Taylorian Institution, Cambridge University Library, Bibliothèque Nationale, Bibliothèque de l'Arsenal, Bibliothèque Mazarine, Bibliothèque d l'Ecole Normale Supérieure, Bibliothèque Sainte-Geneviève, Bibliothèque Municipale de Versailles, Musée Condé, Chantilly, Archivio di Stato, Turin, and Biblioteca Nazionale, Turin.

For money to carry out this research I would like to thank the following: the Ministry of Education and its successors; the Curators of the Taylorian Institution, Oxford, for a Zaharoff Travelling Scholarship, which enabled me to work in Paris; the Research Committee of the University of Newcastle upon Tyne for a grant towards further work in Paris.

It is a pleasure to acknowledge my debt to Dr. R. A. Sayce, who supervised the thesis on which this book is based, and who has been unfailingly generous in his advice and encouragement. I should also like to thank Professor I. D. McFarlane for many valuable suggestions about sixteenth-century epic. I am most grateful to Professor P. J. Yarrow and to Dr. N. E. Ratcliffe for reading the entire typescript and suggesting many improvements; to Professor J. Levine for his help on Renaissance historiography; and to many other friends and colleagues who have given assistance. For the final result, responsibility is, of course, mine.

DAVID MASKELL

Newcastle upon Tyne
1972.

CONTENTS

PART III: THE GENRE

ABBREVIATIONS

BOOKS AND PERIODICALS

BHR	*Bibliothèque d'humanisme et renaissance*
DBF	*Dictionnaire de biographie française*
MLN	*Modern Language Notes*
MLR	*Modern Language Review*
RHLF	*Revue d'histoire littéraire de la France*

LIBRARIES

ARS	*Bibliothèque de l'Arsenal*
BM	*British Museum*
BN	*Bibliothèque Nationale, Paris*
BOD	*Bodleian Library, Oxford*
CHA	*Musée Condé, Chantilly*
CUL	*Cambridge University Library*
ENS	*Bibliothèque de l'Ecole Normale Supérieure, Paris*
MAZ	*Bibliothèque Mazarine*
TAY	*Library of the Taylorian Institution, Oxford*
TUR	*Archivio di Stato, Turin*

Full titles of works referred to in abbreviated form in the foot-notes are given in the Bibliography, which also indicates which editions quotations are taken from. Quotations reproduce the spelling and punctuation of the edition cited, except that occasional misprints have been corrected.

PART I
BACKGROUND

I

DEVELOPMENT

Personarum illustrium illustres actiones
illustri narrans oratione

(Vossius)

The epic genre

IT is easier to sum up the aspirations of epic poets in the six-teenth and seventeenth centuries, than to contrive a definition by which one poem may be called an epic, another not.[1] In France the professed aim of would-be poets was to produce a poem in Latin or French which would rival or outshine the epics of Homer and Virgil. To the ancient[2] models were added, when it appeared, Tasso's *Gerusalemme liberata*, and, with less un-animity, the poems of Ariosto or of other modern writers, amongst whom we must include Ronsard, whose *Franciade* was considered by his admirers, if not by posterity, to be the authentic example of a French epic poem.

Into an epic structure fashioned from the topoi which these diverse sources provided, was fitted an abundance of material, which defies neat classification. The epic poet could take his subject from sacred or profane history or from his imagination: the result might be encyclopedic, didactic, satiric, pastoral, or laudatory.

The Biblical epic has already received full and sympathetic treatment from Dr. Sayce, the first twentieth-century scholar to study French epic of this period as a genre in its own right. He set out not to rehabilitate Biblical epic but to show how it 'touches the seventeenth-century attitude to the relationships between religion, literature, and art'.[3] My purpose here is similar: to assess the aims and achievements of writers of historical epic in the sixteenth and seventeenth centuries and through their poems to explore the relationships between history and epic in the period. By 'historical epic' I mean epic based on history, even where, as in the *Franciade*, history dis-solves into legend. I take as history what was narrated by his-torians or what were in some cases contemporary events. This

criterion brings together the major epics not treated by Sayce:
the *Franciade, La Pucelle, Alaric, Clovis,* and *Saint Louis.*[4]
Biblical and historical epics do not exhaust the epic field.
There remain fictitious, pastoral, and hagiographical epics,[5] as
well as a mass of other poems of epic inspiration related to the
genre. Eulogies of towns and countries were popular in the
sixteenth century.[6] These 'laudes' were themselves a topos of
epic poetry.[7] Wars, campaigns, or battles were often chronicled
in verse, likewise the deeds of kings.[8] A lament on the state of
the country[9] or the assassination of a king[10] could be decked out
with the devices of epic. The frontiers of epic are ill defined;
I have confined myself to poems which by their length or projected length were intended to rival Homer or Virgil.[11]

Influences on the structure of epic

The epic genre has been introduced as a structure made up
of conventional topoi. This view of it is no more superficial
than that of the practitioners of the genre, who were concerned
above all with the external appearance of ancient epic. There
was little attempt to extract and recreate the essence of epic—
whatever the essence of epic might be—for though the theorists
did make some effort to define the purpose of epic, it was never
suggested that this purpose could be achieved otherwise than
in accordance with the precepts concerning externals which
formed the main bulk of their treatises. One must not, however,
exaggerate the uniformity of the structure of epic nor the influence of the theorists. Epic provided enough topoi for the
structure to be variable and the major theoretical works were
published after the most important epics had been composed.
Indeed the inconsistency between theory and practice is strikingly exemplified by Deimier, Delaudun, or Le Moyne, who
wrote theoretical works and epics, but whose achievement in
their poems is quite other than the often admirable principles
outlined in their treatises. Yet there was in practice a considerable body of topoi believed to be essential to the epic genre.

The revival of any ancient genre is a process by which the
characteristics of that genre are isolated and formed into a new
structure, which is then modified by contemporary influences
on the writers and by the material which they fit into that
structure. The success or failure of the genre depends on the

nature of the material and on the response of the writers to the challenge of contemporary influences. The main influences on the writers of epic were noble patronage and the demands of the Christian religion.

Patronage was, of course, a factor in any literary production of the time but it had profound effects on the matter and tone of epics, because the need to glorify the patron's ancestors governed the choice and presentation of the historical material. Glorification of ancestors remained the most important constant in epics throughout the period, though not every poet was necessarily overwhelmed by its effects. It did mean that epic was above all a means of flattery and explains the large number of abortive epics which seem to have been started for the purpose of self-advertisement rather than as serious attempts to rival Homer or Virgil. Even when the motive was more profound, the necessity of pleasing a man who had a vested interest in the *status quo* would discourage ideas that threatened the established order, and, if the patron's tastes were conventional, the poet had little to gain from daring literary innovation. The tie between patron and client obliged poets not to neglect the dynastic and genealogical aspects of epic, and the demands of the patron might even extend to such matters as metre, if we are to believe Ronsard that Charles IX insisted on the decasyllable in the *Franciade*.

The other influence was Christianity, and in the end only Christian subjects were acceptable for historical epic. The poet's attitude to religion might be the conventional orthodoxy of Chapelain, the polemical fervour of Sébastien Garnier, or the obsessive fanaticism of Desmarets, but all were agreed that the ancient and pagan apparatus of epic must be adapted to the requirements of the Christian religion. Herein lay a source of tension similar to that which may be observed in the Biblical poets' attitude to the Old Testament.[12] Le Moyne indeed chose historical epic precisely because he believed that the Bible was too sacred to be the subject of epic[13] but for him the epic still had to be Christian in content. The tension between Christianity and Antiquity might be resolved by Tasso, but it could be a treacherous foundation for lesser men,[14] and when the poets of the mid-seventeenth century realized that Tasso had successfully solved the problems that confronted them, they ceased to look further afield, and gratefully accepted Tasso's solution.

Important though Christianity was for writers of historical epic, there was little attempt to demonstrate its doctrines,[15] and the religious preoccupations are less interesting for their own sake than for their influence on the poets' treatment of history. History was the material which had to be fitted into the epic structure, a structure derived from the models of Antiquity and influenced by the pressures of patronage and Christianity. History was, of course, also a literary genre in its own right, which developed its own conventions during the two centuries under consideration. We shall have occasion to observe the similarities and differences between the two genres both developing simultaneously. That neither genre attained greatness does not invalidate the investigation: the very deficiencies of second- or third-rate writers can illuminate the process of literary creation and afford a clearer picture of the literary climate in which they worked.[16]

Categories of historical epic

Historical epic can be divided into three categories, not to be considered as rigid compartments but as a convenient method of grouping poems of similar inspiration but widely different in their final form. The three categories we shall call annalistic, heroic, and romanesque. Annalistic epic narrates a sequence of events, usually the careers of kings, to which unity is given by the people or nation over whom they rule. Heroic epic,[17] the most important, is given greater unity by the career of a single hero, to whom other characters and episodes are more or less successfully subordinated. Romanesque epic is often nominally unified by a single hero, but contains so much episodic, fantastic, or chivalric material that unity of action is destroyed.

Repeating the caution against rigid classification, one might sum up the objectives of these types of epic as follows: the annalistic usually seeks to inform and to moralize; the heroic to instruct and glorify; the romanesque simply to entertain. Under these three headings the historical epics will be analysed in detail. The categories obviously overlap but on balance they help to explain the disparate achievements of poets who apparently started from the same principles.

Periods of development

The grouping of the epics[18] according to their literary characteristics entails some sacrifice of chronological perspective. The
following summary is intended to remedy this and at the same
time to provide a brief survey of the whole field of historical
epic in this period.

1500–1550 RONSARD'S PREDECESSORS

The categories just outlined are perhaps least applicable to
epics composed before Ronsard's *Franciade*, all of which were
in Latin. The monastery of Saint Dié in Lorraine produced two
epic poets whose poems are essentially heroic, but with annalistic tendencies, since the writers conceived their task as the
recording of historical events for posterity. Blarru's *Nanceid*
(1518) describes the victory of René, Duke of Lorraine, over
Charles, Duke of Burgundy, at the siege of Nancy in 1477.
Pillard's *Rusticiad* (1541) describes the suppression of the
Peasant Revolt by Antoine, Duke of Lorraine in 1525.

The *De gestis Joannae virginis* (1516) of Valerand de
Varanne is also heroic in tone. The emphasis is less on Joan
of Arc, the national heroine, whom Chapelain was later to
depict, than on Saint Joan, the victim of English treachery,
triumphantly vindicated after the second inquiry.

The only sign of a possible epic in French is Marot's promise
to the Duc d'Enghien in 1544, but the poet died two months
later.[19]

1550—1572 RONSARD

It would be fair to describe Ronsard's predecessors as poets
who embellished historical narratives with the trappings of
epic, whereas Ronsard, alone of epic poets in these two centuries, tried to distil the essence of epic from its ancient sources.
He chose to write in French not Latin, but there were no
vernacular models to guide him. Nor was there a coherent body
of theoretical writings to mould his conception of epic. It was
Ronsard's own prestige, and his publicly declared intention of
endowing France with an epic, which dominated the epic scene
until the publication of the *Franciade*; and the *Franciade*, for
half a century afterwards, continued to exercise the greatest
influence on epic composition, even if many of the poets mis-

understood the nature of Ronsard's achievement. Because of Ronsard's original and independent approach to epic and because of his enduring reputation, the *Franciade* must be seen as the focal point of sixteenth-century epic in France.

What were the characteristics of Ronsard's epic which so shaped the epics of his successors? The *Franciade* was in French; it was indebted to Virgil not only for its theme, the founding of a dynasty and a nation, but also for its structure and for innumerable verbal details; it had authentic but not preponderant Homeric colouring; its gods were pagan; it was a heroic epic but contained a long prophetic enumeration of the kings of France; it was incomplete. These were to be the main features of epic in the fifty years after the publication of the *Franciade,* yet for all its influence it was ultimately a dead end. The future lay with the *Gerusalemme liberata* of Tasso, which was being composed at the time of the *Franciade's* publication, quite independently but with similar aspirations. Because Tasso solved the problems of epic more successfully than Ronsard, his poem was to supersede Ronsard's as the model for epic poets of the mid-seventeenth century.

That Ronsard was writing an epic was well advertised between 1550 and 1572 and doubtless deterred his friends and most others from competing in this field. Yet there are signs of others at work. Bouju's *Royal*[20] and Pouges's *Vandoméide*[21] were perhaps even complete before Ronsard began serious work on the *Franciade,* though everything suggests that they inclined to the annalistic tradition.

Jacques Peletier had abandoned his project of a *Herculéide*[22] by the time he wrote his *Art poétique* (1555), in which he none the less exhorted others to aspire to the glorious task.

1572—1623 RONSARD'S SUCCESSORS

Ronsard had shown the way: a host of others followed, often under his influence, but with an eye on du Bartas as well. The most significant event of the period, the publication in Italy of the *Gerusalemme* in 1581, passed unnoticed by epic poets except for d'Urfé certainly and perhaps Delbene, though Italian influence can be seen at work in Boyssières and Deimier, both inspired by Ariosto.

Delbene, to whom Ronsard had dedicated his *Art poétique*

(1565), left only the first book of his *Amédéide* (1580–4) in manuscript. With his hero, Amadeus VI of Savoy, he is the first to attempt heroic epic after the *Franciade*. Two epics before 1584, which do not survive, are du Faux's *Angiade*[23] and Le Loyer's *Thierry d'Anjou*.[24] Later we have Beaujeu's *La Suisse* (1589), one book on the annals of Switzerland, and Boyssières's *Croisade* (1584), inspired by Ariosto, which shows that in the 1580s romanesque as well as heroic and annalistic tendencies were all at work.

The reign of Henry IV was fertile in epics, many of them soliciting favours from the king. Of these, Sébastien Garnier's *Henriade* (1593–4) makes the reigning monarch hero of his epic, while his *Loyssée* (1593) is a contribution to the succession controversy. In 1594 Godard offered Henry a *Franciade*[25] similar in plan to Ronsard's; around 1604 Le Blanc was meditating a *Henriade*;[26] between 1606 and 1615 Navières published fragments of his *Henriade;* none of these poets received any encouragement from the king and nothing survives of the epics of the first two. Neither did Henry smile upon Pierre Delaudun, whose *Franciade* (1603), incomplete in nine books, ends on a begging note. This youthful work ridicules Ronsard for choosing the Trojan Francus as his hero and makes Francus a German chieftain at war with the Romans. Though an anti-Ronsardian effort, its debt to the *Franciade* is none the less manifest. Apparently a more faithful disciple, Claude Garnier added a fifth book (1604) to the unfinished *Franciade*, but in fact his work is a hopeless diversion of Ronsard's plot, intended simply to draw the attention of Henry IV upon the author. Jacques Guillot's continuation is more faithful. His Book v dealt with the Carolingians[27] and Book vi returns to Francus and Dicæe. All the above works were dedicated to Henry IV and all the poets went unrewarded.

Others composed in the same spirit but looked to other patrons: Honoré d'Urfé dedicated his unpublished *Savoysiade* (1599–1606) to Charles Emmanuel of Savoy and Jean de Schelandre his *Stuartide* (1611) to James VI of Scotland and I of England. Together with the works of Sébastien Garnier and Delbene these two, both heroic epics, are the most important of the period; for d'Urfé was the first to profit from Tasso's example whilst Schelandre was the only one to understand the lesson of the *Franciade* and to seek to recreate epic on the lines laid down by Ronsard.

The main tendency under Henry IV, to judge from the projected poems of Godard, Le Blanc, or Navières, and from the surviving ones by Sébastien Garnier, Delbene, d'Urfé, and Schelandre, was undoubtedly heroic, but annalistic and romanesque epic were also attempted. Palma Cayet's *Heptaméron* (1602) was annalistic. Montreux's *Espagne conquise* (1597) treated Charlemagne's campaigns after the fashion of Ariosto. Deimier expanded his *Austriade* of 1601 into the *Néréide* of 1605, by making the original description of the battle of Lepanto the framework for the romanesque tale of Cléophile and Néréclie.

The death of Henry IV stemmed the tide of *Henriades* and the early years of Louis XIII saw a definite slackening in the production of historical epic. The *Lutetiad* of Paul Thomas I, published in 1617, concerned the conversion of Henry IV, and had perhaps been composed much earlier. Apart from the *Lutetiad* and the poems of Schelandre and Guillot already mentioned, we have only Geuffrin's *Franciade* (1623), which is another supposed continuation of Ronsard's *Franciade*, but again distorts the original plot, being merely a moralized version of the catalogue of kings. Geuffrin's admiration for Ronsard is none the less genuine and his poem is a fitting close to the half century in which Ronsard's example dominated epic poetry.

That Ronsard's influence should be held up as the main thread in the development of epic in the years 1572 to 1623 is just, but not, of course, the whole story. Other influences, Ariosto, Tasso, and du Bartas, were at work and the varied fortunes of the *Franciade* by no means guaranteed uniformity. Diverse tendencies have been noticed, the saddest perhaps the debasement of the epic genre into an ill-considered vehicle for self-advertisement. The ambition to become court poet by means of epic foundered on the illiberality of Henry IV and on Malherbe's conquest of that position by his success with shorter poetic forms. Epic during these years assumed strange and bewildering shapes: the period might charitably be called one of experiment but more accurately one of confusion.

1623–1653 INTERVAL

The next thirty years saw no important historical epics published and the silence of Biblical epic between 1620 and 1650 is equally striking.[28] What had happened to epic? The answer lay beneath the surface. A new conception of epic was being elaborated from the example of Tasso's *Gerusalemme* and there was a new insistence on regularity of structure and clarity of expression. 1623, the very year of Geuffrin's backward-looking *Franciade,* saw the publication of Chapelain's preface to Marino's *Adone.* The importance of this preface is threefold. That an aspiring young French writer should seek to make his name with a preface to the work of a visiting Italian demonstrates the admiration for Italian poetry in French literary circles. Secondly, the preface was intended to prove that the *Adone* was a genuine epic:[29] here was firm commitment to the idea that literature in general and epic in particular should rest on rational foundations, an idea reinforced by prevailing respect for Italian critics. Thirdly, admiration for the style and substance of Marino's poem encouraged verbal virtuosity and flights of fantasy, which, curiously combined with a desire for clarity of expression, were the distinguishing features of the epics which were soon to appear. Nevertheless the very peculiarities of the *Adone* which had called forth Chapelain's preface prevented it from being more than a secondary influence on French epic. To a literary circle in whose hands epic theory grew from an assortment of precepts into a serious study in its own right, Tasso's *Gerusalemme* and above all his *Discorsi* seemed like a gift from heaven. Here was not only a poem that brilliantly synthesized Christianity and Antiquity but also a corpus of theory. These sources had earlier been tapped by d'Urfé, but now in favourable circumstances the urge to exploit them was irresistible. As France developed national consciousness, epic poets looked almost exclusively to French history for their subjects and in their grandiose epic designs they aspired to bring the French language to greater heights of clarity and elegance.

The interval of the years 1623 to 1653 is therefore no sign of abated interest in epic but rather of the serious and careful preparation now accorded to it. Chapelain began in 1625, Desmarets in 1630, Scudéry in the 1640s and Le Moyne about

1650. The first three were Academicians and under the aegis of the Académie a torrent of epics was to burst on the French public. If only they had been published at the time that they were conceived, they might have received the applause their authors expected. Delayed, however, by the labours of composition and the turmoil of the Fronde, these epics appeared when fashions were changing and old values disappearing.

While others laboured at composition, two poets published epics, both backward-looking. The *Rupellaid* (1630) of Paul Thomas II celebrated the campaign of La Rochelle in the fashion of a Blarru or Pillard; the *Chevalier sans reproche* (1633) of Jean d'Ennetières was an episodic romance, full of nostalgia for the past, and quite unconnected with the main trends of epic just described.[30]

1653–1658 TASSO'S SUCCESSORS

Into the space of five years was packed the publication of the most famous epics of the seventeenth century. Not only Le Moyne's *Saint Louis* (1653 and 1658), Scudéry's *Alaric* (1654), Chapelain's *Pucelle* (1656), and Desmarets's *Clovis* (1657), whose authors we have seen at work during the preceding years, but also Saint-Amant's *Moyse sauvé* (1653), Godeau's *Saint Paul* (1654), and Mambrun's *Constantinus* (1658).

Historical epic had now achieved a moment of precarious equilibrium under the potent spell of Tasso. Ronsard and ancient sources were forgotten; the annalistic trend was checked. The new heroic epic had Christian heroes and, except for *Alaric*, themes of national interest. The influence of theoretical discussion was evident in the ponderousness of the poems; the progress of the language evident in their clarity and elegance. One can detect the finger of Marino directing poets' attention to the ingenious or romanesque passages of Tasso, without, however, involving a sacrifice of their serious moral purpose and their Christian and national pride.

1658–1700 NEW DIRECTIONS

The publication of *La Pucelle* involved Chapelain in a situation similar to that which faced Ronsard after the publication of the *Franciade*. Chapelain enjoyed a prestige far above that of the other poets mentioned, by virtue of his position in the Académie, his influence on the distribution of pensions to men of letters, and his enormous reputation as a critic, fostered by correspondence with leading literary figures all over Europe. Yet *La Pucelle,* like the *Franciade,* did not live up to the expectations generated during the long years of its composition. Not that it was unsuccessful commercially: six editions spread its fame far and wide. But the more it was read, the more it was criticized for its harsh and monotonous style and for its lengthy tedium. The same criticisms were levelled against the other three poets, but being less eminent they had less far to fall. By a curious paradox the very men who had done most to elevate the conception of epic from its fallen state in the reigns of Henry IV and Louis XIII now by the publication of their poems did most to discredit the whole genre.

After 1658 there was a pause, one might almost say a gasp for breath, and until 1664 the only historical epics to appear were re-editions of the four mentioned. The stage would seem at this point to be set for the appearance of a really great epic. There was now a long tradition of epic theory and practice, an informed and eager public, and plenty to be learnt from the mistakes of others. Other genres, tragedy, comedy, fable, and satire, were reaching pinnacles of achievement: why not epic? Abandoning something of the austere and elevated conception of epic which had intoxicated earlier epic poets whilst depressing their readers, the new generation of epic poets, as is evident from the prefaces to their works, addressed themselves unanimously to the task of captivating their audience. All aimed at brevity; all tried new approaches; all failed.

Le Laboureur tried the instalment plan: three books of
Charlemagne in 1664, another three in 1666, then
Carel de Sainte-Garde offered six books of *Ch*
1667, each book divided into short
poem (167
a compendium
historical epic. Desmarets's *R*
the extreme with a mere 388 li
(1666) struck a happier balance and
length something of the grandeur and
these poets aspired. His *Charlemagne*

the qualities of his earlier poem and introduced a new concept of heroism, the victory of the hero over himself.

No poet therefore really rose to the challenge of epic in the late seventeenth century. Despite the advantages mentioned above, the resounding failure of the Academicians and the reaction against epic expressed in Boileau's satires was perhaps an overwhelming discouragement to any who were seriously attracted to the genre. Indeed, the poets who did write epic seemed anxious to differentiate themselves as far as possible from the poets of the preceding generation and this may explain why in this period historical subjects are less numerous than Biblical ones.

Summary

It is clear that the development of epic hinges on Ronsard and Tasso. Despite Ronsard's numerous followers he was superseded as a model by the Italian poet. Just as Sébastien and Claude Garnier, Guillot, Schelandre, and Geuffrin had been Ronsard's disciples, so Chapelain, Desmarets, Scudéry and Le Moyne were Tasso's disciples. Obviously the seventeenth-century Academicians enjoyed far greater prestige than the scattered provincials who vied for favour under Henry IV, but the disciples of Tasso had few followers themselves, for when a younger generation came to appraise the works of the 1650s, it either abandoned epic altogether or saw that the only hope of being read lay in as much differentiation as possible from the epics of the previous generation.

NOTES TO CHAPTER I

1. See Marni, *Allegory*, pp. 91–101, 'The indefiniteness of the seventeenth century idea of the epic genre'.

2. Because of the ambiguous overtones of the word 'classical'—canon, literary doctrine, value judgement—the words 'ancient' and 'Antiquity' are here used to refer to Greek and Latin literature before A.D. 500 and to approximate to the words 'ancien' and 'antiquité', by which the poets of this period referred to such literature.

3. *French Biblical epic in the seventeenth century*, p. 4. There is a chapter on sixteenth-century epic, pp. 27–48.

4. D'Aubigné's *Tragiques* is a very difficult case. It certainly can be considered a historical epic but it is not profitable to compare it with the poems considered here because hardly any generalization about them applies to the *Tragiques*. Moreover d'Aubigné was not writing epic as the other poets understood it.

5. François Descallis's *Lydiade* (1602) relates the fictitious adventures of Lydie, daughter of the King of Lydia (Goujet, xiv. 24–7; Toinet, i. 31–2). Segrais's *Athys* (1653) is pastoral. Saints' lives are the subject of *Saint Paul* (1654) by Godeau (Toinet, i. 162; Duchesne, pp. 223–8); *Saint Paulin* (1687) by Charles Perrault (Toinet, i. 273; Duchesne, pp. 312–16); and *La Sainte Franciade* (1632) by Jacques Corbin on Saint Francis of Assisi (Toinet, i. 121–2; ii. 100–4).

6. e.g. Germain Audebert's *Venetiae* (1583), *Parthenope* (1585), *Roma* (1585); see Cioranescu, *XVIe*.

7. See Curtius, *European literature*, p. 158; Griffin, *Coronation*, p. 152.

8. e.g. Germain de Brice, *Herveus* (1514), see Cioranescu, *XVIe;* Humbert de Montmoret, *Bellorum britannicorum . . . prima pars* (1512) (Adams, *Catalogue,* H.1154) and *Herveis* (1514?) (Adams, H.1156, wrongly attributed to Humbertus de Romanis); Jacques de Vintmille, *De Bello Rhodio* (*c.* 1527); Etienne Dolet, *Francisci Valesii ·Regis fata* (1539); du Bartas, *Cantique d'Ivry* (1590); Nicolas Courtin, *Sur la nouvelle conquête de la Franche Comté* (1674); see below, pp. 129–32, for Courtin's *Charlemagne*. Many poems of this nature are listed in Lelong, ii. 201–612, under the kings from Charles VIII to Louis XIV.

9. e.g. Geoffroi de Malvyn's youthful *Gallia gemens* (1563); see Courteault, *G. de Malvyn,* pp. 41–62.

10. Jean Prévost, *Apothéose de Henry IV* (1613), see Goujet, xiv. 245; Toinet, ii. 66–8.

11. Sometimes epic-sounding titles can be misleading. Guy Le Fèvre de la Boderie's *Galliade* (1578) is a history of the arts and sciences which the author expressly states is not a 'poème héroïque' (see Secret,

L'Esotérisme, pp. 123–52; *Kabbalistes chrétiens,* pp. 192–8). Jean Godard's *Franciade* is a tragedy and can be found in *Les Oeuvres* (1594), vol. ii, or in *Meslanges* (1624). For his epic projects see below, p. 15 n. 25; *La Montmorenciade* is eight pages of insignificant verse in praise of Montmorency's part in the La Rochelle campaign. Léon Gautier calls the *Guisiade* an epic (*Epopées françaises,* ii. 638 n. 2) but is a tragedy about Mary Stuart (Quérard, *Supercheries,* ii. 344d). The *Milliade* is a satirical poem in 1000 verses, hence its title, against Richelieu, attributed to Charles de Beys (Barbier, *Dictionnaire des anonymes,* ii. 551a). François de Rémond's *Alexias in Sacrarum elegiarum deliciae* (1648), pp. 291–310, is a series of Latin elegiacs described as 'uxoris sancti Alexii querimoniae'.

12. Sayce, pp. 159–61.

13. 'Ce n'est pas qu'il y ait vn fonds plus riche que celuy-là, ny plus fertile en rares materiaux. Mais ce sont des materiaux sacrez; il est deffendu de les toucher du marteau; il n'est pas permis d'en faire aucune figure.' ('Traité,' sig. elr; 'Dissertation,' e3r.)

14. See Greene on Renaissance poems, which are 'imperfectly coherent, uncertainly unified, divided by powerful forces not altogether controlled and understood' (*Descent from heaven,* p. 4).

15. Such as could be found in *Polyeucte* or Godeau's *Saint Paul.*

16. Cf. Sayce, p. 3.

17. Not to be taken as a translation of 'poème héroïque', which the poets used to describe any poem with epic pretensions.

18. From now on I use the word 'epic' alone to refer to historical epic in the sixteenth and seventeenth centuries.

19.   . . . soneray la Trompete bellique
               D'un grand Virgile ou d'Homere ancien:
               Pour celebrer les haults faictz d'Anguyen,
               Lequel sera (contre Fortune amere)
               Nostre Achiles, & Marot son Homere.

(*Epître,* lvii. 72–6, ed. Mayer.) See Cioranescu, 'La Pléiade et le poème épique', p. 85.

20. Jacques Bouju (1515–77) was a scholar and lawyer from Anjou. Befriended by Francis I, Margaret of Navarre, and Catherine de' Medici, he became President in the Parlement of Rennes in 1559. La Croix du Maine is our only source for the *Royal:* 'Voici ce qu'il a écrit en notre langue, dont la plupart n'est imprimé: le *Royal,* qui est un Oeuvre écrit en vers François, contenant un succinct Discours de toutes les choses mémorables qui ont été faites par les Rois de France jusqu'au règne d'Henri III. Ce Livre n'est encore imprimé.' (i. 395.) Lelong (ii, no. 15737) and Moréri (s.v. BOUJU) merely repeat La Croix du Maine, but Moréri (s.v. BONJU) seems to draw on another source,

giving 1588 as the date of his death. Prévost confirms it as 1577 (*DBF*, vi. 1337).

21. 'Jean de Pouges . . . a écrit en vers François un Poëme historial, appelé la Vandomeide, qui est un Oeuvre contenant les louanges du Roi de Navarre . . . Je ne l'ai point encore vue imprimée.' (La Croix du Maine, i. 577–8.) Both Bouju and Pouges are praised by Albert Babinot in his *Christiade* (1559), pp. 112–13. Apart from this nothing is known of Pouges.

22. *Art poétique*, ed. Boulanger, p. 86. See Chamard, *Hist. Pléiade*, ii. lll; Cioranescu, 'La Pléiade et le poème épique', p. 85.

23. Perhaps annalistic. Pascal Robin du Faux (1538–*c.* 1584) was another Angevin scholar. See La Croix du Maine, ii. 218–19; Mouflard, *Robert Garnier*, pp. 315–16; Cioranescu, *XVIe*, p. 607; and the next note.

24. Possibly heroic. 'Pierre Le Loyer a composé en vers François un Poëme à l'imitation de Ronsard en sa Franciade, & du sieur du Faux en Anjou, Paschal Robin, en son *Angiade,* ou histoire d'Anjou, lequel Oeuvre il intitule *Thierry d'Anjou,* il n'est encore imprimé.' (La Croix du Maine, ii, 295.) Pierre Le Loyer, sieur de la Brosse (1550–1634) translated Tasso's *Aminta* and Ovid's *Ars amatoria.* See Cioranescu, *XVIe*, p. 427.

25. Jean Godard (1564–1630) was a Parisian lawyer and prolific poet. The plan of his proposed *Franciade* is outlined in 'Au Roy Henry IV', *Oeuvres* (1594), vol. i. His *Oracle ou chant de Protée* (1594) gave a specimen of his epic style and summarized Book i of Ronsard's *Franciade*. The commentary by Claude Le Brun which accompanies this poem (pp. 20–37) offers comparisons between Godard and Ronsard, and details of Godard's planned *Franciade*. The project fell through and Godard consoled himself by writing a tragedy with that title instead (see above, p. 14 n. 11). See also Goujet, xv. 245, 251–3; Allais, *De Franciadis epica fabula*, ch. iii; Toinet, i. 22–30; Edelman, *Attitudes*, p. 205, n. 8; Cioranescu, *XVIᵉ*.

26. Jean Le Blanc was a Parisian who lost his inherited wealth in lawsuits and the civil wars. He served in the Venetian army and returned to France when Henry IV had restored law and order. According to Lelong, ii, no. 19500, he published the first book of a *Henriade* in 1604. This information is repeated by Toinet, ii. 21–4, Fleuret et Perceau, *Satires du XVIIe*, i. 42, but I have found no copy of the book. He published prose and verse between 1604 and 1628. See Cioranescu, *XVIIe*.

27. Lost but well attested; see below, p. 82 n. 39.

28. Sayce, p. 74.

29. Doubts were cast on it, because its action was peaceful, not warlike. Chapelain's sincerity or insincerity in undertaking the defence of the

Adone did not invalidate his arguments as a tenable critical position; cf. Sayce, p. 19.

30. Compare the case of the *Tobie* and *Joseph* (1648) of Saint-Peres (Sayce, pp. 79–80).

II
THEORY

Sources of epic theory

THE numerous theoretical writings relating to epic may be
divided into those written by critics, who never wrestled with
the problem of composition, and those written by poets, who
did. Critics either wrote chapters on epic in more generalized
Arts poétiques, or devoted whole treatises to epic. Poets often
prefaced their poems with treatises on epic, or confined themselves to brief remarks explaining or justifying their intentions.
Epic poets were also authors of *Arts poétiques* and sometimes
entered into controversies on specific topics.

Until the mid-seventeenth century epic theory in France
consisted mainly of scattered precepts. Mambrun's *Dissertatio* (1652) is the first treatise devoted to epic alone. Divided
and subdivided like a theological treatise, it bristles with
references to irrefutable authorities. Indeed epic theory became
something of an ecclesiastical monopoly. Marolles, Le Bossu,
Rapin, and Le Moyne were all clerics, though their works, in
French, are less formidably scholastic than Mambrun's. Although the critical activity helped to mould poets' conception
of epic, poets did not turn to specific treatises on epic as to a
text-book. The most important treatises appeared after the
major epics had been published, and the theory and practice of
a writer who was both critic and poet were often startlingly inconsistent. Epic theory is best viewed as a genre in its own
right. It had its own topoi, its own forms. Writers of epic
treatises were less concerned with influencing writers of epic
than with constructing imposing and rational edifices.

French epic theory derived mainly from Italian sources.
Starting as scattered precepts culled here and there, it developed into a complex system.[1] The disproportion between
the material of the sixteenth and seventeenth centuries makes
it difficult to treat the theory of both centuries on the same
level. One cannot readily compare the recommendations of
Sebillet, du Bellay, or Peletier with the treatises of Mambrun,

Le Moyne or Le Bossu. Drawing therefore mainly on seventeenth-century works, I propose first to discuss theoretical attitudes to the main problems of epic—its definition, *vraisemblance,* the *merveilleux,* allegory, choice of material, and structure—for these were the topics which the seventeenth-century critics debated in detail. Then, turning to the broader view of epic, I shall contrast the attitudes of the sixteenth and seventeenth centuries. Later, in chapter IV, I shall discuss the special problem of the theoretical relationships between epic and history.

The definition and objects of epic

Sayce has usefully summarized the seventeenth-century conception of epic and this may serve as a point of departure:

The highest common factor of critical opinion was, it may be said, that epic was the narration (as opposed to the representation) in verse of an illustrious action within very wide limits of length. 'Illustrious' meant that the main characters should be of high rank (and according to some critics of exemplary virtue). . . . The other elements of illustriousness were the *merveilleux* and the allegory. . . . The last essential of epic is contained in the word 'action' which is in a way equivalent to *fable.*[2]

This definition shows the relationship between those characteristics of epic which at once strike the reader and which most occupied the critics. The princely hero, the *merveilleux,* and allegory are all aspects of the illustrious nature of epic. The fact that its action is narrated gives epic the particular structure which distinguishes it from other genres. The nature of the action raises the questions of *vraisemblance* and *vérité,* which in their turn are important, because the object of epic was to improve man, earlier in a general moral sense, later in a political sense.[3] In the sixteenth century the emphasis was on the celebration of warlike deeds which without the poets' help might be lost for ever. On the other hand the annalistic epic was always strongly moral in tone, and Blarru inserts many moralizing comments into the *Nanceid.* In all the critics' discussions on the *merveilleux, vraisemblance,* the choice of material, structure and adornment, the guiding principle seems to have been the question: in what way can epic be made different from other genres? This offers the key to the constant appeals to the practice of the ancients, because they had written what was universally recognized as epic.

That epic was the supreme literary genre was accepted almost unanimously by critics in the sixteenth and seventeenth centuries. The prestige of Virgil and Homer over other ancient writers had much to do with this, and also the fact that epic did not only have a moral purpose—this was the purpose of most literature—but was also directed towards the most illustrious audience, the ruler.

Plausibility, the supernatural, and allegory

Epic theory generated fruitless argument because critics and poets tried to apply to literature philosophical concepts that they did not define. Nearly all were in agreement that the epic poem must be plausible (*vraisemblable*). There were two reasons for this. Because the main object of epic was to excite princes to virtue, only situations that might occur in real life would have this effect. Secondly the possible and the probable were the very features which distinguished poetry from history, for history dealt with fact and literal truth. The problems of the essence of poetry were far more formidable than those of exciting princes to virtue.

Aristotle suggested that poetry is what should happen and that history is what did happen. Poetry will grip its audience if it seems plausible and it will be so if it is based on the facts of history. Sayce has pointed out two difficulties here which help one to understand why the arguments about fact and fiction, *vraisemblance* and *vérité*, history and poetry went round endlessly in circles. Firstly, 'there seems to be a contradiction here. If the public will believe a thing more easily because it is historical, why should not everything historical be probable?' Secondly, Aristotle 'did not make the beliefs of the public the only criterion of probability. He is concerned also with general philosophic truth, whether apparent to the public or not. This distinction was, I think, missed by most Italian and French critics.'[4] It was missed because critics did not attempt a philosophical definition of *vraisemblance* or *vérité* yet tried to apply these concepts to literary criticism. When these undefined concepts were applied to the relations between epic and history, the confusion was greater still.[5]

That the *merveilleux,* the intervention of supernatural beings in the action of the poem, was an essential part of the poem, was accepted unanimously. It did not violate the rules of *vraisemblance* because the intervention of the supernatural in human affairs was essential Christian dogma, besides being attested by historians. What did exercise critics was the choice between the Christian supernatural and the pagan mythology bequeathed by the ancients. On this point, the conflict between religion and literature inherent in the epic genre was intense. Religious passion and the imitation of the ancients, which had separately agitated life and literature in the sixteenth century, became in the seventeenth century the main source of tension in epic poetry, a tension which critics and poets attempted to resolve.

The *merveilleux païen* was practised by Ronsard and some of his successors in the sixteenth century but was not the subject of critical writing. Their scattered efforts quickly gave way to an overwhelming conviction that only the *merveilleux chrétien* was permissible. The first to call for it were du Bartas and Vauquelin; Godeau amplified the argument in 1633[6] and, in the 1650s, under the influence of Tasso, the victory of the *merveilleux chrétien* was complete. Critical controversy really only started in earnest around 1670 with a series of progressively more violent pamphlets by Desmarets in defence of Christian inspiration. He started by accepting the authority of the ancients, whose practice needed only to be modified by substituting the true deities of Christianity for the false ones of paganism. Gradually, however, his attack on the errors of paganism extended to undermining the authority of the ancients and he ended by denigating Virgil and Homer, especially when his own Christian epic, *Clovis,* was compared unfavourably with them. The weight of Desmarets's argument was supported by his claim that the Christian religion was superior to paganism. Boileau produced two arguments against this in his *Art poétique* (1674): Christianity is degraded by the contamination of epic fiction and in practice the *merveilleux chrétien* is either dull or ridiculous.

The controversy highlights the deeply felt problems of reconciling Antiquity with Christianity and the commitment of writers to the view that if a poet based himself on sound first

principles then success would follow. Desmarets's principle was
sound and appropriate to the period in which he lived. A poet
writing under the inspiration of a superior religion should produce superior poetry. 'We have here, expressed in a noble form,
an idea . . . which takes into account both the religious devotion
and the monarchical nationalism of the time. *Clovis* is not the
true poem of France, but its guiding principle might have made
it so.'[7] Had Desmarets devoted the energy he consumed in
polemic to bringing *Clovis* to perfection, he would have needed
no further justification. As it was, *Clovis* gave Boileau scope
for justified criticism of its literary defects, but led him to the
unjustified conclusion that the defects of a particular work in-
validated the principles on which it was founded. Desmarets
erred in believing that sincere inspiration and sound principles
guaranteed success; Boileau erred in equating defective practice
with faulty principles.

The *merveilleux* demonstrated graphically the interaction
between the human and the divine. What was incomprehens-
ible from one point of view was explained by knowledge of
the other. Such an atmosphere was favourable to allegory,
where one thing is said and another is meant. Most seventeenth-
century epic poets left indications that their plots had an
allegorical meaning, and this was appropriate to the serious and
moral tone of epic. If the historical events were lacking in
dignity, if the poet's fictions, his amorous or romanesque
episodes, savoured too much of entertainment, all could be
justified by elevating them to universal significance by the
application of allegory. Chapelain argued that allegory was an
essential part of the structure, Le Bossu made its presence or
absence the distinguishing mark of epic.[8] How seriously we
take its interpretation will be examined later. What cannot be
denied is the emphasis placed on it in theoretical writings.

Vraisemblance, merveilleux and allegory were debated endlessly by critics and poets. Rightly so. The problems of truth
and falsehood, possibility and probability, human and divine,
religion and literature, universal and particular, conferred on
epic the illustriousness to which it justly laid claim.

Choice of material

Burdened with such weighty preoccupations, poets obviously had to choose their material carefully. Although we have admitted the distinction between Biblical and historical epic to be in some respects an artificial one, nevertheless it did represent a real choice for poets, and, in the light of their strong religious preoccupations, a controversial one.

The choice between history and the Bible was seen as one between *Histoire chrétienne* and *Histoire sainte*.[9] Scudéry and Le Moyne opposed Biblical subjects because the fictions necessary to epic were detrimental to the revealed truth,[10] an argument we have seen Boileau apply to Christian epic in general. The defenders of Biblical subjects, Desmarets and Saint-Amant, argued that the Bible offered precisely those miraculous but true situations capable of making Christian epic superior to ancient epic, and that if the poetic form necessitated occasional fictions, these need in no way affect the central revealed truth. When we examine the subjects of historical epic, we must remember that they were chosen because they illustrated the triumph of Christianity yet also gave scope for embellishment with fiction, a licence which the poets readily exploited. Hence the crowd of medievàl heroes and the absence of the Romans who were so popular in the theatre.

In the light of these requirements, what parts of Christian history were most suitable for epic? War, especially crusades, provided illustrious participants and a Christian cause. Chapelain, it is true, to justify the *Adone* argued that epic might be peaceful, and Le Bossu argued from the *Odyssey* that war was not essential. But Chapelain chose a war as the subject of *La Pucelle* and Le Bossu did not write an epic. Peaceful epic therefore remained largely theoretical, and war was the most popular subject. This was reinforced by the sixteenth-century tradition of epic as the celebration of martial exploits.[11] The nature of historical writing at the time helped poets in their choice, for history was mostly concerned with war and illustrious characters; neither economics nor the man in the street had made their appearance. Epic theory recommended kings and princes as the only suitable characters and history provided them.

What of the hero himself? The treatises, by devoting chapters to the hero, implicitly recommended as the best form of epic that which we have called 'heroic', as distinct from annalistic or romanesque. The kind of hero the poets sought is summed up by Le Laboureur: 'Ie cherchois vn Heros Chrétien & braue, vn Heros sage & vaillant, vn Heros pour qui tout le monde generalement fut preuenu d'estime . . .'[12] Some heroes came close to this ideal, or could be made to do so; others caused poets to expend considerable ingenuity in demonstrating that they were suitable. Chapelain apologized for Joan's being a woman and for her death at the stake; Le Moyne for Saint Louis's captivity. The conflict between the ideal hero and the recorded career of an individual could be a severe challenge to poets and a further source of creative tension.

Structure

We have characterized the structure of epic as an assemblage of topoi derived from the ancients. The theorists confirm this. Tasso laid down that the plot chosen from history should not be too full of incident, as this would leave no room for the poet to add episodes and adornment.[13] This proves the importance attached to the conventional topoi; if there was no room for them how could the poem be recognized as an epic? The problem did not worry sixteenth-century writers like Blarru or Sébastien Garnier, to whom the course of historical events dictated the structure of their epic; but when the characteristics of epic were subjected to scrutiny by the theorists, the episodes and adornments, by which an epic could be recognized, became all important. In the interests of unity it was laid down that the structure of epic should be hierarchical. The episodes had to be subordinate to the main narrative, whilst remaining intimately connected with it. Le Bossu dealt with the question systematically; his views were echoed by Le Moyne.[14] On this point the recommendations were most impressive and the practice of the poets most disappointing.

It was also recommended that the narrative should not follow the chronological order of history, but use recitals and prophecies to disturb the relations between past, present, and future. This seems to be a development of the 'in medias res' of Horace, which in itself simply recommends that the action should get under way without lengthy explanations. The consequence of this was that past history had to be related elsewhere than at the beginning of the story. This easily developed into a policy of deliberately disturbing chronological order, and the rule was formulated by Chapelain.[15] It suggests again that epic theorists were seeking ways in which epic could be distinguished from other genres. The forcing of a historical narrative, which tends to be chronological, but can never be quite so, into an epic structure which deliberately disturbed chronology, was another problem generated by the theorists to exercise the ingenuity of poets.

Different theories of epic

Detailed discussion of epic theory tends to centre on the seventeenth century because of the abundance of critical writing and the continuous polemical debate over fine distinctions at that time. If one ignores the fine distinctions, two stages in the theoretical conception of epic can be distinguished.

In the sixteenth century epic theory confined itself to recommending imitation of existing epics and to unsystematic observations on the salient characteristics of the proposed models. The models, however, were inconsistent. Virgilian epic, prized for its greater antiquity, was unified, nationalistic, and elevated in style. Ariosto and the medieval romances, to which the poets were closer in time and whose popularity they could observe, were disordered, entertaining and, by comparison, less elevated. Du Bellay, Peletier, and Ronsard in theory recommended medieval romances, and especially Ariosto, as models. Ronsard even called the *Iliad* and the *Aeneid* 'romans' to imply that they could lay claim to the popularity which he knew the romances enjoyed. But when in practice he had to choose between the irreconcilable examples of Virgil and Ariosto, guided by the elevated pretensions of epic, he invariably leaned toward the superior status and greater antiquity of Virgil. Thus the Pléiade recommended direct imitation of models but failed in their theoretical writings to resolve the conflict between the popularity of the romanesque tradition and the austerity of Virgil.[16]

When to these models were added the example of Tasso and Marino and when, on closer examination, the innumerable inconsistencies between the recommended models became manifest and inescapable, it no longer sufficed for the thoughtful theorist simply to bid the poet to imitate. The inconsistencies had to be resolved and logic came to the rescue. Thus it was that between the poet and his models the seventeenth-century critic erected a barrier of theory, intended as a helpful intermediary, but which in fact either misled poets as to how they might best capture an audience or ultimately reduced them to silence.

NOTES TO CHAPTER II

1. Epic theory has been the subject of more discussion than epic poetry. The most helpful accounts are: Saintsbury, *History of criticism*, ii. 120–7 (Ronsard), 256–7 (Chapelain), 266–7 (Mambrun); Cottaz, *Influence*, pp. 33–52 (history), 53–72 (*merveilleux*), 73–84 (allegory), 85–90 (love); Egger, *Hellénisme*, i. 391–410; Spingarn, *Literary criticism*, pp. 107–24, 210–13, 241–6; Patterson, *Three centuries*, i. 471–6, 590–8; Sayce, pp. 6–26; and works by Williams, for which see Bibliography.

2. Sayce, p. 26.

3. Chapelain stressed the action of epic on the individual, Marolles, Rapin, and Le Bossu, its relevance to the conduct of princes; cf. Sayce, pp. 8–9.

4. p. 10.

5. See below, pp. 42–7.

6. In the 'Discours' prefaced to his *Oeuvres chrétiennes*, pp. 23ff.; cf. Sayce, pp. 12–13.

7. Sayce, p. 16.

8. Cf. Sayce, p. 10.

9. Scudéry, Preface to *Alaric*, a7ᵛ; cf. Sayce, p. 17.

10. See above, p. 3 and p. 14 n. 13.

11. 'Le Poëme Heroïque . . . est tout guerrier' (Ronsard, 'Preface sur la Franciade', xvi. 335).

12. Preface to *Charlemagne*, a5ᵛ.

13. *Discorsi del poema eroico*, Book ii (*Prose diverse*, i. 91ff.); cf. Sayce, p. 19.

14. See Sayce, p. 20; Le Moyne's words are quoted below, p. 123.

15. In the *Preface de l'Adone* (*Opuscules critiques*, p. 99); cf. Sayce, p. 21.

16. See Cioranescu, 'La Pléiade et le poème épique', pp. 75–86.

III

MODELS

Diversity of sources

POETS and critics often gave extensive lists of authors who were deemed to be suitable models for epic, though names were also mentioned for their unsuitability. Scudéry claimed,

> . . . j'ay releu fort exactement l'Iliade & l'Odyssée d'Homere; l'Eneïde de Virgile; la Guerre civile de Lucain; la Thebaïde de Stace; les Rolands amoureux & furieux de Boyardo & de l'Arioste; l'incomparable Hierusalem delivrée du fameux Torquato; & grand nombre d'autres Poëmes Epiques en diverses Langues: tels que sont les premiers Livres de la Franciade de Ronsard, & du Saint Loüis du Pere Le Moine: & ce beau Poëme de la Conqueste de Granade. . . .[1]

Too much importance cannot be attached to these lists, since they were as much a commonplace of epic theory as were storms or shipwrecks of epic poetry. A list of authors was a decoration to the preface rather than an honest statement of the poet's studies. Nevertheless the extent of reading indicated gives an idea of the various models considered suitable for epic.

It is obvious that the range of borrowings by French epic poets goes well beyond the epic genre alone. Lyric and drama, the whole corpus of earlier literature indeed, could contribute. We shall therefore consider the epic models mainly in the light of the types of epic structure they provided.

Greek epic

Homer was certainly more talked about than read. Ronsard was probably the only epic poet to study Homer in Greek,[2] but although he embellished the *Franciade* with impressive Homeric colouring—Olympian councils, sacrifices, epithets, and names—his epic remained fundamentally Virgilian. Translations of Homer seem to have done little to make him more widely used.[3]

The *Iliad* undoubtedly helped to consecrate war as a major theme in epic. Unfortunately poets missed the point that the *Iliad* usually analyses the motives and reasons for fighting, and even where numerous deaths are narrated in quick succession, the combatants are characterized by some detail that renders them memorable. The extent to which uncritical copying of this procedure could generate tedium is best illustrated in Deimier's *Néréide*, where lengthy catalogues of duels and deaths are enlivened neither by probing the motives of the combatants nor by memorable details.

The real effects of the *Iliad* reached French epic by the devious route of Tasso's *Gerusalemme*,[4] whose rich synthesis of Antiquity and Christianity so often gave his imitators the spurious air of having made the discoveries themselves. The structural element common to the *Iliad* and the *Gerusalemme* is the quarrel between two heroes: the chief (Agamemnon, Goffredo) and the right-hand man (Achilles, Rinaldo). Much simplified, the epic then falls into three parts: (i) quarrel; (ii) absence of the right-hand man permitting enemy advantages; (iii) return of the right-hand man resulting in enemy defeat. This is the basic structure of *Alaric* and *La Pucelle*, and is used as a topos in *Saint Louis* and *Clovis*, which might all therefore seem directly inspired by the *Iliad*, if their dependence on Tasso were not so well attested. Their variations on the Iliadic theme will be dealt with later.[5]

Tasso was well aware of the Iliadic nature of his *Gerusalemme* and intended to write a sequel related to the *Gerusalemme* 'com'è l'Iliade con l'Odissea'. The hero of this Odyssean sequel was to have been Tancredi.[6] There are no Odyssean epics in France, but the *Odyssey* left its mark by consecrating travel as an epic theme and showing what effects could be achieved by the use of recitals. However, since both travel and recitals are equally prominent in the first half of the *Aeneid*, the *Odyssey* must be assigned a secondary role.

Other Greek epics, occasionally mentioned, were rarely used. Ronsard alone seems to have drawn seriously on Apollonius for the love affair between Francus and Hyante, and, when Homer failed him, on Quintus Smyrnaeus for details of the Trojan war. Hesiod might have contributed to the type of epic that consisted of detached episodes, such as Heudon's *Adventures*, but epic theory did not analyse or regulate didactic poetry and its peculiar features remained incidental to epic practice.[7]

Latin epic

Since the prestige of Virgil went far beyond the confines of epic, it is not surprising that his is the name most frequently mentioned in connection with epic. Virgil took over from the Homeric poems the themes of war and travel and treated them anew. Two aspects of his treatment found favour.

The first is structural and particularly affected sixteenth- and early seventeenth-century epic. In Books i–iii of the *Aeneid* a storm shatters Aeneas's fleet; he is cast up at Carthage, and recites his adventures to Dido. For brevity I call this the Storm–Shipwreck–Recital structure. It formed the basis of Ronsard's *Franciade* (1572), Delbene's *Amédéide* (*c.* 1585), Garnier's *Loyssée* (1593), d'Urfé's *Savoyside* (*c.* 1600), and Schelandre's *Stuartide* (1611). The popularity of the theme is of course as much due to Ronsard's example as to Virgil's prestige. Its variations will be considered later.[8]

The second Virgilian contribution was the concept of the hero's mission. The end of the *Aeneid* opened wider perspectives than the duel which closes the *Iliad* or the vengeance which crowns the *Odyssey*: Aeneas' mission is to found the Roman Empire. The hero's mission was a feature of the poems from 1572 to 1611 mentioned above but took on a new significance in the 1650s when Tasso replaced Virgil as a model and the mission was infused with religious and nationalistic fervour. All the heroes of the 1650s had a mission of consequence to Christianity and all, except Alaric, a national one, whereas earlier only Francus's ultimate objective could be called national, and that only by a stretch of imagination. Of the others, Delbene's Amadeus set out from Savoy to rescue John Paleologus, d'Urfé's Beroldo from Spain to found Savoy, and Schelandre's Fleance from an Atlantic island to find his father. None of these missions was specifically Christian nor, from a French point of view, national; and, though Garnier's *Loyssée* was Christian, in that it dealt with a crusade, it was inspired by the polemic surrounding Henry IV's claim to the throne, and its structure was dictated by the historical material.

Virgil's influence is therefore most apparent among Ronsard and his successors. These epics owed their structure to Virgil and to him the idea of their heroes' mission. Later the structure owed more to Tasso and, as in the *Gerusalemme*, the hero's mission became Christian. The same shift can be observed in the use of the *merveilleux païen*. Ronsard, Schelandre, Guillot, Claude Garnier, and Delaudun followed the Virgilian pattern, which yielded thereafter to the *merveilleux chrétien*.

I have stressed Virgil's influence in the matter of structure, mission, and *merveilleux païen*, because these relate specifically to the epic genre; but Virgil of course influenced epic in other ways, just as Virgil influenced literature as a whole. The details of Ronsard's debt to Virgil have been exhaustively catalogued.[9] These topoi and verbal reminiscences reached Ronsard's followers through the *Franciade*. Even without the example of Ronsard, Virgil's influence was pervasive. He was used as a school book; Ravisius Textor drew on him for his *Epitheta;* Natale Conti for his *Mythologia*; Erasmus for his *Adagia;* nor were translations lacking.[10] Knowledge of Virgil could be gained in many other ways than by reading the *Aeneid,* though Ronsard seems deliberately to avoid the hackneyed phrases, and his use of the *Aeneid* is the result of a profound and personal knowledge of the poem.

Other Latin epics of Antiquity contributed little to the structure of French epic, though the annalistic poems of Ennius or Silius might have served as models for annalistic epic. There were, however, some strange misconceptions, and to the poets of Antiquity could be attributed achievements that were hardly their principal concern. If Sébastien Garnier could think that the famous *Aeneid* contained the exploits of Augustus,[11] it is not surprising that the fragmentary Ennius could be praised by Godard as the flatterer of Scipio rather than as an annalistic poet.[12] More frequently Virgil's successors were criticized for their deficiencies. Ronsard blamed Lucan and Silius for allowing history to dictate the shape of their poems[13] and had he known the works of his predecessors, Blarru or Pillard, he would doubtless have blamed them too for this. None the less, if the later Latin epics did little to mould the structure of epic, they had other lessons to offer. Lucan and Claudian were masters of rhetoric. Ovid was a fruitful source of mythology and had long been numbered among the epic poets.[14] Modern Latin epics, such as Sannazaro's *De partu Virginis* (1526) or Vida's *Christiad* (1535), were by virtue of their subject more likely to influence Biblical epic,[15] though

Pillard's *Rusticiad* (1541) shows many borrowings from Vida.[16]

The real contribution of ancient epic, which in practice meant Virgil, was somewhat different from what the theorists or poets with their exaggerated claims might have us believe. Ronsard alone made ancient epic the substance of his poem and bequeathed the Storm–Shipwreck–Recital structure to his successors. For the most part imitation of the ancients meant borrowing and rearranging topoi from earlier epics. On the strength of a versified historical narrative decorated with a touch of mythology, a few similes, and a pompous invocation, aspiring epic poets might be saluted by indulgent friends as the rivals of Homer or Virgil.

Italian epic

Subservience to Virgil or haphazard imitation of the ancients satisfied poets till about 1623—then attention was devoted to the complex of new factors which Tasso's *Gerusalemme* presented.[17] Even without Tasso's example, the authority of the ancients would have been questioned, for with the infiltration of Italian criticism into French epic theory and with theorists wielding logic and reason as instruments of criticism, reverence for Homer and Virgil was undermined. Tasso's influence on French epic can be seen in the new features of epic after 1623: Christianity, Iliadic structure, love, and magic. The repeated manipulation of these features proves that in the seventeenth century Tasso replaced Virgil as the chief model.

The idea of the hero's mission, originally derived from Virgil, now became essentially Christian. Alaric, Clovis, Saint Louis, and Joan of Arc, like Goffredo, were all instruments of God.

The Iliadic structure mentioned above was now employed as follows. Just as the absence of Achilles and Rinaldo in the *Iliad* and the *Gerusalemme* led to the defeat of the armies they served, so the absence of Joan and Alaric in *La Pucelle* and *Alaric* imperilled the French army and the Gothic expedition. The cause of Rinaldo's absence in the *Gerusalemme* is twofold: partly, as in the *Iliad*, the result of a quarrel, partly, Tasso's own contribution, the result of Armida's intervention. These two features were variously developed. Of those who employed the Iliadic structure, Scudéry made Amalasonthe

perform the same function as Armida, whilst Chapelain introduced a new cause for his heroine's absence, her capture by
the English, a fact offered by history. Chapelain used the
quarrel motif elsewhere, in the relationships between Charles
VII and Joan.

The role of love in epic was transformed by Tasso's example.
Ronsard certainly did not neglect love in the *Franciade* but
nothing illustrates better the distance between him and Tasso
than a comparison of their treatments of this theme. Francus
is loved by two sisters: Clymène, like Apollonius' Medea,
commits suicide, while Hyante performs the double function
of Dido and the Sibyl in the *Aeneid*, and after her prophesying
it is certain that Francus is to abandon her. Both affairs were
strictly modelled on ancient authorities. The poets of the 1650s
did not look so far back: Tasso offered all they needed and
more. Like Rinaldo and Armida, Tancredi and Erminia, the
new heroes might legitimately love and be inspired to great
deeds. Clovis and Clotilde, Alaric and Amalasonthe, Dunois
and Joan illustrate this. Or love could embroil lesser characters:
examples are endless. Or we find detachable episodes modelled
on Sofronia and Olindo: the story of Jameric's daughter and
the Lusitanian in Book ii of *Alaric*. Wherever love plays a
part in the epics of the 1650s, we find Tasso's inspiration
behind it.

The magician Ismeno spawned a numerous progeny: Rigilde
in *Alaric*, Auberon in *Clovis*, Mirème in *Saint Louis*, Géronde
in the *Charlemagne* of Le Laboureur, Arons in the *Charlemagne* of Courtin. No magician troubles *La Pucelle* but Bedford's dabbling in astrology performs a related function.

On all these counts it is clear that Tasso's influence superseded that of the ancients and, because he was better understood, his influence was more profound. We have described
the *Franciade* as the French *Aeneid;* we might describe as the
French *Gerusalemme* any one of the epics of the 1650s.

Another parallel suggests itself. Just as Homer's influence
reached French epic through Virgil and Ronsard, so Ariosto's
was diffused chiefly, but not exclusively, through Tasso.
Boyssières, Montreux, and Deimier, it is true, wrote poems
directly inspired by the technique of the *Orlando furioso;*
isolated episodes were used by d'Urfé[18] and by Ronsard;[19] but

the *Furioso* was above all the source of the romanesque atmosphere which Tasso harmonized with the ancient models and
which Tasso's imitators welcomed to soften the austerity of
epic.[20]

Marino's case is similar to that of Aristo. His influence was
ill-defined but certainly at work. He contributed a taste for
ingenious and extravagant language rather than a structural
model to follow. Stylistically Scudéry and LeMoyne rivalled
him; Chapelain, defender of the *Adone*, was less affected. The
Adone may have encouraged the poets of the seventeenth
century to attempt epic again. It did not exert a dominant
influence.[21]

Independence of models

To Virgil and Tasso principally, to Homer, Ariosto, and
Marino partly, French epic of the sixteenth and seventeenth
centuries owed almost everything. But not everything. Alongside critics theorizing about ancient and modern epic, alongside poets borrowing topoi or structures from the same sources,
stood those who followed neither, but forged poems from
history, thus side-stepping the problems of reconciling a preconceived epic structure with the demands of a historical
narrative. Blarru's *Nanceid*, Garnier's *Henriade*, Courtin's
Charlemagne pénitent owe little to the models mentioned
above. The structure of their poems was dictated by the
sequence of historical events, yet all three managed to rise
above the level of versified history.

Epic poets could adopt towards their models an attitude of
dependence or independence. Neither approach of itself
guaranteed success, and each approach requires us to ask
different questions of it. Of those closely dependent on their
models we must ask how well they responded to the challenge of
adapting fresh historical material to a preconceived epic structure. Of the independent we must ask how far they were successful in creating new structures.

NOTES TO CHAPTER III

1. Preface to *Alaric*, A6 ʳ⁻ᵛ. See also Rapin, *Réflexions*, ed. Dubois, pp. 24–5, 93–6, for similar lists.

2. Silver, *Ronsard and the Hellenic Renaissance*, pp. 85–115; Gandar, *Ronsard*, pp. 15–21.

3. *Iliad*: J. Samxon, i—xxiv (1519–30), based on Valla's Latin translation; H. Salel, i—ii (1542), i—x (1545), xi—xii and the beginning of xiii (1554); A. Jamyn, xii—xvi (1574), xii—xxiv (1577). *Odyssey*: J. Peletier, i—ii (1547); A. de Cotel, xiv (1578); Jamyn, i—iii (1584); S. Certon, i—xxiv (1603). On the translations see Egger, ch. vii, 'Revue des traductions françaises d'Homère', in *Mémoires de littérature ancienne*, pp. 164–217; *Hellénisme*, i. 191–5; ii. 128–34; Hennebert, 'Histoire des traductions', pp. 106–10. On the fortunes of Homer see Finsler, *Homer in der Neuzeit* (Leipzig, 1912); Hepp, 'Homère en France au XVIᵉ siècle', *Atti della Accademia delle Scienze di Torino*, 96 (1961–2), 389–508; *Homère en France au XVIIᵉ siècle* (Paris, 1968).

4. See Chiaradia, *L'imitazione omerica nella 'Gerusalemme Liberata'*, (Naples, 1903).

5. See below, pp. 203–5.

6. Letters 1337 and 1480 (ed. Guasti). The sequel was provided by Ascanio Grandi's *Tancredi*, but this too is basically Iliadic in structure. See Belloni, *Epigoni*, pp. 265–6.

7. See Sayce, p. 19.

8. See below, p. 000.

9. Lange, *Ronsards Franciade und ihr Verhältnis zu Vergils Aeneide* (Wurzen, 1887), contains a full list. See also Storer, *Virgil and Ronsard*, pp. 12–19, for the *Franciade;* and pp. 100–24, for a list of Virgilian reminiscences throughout Ronsard's work.

10. For Virgil's fortune in general, see Comparetti, *Vergil in the Middle Ages* (London, 1908); Zabughin, *Vergilio nel Rinascimento italiano* (Bologna, 1921–3); Hulubei, 'Virgile en France au XVIe', *RSS,* 18 (1931), 1–77. The main translations of the *Aeneid* are those of Octovien de Saint-Gelais (1509), Louis des Masures (1560), and Michel de Marolles (1655); see Hennebert, 'Histoire des traductions', pp. 115–20. On Conti, see Seznec, *Survivance,* pp. 196–225, 273–5.

11. 'Elégie au Roy' in *Henriade* (1770), p. 9:
    Le chant qu'il [Virgil] auoit faict en la gloire & l'honneur
    Contenant les haults faicts de ce grand Empereur [Augustus].

12. 'Au Roy Henry IV' in *Oeuvres* (1594), vol. i:
> Sur tous il [Scipion] aimoit tant la douce compagnie,
> Et les deuis priuez du Rudien Ennie,
> Son chantre & son poëte . . . (sig. † 6ᵛ.)

The idea had been fostered by Petrarch's *Africa*, Book ix.

13. '. . . Lucain & Silius Italicus ont couvert l'histoire du manteau de Poesie' ('Preface sur la Franciade', xvi. 338–9). Not a very fair comment on Lucan; the witch Erichtho in *Pharsalia* vi was only the most popular of Lucan's fantasies.

14. See Otis, *Ovid as an epic poet* (Cambridge, 1966).

15. On Sannazaro's and Vida's poems, see Sayce, pp. 49–50, and di Cesare, *Vida's Christiad and Vergilian epic* (Columbia, 1964).

16. See below, p. 64 n. 20.

17. For borrowings from Tasso in French epic, see Marni, *Allegory*, pp. 32–45; Simpson, *Le Tasse*, pp. 90–5; Beall, *La Fortune du Tasse*, pp. 80–104; and in general Belloni, *Gli epigoni della Gerusalemme Liberata* (Padua, 1893) for Tasso's fortunes in Italy.

18. e.g. Giocondo: *Furioso*, 28, 4–74; *Savoysiade*, vi, fol. 171ᵛ ff. See also Boyssières, *Croisade*, fol. 18ʳ ff.

19. See Parducci, 'Le imitazioni ariostee nella *Franciade* del Ronsard', *Archivum Romanicum*, 14 (1930), 361–94; Cameron, *Ariosto*, pp. 79–84.

20. See especially Cioranescu, *L'Arioste*, i. 174–80 (Ronsard); 189 (Ariosto and Tasso); 190–2 (Boyssières); 195–7 (Deimier); ii. 42–4 (Scudéry); 44–6 (Chapelain); 46–7 (Le Moyne); 47–8 (Desmarets); 48–9 (Courtin); 49–50 (Carel).

21. See Sayce, pp. 54–5, 76, 93; Cabeen, *Marino*, p. 160; Adam, *Théophile*, pp. 443–54; and in general Damiani, *Sopra la poesia del cavalier Marino* (Turin, 1899); Borzelli, *G.B. Marino* (Naples, 1927).

IV

HISTORY

HAVING examined the epic theory which helped to create the conception of a distinct epic genre, having considered the epic models from which poets borrowed the structures, episodes, and topoi which made their poems recognizable as epics, we turn to history, the raw material of epic, which we shall consider from three points of view. Firstly, a brief account of the development of historical writing; secondly, the manner in which poets used this material; and thirdly, a comparison between the genres of epic and history.

Historical writing from 1500 to 1700

The conception of history in these two centuries was as varied and fluid as the conception of epic. Both, in form and content, could take surprising shapes. The writing of the history of France best illustrates the development. It was the theme that most French historians treated and was the source on which poets most frequently drew, though the history of other countries also made its contribution.

The sixteenth century saw the abandonment of annalistic history in favour of two new forms of historical writing, both of which may broadly be termed humanist. Firstly, 'rhetorical' history, by which I mean the attempt to recreate the ancient genre of history by rewriting the annals of one's country in a manner reminiscent of Livy or Thucydides. Secondly, 'methodical' history, by which I mean the attempt to sift the evidence of the past in order to arrive at historical truth. This, the ancestor of modern historical method, was usually presented not so much as an elegant narrative but as a series of well-documented essays.[1]

The epic poets drew on annalistic and rhetorical history, with excursions into methodical history for the purposes of controversy. Though methodical history represents the most progressive aspects of the historical genre, I shall concentrate on the annalistic and rhetorical types because they were the most frequently used by epic poets.

When Ronsard described his historical sources as 'nos vieilles annales' or 'croniques', to what was he referring? There were two kinds of annals, ecclesiastical and secular. Of the former an example is the *Grandes chroniques de France,* a collective title for a series of works in large part due to the monks of Saint-Denis. Of the latter the *Annales et chroniques de France* (1492) of Nicole Gilles were the best known in the sixteenth century.[2] Annals were the chronological record of the reigns of the kings of France and could be extended indefinitely by continuators. Gilles's *Annales* were added to right through the sixteenth century, the amount of revision varying with each editor. Denis Sauvage in 1549 simply brought the annals from the death of Louis XI, where Gilles ended, down to the death of Francis I. In 1573 François de Belleforest substantially revised the whole work mainly to bring it into line with contemporary taste rather than in any critical spirit. He added the reigns of Henry II, Francis II, and the beginning of Charles IX. This was the last major revision. In 1585 Guillaume Chappuys merely added the rest of Charles IX and started on Henry III. In 1621 Jean Savaron finished Henry III, and added Henry IV and Louis XIII. When Ronsard said, 'le bon Poëte jette tousjours le fondement de son ouvrage sur quelques vieilles Annales du temps passé',[3] it was to such works that he was referring.

What of rhetorical history? The first attempt to revive history as a literary genre was made by Robert Gaguin in 1497 with his *Compendium de origine et gestis Francorum.*[4] But for all his learning Gaguin failed sufficiently to distinguish himself from the annalists. This was achieved by the Italian Paolo Emilio who performed for French history the service rendered to English history by Polydore Vergil. Of Emilio's *De rebus gestis Francorum* four books were published in 1517 and all ten in 1539. Like Gaguin's work it was translated and ran through many editions.[5]

In 1549 du Bellay made the following plea to those who were wasting their time on novels:

d'employer cete grande eloquence à recuillir ces fragmentz de vieilles chroniques francoyses, et comme a fait Tite Live des annales et autres anciennes chroniques romaines, en batir le cors entier d'une belle histoire, y entremeslant à propos ces belles concions et harangues à l'immitation de celuy que je viens de nommer, de Thucidide, Saluste, ou quelque autre bien approuvé . . . .[6]

Clearly he did not consider that Emilio's achievement, being in Latin, counted. But Emilio's example did not escape du Haillan, who in 1576 supplied France with her first rhetorical history in the vernacular. In the preface to his work du Haillan reviewed the efforts of his predecessors in order to point the difference between his work and theirs. Dismissing the amusing but tedious prolixity of the medieval chroniclers he describes his conception of history, which 'ne doit traicter qu'affaires d'Estat, comme les conseils des Princes, leurs entreprinses & les causes, les effects, & les euenemens d'icelles, & parmy cela mesler quelque belle sentence qui monstre au lecteur le proffit qu'il peult tirer de ce qu'il lit'.[7] We note here three points of contact with epic. The illustriousness of the chief characters ('conseils des princes'); the need for interpretation to give cohesion to the whole work ('les causes, les effects'); and the desire to moralize ('quelque belle sentence'). Elsewhere in the preface du Haillan lumps Emilio in with other earlier chroniclers, amongst whom he names Gaguin. Doubtless the reason why he failed to pay tribute to Emilio's originality was that he wished to conceal his plagiarism. For du Haillan lifted most of his speeches, the hall-mark of rhetorical history, as du Bellay's words show, from the work of Emilio.[8]

The annalistic and rhetorical forms of history appealed most to epic poets. The former as a source of well-established legends, the latter because of the affinities between history and epic, which I shall presently discuss.

In the last quarter of the sixteenth century, historical writing had reached the following position. The annalistic tradition had yielded on the one hand to rhetorical history such as has been described, on the other to methodical history, such as the *Recherches* of Pasquier, which exemplify the manner of amassing and assessing evidence,[9] or the *Methodus* of Bodin, which attempted to work out a philosophy of history, uniting its two branches, research and narrative.[10] On the threshold of the seventeenth century it seemed that the synthesis adumbrated by Bodin could be realized, but this was not to be. Historical writing in the seventeenth century shifted emphatically in the direction of rhetoric. The new presentations of traditional

material were moulded by the pressures of contemporary
events rather than by the results of critical research.

Shifts of public opinion can be seen at work in the histories
of Dupleix and Mézeray. To many in the 1620s, and especially
to Richelieu, a strong Catholic monarchy seemed the cure for
religious and civil strife. This was the bias of the *Histoire
générale de France* (1621–8) of Scipion Dupleix. But the public
that applauded Dupleix discovered that absolutism and orthodoxy could be a high price to pay for law and order.[11] On the
tide of feudal opposition and Parlementary reaction Mézeray's
Histoire de France (1643) made its appearance. It appealed to
the spirit of the Frondeurs and continued to enjoy popularity
even when the reaffirmation of absolutism discouraged further
historical writing in the same vein. Mézeray's history appeared
too late to affect the bulk of historical epic but in fact it re-
introduced into the historical genre many of the legendary
stories of epic flavour which had been challenged or discredited
in the late sixteenth century.[12]

Such in outline was the development of French national
history, the predominant but not exclusive hunting ground for
epic poets. To Ronsard's successors national frontiers were no
boundary to their literary ambitions. For the history of Navarre
Palma Cayet acknowledged his debt to the Spanish chronicle
of Don Carlos, Prince of Viana. Paradin's *Chronique de Savoie*
served d'Urfé and Delbene. Most of Beaujeu's material could
be found in the works of Loritus or Simler on Swiss history.
For Scotland Schelandre indicated in many marginal notes the
histories of Hector Boethius and George Buchanan.[13]

Ancient historians were readily available in contemporary
editions or translations but neither Greek nor Roman history
attracted either poets or historians to any extent.[14] The historians of later Antiquity were more useful. Desmarets drew on
Gregory of Tours for the careers of Clovis and, for the account
of Alaric's destruction of Rome, Scudéry turned to Procopius
and Orosius.

Historians and poets

Historical writing therefore provided a rich and varied
source of inspiration; but when a poet turned to history, what
was he looking for, and how did he use it?

The simplest approach was the annalistic. The poet recounted in verse what the chronicle related in prose. The
moralizing element was strong. The poet embellished his
narrative with digressions on moral topics suggested by the
historical events, and condensed his judgements into *sententiae*.
To give a poetic framework, poets sometimes introduced the
historical material by means of a prophecy. Cayet imagined a
Sibyl discoursing on the history of Navarre; Geuffrin made
Hector recount the vicissitudes of the French monarchy.

Heroic epic demanded a greater selectivity and a more
complex process of adaptation. The poet made either his hero's
career or an episode of his life the argument of his epic.
According to the structure he had determined, the historical
account would need more or less adaptation. The historical
material might itself dictate the structure of the epic as in the
case of Blarru's *Nanceid*, Pillard's *Rusticiad*, Garnier's
Henriade, or Ennetières's *Chevalier*, where structural fictions
are relatively few. Alternatively the epic structure might impose
itself on the historical material. The Virgilian model moulded
the poems of d'Urfé, Ronsard, Delbene, or Schelandre; Tasso's
example those of Le Moyne, Desmarets, Scudéry, or Chapelain.
Ronsard represented the extreme example of this process. The
historical material on which the story of Francus rested was
barely a few sentences. Ronsard's epic structure expanded
these scanty indications into an entirely fictitious but detailed
and plausible career.[15]

Poets debated the distance that should separate them from
their heroes. Recommendations were based on the requirements of *vraisemblance*. Ronsard argued that three or four
hundred years should elapse before a subject became suitable
for epic treatment.[16] For Ronsard, therefore, events after about
1250 were unsuitable. In fact he made sure of having a free
hand by turning to the very dawn of history. Le Laboureur,
however, believed that so distant a time would prevent the
reader from becoming fully engaged by the theme, but equally
that events which were too close would render the poet's
fictions implausible.[17] In the sixteenth century, when fictions
tended to be more decorative than structural, this was of no
great consequence, and epics frequently dealt with contemporary events.[18] Le Moyne seems to share Ronsard's opinion and

claimed that the four-hundred-year interval between himself and his subject was just right. However, the reason for most of the heroes in the seventeenth-century poems appearing to conform to Ronsard's recommendation is less a preoccupation with chronology than the exigencies of Christian epic. Their heroes are mainly what we would call medieval, though scattered over a wide period of time. What they all offered was the opportunity to treat a Christian theme.[19]

Epic theory recommended that these characters chosen from distant periods should be depicted in a manner appropriate to their nationality and social position.[20] But how were Frenchmen of the sixteenth and seventeenth centuries to paint a convincing picture of sixth-century Merovingian Gaul, fifteenth-century England, not to mention such far-flung settings as the Outer Hebrides or the Euxine sea, and peoples as diverse as the Saracens, the Goths, or the Swiss?

Various solutions were attempted. One was to treat the distant period as the present. Desmarets transformed Clovis, the barbarian chieftain, into a figure who would not have seemed out of place at the court of Louis XIV. The literary modernization was supported visually by the engravings that illustrated the poems. The pressure of the patron played its part in this process. The poet could hardly flatter Louis XIV by depicting his predecessor in a manner, however accurate, that made him seem ridiculous by contemporary standards. This does not mean that a sense of historical perspective was lacking. Sixteenth-century historians were well aware that different periods and countries had different customs, and that they had to be judged in that light.[21] The recognition that each age had its peculiar and valid characteristics underlay the position of those who objected to the slavish imitation of the ancients.[22]

Those who did attempt to portray the authentic flavour of a period or country could turn to the topographical or anthropological surveys which prefaced many historical works. Buchanan's history provided Schelandre with the details of the austere life of the primitive Hebrideans.[23] Chapelain consulted Camden's *Britannia* for a survey of the counties of England, and based thereon his review of the innumerable contingents of the English army.[24] In other instances the historical source was itself close enough to events to furnish local colour. Join-ville's *Histoire de Saint Louis* gave Le Moyne not only his plot but also an eye-witness account of Saracen Egypt. No historical work of course yielded information about the world of Francus, but Ronsard, assuming that it was the same world as that of Aeneas or Achilles, used the *Iliad* or *Aeneid* not only as models for epic structure and episodes but also as a historical source for local colour.

When historians disagreed, what should the poet do? Ronsard, believing that their dissensions were irrelevant to poetry, disdained mere questions of historical fact, whereas his impertinent rival, Delaudun, prided himself on acquaintance with the most recent historical research on the origin of the Franks. To incorporate into his poem current theories concerning the Germanic origin of the Franks would, Delaudun believed, raise his *Franciade* above that of Ronsard; but keeping abreast of the latest historical research was no substitute for lack of poetic talent. The same is true of Carel de Sainte-Garde, who immersed himself in the most recent speculation about the origins of the Capetian kings. Yet, not only did Carel fail to construct a coherent narrative, but he managed to choose the wrong side in the historical controversy as well. Detailed research had decidedly pernicious effects on epic poets, and was invoked as a despairing gesture when they had little else to offer. Chapelain's view was the most sensible: the poet should adhere to the traditional accounts, developing them with imagination rather than erudition. Delaudun and Carel, soliciting applause for their historical exactitude, when their poems were so defective in style and structure, invited merely ridicule.

History and epic

History and epic had much in common, more than historians and poets, both asserting their respective superiority, would care to admit. Du Haillan's conception of history, we have seen, might almost be a definition of epic: emphasis on cause and effect, illustrious exploits, and moralizing.[25] Equally, much of the material in the older annals—legends, miracles, prodigies, and superhuman feats—is typically epic material.

The differences that poets seemed most anxious to underline were the ordering of the narrative and the contrast between truth and plausibility. Ronsard stated that the historian's task was to narrate events 'de fil en fil', while the poet should make use of recitals to disturb chronology. This is a legitimate difference, and one which immediately strikes the reader who compares, say, Livy and Virgil. Later poets, in order to establish their claim to be writing epic, exaggerated the disturbance of chronology to prove their point. Yet no historian can be strictly chronological. The domestic and foreign affairs of a ruler often need to be grouped and narrated in successive blocks, even where the events dovetail each other chronologically. A foreign invasion has to be explained by relating its background after mentioning the point of time at which it occurred. Speeches in rhetorical history frequently rehearsed the past to illuminate the present, and the historian who pointed to the consequences of an event was indulging in prophecy on the basis of hindsight. All are quite natural procedures. Strict chronology, the procedure of certain more arid annalists, is highly artificial, since past, present and future are closely interdependent, and such a procedure is likely to fragment a sequence of events pertaining to a single person or locality. The change from annalistic to rhetorical history permitted a more faithful imitation of reality. Despite their claim that disturbance of chronology was a peculiarity of epic, poets were doing no more than develop a device that was inherent in rhetorical history and which had perhaps in the first instance been suggested to ancient historians by epic poetry.

The application of criteria of plausibility (*vraisemblance*) to history and epic was fraught with far greater problems, though it was often treated as though it were simplicity itself. Ronsard is a case in point, though to his credit he showed more common sense than later theorists, who had pretensions to discussing the question more profoundly. The following statement assigning truth to history and plausibility to epic seemed to leave no further room for argument: '[Le Poëte heroïque] a pour maxime tresnecessaire en son art, de ne suivre jamais pas à pas la verité, mais la vray-semblance, & le possible: Et sur le possible & sur ce qui se peut faire, il bastit son ouvrage, laissant la veritable narration aux Historiographes . . .'[26] We note here what is not often explicitly stated, that, for Ronsard at least, *vraisemblance* embraced the wider field of possibility rather than the narrower one of probability. In an earlier passage, however, Ronsard was careful to distinguish between particular historical truth and general philosophical truth, which when confused, as so often happened, made nonsense of the whole theory of *vraisemblance*:

> Encore que l'Histoire en beaucoup de sortes se conforme à la Poësie, comme en vehemence de parler, harangues, descriptions de batailles, villes, fleuves, mers, montaignes, & autres semblables choses, où le Poëte ne doibt non plus que l'Orateur falsifier le vray, si est-ce quand à leur sujet ils sont aussi eslongnez l'un de l'autre que le vraysemblable est eslongné de la verité.[27]

Ronsard was here acknowledging that in certain matters the poet must stick to the truth as closely as the historian, that is in eloquence, speeches, and war etc., which are common to both genres, but that in their theme as a whole (*sujet*) the poet's province was general philosophical truth, whilst the historian's was particular truth supported by evidence. For example the speeches of Hyante must seem to be the true words of a woman in love, Francus's duel with Phovère a real fight. That neither episode took place, provided they were presented plausibly, not only did not detract from the poet's credibility, but actually made him superior to the historian, who, shackled by the demands of particular truth, would for the career of Francus have nothing to say at all. Common sense, it seems, enabled Ronsard to preserve the distinction between truth based on general experience and truth based on historical evidence, though special pleading may have played its part, for the *Franciade* was based on the scantiest of indications from the historians, and those highly dubious.

When later poets confused general and particular truth they were forced into positions from which only logical gymnastics could rescue them. Delaudun criticized Ronsard for building his epic on discredited historical foundations, but still concedes the validity of *vraisemblance* based on general experience: '. . . il est permis au poëte de mentir, poureu que ce qu'il controuue puisse estre ou auoir esté . . .'[28] Le Moyne expressed the shift in attitude which made the truth of history the basis of plausibility: 'Le premier soin du Poëte sera de bastir sur vn fond ferme & solide; sur vne verité prise de l'Histoire ou receuë de la Tradition.'[29] This view presented the poet with a dilemma. If he did not follow history he was accused of implausibility, but since historical truth is often implausible, he would be accused of implausibility if he did follow it. Desmarets lamented the injustice: 'Elle [l'Envie] est encore si injuste, que tantost elle n'approuve pas certaines choses ausquelles la verité de l'Histoire nous oblige, & tantost elle pretend nous assujettir à suivre exactement l'Histoire . . .'[30] To this paradox Chapelain supplied a logical answer and stood the concept of *vraisemblance* on its head: '. . . il est vray-semblable qu'il arriue quelquesfois des choses, qui selon le cours ordinaire, ne deuroient point arriuer.'[31]

These hair-splittings were the very stuff of which prefaces and treatises were made. The practice of the poets was more down to earth. If they wished to entertain the reader with fiction, they justified it on the grounds of *vraisemblance*. If, like Desmarets or Courtin, they sought to astonish the reader, they would comb the historians for wildly improbable incidents, include them in the epic, and justify them on the authority of the historians.

Criteria of plausibility were also applicable to history. Historians might, on the grounds of plausibility, discard the fabulous material that clustered round the origins of their nation. Plausibility also had to govern the historian's interpretation of the causes and effects of events.[32] There is therefore, no essential distinction between *vérité* and *vraisemblance*. Distinctions certainly were made by both historians and poets, but only as ammunition in their polemics, when they wished to insist on the particularities of their respective professions.

When the writing of history is based mainly on literary sources, the historian's task resembles that of the poet who borrows from him, in that both are recasting the narrative of a predecessor into a new form. The historian seems to be bound by a body of fact which the poet can handle more freely by changing, omitting, or selecting whatever suits his purpose; but this freedom was also enjoyed by historians, and they were not slow to take advantage of it. For example Boethius offered a version of the events leading to Macbeth's usurpation, which Buchanan recast for his own history. On the surface their narratives seem much the same. But what has Buchanan done with his predecessor's account? Some parts of it he omitted because, he says, they sound fictitious. Other parts he omitted because he wished to give a briefer account of Macbeth's career; he therefore selected what he thought was most important. Further parts of Boethius's narrative he modified because he was offering new interpretations of events, or assessments of character. Buchanan's choice in these matters was determined by the length, method, and bias of his history. The poet Schelandre employed exactly the same procedure when, the works of both Boethius and Buchanan before him, he modified their narratives according to the structure and argument of his epic. Naturally the distinguishing features of epic—the disturbance of chronology, the fictions and the *merveilleux*—place particular constraints on the poet's adaptation of history. Epic thus becomes an interpretation of history, usually a poetic interpretation, which, when both historical sources and epic models are known, can illustrate the workings of both poetic and historical creation.[33]

Schelandre's example is profitable because both his historical sources and his epic models can be identified and it is clear that he had a particular epic structure in mind. With other poets the case is different. Where the epic element is reduced to decorative embellishment, the interpretative function becomes more historical than poetic. Epic then verges on history as Ronsard pointed out.[34] But whilst Ronsard intended to denigrate the poet who was too much of a historian, we must ask whether the epic poet was not in fact fulfilling a function that was lacking in annalistic history. The most complex annals could be extended indefinitely with no overall plan except chronology, but even the crudest attempt at epic presupposed some interpretative effort. What we notice about the early sixteenth century is that history was mainly annalistic whilst epic was structurally historical rather than poetical. Blarru or Pillard were in a sense doing what Gilles or Gaguin failed to do, namely giving cohesion to scattered fact. In the course of the sixteenth century the work of men like Le Roy, Baudouin, Vignier, La Popelinière, Bodin, or Pasquier quite transformed historical method. At the same time Ronsard gave an emphatically poetic structure to historical epic. His successors wavered between the two. The work of Sébastien Garnier was not substantially different from that of Blarru or Pillard, but Delbene, d'Urfé, and Schelandre inclined towards a poetic interpretation of history. The poets of the 1650s also illustrated this poetic interpretation of history whilst their contemporaries, the historians Dupleix and Mézeray, were, in strange retreat from the more scholarly and philosophical methods of the sixteenth century, readmitting into the historical genre of their day the legendary material and rhetorical approach that were characteristic of epic.

Clearly history and historical epic share the function of narrating historical events within a structure that gives cohesion to the facts and an interpretation to the events. In the sixteenth and seventeenth centuries certain techniques of research, interpretation, and narration oscillated between the two genres, so that we can never firmly fix the boundaries between epic and history.

NOTES TO CHAPTER IV

1. See Kelley, *Foundations of modern historical scholarship* (Columbia, 1970), a most useful work for sixteenth-century historiography, which traces the rise of methodical history from the philological researches of Valla and the legal humanism of Budé and Alciato. See especially the chapter on François Baudouin, pp. 116–48, for the first attempt 'to promote history from an art to a science by organizing it in a methodical way'. See also Huppert, *The idea of perfect history* (Illinois, 1969), pp. 12–27. The works of Kelley and Huppert provide bibliographical information on the historians mentioned in this chapter.

2. According to Tilley, 'first published in 1492, but no copy of this edition is known' (*Studies*, p. 180). Cf. Huppert, *Perfect history*, p. 13 n.1.

3. 'Preface sur la Franciade', xvi. 339.

4. Further editions in 1499, 1500, 1507, 1511, 1521, 1524, 1548, 1577. Translated by Pierre Desrey 1514. Further editions of the translation 1515, 1516, 1518, 1520, 1525, 1527, 1530, 1536. See Kelley, p. 55; Simone, *Rinascimento*, p. 50; and Tilley, *Studies*, pp. 174–5.

5 It was re-edited and brought up to date in 1544, 1548, 1549, 1550, 1555, 1565, 1569, 1577, 1598, 1601. Translated by Simon de Monthières (1556) and Jean Regnart (1581 and 1598). See Huppert, pp. 15–17.

6. *Deffence* (ed. Chamard), pp. 237–8.

7. Preface to *Histoire de France* (1576), sig. *8^r.

8. Evans, *Mézeray*, p. 15; Huppert, p. 17.

9. See Huppert, pp. 28–71; Kelley, pp. 271–300.

10. See Huppert, pp. 93–103; Kelley, pp. 136–8; and the introduction to Reynolds's translation of the *Methodus*.

11. See Evans, p. 21.

12. See Evans, p. 22; Huppert, pp. 84–6.

13. See below, p. 101 n. 40.

14. Cf. Huppert, p. 20.

15. 'Or' il est vraysemblable que Francion a fait tel voyage . . . & sur ce fondement de vraysemblance j'ay basti ma Franciade de son nom.' ('Au lecteur', xvi. 7–8.)

16. . . . le Poete ne doit jamais prendre l'argument de son oeuvre, que trois ou quatre cens ans ne soient passez pour le moins . . .' ('Preface sur la Franciade', xvi. 345).

17. Preface to *Charlemagne*, a5^r.

18. Events of 1476 are narrated in the *Nanceid* (1518); of 1524 in the *Rusticiad* (1548); of 1589–90 in Garnier's *Henriade* (1594).

19. The dates of the events narrated in these epics are: *Alaric* (410), *Clovis* (481–96), the *Charlemagnes* of Courtin and Le Laboureur (774–814), *Saint Louis* (1249–50), *La Pucelle* (1429–31).

20. Mambrun, *Dissertatio,* p. 439; Marolles, *Traité,* pp. 77–9; Le Moyne, 'Traité', ol^r; 'Dissertation', i3^v.

21. Starting with Alciato (see Kelley, p. 97). See also Huppert, pp. 161–6, on 'historical relativism'.

22. 'Il faut examiner et considerer [les methodes des anciens] par les circonstances du temps, du lieu et des personnes pour qui elles ont esté composées . . .' (Ogier, preface to Schelandre's *Tyr et Sidon* (1628), in Lawton, *Handbook,* p. 124).

23. *Rerum scoticarum,* i, fol. 7^{r-v}.

24. *Pucelle,* Bk. xviii. Chapelain had the 1607 edition of *Britannia* in his library (see Searles, *Catalogue,* p. 111, no. 3863).

25. See above, p. 38.

26. 'Preface sur la Franciade', xvi. 336.

27. 'Au lecteur', xvi. 3–4.

28. *Art poétique,* p. 263.

29. 'Traité', a12^r; 'Dissertation', e2^v.

30. *Clovis,* 'Avis', e2^v.

31. Preface to *La Pucelle,* b4^v. Cf. Aristotle, *Poetics,* 1456a, 23–5; Boileau, 'Le Vrai peut quelquefois n'estre pas vraisemblable.' (*Art poétique,* iii. 48).

32. Buchanan at the beginning of *Rerum scoticarum* refers to the fables related by Boethius and discards them on the grounds of implausibility. The attitude is summed up by Elton: 'Even when the right questions have been asked . . . the answers must be probable; they must agree with what is known to be possible in human experience.' (*Practice of history,* p. 111.).

33. See Maskell, 'The transformation of history into epic: the *Stuartide* (1611) of J. de Schelandre', *MLR,* 66 (1971), 53–65.

34. See above, p. 35 n. 13, for his criticisms of Lucan and Silius.

PART II
THE POEMS

V

CONTEMPORARY HEROES

HAVING considered how theory moulded the conception of epic and how the task of reconciling historical sources with literary models created a challenge to which the poets responded in different fashions, we are now in a position to examine individually the epics of the sixteenth and seventeenth centuries.

The first three poems to be dealt with belong respectively to the beginning, middle, and end of the sixteenth century. They all show how, when faced with a particular kind of hero, namely a patron and a contemporary, the poets used poetic structures sparingly and for the most part allowed the sequence of historical events to determine the structure of the epic.

Blarru and René, Duke of Lorraine

Pierre de Blarru was born in 1437 in Paris[1] six years after François Villon.[2] Blarru took a degree in theology and law at the University of Paris after which we lose track of him until 1475, when he is found in the service of René, Duke of Lorraine. Though Blarru finally settled in Lorraine and though his name is mainly linked with that duchy as a result of the *Nanceid*, his formative years were spent in Paris, and reminiscences of Paris can be found in the *Nanceid*.[3] Pensioned by René after the defeat of Charles, Duke of Burgundy, Blarru, through the influence of his patron, became shortly before 1498 a canon of Saint Dié. In 1510 he died.

His epic, the *Nanceid*, describes the overthrow of Charles of Burgundy by René of Lorraine (May 1475 to January 1477). The exact date of composition cannot be determined, since the poem was published posthumously in 1518 by Jean Basin, a friend and admirer of Blarru.[4] Towards the end of the sixteenth century the *Nanceid* was translated into French Alexandrines by Nicolas Romain.[5] In 1840 Ferdinand Schütz's edition provided a French translation facing the Latin text.[6]

What historical sources did Blarru use for this the first epic of the sixteenth century? Firstly, his own experience; he was in Epinal when Charles besieged it and in Nancy when Charles's funeral took place there.[7] Secondly, the accounts of other eye-witnesses; thirdly, written sources. From the account of the siege of Nancy by René's secretary, Chrétien, based on the letters of René, Blarru derived such details as the names of René's captains and the numbers of troops deployed.[8] The *Chronique de Lorraine* also contained many details about this campaign. Unlike Sébastien Garnier, who revelled in a whole gallery of noble characters, or Voltaire, who flattered the ancestors of his contemporaries,[9] Blarru omitted people or episodes which detracted from his theme, the duel between Charles and René. Notable among such omissions is the account of the defection of the Count of Campo Basso which badly weakened Charles's army and hastened his defeat.[10]

Such were the diverse sources available to Blarru for the matter of the *Nanceid*. How did he shape these events and to what extent did he borrow a structure from his predecessors in epic? The title of the poem is important. It is the city of Nancy which occupies the central place in the poem: Nancy is thrice besieged. Important too, is the relationship between the protagonists, Charles (the Lion) and René, neatly balanced in the opening lines:

> Proelia magnanimum quae te fregere *Leonem*
> . . . scribo . . .
> Victoris sinat haec [Clyo] iam principis arma *Renati*
> Surgere perpetuo (patitur si livor) honore.[11]

Charles's defeat is mentioned before René's victory; this is no 'Renatiad'; there are no trumpetings for a superhuman hero. Indeed, Charles's virtues and vices are depicted with such impartiality that at times he even eclipses René.[12] The structure of the poem is based on the account of the vicissitudes of the city of Nancy interwoven with the theme of Nemesis. In Book i René defies the ambitious Charles, who promptly ousts him from his capital, Nancy. Nancy changes hands again in Book ii. De Rubempré, holding it for Charles, loses it to René. Books iii–vi relate the drama of the final siege: a single city, one hero inside the walls and another without. Finally, Charles is crushed by René. Of the two heroes, he whose character is flawed is ruined. A fate envisaged at the start of the poem, threatened during the course of it, is accomplished at the end.

To ancient models this treatment owed nothing. The downfall of the proud was a medieval commonplace. Blarru followed medieval tradition in his adornments as well. There are reminiscences of Virgil, Lucan, and Ovid; also of the satirists, Horace, Juvenal, and Persius.[13] There are many *sententiae* and renderings of popular wisdom into latin.[14] The prevailing tone of Blarru's epic is moral, but morality does not knock all the life out of it. His erudition serves not to stimulate a new conception of epic but rather to reinforce the moralizing tendency.

In one respect however the influence of ancient epic may perhaps be seen at work. The introduction of events previous to the start of the poem is a technical problem which any writer of historical epic must grapple with. Blarru at one point gives Charles a long speech in which he recounts his earlier campaigns.[15] If we inquire what is the context of this speech we find that it is intended to encourage Charles's men before battle. The topos of encouragement occurs frequently in epic. The obvious Virgilian example is Aeneas reminding his comrades, briefly, of the trials they have undergone together.[16] We may suppose that Blarru developed this topos to serve a structural purpose, namely the disturbance of chronology. Thus a technical problem is solved by giving a topos a new twist, an example of the creative use of the topoi and structures of epic.

Clearly Blarru's *Nanceid,* by virtue of the unity which the theme of Nemesis gives it, set a reasonable standard in the matter of structure. But it is not by structure that a poem must finally be judged. We shall see later how brilliantly Chapelain conceived his epic, how unmercifully his handling of language let him down. This Blarru for the most part avoided. He has faults indeed, and Collignon has catalogued them.[17] But more often Blarru's imagination works constructively:

> . . . ora
> multa bibunt mortem, duri sine vulneris ictu.
> atque siti moriente bibunt; interque bibendum
> 'Mergimur,' exclamant, 'heu mergimur. O tamen auro
> quod latebris gerimus veniam date. Dignius aurum
> est homine; ob nostros salvate haec corpora nummos.'
> talia dum iactant in caelum verba, refusus
> humor adit vitae penetralia.[18]

The Burgundians sought escape from the enemy by diving into a lake. If they did not drown at once, they drowned as they opened their mouths to offer gold for mercy. The uncontrollable water fascinates Blarru; he renders his fascination by the paradoxical 'bibunt mortem' and 'siti moriente'. The aimless desperation of their dying words is contained in the vague 'auro quod latebris gerimus' and 'iactant in caelum': they are past addressing their pleas for mercy to any particular aggressor. The tense nervous sentences, often over-running the line, are typical of Blarru. He ends his epic telling us how the Muse commanded him to set to work: 'I, pluteo incumbe.'[19] Such vigour is characteristic of Blarru.

Pillard and Antoine, Duke of Lorraine

The next epic with a contemporary hero also issued from Saint Dié. Laurent Pillard, unlike Blarru, was a native of Lorraine.[20] He was born around 1480 in a village near Pont-à-Mousson. His origins were humble: 'Exilis genuit me sine luce domus.'[21] Fatherless at the age of two, Pillard received a good education thanks to a devoted mother and money from an uncle. He entered the Church and some time before 1513 succeeded his uncle as a canon of Saint Dié. Amongst other minor administrative functions he collected dues owing to the Chapter from the inhabitants of the surrounding countryside, a task not without significance for the subject of his epic, the Peasant Revolt of 1525. Pillard's life was uneventful and unpretentious. So too is his epic, the *Rusticiad,* completed in 1541. It is Pillard's only claim to fame. He died in 1553.

The diligence of scholars who have treated the history of Lorraine has ensured the *Rusticiad* a degree of attention that its qualities would not otherwise have attracted. The first edition, published at Metz by Jean Palier in 1548, became over the years hard to obtain. To remedy this Calmet reprinted the text in his *Bibliothèque Lorraine* (1751). In 1876 Dupeux performed for the *Rusticiad* the same service that Schütz had rendered the *Nanceid;* he provided a French translation with the Latin text. Many misprints mar Dupeux's text and a preference for generalized words in his translation tends to conceal what little colour there is in Pillard's original.[22]

To Pillard, succeeding his uncle as a canon of Saint Dié,

Blarru must have seemed a venerable figure. The Parisian man of affairs and poet had died in 1510, just about the time Pillard joined the community. Clearly Pillard knew Blarru's *Nanceid*; reminiscences in the *Rusticiad* prove it.[23] Indeed there can be little doubt that the *Nanceid* in fact inspired the *Rusticiad*. Pillard's subject, however, was far more recalcitrant epic material than Blarru's.

In April 1525 the Peasant Revolt, which had started in Germany, reached Alsace and thence, under the leadership of Erasmus Gerber, spread to the Sarre valley in Lorraine.[24] Antoine, Duke of Lorraine, raised an army against the peasants; the command was entrusted to his brother Claude de Guise. The peasants wanted no trouble with Antoine and sent him a spokesman, assuring him of their loyalty and asking only permission to preach the Gospel. Antoine had their spokesman put to death. Fearing further trouble, the peasants submitted. Antoine promised there would be no reprisals and the peasants laid down their arms at Saverne. His enemies defenceless, Antoine broke his word, had Gerber hanged, and started a massacre of the rest. Sixteen thousand were murdered; some escaped. Antoine pursued them to Sherwill and won a bloody victory. Another 12,000 died. Ten days after the army had taken the field Antoine made a triumphal entry into Nancy. Hardly a heroic tale. To Pillard, however, it was. As a canon of Saint Dié, as a local administrator, he saw in the Peasant Revolt a threat to religion and to society. That the Duke should have removed that threat so efficiently and expeditiously was a matter for the greatest rejoicing.

Like Blarru, Pillard's own experience furnished material for his epic; eye-witnesses returning from the scene of battle could fill in the gaps. If this did not suffice, Antoine's secretary, Nicholas Volcyre, had composed a *Histoire et recueil de la triumphante et glorieuse victoire*. Everything indicates that Pillard had this work before him as he composed. Lists of captains are reproduced in the *Rusticiad* in the same order as they appear in Volcyre, even at the expense of awkwardness in his verse.[25]

Animated by the passion of a man who saw his security threatened, aided by detailed sources and his own experiences, Pillard might yet have breathed life and fire into the *Rusticiad*

despite its faithless and unheroic hero. We can see he felt the
inadequacy of his subject-matter. Why else should he have
decked out these paltry events with no fewer than eighty-one
speeches? We can see he felt that Antoine of Lorraine, however
admirable as the protector of law and order, was not quite the
stuff of which epic heroes are made. Yet how did he remedy
this? Again by speeches (of which Antoine makes eighteen)
and prayers (of which he offers eight.)[26] In such a climate
sententiae not surprisingly abound. Pillard favoured them at
the conclusion of speeches and derived repeated pleasure from
the exercise.[27] The chronicle of which the *Rusticiad* is little
more than a versification was already ornate with quotations
from the ancients. Pillard's originality seems confined to his
adaptation of the infernal council from Vida's *Christiad* which
had appeared in 1535. Pillard's style may be 'purer' than
Blarru's in that it contains fewer neologisms, but it is far inferior in vigour and imaginative power.[28] There is no excitement in the *Rusticiad*. Pillard's epic inspiration was irremedi-
ably dulled by the dead hand of religion and morality.

Garnier, Navières, Thomas I, and Henry IV

To understand the piecemeal publication of Garnier's *Henriade* we need to know something of the poet's life, details of
which may be gathered from his published works and from the
archives of Blois.[29] He was born in that town between 1548 and
1551 and held the office of *procureur du roi*. He was a determined opponent of the League and profoundly deplored the
assassination of Henry III. His literary activity was confined to
the years 1590 to 1594.[30] He was an ardent champion of legitimacy and this prompted him to write. Five years after the
murder of Henry III the poet was condemning the authors of
the crime, even though public opinion was against him, and in
all his works he insisted on the justice of Henry of Navarre's
claim to the throne. As a writer of historical epic Garnier held
strong political convictions and his poems are more polemical
in tone than any others. He died in 1595.

The *Henriade* was published in two parts. Books ix–xvi, the
second half, in 1593, and Books i and ii, in 1594.[31] Also in 1593
he published the first three books of a *Loyssée* which he never
finished. The following discussion of the publication of the

Henriade is relevant to the understanding of the *Loyssée* but I shall deal with the *Loyssée* itself later, together with the *Saint Louis* of Le Moyne.

There is some contradiction in what Garnier tells us about the origins of his epic. He claims that, even before the murder of Henry III, Henry of Navarre's generous character and high ideals so impressed him, that he conceived the idea of writing an epic on the life of the Bourbon prince.[32] But it is doubtful if Garnier really began to write as early as this. The earliest events described in Book i of the *Henriade* are subsequent to the battle of Arques (September 1589). In Book ii he refers to the siege of Paris (April to August 1590). Obviously Books i and ii of the *Henriade* could not have been written before the murder of Henry III. It is much more likely that Garnier conceived his epic after the provisional recognition of Henry IV in August 1589. This is made plausible by another remark. In October 1594 Garnier wrote in his 'Elégie au roi':

> Il y a ja cinq ans que sans aucun salaire
> Je travaille pour vous . . . [33]

Probably he is unintentionally revealing that he only started work on the *Henriade* in October 1589, just after the battle of Arques. This is in fact where the action of the *Henriade* begins.

Garnier's detestation of the League is clear throughout his poems and earned him many enemies in Blois, which, if it did not openly support the League, harboured influential partisans of Mayenne. This may have been the reason for having the *Henriade* printed in secret.[34] In July 1593 he published Books ix–xvi of the *Henriade*. Did he have the whole poem in manuscript at this stage, or had he for some reason started to compose his poem in the middle? The last eight books form a complete account of the battle of Ivry; they are self-contained and intelligible without reference to the earlier part of the story. If the whole poem had been written, there might have been a reason for publishing the second rather than the first half. The first eight books, whose action begins after[35] the battle of Arques, would have been based on a series of sporadic events, 'les reprises de villes, des forts & des châteaux', and therefore probably inferior in dramatic interest to the unified account of the battle of Ivry. So Garnier may have thought that the second eight books had a better chance of success. But if the whole poem was ready, why not publish it all? Probably the desire for reward played its part. In the dedicatory letters of the *Henriade* and *Loyssée* of 1593 there is no mention of money; doubtless Garnier expected recompense without the indelicacy of claiming it. He was disappointed. So the publication of only two books of the *Henriade* in 1594 suggests a determination from then on to harbour his resources until rewards came. In 1594 he reminded the King of his duty for the first time:

> N'aurez vous point mon Roy memoire & souvenance
> De moy vostre GARNIER? me faisant recompense
> De mes labeurs passez . . .[36]

Garnier was not rewarded and Books iii–vii of the *Henriade* are lost to us.

In what survives the guiding theme is politics. Garnier condemns extremists on both sides. Into Châtillon's mouth he puts a speech reproaching supporters of the League with the massacre of St. Bartholomew:

> Ne vous souvient-il plus, cruelz & inhumains,
> Du jour où tant de gens passerent par vos mains?
> Avez-vous oblié l'incroyable carnage
> Que vous fistes ce jour, pleins de fureur & rage;
> Massacrant, transportez d'extrême passion,
> Sans avoir ni de sang, ni d'âge acception . . .[37]

For the assassination of Henry III he lays entire responsibility on the Jesuits:

> . . . La conspiration
> D'un si horrible faict en fut faicte à Lyon,
> En leur maudit College, & depuis confirmée
> Par Varade à Paris, comme est la renommée.
> Jésuiste que dis-tu? Quel pilier de la Foi!
> Sus respons à mes dicts; & où est ceste loi
> Qui permet de tremper d'une main violente
> Dans le sang de son Roi l'espée flamboyante,
> Voire fust-ce un Néron; & encore qui est pis,
> De promettre aux meurtriers de leur Roi Paradis?[38]

All forms of political activity which disrupt the peace and unity of France are abhorrent to Garnier. He condemns the intervention of the Pope and his abuse of spiritual authority.[39] He condemns the League for inviting foreigners to support their cause.[40] Only loyalty to Henry can save the country from ruin, and his claim to the throne is constantly justified:

> Je ne suis point issu d'un Hespagnol marrane,
> Ni par mere sortie de quelque Italienne . . .
> Mon pere a pris sa source et sa vraie origine
> De Robert de Clermont, race saincte & divine,
> Fils du Roi Sainct Louis . . .[41]

Noteworthy is Garnier's use of the topoi of epic to emphasize the legitimacy of the Bourbon cause. On Henry's shield is depicted the life of Saint Louis, thus reminding the reader of the origins of the Bourbon family. When Henry asks for a sign of divine approval, thunder and lightening appear on the left.[42] When Henry is hard pressed, God sends Saint Michael himself to help.[43] Garnier uses the machinery of epic to further the cause he firmly believes in.

Sometimes the epic adornment sits awkwardly on Garnier's narrative. First he rejects the inspiration of the Muses as impotent liars;[44] later he invokes their omniscient aid.[45] The divine machinery is meant to be Christian. God and his angels intervene in battle, but we find Mars and Minerva taking part too. Curiously Mars is armed with a pistol.[46] Indeed Garnier's taste in epic adornment is remarkably diverse. There are reminiscences of the *chansons de geste,* whether deriving from medieval or Italian sources it is impossible to say. Henry's sword is none other than Durandal; his horse is descended from Renaud's Bayard.[47] The Old Testament is evoked in some similes: the mists which conceal Châtillon's advance from the Parisians are compared to those which veiled the Israelites' flight from the Pharaoh;[48] Henry's fright at the appearance of an angel is likened to that of Moses or Gideon when confronted by God's messengers.[49]

Garnier's flaccid monotonous style deprives his poem of real distinction, yet he is capable of accumulating detail in such a way as to produce a memorable picture. The effects of battle on the peaceful countryside suggest an eye-witness account: riderless horses running aimlessly, bodies abandoned to crows and wolves, uniforms fresh in the morning stained with blood and dirt after battle.[50] Sometimes an imaginative detail is marred by clumsy expression:

> Comme le cerf liger extrêmement lassé,
> Qui tout le long du jour a esté pourchassé,
> Desire de trouver au milieu de la plaine,
> Pour se désaltérer, quelque froide fontaine:
> De mesme nostre Roi desiroit, oppressé,
> Trouver quelque ruisseau d'extrême soif pressé,
> Mais quoi? vous ne pouviez; car les eaux des fontaines,
> Coulantes doucement, de nostre camp prochaines,
> Estoient teintes du sang sorti des ennemis,
> Qui par noz gents avoient esté à la mort mis . . .[51]

Henry's thirst after the exertion of battle and his frustration at finding every stream blood-polluted and undrinkable is well conceived. Less happy is the unnecessary *coulantes doucement* and the harsh inversions in the last line for the sake of a rhyme. Elsewhere we find striking reminders of the unpleasant realities of civil war. The survivors of the defeated army of the League straggling in twos and threes along the road; the weak and wounded, deserted by their stronger comrades, hiding if possible in the woods, mercilessly hunted out by the peasants in revenge for the disruption of their daily life.[52]

If the *Henriade* of Charles de Navières[53] had survived complete it would doubtless present an interesting contrast to Garnier's. It probably ran to 30,000 lines, and, between 1601 and 1610, numerous extracts, varying in length from three to nearly 700 lines, were published. About 1,000 lines survive altogether and enable us to form some estimate of it. The poem starts in a blaze of alliteration and assonance:

> De Valois alarmé j'enlarmerai l'armée
> Qui lamente sa fin si sanglante tramée
> Si le Diuin Donneur dont la dextre domine,
> Nous douër d'assez d'heur & d'heures determine
> Pour limer & liurer l'oeuure laborieus
> A l'oeil & au loisir du Roy victorieus . . .[54]

Navières, however, does not manage to keep this up in the rest of the fragments. His progress through Henry's career was more leisurely than that of Garnier. From the published extracts and some remarks by Navières's publisher, Pierre

Mettayer, we may conjecture that Books i and ii traced the career of Henry as King of Navarre up to the assassination of Henry III. In Book iii some of his supporters threaten to leave the new King, and Book iv begins with Henry's reply to these would-be deserters.[55] The council is then addressed by three speakers in turn, occupying perhaps Books iv, v, and vi. The speech of the 'tiers harangueur' is preserved more or less complete and takes up most of Book vi. Book vii must have described how the nobles rallied to Henry.[56] Book ix dealt with the battle of Ivry. Henry's assassination deprived Navières of his patron and his hero. He did not despair. In 1610 he tried to interest the Queen Mother and the young king in the epic, by treating the murder, and, of course, violently condemning Ravaillac.[57] Another fragment followed the death of Queen Marguerite[58] but does not add much to our knowledge of the poem. What survives suggests that Navières's *Henriade* would have been a frenzied and interminable outburst of every kind of stylistic excess.

In 1617 Paul Thomas I (so called to distinguish him from his nephew, Paul Thomas II) produced the first edition of his *Lutetiad* in a volume of *Poemata*, which had originally appeared without the *Lutetiad* in 1593. The five books of the *Lutetiad* were again published in a third edition of the *Poemata* in 1640. At first sight the title might seem to indicate a poem in praise of Paris, like Audebert's *Roma, Venetiae,* or *Parthenope;* but the proposition dispels this error:

> Civiles furias, sacrisque profana tuendis
> Bella cano, & regale iugum ceruice rebelli
> Gallorum excussum; totamque ardentibus actam
> Europam in partes studiis, & moenia circum
> Parisidûm exhaustos longa obsidione labores.[59]

His subject is in fact the religious wars and the siege of Paris. His hero is Henry IV, and Thomas I thus finds his appropriate place after Garnier and Navières.[60]

Like Garnier, Thomas enlivens his poem with religious polemic. His very first words, after proposition and invocation, concern the poison from across the Rhine, which overthrew the long-established and pious customs of the French nation. The poet has a happy touch for thumb-nail sketches—

Catherine de' Medici is not content to sit at home and spin:

> Mater ei [Henry III] ab genere Hetrusco Catharina, domusque
> Sanguine Mediciae: non illa exercitat curis
> Foemineis, neque acu, vel agendo callida fuso:
> Sed populos regere, & pacem bellique tumultus
> Ingenti moderari animo, communibus illa
> Tum quoque cum nato regnum flectebat habenis.[61]

The poem moves swiftly from the murder of Guise (Book iii) to Henry's conversion (Book v). The beleaguered Parisians ascribe their troubles to Henry's adherence to the heretical cult:

> . . . [Borbonius] qui tot post ordine Reges,
> Omnes Christicolas, omnes pietatis amantes,
> Immemor ipse sui, Lodoïcique immemor huius,
> Vnde genus ducit; pollutis ritibus haeret . . .[62]

They beg Henry to abandon his heresy. He, blaming his errors on his mother, Jeanne d'Albret, and thus easily rid of them, promises to submit to the Pope and spare them their troubles. His triumphal entry into Paris soon follows. Such a straightforward and stirring evocation of the establishment of the Bourbon monarchy clearly appealed to readers during the regency of Mary de' Medici, and doubtless accounts for its republication in the last years of Louis XIII.

Thomas II and Louis XIII

The uncle celebrated the father; the nephew celebrated the son. The *Rupellaid*, in six books, was published by Paul Thomas II in 1630, and, whilst it duly ascribed the victory of La Rochelle to Louis XIII, it did not neglect to credit Richelieu with his miraculous dyke.[63] The personalities of the war make heroic appearances in the epic, splendid in their Latin names, their deeds resonant with Virgilian echoes. La Rochefoucauld brings his fleet to the Ile de Ré:

> Interea Engolimis Rupisfulcaldus ab oris
> Idem Pictonici Dux limitis, insula portu
> Quà facili patet, aduertit longo ordine proras.[64]

Buckingham, treacherous and handsome, appears in a review of the English fleet:

Ipse regit classem Dux Bucquincamius, armis
Aureus, imperique ferox, authorque soluti
Foederis, & forma ante omnes pulcherrimus Anglos.[65]

Richelieu, Aeneas incarnate, encourages his men before battle:

. . . Nec enim ille quiescit,
Non magni mens Richelij, quam prouida Gallis
Natura eduxit: 'Vos ô durate, animosque
Colligite, obtestor, durisque obsistite rebus . . .[66]

When Louis falls sick, God sends Iris to reassure him that
Richelieu will take care of everything. The dyke reduces the
Rochellois to despair, and, after the envoys have sued for
peace, the poem ends abruptly with the clemency of the
victors.[67] Like his uncle, Paul Thomas II knew when to stop.

The epics devoted to contemporary heroes had more chance of
completion when written in Latin: Blarru, Pillard, Thomas I,
and Thomas II finished theirs; Garnier and Navières, writing in
the vernacular, did not. Not surprisingly these poems show
great respect for the established order—writing otherwise, the
poets would hardly have appealed to their patrons.

The alliance of epic and the living hero had a cramping effect
on the poets who tried this experiment. The interest of these
poems therefore remains largely historical. As epics they are too
violently distorted by the weight of contemporary events.
Pillard's neurotic obsession with heresy was fatal to the balance
of his poem. We cannot properly judge Navières's epic because
it is too fragmentary; but, having sampled the ecstatic flattery
of the specimens he chose to publish, we cannot grieve too
keenly over the disappearance of the rest. Blarru did indeed
manage to invest his work with some kind of universal significance; the firmness and moderation of Garnier's views may
command respect; the *Lutetiad* and the *Rupellaid* told a simple
story with competent brevity; but the restraints imposed by the
contemporary hero caused this type of epic to remain a
minority pursuit. Other ways had to be sought to explore the
full potential of the epic structure.

NOTES TO CHAPTER V

1. See articles by Rouyer in *Mém. soc. arch. lorraine*: 'P. de Blarru et son poème la *Nancéide*', 4 (1876), 360–420; 'Recherches biographiques sur P. de Blarru', 11 (1883), 213–25; 'Testament de P. de Blarru', 16 (1887), 173–5; Collignon, *De Nanceide Petri de Blaro Rivo* (Nancy, 1892); Gaguin, *Epistolae et orationes*, ed. Thuasne, ii. 183–9; Couderc, 'Oeuvres inédites', *Bibliographe moderne*, 4 (1900), 86–112; de Morembert, *DBF*, vi. 648–9.

2. Not the Blarru mentioned by Villon (*Lais*, xii. 91). See *Oeuvres*, ed. Thuasne, ii. 17–18; Couderc, 'Oeuvres inédites', p. 88.

3. v, pp. 128–32.

4. A manuscript of the poem was presented by the Baron de Landres to the Société d'Archéologie lorraine. It is described in detail by Rouyer '*Nancéide*', pp. 379–408. Rouyer compared the manuscript with the edition of 1518 and found only 'quelques variantes très-légères, et généralement de peu d'intérêt', which he lists (p. 401). For another description see Collignon, *Nanceid*, p.vi.

5. See Rouyer, '*Nancéide*', p. 381, n. 4; Collignon, *Nanceid*, pp. viii–ix. The translation remains in manuscript.

6. I quote from this edition, modernizing the spelling and punctuation for clarity.

7. 'Reddita tum caeso peregrini iura sepulchri/visa, canam.' (i, p. 4); see Collignon, *Nanceid*, p. 33.

8. See ibid., pp. 34–6, for quotations from Chrétien and Blarru.

9. '. . . une majorité des hommes puissants, influents ou haut placés sous la Régence ou sous le gouvernement de Fleury avaient leur place dans les vers ou dans les notes de Voltaire . . . Le poète saisit avidement une occasion unique de faire sa cour aux grands.' (*Henriade*, ed. Taylor, p. 186).

10. See Collignon, *Nanceid*, pp. 37–41.

11. i, p. 2 (my italics).

12. Cf. Collignon, *Nanceid*, p. 42.

13. For details see ibid, pp. 82–5.

14. See ibid., pp. 56, 79. In the 1518 edition *sententiae* are indicated by that word in the margin. These marginalia are not unfortunately reproduced by Schütz.

15. v, pp. 118–36.

16. *Aeneid* i. 198–207: 'o passi graviora . . .'

17. *Nanceid,* pp. 92–4.

18. ii, p. 102.

19. vi, p. 298.

20. See Collignon, *Nanceid,* pp. 96–103, for a comparison between the *Rusticiad* and the *Nanceid;* and, also by Collignon, 'Etude sur la *Rusticiade*', *Mém. Acad. Stanislas,* 15 (1918), 230–58, and 16 (1919), 108–144; 'Quelques imitations dans la *Rusticiade*', *Annales de l'Est,* 7 (1893), 594–601 (mainly on Pillard's debt to Vida's *Christiad*). See also Klippel, *Darstellung,* pp. 55–6.

21. *De Seipso,* line 2, quoted by Collignon, '*Rusticiade*', (1918), p. 231.

22. See Collignon, '*Rusticiade*', (1919), pp. 141–4.

23. A list in Collignon, *Nanceid,* pp. 98–100.

24. For further details see Collignon, '*Rusticiade*' (1918), pp. 235–40.

25. See ibid., pp. 242–52.

26. Full list in Collignon, '*Rusticiade*' (1919), p. 109.
27. See ibid., p. 123.

28. For Blarru's neologisms see Collignon, *Nanceid,* pp. 85–89, and for Pillard's greater debt to Virgil, pp. 101–2.

29. Evidence from this source is summarized by Dupré, 'Observations', pp. 506–11.

30. See Plée, 'Notice sur la première *Henriade*', pp. 460–505; Toinet, i. 152, ii. 21n; Mouflard, *Robert Garnier,* p. 378.

31. Not 'les huit premiers livres' as the title claims. After the publication of Voltaire's *Henriade,* Garnier's epics were unearthed, and received a second edition in 1770, so that readers could compare the two poets. There is no sign that Voltaire owed anything to Garnier. (See Voltaire, *Henriade,* ed. Taylor, p. 200.)

32. '. . . depuis le jour que je vis la courtoisie dont il pleu à VOSTRE MAJESTE user en mon endroit à vostre retour de Tours, repassant en ceste ville pour aller retrouver vostre armée (le Roi dernier encores vivant), je fuz tellement espris de la grandeur de vos conceptions, que deslors je proposé me desdier du tout à coucher par escrit vos faicts généreux . . .' ('Epître au Roy', 26 March 1593, p. 70).

33. p. 9.

34. '. . . & d'autant que je sçay avoir infinis ennemis & envieux, pour m'opposer ordinairement à ceux qui détractent de vous, & deffendre en tous lieux vostre juste querelle, mesme des principaux, qui me devroient supporter, estans mes supérieurs . . .' ('Epître au Roy', p. 72). See Plée, 'Notice', p. 468.

35. Not, as Mouflard says, 'à la bataille d'Arques' (*Garnier,* p. 378).

36. pp. 9–10.

37. p. 25.

38. p. 55.

39. pp. 57, 103–5.

40. p. 56.

41. p. 48.

42. p. 97.

43. p. 195.

44. p. 80.

45. p. 195.

46. p. 180.

47. pp. 86–7.

48. p. 24.

49. p. 109.

50. p. 193.

51. p. 235.

52. pp. 238–9.

53. Born in Sedan 1544, died in Paris 1616. He combined poetry with soldiering, as did Schelandre and d'Urfé. Navières served the Prince of Orange and the duc de Bouillon. He wrote music for his translation of the Psalms and scored the opening lines of his *Henriade* for trumpet. For the many opuscules in which fragments of his epic may be found see the bibliography. See Cioranescu, *XVI*, for a list of his works, and Toinet, ii. 73–8.

54. *Baptême*, pp. 19–20.

55. *Entrée*, p. 21.

56. *Entrée*, pp. 10–11.

57. In the *Heureuse entrée au ciel du feu Roy Henry le Grand*, which contains most of the fragments mentioned above.

58. In the *Trépas de la Royne Marguerite* (1615).

59. *Lutetiad*, i, in *Poemata*, p. 1.

60. In *Les sept livres des honnestes loisirs* (1587) François le Poulchre de la Motte-Messemé published versified memoirs of his activities in the religious wars from 1562 to 1572. Being a soldier, he apologizes for his unpolished verses. He mentions Commines and the du Bellay memoirs as his models (sig. †4ʳ). His work has no epic pretensions, though there are some imitations of Ariosto (see Cioranescu, *L'Arioste*, i. 182–3).

61. i, pp. 5–6.

62. v, p. 112.
63. *Rupellaid,* vi, pp. 109 ff.
64. i, p. 20.
65. iii, pp. 53–4.
66. iv, p. 77.
67. vi, pp. 128–31.

VI

FRANCUS

It is against the background of epics on contemporary heroes
that the originality of Ronsard's conception of epic can be
justly appreciated. The epics we have just considered owed
their structure to the sequence of historical events; we now pass
to an example of a wholly poetic structure in which the part
played by history in shaping the epic was minimal. We shall
consider Ronsard's poem as the focal point of sixteenth-century
epic, and then the small additions made to it by Claude Garnier
and Jacques Guillot. We shall conclude with Delaudun's
attempt to react against Ronsard. Before discussing the poems,
however, let us look briefly at the origin and significance of the
Franco–Trojan myth.

The Franco–Trojan myth

To a French epic poet eager to glorify his country the historians of the sixteenth century offered various accounts of its
origins. The one with most appeal to a poet steeped in the epics
of Antiquity was that Francus, son of Hector, escaped from
the sack of Troy, migrated to central Europe, and established
the Frankish nation. The French were thus descended from the
Trojans, and could claim kinship with the Romans, who owed
their origins to Aeneas, another survivor of the sack of Troy.

How did this curious legend come into being? Faral has
shown that the first seeds of the Franco–Trojan myth are to be
found in the seventh-century chronicle of Fredegar.[1] By a close
analysis of Book ii, chapters iv-ix, he demonstrated that two
authors, both inspired by the bare narrative of Saint Jerome's
Interpretatio chronicae Eusebii,[2] of which Fredegar's chronicle
is an expanded version, contributed successively to the formation of the myth.[3] It was repeated in a slightly different form
in the *Liber historiae Francorum*[4] of the eighth century and
thereafter the story was expanded and developed in numerous
medieval works.[5]

By the sixteenth century some writers were still repeating the legend while others were pouring scorn on it. Nicole Gilles, citing Hugh of Saint-Victor as his authority, explained the origin of the Franks as part of the dispersion of Trojan princes over Europe: Francio settled near Hungary, built Sicambria and gave his name to the Frankish people; 200 years later their chief, Ybros, led them to the Seine, where they founded Lutecia, calling it Paris in honour of Francio's uncle.[6] Gaguin repeated the story at the beginning of his *Compendium,* whilst Lemaire de Belges claimed that Francus, son of Hector, actually came to Gaul.[7] Jean Bouchet's version of the story closely corresponded to that elaborated by Ronsard. After explaining how Helenus and Andromache, the prisoners of Pyrrhus, acted as guardians to Francus, Bouchet has Francus reconquer Ilion, and then continues:

. . . Francus filz de Hector acompaigne de grant nombre de Troyens, ou dict an laisserent Ilion, & allerent en la basse Scithye premiere region de Europe, commenceant est maretz Meotides entre la riuere du Noue, & la mer Septentrionale, & se arresterent en la terre de Pannonie, quon appelle de present Hongrie, qui est en Scythie, pour y faire leur perpetuelle demourance, soubz leur duc Francus ou Francion filz de Hector.[8]

There was clearly justification for Ronsard's assertion that the legend of Francus was widely accepted by the French people.[9]

Of course others by this time were ridiculing the story. It could hardly stand up to the scrutiny of those who, like du Tillet, Bodin, Pasquier, Hotman, or Fauchet adopted a critical approach to historical evidence.[10] But this was of no consequence to Ronsard. Even historians who were Ronsard's friends and who dismissed the Franco–Trojan myth did not blame Ronsard for using it. Belleforest rejected the legend with some asperity: 'les Annalistes de France . . . se sont aussi arrestez sur ne sçay quelle folle opinion que les Troyens (peuple effeminé d'Asie) estoient ceux qui ont donné source & nom à celle braue nation Françoise . . .'[11] Yet he did not criticize Ronsard for making it the basis of a poem. To Belleforest Ronsard is 'le pere & ornement de la poësie Françoise'. Indeed because 'c'est des seuls poëtes qu'est sortie l'histoire des Troyens', it is appropriate that it should come to rest in an epic poem. Du Haillan was another who emphatically rejected the legend: 'Il est tout asseuré qu'il n'y eut iamais de Francus ny de Francion fils de Hector . . .'[12] But du Haillan collaborated in the composition of the annalistic parts of the *Franciade*, and was present to comment on the history in the poem when it was read to Charles IX. Clearly among poets and historians alike, criticism of the *Franciade* for being based on legend was merely pedantic.[13]

Yet pedants there were, and, to understand Delaudun's *Franciade*, we must examine that opinion which stood mid-way between acceptance and rejection of the Franco–Trojan myth. Amongst those who believed in an eponymous founder of the Franks there was some perplexity at the long gap between the Trojan war and the first authenticated incursions into Roman history of the Germans, in the first century, or of the Franks, in the third century A.D. Consequently it was an attractive idea to bring Francus forward from the remote era of the Trojan war and fit him into the Germanic invasions described by the Roman historians. This Trithemius did in his *Compendium* (1515),[14] and from his line of German kings, starting with Marcomir in 440 B.C., Delaudun chose his Francus, the son of Antharius not of Hector. Delaudun thought he was being more up-to-date than Ronsard, and Allais has praised him for it;[15] but I have shown that this criticism of Ronsard was mere pedantry, for the developments in historical research in the late sixteenth century rendered ridiculous a Francus of any description, Trojan or German.

Ronsard and the Trojan Francus

Indifferent as he clearly was to historical veracity, Ronsard was obviously going to produce quite a different kind of epic to that conceived by Blarru or Pillard. Imbued with a profound knowledge of the epics of Antiquity, he selected a hero, who had begun his nebulous life in the pages of Fredegar, to be the cornerstone of an epic which he hoped would be the crowning achievement of the revival of French letters. He needed only to read in the pages of Gilles, Gaguin, Lemaire, or Bouchet that a son of Hector had survived the sack of Troy, had been brought up in Epirus by Helenus and Andromache, had travelled by land and sea, had founded a town on the Danube, had eventually reached Gaul—and here was the basis of an epic which could include almost any device adapted from the *Iliad, Odyssey, Argonautica,* or *Aeneid.* Francus was son of Hector, so he could be linked with any episode from the Trojan War. He founded a dynasty; in this he resembled Aeneas. He ploughed the seas; Odysseus and Jason provided models. Ronsard had only to make his choice.

From conception to execution was a long step. The circumstances of the composition of the *Franciade*[16] help us to appreciate why the erudite solemnity of the unfinished result failed to match the passion and intensity of its inspiration. In 1549 du Bellay's *Deffence* called for a 'long poëme'. A few months later Ronsard spoke in his *Hymne de France* of the French as descendants of Priam, a vital factor linking the epics of Antiquity and the French nation. In 1550 Ronsard outlined the career of Francus, and begged Henry II for some benefice to support him whilst he worked for the glory of France and the King. Not till 1554, however, did Henry show any sign of interest and then only to make it clear that he would not bestow the reward until after the poem's completion. Repeated prodding from the poet failed to change his mind. Perhaps the King and his court were even apprehensive: 'Scilicet, ut eos minime movebant Trojani illi atavi, ita eosdem pavore affectos esse verisimile est, imminente epica mole.'[17] Henry's death in 1559 undid what little Ronsard had achieved in his lifetime, and the poet, discouraged, dropped the matter for some years. The project revived when appeals to Catherine de' Medici bore fruit. In 1565 Ronsard received the priory of Saint Cosme and Charles IX took an official interest in the *Franciade.* Perhaps Ronsard had been contemplating an epic in Alexandrines; Charles insisted that it should be decasyllables, though, by the time he came to write the preface to the *Franciade,* Ronsard was so far reconciled that he claimed to prefer the decasyllable for aesthetic reasons.[18] Charles also, it seems, insisted that all his ancestors must appear in the poem, but the part he played in influencing the poet must be assessed with some caution, since Ronsard's remarks on the subject, which are our main source of evidence, are doubtless coloured by his disappointment with the failure of his grandiose projects.

Composition was proceeding in earnest. Amadis Jamyn

indexed the *Iliad* for similes, epithets, and other ornaments, which might be used in the poem. As each book was completed, a copy was probably sent to Charles.[19] In September 1571 Charles listened to Jamyn reading Book iv at Blois, while du Haillan stood by to comment on the history of the Merovingians.[20] The first four books were published in September 1572, a month after the massacre of Saint Bartholomew, and other editions followed. The *Franciade* appeared in the sixteenth volume of the *Oeuvres* of 1573, and in 1574 a pirated edition bore the imprint 'Turin'. 1574 was the year of Charles IX's death. When the *Franciade* was next published, in the *Oeuvres* of 1578, Ronsard took leave of his project:

> Si le Roy Charles eust vescu
> J'eusse achevé ce long ouvrage:
> Si tost que la mort l'eut vaincu,
> Sa mort me veinquist le courage.[21]

By now the star of Desportes was rising. Henry III had no favours for Ronsard, and the poet was not going to continue to glorify the Valois for nothing. The inspiration to write epic was there, but the grandeur of the enterprise would only sustain him so long as it brought adequate rewards.[22] Ronsard was no Tasso to produce an epic struggling against adversity. Hence twenty-five years of hopes and promises, and only four books of the *Franciade*.

Ronsard's epic is based on a nodding acquaintance with the French historians and a profound knowledge of ancient epic.[23] The *Iliad, Odyssey, Argonautica*, and *Aeneid* are the main epic sources, supplemented by Hesiod, Callimachus, Catullus, Ovid, and Propertius for adornment.[24] Ronsard uses ancient literature in three ways. In one sense they are historical sources. By introducing Neptune's building of the walls of Troy, Laomedon's treachery, the Trojan horse, or the death of Priam, Ronsard accorded the legends preserved in the *Iliad* or *Aeneid* the status of historical background.[25] Secondly, Ronsard used episodes or topoi from ancient epic as the building material for the structure of his own epic. This we shall examine presently. Thirdly, there were innumerable cases of probably unconscious reminiscence echoing some ancient author.[26] It is remarkable that despite the variety of this borrowed material, the style is har-

monious throughout. From a stylistic point of view, what
Ronsard borrowed he made fully his own. The lengthy catalogue of borrowings is no list of substitutes for inspiration; it
is his inspiration itself.

There can be no doubt that the *Franciade* is primarily a
Virgilian poem. Let us now examine the poetic structure that
Ronsard fashioned out of the early books of the *Aeneid*.
Broadly speaking he rearranged the major episodes of Books
ii (Troy), i (Storm-Shipwreck-Recital), iv (Dido), and vi
(Shades), to form Books i, ii, iii, and iv respectively of the
Franciade. The pattern is varied by borrowings from the
Argonautica and from other parts of the *Aeneid*.

The foundation of this structure is the Storm-Shipwreck-
Recital of *Aeneid* i–iii. This pattern corresponds most closely
with the story of Francus as related by the chroniclers, and
other episodes could be worked in round it. This gives us the
essence of the *Franciade*: Francus sets sail from Buthrotum,
loses his ship in a storm, lands in Crete, tells his own story,
briefly, and, at greater length, listens to Dicæe's story, fights a
duel, and resists two lovers. A more detailed examination of
each book shows how Ronsard departed from the Virgilian
structure.

Book i is a fairly lengthy introduction. Jupiter expounds the
fall of Troy to a council of gods; most of this derives from
Aeneid ii. In setting Francus in motion, Ronsard draws on
several episodes from *Aeneid* iv and for the building of the
ships from *Argonautica* i. This long introduction is perhaps an
attempt to cover up his tracks, and conceal the essentially
Virgilian structure. As an objective this is sound. Topoi usually
gain from fresh contexts. Unfortunately the first book of an
epic needs more than a rearrangement of topoi to get it off to a
good start. He might have done better to follow Virgil and
begin with the storm and shipwreck, which in fact are the main
events of *Franciade* ii, and derive from *Aeneid* i. Then, at the
end of *Franciade* ii, we have the duel between Francus and
Phovère, which, though it contains reminiscences of *Aeneid* v
and xii, is clearly intended to break up the Virgilian structure.
This is partly to show his independence of Virgil, and partly
because the duel was an essential feature of the romanesque
tradition, of whose popularity Ronsard, though imbued with

ancient epic, was anxious to take advantage.[27] This time the variation is more successful. The same technique of variation can be seen in Book iii, where Clymène is clearly modelled on Dido (*Aeneid* iv), but adornments are taken from elsewhere. Ronsard achieves variety in a technical sense, by breaking up the Clymène affair with other episodes, but the tedium of the Clymène affair is not thereby diminished, nor are the intercalated episodes interesting in themselves.[28] In Book iv Ronsard adorns Hyante with the characteristics of Apollonius' Medea, and the exercise of magical rites lead to an imitation of *Aeneid* vi. After a philosophical discourse, the shades of the Merovingian kings are conjured up, a pale shadow of Virgil's heroes of the Roman Republic.

If we ask why the *Franciade* failed, and it did fail because Ronsard gave it up, we cannot blame either the conception,[29] or the subject.[30] Ronsard's ideas on epic were original, his understanding of ancient epic much deeper than that of his predecessors, his choice of hero in no way unsuited to the genre he was attempting. Nor can his style be held responsible; any passage of the *Franciade* shows that as a manipulator of words Ronsard commanded unrivalled technical resources and could harmonize an endless diversity of inspiration.[31] It is the structure of the *Franciade* which is clumsy. The bareness, even barrenness, of the historical account of Francus obliged Ronsard to construct an epic structure that was entirely dependent on literary models. His dependence on Virgil prevented that creative tension which might have resulted from a greater conflict between historical sources and epic structure. Certainly he tried to shake himself free from the Virgilian structure, but in a manner that suggests a plodding critic who knows that a poem should be varied, rather than a poet inspired by divine frenzy.

How then did Tasso succeed where Ronsard failed? Both were inspired by similar ideals; both brought similar qualifications to the task; both published their epics at about the same time. In the light of the analysis I have made of epic structure and historical material, we can see at once that Tasso's historical material was more substantial than Ronsard's. Therefore it created greater problems when he tried to adapt it to a structure derived from Homer, Virgil, and his romanesque predecessors.

These problems were the challenge to which Tasso responded; the tension generated by this struggle is what keeps the *Gerusalemme* alive. If we compare the two poets in their approach to the *Aeneid,* we find that Tasso nearly always uses the topoi actively, that is, he places them in new contexts; Ronsard accepts the topoi passively and serves them up in contexts not much removed from the original. This may be illustrated from the preparation of the storm in *Aeneid* i. 50–64. Almost every line of *Franciade* ii. 71–82 echoes some feature of Virgil's account, and the contexts are the same. In the *Aeneid,* Juno, planning a storm, visits Aeolus; Virgil describes how the winds are confined to their cave. In the *Franciade,* Neptune is planning a storm; he reminds the winds how they come to be confined in their cave. All is transformed in the *Gerusalemme.* The Virgilian passage is evoked in two different contexts: Solimano remembers the harm done him by the Christians in Egypt (ix. 7); escaping demons are likened to a storm (iv. 18). If we liken poetic composition to a chemical reaction, Tasso fuses the elements into something new; in the *Franciade* fusion has not taken place, and we are left with the debris of a failed experiment.

Ronsard's continuators

Attracted by the incompleteness of Ronsard's *Franciade,* two poets published works which claimed to be continuations of it. Claude Garnier, co-editor of Ronsard's *Oeuvres* in the early seventeenth century, added a fifth book in 1604; Jacques Guillot, an obscure ecclesiastic from Bourges, a fifth book in 1606, and a sixth in 1615.

Garnier's *Livre de la Franciade à la suite de la celle de Ronsard*[32] is hardly a serious attempt to continue the *Franciade* according to the plan conceived by Ronsard, but rather a piece of self-advertisement intended to impress Henry IV with Garnier's abilities. Ronsard had left Francus and Hyante near a sombre cave, watching the shades of the French kings; Garnier progresses as rapidly as possible to the appearance of the shade of Hector, who is to describe for Francus's benefit the glorious career of Henri de Bourbon. No sooner, however, has Hector opened his mouth to begin this prophecy, than Garnier brings the book to an abrupt end. His concluding words convey his message, one with which we are familiar: he will immortalize Henry IV if the King will pay him well.[33] Garnier had an intimate knowledge of Ronsard's poem, but his Book 5 is clearly a hopeless diversion of the original plot. He might, like other poets of the day, have produced some books of a *Henriade* as specimens of his epic talent; instead he counted on the reputation of Ronsard's *Franciade* to attract attention to his own work, even at the risk of disappointing those who hoped to read a faithful continuation of Ronsard's epic.

Most of Garnier's poem is calculated to show his competence to deal with any aspect of Henry's career were he asked to do so. He candidly reminds Henry of the sweetness of flattery.[34] Much of the book is taken up with the engravings on Hector's armour;[35] irrelevant to the *Franciade*, they show the full range of Garnier's talents. He depicts Priam's peace and prosperity shattered by the horrors of the Trojan war; in reverse order these were the main features of Henry's reign.

Though Garnier abandoned Ronsard's plan, his poem is not wholly disrespectful or irrelevant to the work of his predecessor. He starts by reminding the reader of the events of *Franciade* iii and iv. He even shows Francus giving thanks to Cybele for sending Dicæe the dream which led the Cretan King to discover the castaway Trojans,[36] though how Francus knew of this is not quite clear. The apparition of Hector is an ingenious development of an opportunity left by Ronsard which admirably serves Garnier's purpose. He uses the fact that Hector last saw Francus at his mother's breast on the eve of Troy's fall to construct a small drama of recognition. Hector refuses to accept Francus as his son until Francus convinces him by pointing to the robe that he is wearing, which once belonged to Hector, and which Andromache presented to Francus.[37] Though the only reason for Hector's appearance is to get round to the subject of Henry IV, Garnier successfully grafts the episode on to Ronsard's poem.

The other continuator was Guillot.[38] His fifth book, probably lost, seems to have been more faithful to Ronsard's intentions in that it continued the catalogue of kings through the Carolingians.[39] Book vi opens with Dicæe's decision to punish Francus for Clymène's death. Believing that the Trojan adventurer violated his daughter, and then drowned her in the sea,

Dicaee urges Orée to forget how Francus saved him from Phovère, and avenge his sister. Guillot introduces a new character, Lictie, Hyante's lover. Dicæe persuades them all to unite against Francus, and prepares to make war on the Trojans.[40] Meanwhile Francus has been hearing about the Capetians from Hyante and, having reached Louis XIII, he prepares to leave Crete. In a dream he learns that Dicæe is going to attack him. While the Trojans wait fearfully on the shore, a ship approaches; Francus is confident that this means reinforcement for him, not for Dicæe. Brennus steps ashore, relates how he helped Andromache to save Francus the night of the sack of Troy, and offers his men to replace those lost in the shipwreck.[41] The Cretans advance; the Trojans have no arms. At this point the book ends.

Guillot's poem is by no means unworthy of the epic that inspired it. He shows considerable knowledge of the first four books of the *Franciade,* develops Ronsard's story intelligently, and prepares for future developments of his own; for example Brennus promises a recital of his adventures when circumstances permit. The theme of his book is the enmity between Dicæe and Francus that arises because Dicæe thinks Francus responsible for Clymène's death. Guillot adds details which are not mentioned by Ronsard but are entirely consistent with the story. Clymène, he says, drowned herself near Francus's ship; this naturally gave colour to the suggestion that Francus killed her. Dicæe was influenced by flatterers into believing that Francus was the murderer; Ronsard says nothing of them but they are quite appropriate to Guillot's version. Guillot's brief contribution to the epic genre ranks with Schelandre's as the most successful development of Ronsard's initiative.

Delaudun and the German Francus

Pierre Delaudun d'Aigaliers[42] read Ronsard's *Franciade* in the last decade of the sixteenth century and decided that the leader of the Pléiade had chosen the wrong hero. He abandoned the Trojan Francus and found another: 'Le suject de mon present oeuure, est la guerre de Francus, seiziesme Roy des Sicambriens & Cimbriens . . . contre Domitius Caluinius, & Asinius Pollio, Consuls Romains . . . quinze ans auant la venuë de nostre Seigneur . . .'[43] Delaudun's *Franciade* is therefore the work of a young man, who believed that he could outshine Ronsard by rejecting his hero and theme. In later life he regretted having published this immature work at the instance of an over-indulgent uncle, who added to the epic a commentary of considerable erudition.[44] Erudition is confined to the commentary; the poem is less abstruse, in places positively pedestrian. The plot divides too readily into three parts. In Books i–iii, the Franks fall foul of the Romans and hostilities begin. In Books iv–vii, interest shifts to the love affair of Clogio and Mantis, with its attendant domestic entanglements, in Herbipolis. This interlude has all the complexity of romanesque epic, even of the comic stage. In Book viii Delaudun returns to the war, and in Book ix leaves it in suspense before the final battle.

Delaudun's style has all the characteristics of youth and inexperience. He manages to express banal thoughts elegantly, but lacks fluency when his thoughts are not banal. Striving to add a note of informality to the elevated material of epic, he lapses into the trivial. The gods of Olympus are the 'bourgeois de la voulte estoilée', who take their places thus:

> Se mirent tous en rang selon leur qualité
> Cà & là du parquet en iuste egalité.[45]

Jupiter is degraded to the level of an impotent mischief-maker whose repeated appearances only emphasize the futility of his opposition to destiny. Delaudun's sense of proportion frequently deserts him. Marcellinus, who ventures to oppose Domitius's aggressive policy, is promptly beheaded; he then receives funeral honours far exceeding in magnificence his importance to the story. At other times Delaudun delights us by unexpected brevity. The Capetian kings who figure on Francus's shield are despatched as a mere list; their careers elaborated only in the uncle's commentary.

To compare Ronsard and Delaudun is to discover two completely different conceptions of epic, not to be explained solely by the change from Trojan to German hero. Gone is Ronsard's single-minded devotion to one hero and a divine mission. Delaudun's Francus is a German kinglet anxious to live in peace, yet capable of resisting two Roman invasions. Having sacrificed the foundation theme, Delaudun's story is naturally less closely knit, though his fertile imagination embellishes each episode with the minutest of details. Francus rebukes his son for spending too much time hunting and sends him abroad to broaden his mind. Clogio first notices Strouta and Mantis at work in a cloth shop. Strouta weeps because Clogio has not held her hand all day. Probably the poet concentrates on domestic life to present the Germans as the peaceful and innocent victims of aggression. There is a clue to this attitude when Presbée delivers the Roman ultimatum. The Romans thirst for bloodshed; as for the Germans,

> . . . ils n'ont point autre cure
> Qu'à leurs esbattements, & viure d'heure en heure
> En soulas & repos, ne demandans plus rien,
> Si ce n'est de passer ce chemin terrien
> Sans noise & sans debat, sans songer aux conquestes
> Que sur eux les Romains de iour en iour ont faictes.[46]

Delaudun does admit that he has no intention of sustaining the dignity normally associated with epic, and for his flaccid straggling verses we might find some excuse in his candid confession: '. . . & ne se faut esmerueiller si le style de mon vers n'est si haut, graue, & remply de fables & Histoires, comme beaucoup eussent esperé de moy . . .'[47]

Despite this change of atmosphere, Delaudun owes a great deal to Ronsard; and we can appreciate how greatly Ronsard influenced epic in general by the extent of his opponent's debt to him. Like Ronsard, Delaudun begins with a council of gods.[48] Jupiter sends Ronsard's Mercury to stir up Francus,[49] whilst Delaudun's is sent to Domitius.[50] Ronsard's Francus dreams of his shipwrecked friends begging for burial;[51] Deludun's is visited by the shades of those who fell in battle.[52] Ronsard has two sets of funeral rites;[53] Delaudun has four.[54] The duel between Capito and Herbanc[55] imitates that between Francus and Phovère.[56] Bellona's visit to Sleep[57] resembles Cybele's to Jealousy.[58] Clogio's departure from Butel[59] corresponds to Francus's from Buthrotum,[60] especially in the tearful farewells to mothers and the itineraries given by Francus to Clogio and by Helenus to Francus. Like Ronsard's Francus, Delaudun's Clogio runs into a storm and loses all his ships;[61] like Clogio, Domitius meets a similar disaster.[62] Delaudun follows Ronsard's example and loads his poem with quaint legends of the origins of the French towns; Lyons and Rouen,[63] Cambrai and Tours.[64] In his enthusiasm for this embellishment, he includes a second version of the origin of Rouen, which contradicts the first.[65] Delaudun's names are, like Ronsard's, based on Greek words.[66] It is quite clear that Delaudun reacts against Ronsard, but cannot escape him.

The legend of Francus was entirely appropriate to the aspirations towards national epic which Ronsard dreamed of. That he remains a shadowy figure to us does not mean he was incapable of life. It is the poem which immortalizes the hero, not the other way round. 'Hectora quis nosset, felix si Troia fuisset?'[67] It was, however, unfortunate that the career of Francus had not been sufficiently embellished by historians to provide that abundance of circumstantial detail which might have acted as a catalyst and brought Ronsard's epic structure to life.

We have seen in the continuations of Garnier and Guillot, and in the perverse manner in which Delaudun both accepted and rejected the example of Ronsard, some indication of how influential the *Franciade* was on later poets. We now turn to another group of poets who seized eagerly on the epic structure that Ronsard bequeathed, and who tried to adapt it to historical material far richer in circumstantial detail than the story of Francus.

NOTES TO CHAPTER VI

1. *La légende arthurienne,* 'Comment s'est formée la légende de l'origine troyenne des Francs', iii. 262–93. See also Joly, *Benoît de Sainte-More,* i. 119 ff.; Huppert, *Perfect history,* pp. 72–87; Ronsard, *Oeuvres,* xvi. v–vi, 6–8; Chamard, *Hist. Pléiade,* iii. 123–30.

2. Migne, *PL,* vol. 27, tom. 8, col. 318.

3. Exinde origo Francorum fuit. Priamo primo regi habuerunt [*sic*]; postea per historiarum libros scriptum est, qualiter habuerunt regi Friga. Postea partiti sunt in duabus partibus. Una pars perrexit in Macedoniam . . . Nam et illa alia pars, quae de Frigia progressa est, ab Olexo per fraude decepti, tamen non captivati, nisi exinde eiecti, per multis regionibus pervacantis cum uxores et liberos [*sic*], electum a se regi Francione nomen, per quem Franci vocantur. In postremum, eo quod fortissimus ipse Francio in bellum fuisse fertur, et multo tempore cum plurimis gentibus pugnam gerens, partem Asiae vastans, in Eurupam dirigens, inter Renum vel Danuvium et mare consedit. (Fredegar, ii, §§ 4–5, *MGH,* ii. 45–6.)

4. §§ 3–4, *MGH,* ii. 243–4.

5. Klippel, *Die Darstellung der fränkischen Trojanersage* (Marburg, 1936), gives a full account.

6. *Annales* (1549), fol. 7$^{\text{r-v}}$.

7. 'Huit ans apres . . . Francus filz d'Hector, commença à regner sur les Gaules Celtiques.' (*Illustrations,* ed. Stecher, ii. 268.) On Ronsard and Lemaire, see Guy, 'Les sources françaises de Ronsard', *RHLF,* 9 (1902), 228–37.

8. *Anciennes et modernes généalogies,* fol. 14^{v}–15^{r}.

9. 'Au lecteur', xvi. 7; cf. Huppert, *Perfect history,* p. 79; Klippel, *Darstellung,* pp. 61–8.

10. See Kelley, *Modern historical scholarship,* pp. 208–10, 229, 292–3.

11. *Chroniques,* fol. 1^{r}.

12. *Histoire,* sig. ***3^{v}–4^{r}.

13. On the matter of the Trojan origins, poets and historians drew particularly close: 'Ronsard might deny that the poet and historian had anything in common, but in reality his *Franciade* appealed to much the same audience, and played upon the same sentimental traditions as the writings of his friends Belleforest, du Haillan, and Pasquier.' (Kelley, p. 306.) See Pasquier's repeated praise of Ronsard (Gillot, *Querelle,* pp. 113–17), and Richter, 'Ronsard and Belleforest on the Origins of France', *Essays presented to Stanley Pargellis,* ed. Bluhm (Chicago, 1965), pp. 65–80.

14. See Joly, *Benoît de Sainte-More,* i. 550ff.

NOTES TO CHAPTER VI

81

15. *De Franciadis epica fabula,* pp. 17–30.

16. See especially Dédéyan, 'Henri II, la *Franciade* et les *Hymnes* de 1555–1556', *BHR*, 9 (1947), 114–28; also Ronsard, *Oeuvres,* xvi. v–xviii; Binet, *Vie,* ed. Laumonier, p. 25; Storer, *Virgil and Ronsard,* pp. 14–18; Chamard, *Hist. Pléiade,* iii. 97–109.

17. Allais, p. 11.

18. *Abrégé,* xiv. 25; 'Au lecteur', xvi. 9; see Lebègue, *Ronsard,* p. 97, 101; Chamard, *Hist. Pléiade,* iii. 120–2.

19. On the manuscripts see Faral, 'Sur deux manuscrits du livre II de la *Franciade*', *RHLF*, 17 (1910), 685–708, 20 (1913), 672–4; Ronsard, *Oeuvres,* xvi. 357–375; Chamard, *Hist. Pléiade,* iii. 107–8.

20. See Chamard, *Hist. Pléiade,* iii. 108–9. For a suggestion that Ronsard's changes to Book iv between 1572 and 1584 were inspired by political considerations, see Cameron, 'Ronsard and Book iv of the *Franciade*', *BHR*, 32 (1970), 395–406.

21. *Oeuvres,* xvi. 330.

22. For Ronsard's attitude to patronage, see Silver, 'Ronsard, panegyrist, pensioner and satirist of the French Court', *RR*, 45 (1954), 89–108.

23. See Silver, 'The birth of the modern French epic', *PMLA*, 70 (1955), 1118–32; *Ronsard and the Hellenic Renaissance,* pp. 85–115; Hepp, 'Homère en France au XVIe', pp. 477–94. Nolhac, *Ronsard et l' humanisme,* pp. 121–9, acknowledges Ronsard's originality in drawing on Homer, but denigrates his conception of epic.

24. The notes to Laumonier's edition are very helpful for the minor borrowings. See for example *Franciade,* ii. 14, 124; iii. 571.

25. For Neptune see *Franciade,* i. 18–19, *Iliad* vii. 252 ff.; Laomedon, *Franciade,* ii. 15–28, *Iliad* xxi. 441 ff.; Trojan horse, *Franciade,* i. 36, *Aeneid* ii. 15 ff.; Priam, *Franciade,* i. 85–94, *Aeneid* ii. 515–58.

26. Storer, *Virgil and Ronsard,* pp. 100–24; Lange, *Ronsards Franciade,* pp. 26–36.

27. Of course duels were not unknown in ancient epic, but in the duel between Francus and Phovère, the debt to Ariosto is greater than elsewhere: 'Le souvenir de l'Arioste n'y apparaît [dans la *Franciade*] qu'aux endroits les plus romanesques; Ronsard se le rappelle et le suit d'assez près, seulement dans la description d'un combat singulier, comme il y en a tant dans le *Roland Furieux*.' (Cioranescu, *L'Arioste,* i. 176, and, for an analysis of the duel, pp. 177–8.)

28. On the weaknesses of Books i and iii, see Gandar, *Ronsard,* pp. 45–50.

29. Gautier, *Epopées françaises,* ii. 636–7; Chamard, *Hist. Pléiade,* iii. 130–1; Spingarn, *Literary criticism,* p. 211.

30. Morçay and Müller, *La Renaissance,* pp. 399–402; Chamard, *Hist. Pléiade,* iii. 122.

31. 'Même quand le sujet ne lui plaisait guère, Ronsard ne pouvait être foncièrement mauvais' (Lebègue, *Ronsard,* p. 103). 'L'artiste scrupuleux qu'il s'est toujours montré n'est pas moins grand ici qu'ailleurs' (Chamard, *Hist. Pléide,* iii. 112).

32. Garnier (*c.* 1588—after 1633) was a Parisian who admired Ronsard, edited his works, and imitated him. For his numerous opuscules see Lachèvre, *Recueils collectifs,* i. 196; Fleuret et Perceau, *Satires du XVIIe,* pp. 163–8; Cioranescu, *XVIe.* See also Allais, p. 97, where he discusses Garnier, describes Guillot as *Guillant,* and conjures up a mythical *Levet,* supposed to have added a sixth book to the *Franciade* (the error probably derives from Maurice Levez, publisher of Guillot's *Franciade 6*); Marni, *Allegory,* p. 110; Goujet, xiv. 235–45; Toinet, i. 72–7, ii. 19–21; Edelman, *Attitudes,* p. 205, n. 9. I refer to Garnier's continuation as *Franciade 5.*

33. *Franciade 5,* pp. 47–8.

34. p. 11.

35. pp. 20–32.

36. p. 13.

37. p. 45. Cf. Ronsard's *Franciade,* i. 1015 ff.

38. Little is known of him. He was a canon at Bourges, devoted to Condé. See Toinet, i. 82; Tchemerzine, ix. 448; Edelman, *Attitudes,* p. 205, n. 9. I refer to his continuation as *Franciade 6.*

39. In the dedicatory letter to Condé of *Franciade 6,* a2^v, he says: 'Ie luy ay desia faict sonner en mon cinquiesme liure, la gloire du victorieux Charlemaigne, & de ses descendans.' I have not been able to trace this work.

40. Sig. Bl^r-3r.

41. Sig. K3^r-4^v.

42. Born at Uzès 1575, died 1629. While he was studying in Paris, his uncle, Robert Delaudun, persuaded him to cultivate poetry rather than philosophy, and was later to edit his nephew's *Franciade.* Pierre's *Art Poétique* of 1597 contains precepts on epic theory, pp. 259–68. See Toinet, i. 65–72, ii. 18–19; Marni, *Allegory,* pp. 73, 75, 82–3, 110.

43. Author's preface to the *Franciade,* all^r.

44. Published in 1603, reissued 1604. According to Robert Delaudun's preface to the *Franciade,* it was composed much earlier: 'L'autheur mon nepueu, l'enfanta lors qu'il estudioit encore a Paris . . . il estoit resolu de nous priuer du doux fruict de cest ouurage, & le laisser eternellement croupir dans son estude, (comme par l'espace de cinq ou six ans il a demeuré sans voir la clairté du Soleil) . . .' (a4^v-5^r). The last

phrase suggests a date of composition about 1598 when Pierre was about twenty-three. Raymond says that Delaudun 'reprend le sujet de la *Franciade* (1608)' (*Influence de Ronsard*, ii. 351); he is wrong both as to the date and subject of Delaudun's epic.

45. i, p. 5.

46. viii, p. 281.

47. Author's preface to *Franciade,* a10^v.

48. Ronsard, i. 24–163; Delaudun, i, pp. 5 ff.

49. i. 287–304.

50. i, p. 12.

51. ii. 641 ff.

52. iii, pp. 76 ff.; cf. viii, pp. 305 ff.

53. ii. 677 ff.; iii. 671 ff.

54. i, p. 15, iii, p. 90, v, pp. 157 ff., viii, p. 307.

55. ii, pp. 64 ff.

56. ii. 1209 ff.

57. iii, p. 72.

58. iii. 1299 ff.

59. iii, pp. 110–20.

60. i. 959 ff.

61. iii, pp. 115 ff.; cf. Ronsard, ii. 124–310, discussed below, pp. 214–5.

62. viii, pp. 271 ff.

63. ii, pp. 41–2.

64. ii, p. 53.

65. iv, pp. 143–4.

66. Catascope, Hierée, Presbée, Hippocome, Strouta, Mantis.

67. Ovid, *Tristia,* iv. iii. 75.

VII

GLORIFICATION OF ANCESTORS

THE next group of epics, which belong to the years 1580 to 1611, show variations on the epic structure that Ronsard had created, whilst at the same time diverging from Ronsard in their main purpose. For Ronsard the task of epic was above all to illustrate the French language and French literature; for Delbene, d'urfé, and Schelandre it was chiefly a vehicle for the glorification of their patron's ancestors. Of course, this was a theme that had appeared before. The epics of Blarru and Pillard in praise of the Dukes of Lorraine clearly glorified that family, even if they did not contain detailed lists of the ancestors of René or Antoine. Long lists of the French kings occurred in the *Franciades,* both Ronsard's and Delaudun's, and in Guillot's continuation. In Garnier's *Henriade* and *Loyssée* the ancestor theme was given a special twist to prove a claim to the throne. In singling out any feature of epic for closer examination, or in trying to group epics so as to make fruitful comparisons, it must always be remembered that epic was an all-embracing genre, and that the predominant features of one poem are usually to be found less conspicuously in many others. What justifies the grouping of the epics of Delbene, d'Urfé and Schelandre, is that they all abandoned the royal family of France: the first two celebrated the house of Savoy, the last the Stuart family. Despite great divergencies of detail, all three used the Virgilian structure on which the *Franciade* was based.

Delbene and Amadeus VI, Count of Savoy

The fire which ravaged the Biblioteca Nazionale of Turin in 1899 served the epics of Savoy ill. The manuscript of Delbene's *Amédéide* perished; so also did two manuscripts of d'Urfé's *Savoysiade.* Fortunately the manuscript of the single book of Delbene's *Amédéide* was edited by Dufour in 1864, and Delbene published a revised version of his manuscript in 1586.[1] The poem must have been composed between 1580, when Charles Emmanuel became Duke of Savoy, since the manuscript

is dedicated to him with that title, and 1586, when Delbene published his revised version.[2] This makes it the first historical
epic to be written after Ronsard's *Franciade*; it was also written
by the man to whom in 1565 Ronsard had dedicated his *Abrégé
de l'art poétique.*[3]

To glorify a patron's ancestors the poets worked as follows.
They examined the patron's family tree, chose from it some
outstanding figure suitable as an epic hero, adapted the career
of this figure as they found it described in the chronicles to
suit whatever epic structure they deemed appropriate, and
finally ensured that all the members of the patron's family were
celebrated during the course of the poem. Delbene, being something of a genealogist and historian himself, was well equipped
to embark on a epic of this nature. From the long line of rulers
of Savoy his choice fell on Amadeus VI (1342–83), an ambitious
and talented soldier whose vigorously aggressive foreign policy
and subtle diplomacy left its mark on the international scene
of the fourteenth century. Having successfully extended the
boundaries of his own domain, Amadeus undertook, at the
suggestion of Pope Urban V, an expedition to repulse the Turks
and Bulgars, who were overrunning the Eastern Empire, and
to liberate the Emperor John Paleologus, who was held in
prison by the usurper Andronicus. Successful in both enterprises, he also brought about a short-lived reconciliation
between the Greek and Roman Churches.[4] None of these adventures, however, is to be found in the *Amédéide,* for Delbene
wrote only Book i, and Amadeus only got as far as Patras.

The unfinished *Amédéide* bears a close resemblance to the
unfinished *Franciade.* It starts with Christian version of the
pagan council of gods. In the storm which follows, 'Neptune'
and 'Jupiter' occur only as synonyms for 'sea' and 'thunder'[5]
and have no individual personality attached to them as do
Ronsard's Neptune, Iris, and Juno. Having lost several ships
Amadeus, through the intercession of Mary, to whom he
addressed prayers for help, lands safely at Patras, whose ruler
is Orytie. Amadeus, like Francus, grieves for his drowned
friends, and we are not surprised to find that Orytie, like Dicæe,
has troubles. Her Turkish neighbour, Amurat, is ravaging her
lands until she submits to the usurper Andronicus. Amadeus
immediately takes up her cause, and we can scarcely doubt that

in Book ii, had it survived, there would have been some duel or battle in which Amadeus released Orytie from her oppressor, just as Francus released Dicæe from the giant Phovère.

Between Amadeus's arrival at Patras and his listening to the recital of Orytie's troubles he visits a picture gallery containing portraits of the rulers of Savoy, from the founder Beroldo to Amadeus V, the hero's father. This historical digression occupies more than a third of the poem.[6] One suspects Delbene brought this feature, which occurs in Book iv of the *Franciade*, to Book i of the *Amédéide,* so that he might include in the first book of his epic the part which would most appeal to his patron, and thus make his main point with a minimum of effort.[7] Faithful though this digression may be to Delbene's intention of glorifying his patron's ancestors, it cannot fail to have a retarding effect on the action of the poem. Nor indeed is the tempo quickened by the insertion of a hymn to Justice, sung by the bard Synope, just before the recital of Orytie's troubles.

Delbene's grip on his story is far from secure. What little cohesion it has derives from the Storm-Shipwreck-Recital structure which he borrowed from Ronsard, distorting it with untimely digressions. In the matter of metre, Delbene was at first more original. He adopted the Alexandrine, discarding the decasyllable, which Ronsard's other main imitator, Schelandre, was to employ again in 1611. The rhyme scheme is in groups of six lines: ababab cdcdcd. Dufour's edition divides the text into tercets, which conveys the mistaken impression that the poem is in *terza rima* (aba bcb cdc ded . . .). As there is frequent enjambment between these tercets, and as there is usually a sentence ending after each group of six lines, the poem would be better divided after each six lines. This would bring out the more appropriate comparison with the metre of Italian epic-romance, *ottava rima* (a b a b a b c c), of which Delbene's stanzas lack only the final couplet. However, Delbene found this rhyme-scheme too constricting and rewrote the poem in rhyming couplets in 1586. Other differences from Ronsard are the use of the *merveilleux chrétien*, and the notable absence of any but the simplest type of simile. Original in some respects, curious in others, Delbene's abortive epic displays most of the vices of the *Franciade* and none of its virtues.

D'Urfé and Beroldo

The first of the portraits in the picture gallery visited by Amadeus VI was that of Beroldo, the Saxon prince who founded the dynasty that ruled Savoy. Nephew and favourite of the Emperor Otto, Beroldo one day discovered the Empress in adultery. To defend his uncle's honour he stabbed the Empress and her lover, a hazardous step, for there was only Beroldo's word to explain away the dead Empress. Otto believed Beroldo's story. But the Count de Monts claimed that the Empress was an innocent victim, accused Beroldo, started a civil war, and succeeded in forcing Otto to sacrifice his nephew. Hounded from Saxony, Beroldo fought for the Spaniards against the Saracens, and for Boson of Burgundy against the Genoese and Piedmontese. Finally he established himself in Savoy. This story of the origins of the ducal family of Savoy could be found in the chronicles of Paradin[8] and the *Novelle* of Bandello.[9] D'Urfé was himself related to this family, and, after serving in the army of Charles Emmanuel in 1598, he retired to his estates at Virieu-le-Grand in 1599, there to start his epic in honour of the Duke. More learned and inventive than Delbene, d'Urfé in his epic was the first to show the influence of Tasso.

Because the *Savoysiade* was never published in the poet's lifetime, it failed to exercise any influence on French epic, and, remaining unread, has been condemned by many critics ever since.[10] The task of studying the *Savoysiade* is complicated by the complexity of the manuscript tradition, but the nature of these manuscripts permits a revealing glance into the poet's workshop.[11] The earliest version of the poem is almost certainly represented by A, in view of the careful dating of the start and finish of each book, and the numerous corrections and alterations to the text.[12] B, to judge from Rua's description, corresponds to Book i of A, but where A has been corrected B seems to accord with the first version before correction.[13] C represents a further stage in the evolution of the poem,[14] but the nine books of C are not merely a continuation of the six books of A. In fact d'Urfé has completely revised and expanded the first three books of A to form Books i–vi of C.[15] D is probably a copy of C before correction, just as B was a copy of A before correction.[16] Finally E seems to have been a copy of C incor-

porating the later corrections, but it lacks Books ii, iii, and ix.[17]
The affiliation of the manuscripts of the *Savoysiade* may therefore be represented thus:

We may leave aside D because it was superseded by later corrections to C. We must leave aside B and E because they are
lost. This means that the important stages in the composition
of the poem are A and C. The few published extracts of the
epic[18] have long served as a convenient means of misjudging
the poem as a whole. To remedy this I shall therefore discuss
the story as it appears in A and, by indicating the revisions and
additions of C, show how the poem evolved in the process of
composition.

The variants of the beginning of the poem in A itself, and
then in C, show that d'Urfé experienced much difficulty in
setting the story in motion and in providing enough historical
background to make it intelligible. In A we learn of the martyrdom of Saint Maurice, which made God specially interested in
Savoy, of the plight of Boson of Burgundy, and of Beroldo's
prayer to the Virgin as he cruises past Montserrat. Suddenly
Beroldo comes upon two fleets drawn up against each other
and prepares for action.[19] These events are given more cohesion
in C. Saint Maurice is introduced as a character instead of
merely being mentioned, and in his conversation with God we
learn that God's choice of Beroldo to found the house of Savoy
is in response to Saint Maurice's request for favour to be shown
to his province. Instead of coming upon the two fleets by
chance, Beroldo learns from some sailors of Boson's predicament and how the two fleets come to be there.[20] This is an improvement on A where the reader is thrown unprepared into the
complexities of a three-cornered sea-battle with little indication
of what it is all about.

Before Beroldo goes into battle on Boson's side, he knights
his son Humbert. The speeches which adorn the ceremony show
d'Urfé's preoccupation with codes of conduct, a preoccupation

which shapes much of *L'Astrée*. Humbert's companions in A are Lindamor and Vuelfe. In C Lindamor is changed to Gaston de Foix, the ancestor of Henry IV of France, and a new companion, Geoffrey of Anjou, is added, whilst Vuelfe, traditionally connected with d'Urfé's own family, is retained. Fighting begins at the start of Book ii in A and in the middle of Book i in C. There are many duels, among which d'Urfé introduces the rescue of Humbert by Brasilda, a fierce female warrior, who falls in love with him.[21] For the most part C preserves the events of A, but there are substantial additions in the shape of recitals, such as the episode of Belmont and the tale of Gonsale di Lara[22] which occupy most of Book iv in C. D'Urfé here yields to the temptation to develop the poem with recitals not directly connected with the principal characters, a technique later exploited by Le Moyne and Carel de Sainte-Garde.

The issue of the sea-battle is decided at the end of Book ii in A and at the beginning of Book v in C, an indication of how much of the additional material of C is devoted to expanding the account of the sea-battle. Beroldo pursues the remnants of Boson's enemies, the Genoans, to Ventimiglia where Humbert, after more glorious deeds, joins him. Ventimiglia is the domain of Anne Lascaris; her ward is Adelis; with Adelis Humbert falls in love; from the marriage of Adelis and Humbert is to spring the family of Charles Emmanuel. Hence the importance of Adelis to d'Urfé's purpose. At this point ends Book ii in A, dated 25 October 1604, and this corresponds to the end of Book vi in C. In the winter of 1604 d'Urfé made a pilgrimage to Loreto and on his return took up the story of Beroldo in Ventimiglia. From February to July 1605, he composed Books iv, v, and vi of A, and these remained virtually unchanged as Books vii, viii, and ix of C. The task of analysis is thus greatly simplified.

The first episode of Book iv in A shows a startling change in d'Urfé's handling of the *merveilleux*. In place of God and the Virgin, he introduces a supernatural element with Neoplatonic overtones. In a remote corner of Scythia, the Demogorgon (l'âme du monde') has constructed an abode for himself and his four daughters: Phossiné ('clarté'), Noussis ('entendement'), Anangué ('fatalité'), and Physis ('nature').[23] Here the fairy Melusine observes in a huge mirror Beroldo's arrival at Ventimiglia. Melusine therefore visits Anne Lascaris to persuade her to make him welcome and in the shape of Adelis's nurse Canuze, prepares the union between Adelis and Humbert. The action is delayed by Beroldo's visit to a temple where he sees engraved portraits of the Saxon emperors. Their history is described to him by Rodolf down to Otto I whom Beroldo recognizes. Beroldo stops the recital as he knows the rest:

> voicy les trois Othons, voicy Hugues mon pere
> fils du second Othon, et, du troisiesme, frere;
> de sorte que ie voix, sans destourner mon oeil
> & mon pere & mon oncle, Ayeul & bisayeul.[24]

At the temple Beroldo meets Anne, and they now return to the castle for a great feast, after which a bard sings a hymn to the Trinity. Anne is curious to know Beroldo's adventures and he obliges:

> Allors chascun se teust & Berol commença . . .[25]

This is the first line of Book vi of A and of Book ix of C. In the last book of the *Savoysiade* in both versions Beroldo relates his expulsion from Saxony, the tale of the Empress's death, and de Monts's rebellion.

Even this skeletal summary indicates the richness and diversity of d'Urfés inspiration. At the centre of it all is a variation on the Storm-Shipwreck-Recital formula: a sea-journey and a sea-battle, which drives the hero to an unexpected shore. The similarities between d'Urfé's account of events there, and Delbene's of events in Patras, are striking. The recitals, the portraits, the hymns, the feasts, all correspond. Certainly d'Urfé could have known Delbene's poem, though he could hardly have needed its inspiration; he may have drawn on Ronsard, though this cannot be proved; he may have drawn directly from Virgil. In any case the thread of continuity is there. It may be a case of similar causes producing similar results. However, if d'Urfé owed anything to Ronsard or Delbene, he undoubtedly went far beyond them. The debt to Tasso is unmistakable. Romanesque elaboration is common to both, as well as individual episodes, such as Lindamor's first sight of Brasilda[26] or the slaughter of Belmont's sons.[27] Ariosto is pressed into service: the drama of the Empress's death is developed along the lines of the Giocondo episode in the *Furioso*.[28] Stories from Spain are included, such as the tale of Gonsale di Lara. In the early stages of manuscript A the Cid was included among the companions of Humbert. Virgilian reminiscences abound: the introduction to Beroldo's recital has just been quoted. Yet the *Savoysiade* is no repository of dead epic borrowings.[29] Its very diversity prevents that. Ideas from different sources clash to give the poem life. Though conceived to flatter Charles Emmanuel, the poem bears witness in its revisions and research to d'Urfé's seriousness of purpose. Others published a couple of books to catch their patron's eye; d'Urfé, perhaps dissatisfied with his own work, did not publish and thereby achieved more.

This conscientiousness is evident in the handling of historical material. The poet took pains to establish an inner logic to his poem and to eliminate inconsistency. To this end he drew on conflicting historical accounts and extracted the maximum drama from them. The chronicles, we have seen, attributed de Monts's rebellion to Beroldo's killing of the Empress, his relation. This view was challenged by Albert Krantz, who affirmed that the Empress was publicly burned for adultery, so that Beroldo could not have killed her.[30] The motive for de Monts's hostility toward Beroldo thus disappeared. But another possibility was suggested by Giovanni Botero: 'Può essere che se ben Beroldo non amazzò l'Imperatrice, ammazzasse qualche parente del Conte di Mons, mentovato dagli storici Savoini.'[31] D'Urfé's version partakes of all these elements. He made the Empress's lover a son of de Monts; Beroldo believed he had killed the adulterous pair, but the Empress escaped. Thus it was possible for Otto to threaten his wife with burning, and de Monts's dead son provided a motive for his hostility to Beroldo.[32]

An unpublished poem provides a good target for repetitive abuse, though the manuscripts of the *Savoysiade* have always been known to be in existence. Of the published passages Toinet in 1907 said: 'Le fragment que nous possédons imprimé n'a aucune valeur historique ou littéraire.'[33] Beall in 1942 declared: 'Ce poème inachevé de Urfé n'a aucune valeur littéraire ou historique. La composition est insignifiante, les vers sont monotones, pompeux et vides.'[34] Edelman in 1946 called all nine cantos 'a pompous and monotonous fragment devoid of historical value,'[35] a judgement which seems to owe more to Toinet and Beall than to a reading of the epic itself. The truth had been uttered in the nineteenth century. In 1839 Bernard wrote: '. . . Honoré d'Urfé était occupé d'un poëme qui, quoique resté manuscrit et inachevé, n'est pas sans importance; c'est la *Savoysiade*, dont beaucoup d'auteurs ont parlé, mais qu'aucun ne s'est donné la peine de lire.'[36] A meticulous study of the poem was published by Rua in 1893, and his judgement deserves more attention:

Tra i varii poemi a cui diedero origine e materia le gesta dei príncipi di Savoia, ci è parso che quello del d'Urfé occupasse uno dei posti migliori e meritasse di essere, più degli altri, conosciuto e studiato. L'opera del nostro poeta non è già la vuota improvvisazione del cortigiano devoto, sibbene il frutto d'un lavoro lungo e diligente . . . non si contenta di tessere una scarna e fredda cronaca versificata; valendosi della licenza concessa ai poeti, colorisce e vivifica il suo canto con elementi di altra natura . . .[37]

Schelandre and Fleance

Jean de Schelandre's contribution to the glorification of ancestors was addressed to James Stuart, King of Scotland and England. From the genealogical tree of the Stuarts, Schelandre selected, like d'Urfé, the founder of the family: Fleance. Delbene and d'Urfé, both under the influence of Italian epic, composed poems that were well in advance of their time, Delbene by his use of the *merveilleux chrétien*, d'Urfé by his romanesque developments. Schelandre, however, though he wrote some years later turned resolutely back to Ronsard for his epic technique, and felt the need to apologize for some aspects of it.[38]

The *Stuartide* survives in one manuscript and a single edition, published in 1611. The manuscript, in one book, is expanded into two books in the published version.[39] The epic opens with Fleance setting out to find his father Banquo. He is thwarted by Mars and Neptune, who fear Fleance's prophesied descendant, King James. A storm summoned up by Neptune drives Fleance from the coast of Scotland to the island of Lewis in the Outer Hebrides. Book ii relates Fleance's reception there by Gothrede, the governor of the island, who recounts for Fleance's benefit the events leading to Macbeth's usurpation of the throne of Scotland.

The Storm-Shipwreck-Recital formula is by now familiar. As a confessed disciple of Ronsard, Schelandre was undoubtedly influenced by the structure of the *Franciade*, yet he is closer to Virgil in plunging straight into the storm in Book i. Not only are Schelandre's literary sources plain, but he also tells us which historians he followed. Numerous marginal notes refer the reader to the histories of Hector Boethius and George Buchanan, first published in 1526 and 1582 respectively. A comparison between Schelandre's account of the usurpation of Macbeth with that to be found in the histories shows that the poet tried to present Banquo in a better light than the historians. He passed over what was detrimental to Banquo's reputation, for example his ignominious pleas for help against the rebels at Duncan's court. He transferred to Banquo Macbeth's victory over the rebels, but entirely omitted Macbeth's savage punishment of the rebels, which would not have been appropriate to the character of Banquo. After the rebellion Schelandre introduced a strange duel between Banquo and Mars not derived from the historians. The purpose seems to be to prepare for the invasion of the Norwegian King, Sueno, the next episode which the historians related. They introduced the episode by ascribing its cause to the rivalry between the heirs of the King of Denmark; Sueno invaded Scotland because Canute had just added England to his kingdom. All this was irrelevant to Schelandre's purpose. In order to give his epic inner cohesion he invented the duel between Banquo and Mars in order to supply a reason for Sueno's success in invading Scotland. The reason is Banquo's absence from public affairs after he had been severely wounded in the duel with Mars. When the poet came to the murder of Duncan he was, like Shakespeare in *Macbeth*, embarrassed by the complicity of Banquo in the crime. He therefore abandoned the historians' account and had Banquo removed to Sutherland by the magic powers of Macbeth's wife. Banquo could thus be absolved of any responsibility for the murder. It is possible therefore to follow step by step the process by which Schelandre adapted the historical material to the composition of an epic and thus illustrate the essential features of heroic epic, namely the presentation of the hero as a paragon of virtue and the omission of events that would distract attention from him. Banquo is not, of course, the hero of the *Stuartide*, but being the hero's father, qualifies for the same treatment.[40]

Schelandre was a follower of Ronsard and his purpose, the glorification of ancestors, the same as that of Delbene and d'Urfé. He managed, however, to avoid some of the weaknesses of his model and one of the inconveniences of his theme.[41] The *merveilleux païen*, which Ronsard treated with such seriousness, caused Schelandre some unease. His apology for using it at all has been noted; his solution to the problems it raised led him to improve on Ronsard. To meet the criticism that he was accepting paganism, he divided the universe into three orders. The lowest, human, was subject to the interference of the next order, the supernatural, represented by Mars and Neptune, who in turn were subject to a higher authority, 'Dyname',[42] an irresistible and omnipotent force in which the Christian could recognize his own God. The pagan deities could either be assimilated to the demons of Christian theology, or, when it suited the poet, they could be considered as personifications: Neptune as the sea, over which King James's navy would rule supreme, and Mars as war and disorder, which the King's peaceful policies would banish. The pagan deities were thus reduced in status and at the same time enriched in significance. This allowed Schelandre to treat them with a lightness of touch, without degenerating into the triviality of Delaudun. When Neptune calms the storm, he is compared to a schoolmaster silencing his students, while the frightened sailors are likened to wary tortoises or snails:

> Cela conclu, l'orage il desmesla
> Par le seul ton d'vn serieux Holà,
> Tout le bruit tombe & la fiere tempeste
> En vn clin d'oeil se resoult & s'arreste,
> Comme on verroit les petits escoliers
> Quitter debats, cris, & ieux familiers
> Quand le pedant au gros sourcil arriue.
> Les matelots d'vne audace tardiue
> Sortants le nez, qu'ils ont tenu caché
> Par dix Soleils dans le coffre bousché
> (Ainsi que tire ou la froide tortuë
> Ou l'escargot à la loge tortuë
> Premier la teste & bien tost le surplus
> Quand le peril ne les assiege plus) . . .[43]

The decasyllable was appropriate to Schelandre's jocular style, whereas it was sometimes a hindrance to Ronsard's solemnity. Schelandre was no innovator in epic structure like d'Urfé, but his discerning handling of the tradition he accepted resulted in one of the few epics whose incompleteness is a matter of regret.

The glorification of ancestors lingered as an epic theme, but never again dominated the work of poets as it dominated the poems of Delbene, d'Urfé, and Schelandre. It might have done in the poem which Scudéry proposed to Cardinal Richelieu in 1634. Scudéry's attention lighted on Robert of Dreux whom Richelieu claimed as an ancestor; he outlined a plan of work which exactly describes the procedure followed by Delbene, d'Urfé, or Schelandre:

> Bref, elle [la Muse] se promet, tant elle a de courage,
> De faire voir le bout de ce penible ouurage
> Que le diuin Ronsard n'osa que commencer,
> Et pour ta seule gloire, elle veut y penser.
> Aprends que chaque iour cette Muse s'aplique,
> A former le projet d'vn POEME HEROIQVE.
> Sur les Maistres de l'Art, qui n'aura rien des leurs,
> Elle esbauche vn dessain, apreste des couleurs,
> Choisit dedans l'Histoire, vn HEROS de ta race,
> S'instruit de sa valeur, & le suit a la trace,
> Le tire du sepulchre, afin que dans ses Vers,
> Il ne puisse finir qu'auecques l'Vniuers.
> Le sang Royal de DREUX, d'où vient ton origine,
> Luy fournit maintenant, tout ce qu'elle imagine,
> Et c'est ROBERT LE GRAND, qu'elle veut esleuer
> Iusqu'où mortel que toy, ne sçauroit arriuer.
> Mais n'ayant pour objet, que ton coeur magnanime,
> Il faut grand RICHELIEV que ta douceur l'anime . . .[44]

Poised between two periods of intense epic activity, that which followed the publication of the *Franciade*, and that which surfaced after the troubles of the Fronde, this is an important statement of the aims and methods of the epic poet, and shows the continuity of the epic tradition despite the changes of structure, adornment, and language which resulted in practice. In fact Richelieu did not encourage Scudéry's project—perhaps he felt that there was some impertinence in the line 'Iusqu'où mortel que toy, ne sçauroit arriuer', and that his own career

would speak more eloquently for him than Scudéry's celebration of Robert of Dreux. Scudéry, however, did not abandon
his epic ambitions, and turned to Queen Christina of Sweden.
Her family was said to descend from Alaric, the Goth who
sacked Rome. The glorification of ancestors continued, but as
part of a conception of epic that embraced much else besides.

NOTES TO CHAPTER VII

1. *Mémoires et documents publiés par la société savoisienne d'histoire et d'archéologie*, 8 (1864), 207–55. Dufour describes the lost manuscript thus: 'Le manuscrit, de vingt-six feuillets sur papier format in –4°, est du seizième siècle et d'une écriture assez lisible. Il porte çà et là quelques corrections qui doivent être de la main de Delbene. J'ai laissé à ce manuscrit sa physionomie tout entière, orthographe et ponctuation' (p. 210). Dufour does not, however, indicate what the author's corrections are. In the catalogue of the royal library the manuscript (Codex lxi.k.1.97 (L.v.24)) is described thus: '*Chartaceus, habens folia 26, saeculi XVI, Premier livre de l'Amedeide a Charles Emanuel Duc de Savoye par Alfonce del Bene Abbé d'Haute Combe*. Incipit Je chante les travaux les faicts & la valeur . . .', and the first six lines are quoted (*Codices manuscripti bibliothecae regii Taurinensis*, ii. 477). There is an account of the poem with extensive quotation in Bernardet, *Un abbé d'Hautecombe*, pp. 41–50, which has a good bibliography, and further extracts in Marie-José, *La Maison de Savoie*, pp 199–200. The revised version, in couplets instead of the form of *terza rima* which Delbene first used, preserves the verses of the original wherever possible, and is thus even clumsier than original version. The general sequence of events remained the same.

2. Dufour, p. 211.

3. See Ronsard, *Oeuvres*, xiv. 3, for Laumonier's note on Delbene as the recipient of the *Abrégé*.

4. For the career of Amadeus see Cox, *The Green Count of Savoy*. He mentions the *Amédéide* on p. 179. See also Marie-José, *Maison de Savoie*, pp. 75–277. Amadeus VI was in the popular tradition one of the most famous of the ducal family. At the marriage celebrations of Margaret and Isabella of Savoy in 1608 a float carried effigies of Beroldo, Amadeus IV, Amadeus VI, and Emmanuel Philibert. Amadeus VI was described thus: 'Amedeo il Sesto, detto il Conte Verde, dominatore del Piemonte, liberatore di Alessio, imperatore di Costantinopoli, dalle mani del Re della Bulgaria, espugnatore di Gallipoli, di Malatia, ecc.' (Rua, *Epopea savoina*, p. 8). Clearly Delbene was choosing a well-known and popular hero.

5. Tercets 21–2, lines 63–8; quoted below, p. 215.

6. Tercets 135–248.

7. Rua compares Delbene's treatment of Beroldo and the princes of Savoy with that of the *Temple d'alliance des Ducs de Savoye*, a manuscript in the Biblioteca Reale of Turin (*Epopea savoina*, pp. 4–6).

8. *Chronique de Savoie*, pp. 33–63.

9. 4a parte, xix (ed. Flora, ii. 755–60). See Rua, *Epopea savoina*, pp. 35–6.

10. e.g. Toinet, Beall, Edelman; but see the excellent study by Rua, and also Benedetto, 'Una redazione inedita della leggenda degli infanti de Lara', *Studi medievali*, 4 (1912–13), 231–70; Duparc, *'La Savoysiade'*, *Revue savoisienne*, 86 (1945), 60–4.

11. No complete account of these manuscripts exists. For partial accounts see Bernard, *Les d'Urfé*, pp. 155–9 (the information given by Bernard is repeated and misinterpreted by Bonafous, *Etudes sur l'Astrée*, pp. 158–9); Rua, *Epopea Savoina*, pp. 12–13; Toinet, ii. 43–9; Reure, *La vie et les oeuvres*, pp. 126–8. I have labelled the five manuscripts A, B, C, D, and E as follows:

A. Paris, Bibliothèque Nationale: fonds français, 12486.

A poem in d'Urfé's handwriting, variously entitled *La Béroldide, Bérol*, and *La Savoye*, in six books, dated between 1599 and 1605, with numerous corrections. This is evidently the manuscript once owned by Bernard: 'Je ne connais que trois copies de ce poëme, dont je possède le brouillon original, portant l'indication des lieux où a été commencé et fini chaque livre ou chant. Cet exemplaire est d'autant plus précieux, qu'on y trouve tous les essais de l'auteur' (p. 156). See also Toinet, ii. 45–6; Reure, pp. 128–9 (A).

B. Turin, Biblioteca Nazionale: Codex clii.k.l.69 (L.v.50).

Destroyed by fire. Description from the catalogue: 'Chartaceus constans foliis 21 (4°) saeculi XVI, *Le premier livre de la Beroldide*, absque autoris nomine. Incipit: D'un grand Prince Saxon je chante les alarmes . . . [four lines are quoted]' (*Codices manuscripti*, ii. 496). According to Rua this fragment had about 810 lines (*Epopea Savoina*, pp. 12–13 (IV)).

C. Turin, Archivio di Stato: Storia della Real Casa, Categoria 2a, Storie generali, Mazzo 7.

A poem in d'Urfé's handwriting entitled *La Savoysiade*, in nine books, preceded by a dedicatory letter to Charles Emmanuel dated 1615. The manuscript ends with the declaration: 'Fin du neufiesme livre de la Savoysiade que j'ay fini à Virieu le 29 d'aost 1606. Laus Deo.' See Bernard, p. 157; Rua, p. 12(I); Toinet, ii. 46n; Reure, p. 129 (C).

D. Paris, Bibliothèque de l'Arsenal: MS. 2959.

La Savoysiade in nine books written in a different hand to d'Urfé's. Ends: 'Fin du neufviesme livre de la Savoysiade que j'ai fini d'escrire à Virieu-le-Grand le 29 décembre 1606. Truffier.' See Bernard, p. 157; Rua, pp. 12–13 (II); Toinet, ii. 45; Reure, p. 129 (D).

E. Turin, Biblioteca Nazionale: Codex cxix.l.v.29 (L.v.3).

Destroyed by fire. Description from the catalogue: 'Chartaceus habens folia 157, saeculi XVII, La Savoysiade d'Honoré d'Urfé. Poema Carolo Emmanueli Primo inscriptum. Incipit: D'un grand Prince Saxon je chante les allarmes . . . [six lines are quoted]' (*Codices manu-*

scripti, ii. 489). According to Rua this is an incomplete copy of the nine-book version and contains only Book i and Books iv-viii. See Bernard, p. 157; Rua, p. 13(III); Toinet, ii. 46n; Reure, p. 129(B).

To determine what relation these manuscripts bear to each other, I have collated selected passages, used the evidence of the dates in the surviving manuscripts (A, C, and D), and relied on Rua's description of those which are lost (B and E).

12. These include five different versions of the opening of the poem, ranging from a sketch in unrhymed verse to a version which closely corresponds to the invocation as it appears in the later manuscripts.

13. This might suggest that B is the very earliest draft of Book i, but this does not account for the great variety of corrections and hesitations in A. It is more likely that B represents a copy of Book i from A at some stage after the earliest hesitations, but that d'Urfé later returned to A and used it rather than B for further corrections and continuation. Thus, in describing the second of Humbert's companions d'Urfé first wrote in A:

> L'aultre c'estoit Artolf beau s'il s'en pouuoit voir,
> Fils de ce sage Vulfs, Vulf de qui le sauoir,
> La prudante valeur la vertu la sagesse
> randoit recommandable a chascun sa vieillesse (i, fol. 75ᵛ).

According to Rua (p. 40 n.4) manuscript B had:

> . . . c'estoit Artolf, beau s'il s'en pouvoit voir,
> Fils de sage Vulfs.

In A, the lines quoted above were crossed out and the following substituted:

> L'aultre Vuelfe d'Altorff, Germain de nation
> Fils du sage Rodolf dont la devotion
> La prudante valeur [etc. as above].

This version was then further expanded in C, where Humbert has three companions:

> Or le dernier des trois qui venoit à son rang
> c'estoit Vuelfe d'Altorf fils de Rodolf le grand
> Rodolf dont la valeur, la vertu, la sagesse
> randoit recommandable a chascun sa viellesse (i, fol. 21ʳ).

14. C was presumably written between July 1605 (the last date in A) and August 1606 (the date at the end of C).

15. The next three books of A (iv-vi) become Books vii-ix of C with scarcely any change.

16. The writing of D is extremely hard to read and some pages are illegible, but the manuscript is not important since corrections made to C after D was copied from it represent a later stage of composition. For example d'Urfé first wrote in C that the second of Humbert's companions was the Cid:

> L'autre Ruy de Vivar honneur de la famille
> des valeureux Laras vieux contes de Castille . . . (i, fol. 18ᵛ),

and the Cid appears in D as one of Humbert's companions (fol. 6ʳ). But in C d'Urfé later crossed out everything relating to the Cid and substituted the ancestors of the Angevin dynasty. On this substitution see Rua, pp. 39–40.

17. 'Il codice della Biblioteca Nazionale (L.v.3) non contiene già otto libri . . . ma solamente sei, essendo stati lasciati in bianco il II e il III. Esso ci sembra una copia esatta dell' esemplare corretto del codice dell' Archivio [i.e. my C], copia che fu riveduta dal d'Urfé, come fanno supporre alcune correzioni autografe di errori incorsi nella trascrizione' (p. 13).

18. Two fragments appeared in Toussainct du Bray's anthologies of 1609, 1615, and 1618: the first, of about 130 lines from Book ii, begins: 'Dessus le haut de Troye horrible en sa Gorgonne'; the second, of about 430 lines from Book iii, begins: 'Mais Vulfe cependant dont l'Ame à toute peine'. See Lachèvre, *Recueils collectifs,* i. 46–58, 182–5; Toinet, ii. 43–9; Reure, p. 221. Magendie, *Du Nouveau sur l'Astrée,* p. 22 n. 1, says of the 1609 *Recueil:* 'J'ai vu un exemplaire de cet ouvrage où le fragment ne figure pas.' BN: Ye. 11442 is a defective copy of this nature. Benedetto, 'Una redazione inedita', pp. 253–70, reproduces 888 lines of Book iv of C.

19. i, fol. 67ʳ—74ʳ.

20. i, fol. 11ʳ—15ᵛ.

21. Part of this episode was published in the anthologies; see Toinet, ii. 46–7.

22. iv, fol. 84ᵛ—98ʳ, summarized by Rua, pp. 22–4.

23. These identifications are given in notes in the margins of manuscript A, iv, fol. 132ᵛ and 133ʳ. The discourse explaining the system is summarised by Rua, p. 28.

24. A, v, fol. 162ʳ (my punctuation).

25. A, v. fol. 169ʳ. Cf. *Aeneid* ii. 1: 'Conticuere omnes . . .'

26. A, i, fol. 79ᵛ; cf. *Gerusalemme,* i. 46–8 (Tancredi and Clorinda).

27. C, iii, fol. 70ʳ—75ʳ; cf. *Gerusalemme,* ix. 27 ff. For imitations of Tasso in *L'Astrée,* see Simpson, *Le Tasse,* pp. 78–9.

28. A, vi, fol. 171ᵛ ff.; *Furioso,* 28, 4–74.

29. Invited to comment on Chiabrera's *Amedeida,* another epic in honour of Charles Emmanuel, d'Urfé criticized it for its repetitions (two angelic visions in cantos i and ii) and *longueurs* (debates in Heaven and Hell). See Belloni, *Epigoni,* pp. 169–71; Rua attributes Chiabrera's failure to his abuse of fictions, and d'Urfé's success to his adaptation of the stories of the chroniclers to epic form (p. 39).

30. *Saxonia et Metropolis* (1574); quoted by Rua, p. 37, n. 1.

31. *De' principi cristiani* (1603); quoted by Rua, p. 38, n. 4.

32. See Rua, p. 38.

33. ii. 46. Magendie is no kinder: 'La gloire de d'Urfé n'a rien perdu à l'obscurité où est demeurée la *Savoysiade*' (*Du nouveau sur l'Astrée,* p. 22, n. 1).

34. *Fortune du Tasse,* p. 47.

35. *Attitudes,* p. 204.

36. *Les d'Urfé,* p. 155.

37. *Epopea savoina,* p. 51.

38. For using the decasyllable in deference to Ronsard 'plustost par deuoir que par inclination'; and for resuscitating the *merveilleux païen:* 'on le prie [le lecteur] qu'auant d'asseoir iugement de blasme il compare la majesté des poëmes anciens, qui sont enrichis & comme animés de ces plaisantes inuentions . . .' (*Stuartide,* 'Argument', p. 34).

39. The manuscript is in the British Museum (Reg. 16.E.xxxiii) and is described by Cohen, *Ecrivains français,* pp. 709–11. Schelandre (1585–1635) was a soldier-poet who led a turbulent life, visited England, and died on active service in Holland. See Cohen, pp. 15–137; Asselineau, *Jean de Schelandre,* pp. 12–13; Toinet, ii. 57–8; Harastzi's preface to his edition of *Tyr et Sidon,* pp. xii–xv; Maskell, 'The transformation of history into epic: the *Stuartide* (1611) of J. de Schelandre', *MLR,* 66 (1971), 53–65. Hankiss, 'Schelandre and Shakespeare', *MLN,* 36 (1921), 464–9, deals only with Schelandre as a dramatist.

40. For details of Schelandre's use of the historians, see Maskell, 'Transformation', pp. 56–60.

41. He does not include a list of ancestors in his poem, though there is a long genealogical table prefaced to it (pp. 15–26).

42. 'Allegorie de la Toute-puissance' (marginal note, p. 61); the system is explained in Book i, p. 67.

43. i, pp. 64–5.

44. *Discours de la France,* p. 13. Robert de France was the fifth son of Louis VI and received the apanage of Dreux around 1135. Richelieu claimed descent from him. See Constans, 'Scudéry's lost epic', *MLN,* 37 (1922), 212–5, where he corrects Toinet's identification (i. 161–2) of Robert le Grand with Robert le Fort, who was entrusted by Charles the Bald with the government of the Duché. Desmarets mentions Richelieu's ancestry in *Clovis,* viii, p. 144.

VIII
ROMAN HISTORY

LOCAL, national, and patriotic feeling governed the choice of hero when poets were writing for the kings of France or Scotland, and the Dukes of Lorraine or Savoy. Roman history, Republican or Imperial, offered a multitude of heroes suitable for the heroic and moral tone of epic, yet attracted the epic poets hardly at all. In tragedy Roman heroes abound: from epic they are almost entirely absent. Patriotism and national and local loyalties explain this to some extent. Those who wished to flatter a patron would find Roman Antiquity too remote for their purpose. Even the most devious manipulations of the family tree could scarcely produce an ancestor from Roman history. Yet Scudéry managed just that. The claim of the Royal family of Sweden to descend from Alaric the Goth provided him with a chance to make an excursion into Roman history, even if only to recount the downfall of Rome. The theme of *Alaric* is anti-Roman: it shows God destroying Rome through his instrument, Alaric the Goth.

The Stoic virtues of Republican Rome, long degenerate by the time of Alaric's invasion, were celebrated by Desmarets de Saint-Sorlin in his *Regulus*, a curious epic of miniature dimensions. The triumph of Christianity was illustrated in Mambrun's *Constantinus*, a Latin epic contemporary with Scudéry's *Alaric*. The grouping of epics derived from Roman history throws two points into relief: their lack of homogeneity, and the pervasive influence of Christianity on the mid-seventeenth-century epic, which will be further illustrated in the next chapter on the Christian kings of France.

Scudéry and Alaric

Incompleteness is the dominant feature of the epics that have been considered so far. One book from Delbene, two from Schelandre, four from Ronsard, nine from d'Urfé and Delaudun; even these last failed to reach their conclusion. Scudéry's *Alaric*, published in 1654,[1] is remarkable for being the first complete epic in French; all previous epics, except those in Latin of the early sixteenth century, were abortive. With Scudéry's *Alaric* the character of French epic changed entirely. The language became more fluent, the influence of Tasso was firmly established, and Christianity became a major source of inspiration. These characteristics *Alaric* shared with the other epics that were shortly to follow: *La Pucelle, Clovis,* and *Saint Louis.* In two important respects it differed from them. By going outside French history for his material, and outside France for a patron, Scudéry resembled his predecessors, not his fellow Academicians whose preoccupations were national and patriotic. In turning to the *Gerusalemme* as a model for epic, he shared the tastes of his contemporaries, but achieved what eluded them: a unified epic. A brief summary of the poem will demonstrate its unity.

God commands Alaric to capture Rome. Book i describes the reactions to this command. Alaric weighs up arguments for and against, and finds a compromise: by conquering Rome he will make himself worthy of Amalasonthe. His Council waver; he sways them to his point of view. Amalasonthe refuses to accept his justification; he fails to persuade her. Amalasonthe allies herself with the magician Rigilde to thwart Alaric, and the next nine books describe their efforts to achieve this.

Alaric's departure is the theme of Book ii. He foils Rigilde's attempts to delay him and reviews his army. Jameric's recital is inserted at this point; like Scudéry's other recitals it is carefully grafted on to the story. It is told to the hero by an interested party; it concerns two members of the hero's army; Alaric's own attitude to the beautiful Laplander, Jameric's daughter, excites interest, coming so soon after his quarrel with Amalasonthe. Alaric's abduction occupies Book iii; it is Amalasonthe's attempt to win him back. Two styles contrast. First, dramatic: Amalasonthe's interview with Rigilde, her farewells to Alaric, her imprecations, her plot with Rigilde; secondly, descriptive: the landscape, palace, garden, paintings of the island to which Alaric is abducted. But as all is seen through the eyes of the hero, unity is not destroyed, and the story is easily picked up when the description is over. In Book iv Alaric is rescued. His loss dispirits his men; his captains discuss whether to proceed with the expedition or not; divine intervention breaks the deadlock. The Bishop of Uppsala is sent to rescue Alaric. A second recital, linked to the main narrative by dramatic irony, prepares for Alaric's departure from the magic island. The false Amalasonthe tells Alaric a long tale of what befell a lover who abandoned his mistress. The tale ends. The Bishop arrives, slips the ring from Alaric's finger, and the island is seen for what it is. Amalasonthe's charms fail; Alaric abandons her.

Book v is the turning point of the poem. Up till now Alaric has been struggling to get started, henceforth he moves forward towards his goal. Scudéry engineers this by bringing Alaric's difficulties to a climax, by introducing what at first sight seems a gratuitous digression, and by working a change in Alaric's character. A storm conjured up by Rigilde drives Alaric to England, where a hermit shows him his library, a panorama of world literature, and prophesies the reign of Christina. Alaric's character is strengthened by overcoming the difficulties placed before him by Rigilde's machinations; the hermit's instruction broadens his mind; the prophecy of Christina inspires him to go on.

An infernal council at the beginning of Book vi prefigures the events of the remainder of the poem, but not in such detail as to exclude the unexpected. The demons resolve on four plans: to incite the Spaniards to resist Alaric's landing; to stir Honorius to action; to persuade Arcadius to send reinforcements to the West; and to bring Amalasonthe from Birch to join Alaric's enemies. The first plan is scotched at the end of Book vi. A Spanish fleet attacks Alaric and is defeated. Alaric now proceeds over land and crosses the Alps. An ambush laid by the Romans comes as a surprise to the reader and to Alaric, the Romans are defeated and many prisoners taken, amongst them Valère. Here Scudéry again shows his skill in attaching recitals to the main narrative. Valère describes his rivalry with Tiburse for the hand of Probé. All three are to play an important part in the defence and betrayal of Rome. Even Tasso does not always link recitals so indissolubly to the plot. The same contrast between dramatic and narrative technique that was employed in Book iii is repeated in Book viii. Love dominates the first part: Valère and Tiburse expend much ingenuity in trying to justify themselves to Probé. Fighting dominates the second part: Amalasonthe enlists the aid of Arcadius; Alaric

embarks on the attack on Rome. As is fitting at this stage—
there are two more books to go—the result is inconclusive.

The last threats to Alaric's success are dismissed in Book ix :
a Greek army is defeated in Sicily; Amalasonthe's jealousy is
overcome; Rigilde's calumnies are confounded; and Alaric wins
his mistress to his side. All is ready for the climax, yet here
Scudéry's sense of proportion seems to desert him. More than
half the final book, considerably longer than the other nine, is
devoted to the glorification of ancestors. The Sibyl enumerates
the kings of Sweden, narrates in detail the campaigns of Gus-
tavus Adolphus, and extols at length the virtues of Christina.
After a siege and Probé's treachery, Rome falls to Alaric.

On the whole the action of *Alaric* presses forward towards
the end. Five books describe successively Alaric's mission, departure, abduction, rescue, education. Three books deal with
different kinds of fighting: sea-battle, ambush, and siege. In
the penultimate book Rigilde is confounded and Amalasonthe
converted. Finally Rome is conquered. To achieve this unity,
Scudéry handles the epic conventions thoughtfully. The hero's
companions are given no chance to distract attention from the
hero. They appear as a group, in debate and in battle, devoid
of individuality. The Bishop of Uppsala stands out for his
rescue of Alaric; Radagaise and Athalaric fight with distinction and merit funerals. The rest—Hildegrand, Theodat, Sigar,
Haldan, Wermond, and Jameric—become familiar through
repetition but lack all personality. Amalasonthe never distracts
attention from Alaric, because she is so bound up with the success or failure of his mission. Initially her resentment at Alaric's
departure seems too trivial a reason for her being the obstacle
to so great an enterprise, but as the story proceeds the portrayal
of her unrequited love rises to the height of the epic's theme.
The manner in which episodes and recitals, always a threat to
unity, are closely tied to the narrative has been noted in the
preceding summary. From the point of view of structure *Alaric*
is the most unified of French epics.

So obvious is the debt to Tasso that it has misled some critics
as to its significance.[2] A comparison of the structure of the
poems shows accurately what the nature of the debt is. The main
points of similarity are the capture of a city—Jerusalem and
Rome—and the use of abductions—Armida and Amalasonthe.[3]

In the first case Scudéry has tightened up Tasso's structure and followed the sequence of historical events more faithfully. For Tasso the capture of Jerusalem is the central theme around which episodes, recitals, and characters radiate and multiply. Scudéry, as we have seen, subordinates everything to Alaric's journey from Sweden to Italy and nothing is included, except the laudatory digressions, which is irrelevant to the capture of Rome. This policy having been adopted, the use of the abduction episode fits less happily. The abduction in the *Gerusalemme* serves the same purpose as the quarrel in the *Iliad*: Rinaldo's absence is the reason for the reverses of the Christians, and for the digressions that arise out of it. The structure of the *Gerusalemme* justifies the dispersal of interest. In *Alaric* the abduction occupies two books, enough to justify examining it as a structural element, but it really leads round in a circle, and fits ill with the forward motion of events.

Scudéry's *Alaric* offers an example of the historian's interpretation of events influencing the poetic interpretation. The poet indicates as his chief sources Procopius, Orosius, and Riccio.[4] Riccio's account of Alaric's career is bald and contributes little.[5] Orosius, on the contrary, must have influenced Scudéry's presentation of Alaric as God's instrument for punishing Rome: 'Itaque post haec tanta augmenta blasphemiarum, nullamque poenitentiam, vltima illa diuque suspensa vrbem poena consequitur.'[6] In the epic God declares that his patience is exhausted:

> Mais il la faut payer, & mesme avec usure:
> Ma longue patience a comblé la Mesure;
> Le temps du chastiment est tout prest d'arriver;
> Et je m'en vay la perde, afin de la sauver.[7]

The point is taken up at the end of the poem. It is essential that, as the instrument of God, Alaric must respect Christian churches when he finally enters Rome. Scudéry here echoes Orosius: 'Adest Alaricus, trepidam Romam obsidet, turbat, irrumpit. Dato tamen praecepto prius, vt si qui in sancta loca praecipueque in sanctorum Apostolorum Petri & Pauli basilicas confugissent, hos in primis inuiolatos securosque esse sinerent.'[8]

> Mais genereux Soldats, espargnez les Eglises,
> Gardez de violler les Droits de leurs Franchises,
> Qu'elles soient un Azyle à l'Enfant innocent,
> A la Vierge pudique; au Vieillard languissant.[9]

Procopius is the most detailed on the capture of Rome itself, and is evidently the source for Probé's treachery:

> But some say that Rome was not captured in this way by Alaric, but that Probé, a woman of very unusual eminence in wealth and in fame among the Roman senatorial class, felt pity for the people who were being destroyed by hunger and the other sufferings they endured; for they were already even tasting each other's flesh; and seeing that every good hope had left them, since both the river and the harbour were held by the enemy, she commanded her domestics, they say, to open the gates by night.[10]

To Scudéry, a version with a woman in it was preferable to one without; the *dénouement* in Book x is inspired by this passage, and is prepared for earlier by the story of Valère and Tiburse. After describing the horrors mentioned by Procopius, Scudéry continues:

> Mais la belle Probé, dans ce commun malheur,
> De la compassion passant à la douleur;
> Et de cette douleur à l'adresse subtile;
> Veut essayer de perdre, & sauver la Ville.[11]

The Christian message of salvation through destruction, that motivates God in the quotation above ('je m'en vay la perdre afin de la sauver'), is here echoed in Probé's betrayal.

Christianity is the guiding inspiration of *Alaric*, Christina of Sweden the occasion for the poem. Decadent Imperial Rome, in the person of Honorius, offered Scudéry no opportunity to evoke Republican virtues, so he invented the opportunity by making Tiburse and Valère the descendents of Cato and Scipio, and by illustrating their Stoicism as they grappled successively with the problems of love and war. By exercising a restraint in embellishment unusual in epic poets, Scudéry produced a poem whose simplicity of structure was not to be repeated until the epics of the 1650s had run their course.

Latin as a medium for epic diminished in popularity after *Mambrun and Constantine* the publication of Ronsard's *Franciade*, but reappeared in 1658 with Pierre Mambrun's epic, entitled *Constantinus sive idololatria debellata.* The epic was again printed in 1661 amongst Mambrun's *Opera poetica*, with the title and sub-title reversed: *Idololatria debellata sive Constantinus.* The epic was followed by a dissertation on epic, *De epico carmine dissertatio peripatetica*, which had first appeared in 1652. The poem was in hexameters, in twelve books.[12]

Rome for Mambrun, as for Scudéry, was pagan Rome. The setting was to be the new Rome, Byzantium. The conflict was between the pagan Licinius and the Christian Constantine. The issue was Constantine's defeat of Licinius in single combat. Constantine derived his heroic status from being the representative of Christianity. The sub-title is more significant than the hero's name, and its elevation to first place in 1661 was appropriate, for the overthrow of idolatry is the main theme.

The main theme of the epic being an abstraction, the structure is not surprisingly flimsy. Were the substance of the episodes more diverse the poem would deserve to be called a romanesque epic. But the embellishments are obviously intended to give the poem the appearance of an epic, an epic on the model of Tasso in particular. The adornments are epic in form; they derive their content from the story of Constantine or the theme of the poem, the collapse of paganism. Some examples of the manner in which they adorn without developing the theme will also give an idea of the content of the poem.

Constantine in Book i is besieging Byzantium. The prefect of the city, Iphicrates, like Tasso's Aladino, orders a massacre of the Christians in the city. After Christian successes in a sea-battle an infernal council in Book iii opposes demons to angels under the command of Saint Michael, who raises a storm and sinks the pagan ships. Familiar epic devices crowd into Book iv. Saint Michael in a dream urges Constantine to change his capital from Rome to Byzantium; the dream at least is concerned with a historical event. Licinius, now also besieged in the city, consults the shades of the Roman emperors, especially Diocletian, through the charms of the magician Magus, another descendant of Tasso's Ismeno. Beroë's burning at the stake, followed by the conversion and martyrdom of Orpheus, recalls Sofronia and Olindo in Book i of the *Gerusalemme.*

Indeed this episode is started in Book i of *Constantinus* and accomplished in Book iv. The poem continues with the funeral of Priscus in Book v, the pageant of Love in Book vi, a banquet and hymn in Book vii, a recital of Constantine's victory over Galerius in Book viii, games in Book ix, and a mutiny in Book x. All familiar topoi of epic, all attached with varying degrees of relevance to the continuing story of the skirmishes outside Byzantium. The climax is reached in Book xi, where Licinius, after being worsted in a general battle, challenges Constantine to single combat. The duel takes place in Book xii. God looks from heaven to see which combatant will favour Christianity, and, when he decides that Constantine will, the reader will hardly doubt the outcome of the duel. Watched by God, Satan, by Asians, Africans, and Europeans, the whole world in fact, Constantine defeats Licinius and idolatry is crushed.

Le Moyne's *Saint Louis* has much in common with *Constantinus*, deriving either from their shared source, Tasso, or, as the pageant of love, peculiar to both poems and not in Tasso, suggests, from personal contact between the poets. Nor does Mambrun cause us surprise by choosing Latin as the vehicle for his epic and a theme that illustrates the triumph of Christianity. If laymen like Scudéry saw in the history of Rome the workings of God's providence, all the more reason for a Jesuit to embroider the same theme; and if the epic poets of the day took Tasso as their chief model, why should not Mambrun do the same? Quite clearly *Constantinus* is an integral part of the epic tradition of the 1650s. The symbiosis of Latin and vernacular literature, taken for granted in the sixteenth century, was challenged but not dissolved by the increasing use of the vernacular in the seventeenth century. Mambrun's *Constantinus* should not, because it is in Latin, be considered apart from the French epics of the 1650s.

Indeed Mambrun's *Constantinus* and *Dissertatio* are very much the Latin counterpart of his coreligionary Le Moyne's *Saint Louis* and 'Traité du poème héroïque'. Though the dates of publication of the two epics make it hard to disentangle the relations between them, there is no doubt that Le Moyne's 'Traité' was intended to be a less demanding introduction to epic than Mambrun's *Dissertatio*. Le Moyne, excusing himself for duplicating the work of his predecessor, expresses thus the

opinions of those who urged him to treat the same matter in
French:

> Si i'opposois à cela, que nostre Pere Mambrun ne m'auoit rien laissé
> à faire sur cette matiere, . . . ils demeuroient bien d'accord que le
> P. Mambrun auoit découuert le secret de l'Art, & qu'il ne se pouuoit
> reduire à vne forme plus reguliere, ny plus methodique que celle
> qu'il luy a donnée, mais ils ajoustoient que cette forme dessinée en
> Grec & en Latin n'estoit pas pour ceux qui ne connoissent que le
> François, & que la Poësie Heroïque estant la vraye Philosophie de
> la Cour, & la partie de la Politique qui est la plus propre à l'institu-
> tion des Grands, il ne falloit pas plaindre la peine de leur en faire
> quelques leçons, purifiées de la teinture du College, & accommodées
> à la delicatesse de leur goust.[13]

Le Moyne thus tried to give more popular appeal to Mambrun's
epic theories, and the two Jesuits shared a liking for epic poems
of loose structure. They both had a fascination for horrific
description.[14] The difference between them is that Mambrun
sought his edifying theme in the history of Rome whilst Le
Moyne illustrated the same themes more aptly from the history
of medieval France.

Desmarets and Regulus

Stoic and Republican virtues, almost completely absent from
the epics based on Roman history considered so far, were portrayed in Desmarets's *Regulus* (1671), a miniature epic, which
we shall examine briefly, before passing on to the medieval
heroes who were so much more suited to the religious and
national preoccupations of the poets of the 1650s. Desmarets
indeed had already made his contribution to this outpouring
with *Clovis* in 1657, an epic of more substantial proportions,
which he was to publish in a revised form in 1673. So completely unlike *Clovis* is *Regulus* that Desmarets's authorship
has been contested:

> Je trouverais les vers de Régulus assez mauvais pour les attribuer à
> Desmarets [wrote Toinet unkindly], je ne pense pas cependant qu'il
> en soit l'auteur, et pour deux raisons: il n'était pas homme à se
> contenter d'une si petite mesure . . . en outre un sujet classique lui
> aurait peu convenu; il était, ou se croyait promu chef d'école, et en
> matière héroïque ses théories ne lui permettaient de s'accommoder
> que d'un héros biblique ou chrétien.[15]

Yet, as Toinet points out, the dedication to de Bartillat is signed
J.D.M., the initials which signify Jean Des Marets in the *Jeux
des roys de France . . . par J.D.M.* published in Paris in 1664.
There was, moreover, in the epics after 1658, a tendency towards brevity, as shown by Courtin and Le Laboureur, though
the revision of Desmarets's *Clovis* of 1673 is certainly not in
that direction. The rapid narrative style of *Regulus*, however
has much in common with that of *Clovis*, the difference being
merely one of length. Certainly *Regulus* cannot in any way be
called a pagan poem; the poet studiously avoids mentioning
the gods of Olympus even when describing a sacrifice in which
they would have been quite appropriate. This peculiarity suggests that the poem might be consistent after all with Desmarets's known obsession with Christianity. One may also note
the justification from history of the slaughter by Regulus of a
monstrous serpent. In *Clovis*, whenever an incident seems really
improbable the source is not usually the poet's fantasy but the
historical works he drew on, though once again this procedure
is not peculiar to Desmarets and the justification of wildly improbable stories from the authority of historians can also be
found in Courtin. The strangeness of *Regulus* does not make
Desmaret's authorship impossible; it shares features which are
to be found in his other works, even though these are not confined to him alone.

The whole poem in five *chants* contains only 388 lines, fewer
than even the shortest single book of most other epics. There is
no *merveilleux*; there are only two similies. The trappings of
epic which in previous years had swollen epics to many thou-
sands of verses have been ruthlessly rejected. Only the essence
remains: a hero's resistance to superhuman trials. The poet
follows the traditional account of Regulus' capture by the
Carthaginians and of his mission to Rome, where he sets aside
all entreaties to break his word and remain in safety. The climax
is brief and sudden:

> Voilà ce qu'au Heros un noble Zele inspire;
> Il ne veut rien entendre, il ne veut plus rien dire;
> Il retourne à Cartage où l'ennemy cruel
> Le fait cent fois mourir & le rend immortel.[16]

The brevity of *Regulus* makes it readable; its intensity, its emphasis on dialogue are more appropriate to tragedy than epic. Its peculiarities show how French epic after 1658 sought new directions and in so doing became almost unrecognizable. Yet *Regulus* obeys the precepts of epic theory more faithfully than many more elaborate poems. If because of its extreme brevity it cannot really qualify as an epic, it certainly cannot be denied the title of *poème héroïque*.

NOTES TO CHAPTER VIII

1. None of the many editions of *Alaric* shows significant alterations to the text. After Courbé's fine folio edition of 1654, illustrated with magnificent engravings, there appeared several pirated editions in 1654, 1655, and 1656. Courbé published a 12mo edition in 1659, also illustrated. The commonest edition is that of Ellinkhuysen, The Hague, 1685, with inferior copies of the 1654 engravings. On *Alaric* see Toinet, i. 153–61; Beall, *Fortune du Tasse*, pp. 86–91 (for his borrowings from Tasso); Cottaz, *Influence*, pp. 37–8; Duchesne, pp. 84–100; Marni, *Allegory*, pp. 131–46; Duportal, *Livres à figures*, pp. 270–3; Canivet, *Illustration*, no. 86; Adam, *Histoire*, ii. 62–3; Picard; *Poésie française, 1640–1680*, pp. 33–5 (Preface to *Alaric*); pp. 173–85 (extracts from the poem: i. 201–95, 346–425; iii. 189–308); Williams, 'Plagiarism by Scudéry of Tasso's epic theory', *Mod. Philology*, 22 (1924–5), 151–8; Sayce, 'L'Architecture dans *l'Alaric*', *Mélanges Lebègue*, pp. 185–93; and in general Reumann, *Scudéry als Epiker* (Coburg, 1911). For Scudéry's other poetry and his plays see Cioranescu, *XVIIe*.

2. e.g. Beall, p. 91, and especially Duchesne, who describes *Alaric* as 'le type de l'Epopée exclusivement romanesque' (p. 84).

3. *Gerusalemme*, Books xiv–xvi; *Alaric*, Books iii–iv.

4. '. . . j'ay choisi ALARIC pour mon Heros: luy dont les Grandes actions sont particulierement descrites dans Procope, au premier Livre de la Guerre des Vandales: dans Orose, au Livre septiesme au Chapitre trente-huit: & dans Ritius, au Livre premier des Rois d'Espagne.' (Preface, A7r.)

5. *De regibus Hispaniae*, i. 3.

6. *Adversus paganos*, vii. 38, p. 594.

7. i, p. 5.

8. vii. 39, p. 595.

9. x, p. 335.

10. *History of the wars* (Loeb), iii. ii. 27; *Historiarum Procopii*, ed. Hoeschel, 1607, p. 93.

11. x, p. 331.

12. On Mambrun (1601–61), see Sommervogel, *Bibliothèque*, v. 451–3, and Chérot, *Le Moyne*, pp. 233–49. Toinet, i. 201, suggests that Berthier's *Constantin* may have been a translation or adaptation of *Constantinus*. Berthier's poem is mentioned by Adam Billaut in *Le Vilebrequin* (1663):

Ie dirois que ta veine en merueilles feconde,
Dans vn liure fameux va charmer tout la monde,
Que le grand Constantin r'animé par tes Vers,
Pour la seconde fois va vaincre l'Vniuers (p. 429).

I have found no trace of the epic either in Berthier's *Oeuvres*, ed.
Minoret, 2 vols., 1889–90, or anywhere else. Edelman, *Attitudes*, p. 203,
n. 4 records the information given by Toinet.

13. 'Traité', a7^r; 'Dissertation', el^r (I have modernized the punctuation).
In some respects the 'Traité' was a reply to criticisms of *Saint Louis*
implicit in Mambrun's *Dissertatio*. On the controversy between Mambrun and Le Moyne, see Chérot, pp. 240–9.

14. e.g. Beroë's self-blinding (*Constantinus*, i, pp. 108–9); the man-
devouring crocodile (*Saint Louis*, iii, p. 84).

15. i. 256–7.

16. v, p. 42.

IX

CHRISTIAN KINGS

DISTORTING as best they could the history of Imperial Rome to the requirements of the Christian religion, Scudéry and Mambrun chose a harder task than their contemporaries who selected the Christian Kings of France as their heroes. Clovis, Charlemagne, and Saint Louis not only satisfied the religious requirements, but were a fitting vehicle for national and patriotic enthusiasm, the glorification of ancestors, and indeed most of the themes deemed suitable for epic poetry.

Desmarets sang of Clovis, Le Laboureur and Courtin of Charlemagne, Le Moyne of Saint Louis. Thus, in the 1650s and 1660s, there arose amongst epic poets the same interest in the French Middle Ages as had inspired the historians of the sixteenth century in their researches into the laws and customs of medieval France. The epic poets, especially Desmarets, approached the subject in a similar frame of mind. They sifted the sources; they searched for clues to traditions that had survived until their own day. Certainly the history that they recounted was resplendent with the miraculous panoply of Christianity and throbbed with the excitement of amorous complications, but beneath it lay a serious preoccupation with the true meaning of sovereignty and national feeling, which the poetic structure was intended to illuminate not disguise.

Desmarets and Clovis

From a strictly historical point of view, Clovis perhaps belongs with Alaric to Roman Imperial rather than to French medieval history, and Desmarets's *Regulus* and *Clovis* could be said to represent the extreme limits of the history of Rome. But in presenting Clovis as the hero of his poem, Desmarets deliberately transformed the barbarian chieftain into a character worthly to be the first Christian king of France, so that, although the poem is set in a Europe ravaged by the wars and migrations of barbarian tribes, Clovis could justly be considered the first in the royal line which later included Charlemagne, Saint Louis, and Louis XIV.

Clovis ou la France chrétienne was first published in 1657 and contained twenty-six books. The same text appeared again, both in a pirated edition of 1657 and in a second edition of the poem in 1661. In 1673 Desmarets published a revised version of his epic, containing only twenty books. The differences between the two versions, however, do not affect the substance of the poem, and the text discused is that of 1657.[1]

Desmaret's purpose in *Clovis* was to narrate the battles by which the Frankish leader made himself sole ruler, and to celebrate the conversion of the Franks to Christianity. The poet also proposed Clovis as a model prince to Louis XIV: 'Ce sera, Sire, en suiuant ces grands exemples de vertu heroïque que vous dompterez tous les vices de vostre Royaume . . .'[2] He was not much concerned with tracing the line of French kings from Clovis to Louis XIV, as Ronsard might have done.[3] Unlike some of his predecessors, Desmarets had something to say about religion and the state. He also found a readable style in which to say it.

The pace of Desmaret's narrative is far more rapid than anything attempted previously. In the heroic epic, narrative technique had mainly consisted in the elaboration of certain scenes by means of dialogue and description. The only time when events were narrated in quick succession was in recitals.[4] Such recitals were often the most readable parts of the poem, because the poet quickly gratified the reader's interest in what would happen next. Desmarets alone seems to have realized that this rapidity was the surest way of securing the reader's attention throughout the poem, and he gave to his whole narrative that forward movement usually only found in the recitals of other epics.[5] Le Moyne also made this discovery, but *Clovis* has a great advantage over *Saint Louis*: whilst Desmarets was even more inventive of episodes than Le Moyne, his episodes represents the rapid progress of the action, not the constant interruption of it.

Despite the multiplication of characters and episodes, Desmarets manages to keep a single theme to the fore: Clovis's conversion can only be achieved by his marriage to Clotilde. Throughout the poem obstacles frustrate the lovers; nearly every episode is a turn of the plot either hastening or postponing their union. In this way, even if Clovis temporarily disappears from the scene, as during Aurèle's encounter with the hermit, the fact that this episode explains how Aurèle came to be Clovis's companion, and why it is necessary for Clovis to marry Clotilde, ensures that unity is preserved.[6] In a few instances Desmarets develops situations involving secondary characters in a fashion irrelevant to the main theme,[7] Clovis's conversion, but the digressions are recounted so briefly, and in the case of Lisois and Aurèle are so closely linked to important characters and the main issue, that they are intervals in the action not distractions from it. Desmarets's achievement is to have produced episodes in abundance without submerging his main theme, and to have narrated his story with such rapidity that the reader has no time to allow momentary loss of interest to mature into boredom.

Although narration predominates in *Clovis*, dialogue is not neglected, and Desmarets develops certain situations after the fashion of a dramatist rather than an epic poet. In general he avoids lengthy speeches. Amalgar's report of Clotilde's loss illustrates the rapid exchange of dialogue:

> Quel sujet te conduit, dit le Prince estonné?
> Amalgar, où vas-tu d'vn cours abandonné?
> Pourquoy laisser Clotilde? ou que me mande-t-elle?
> Ie l'ay, dit-il, laissée en la garde d'Aurele.
> D'Aurele? et tu le vois marchant à mon costé,
> Dit le Prince.[8]

The second half of Book xxii[9] might almost be the last act of a tragedy. Clovis is asked to give judgement whether Aurèle or Arismond has a better claim to Agilane. Here the speeches are long: Arismond sets out his case; Aurèle replies; Clovis refers the matter to Agilane, and she gives the decision. Elsewhere Desmarets handles situations to give maximum effect to the clash of personalities, displaying dramatic rather than epic technique. Doubtless his experience of the stage helped him in this respect.[10]

Ponderousness avoided, Desmarets found neat solutions to other problems. His approach to the *merveilleux* rid him of the literary and moral conflicts between Christian and pagan supernatural. Jupiter, Juno, Mars, and Mercury appear in the poem alongside God, the Virgin, and Saint Michael, but only as devils in disguise. The gods of Olympus, abandoned by Ronsard and his successors, were put to new use by a Catholic fanatic. The *merveilleux chrétien* absorbed them. When Jupiter, Mars, Hercules, and Venus visit Clovis to rebuke him for his flirtation with Christianity, they represent pagan super-stition making a last effort to reassert itself.[11] This attitude may be traced to Gregory of Tours, whose *Historiae Francorum* was the most important source for the career of Clovis. Gregory described how Clotilda reproached Clovis for adoring impotent gods. Jupiter is condemned as a foul adulterer: 'ipse Iovis omnium stuprorum spurcissimus perpetratur, incestatur virorum, propinquarum derisor . . .'.[12] This inspires Clovis's remark when Clotilde has been abducted:

> Mais j'apperçois du Ciel les embusches traistresses
> Et le seul Iupiter, pour m'oster mes amours,
> Avoit des autres Dieux emprunté le secours.[13]

According to Gregory's Clotilda, Mars and Mercury were mere conjurors: 'Quid Mars Mercuriusque potuere? Qui potius sunt magicis artibus praediti, quam divini nominis potentiam habuere.'[14] In the epic Auberon, the magician, tells his daughters how he came to patronize Mercury:

> I'habite l'Austrasie aux bois les plus épais.
> Là je consacre vn temple à ce puissant Mercure,
> Qui m'ouvre les clartez d'vne science obscure:
> Qui m'apprend loin du bruit les secrets curieux
> Des Enfers, de la Mer, de la Terre, & des Cieux . . .[15]

Clovis is only finally converted when God responds to his request for victory over the Germans: 'Iesu Christi quem Chrotchildis praedicat esse filium Dei vivi . . . si mihi victuriam super hos hostes indulseris . . . credam tibi et in nomine tuo baptizer.'[16]

> Clovis dit à genoux: Dieu que Clotilde adore
> Ie fay voeu qu'au baptesme on me verra soumis,
> Si tu me rends vainqueur de mes fiers Ennemis.[17]

As Desmarets points out, 'ce sont les mots de l'histoire'. The historical interpretation of the seventh-century chronicler became the poetic interpretation of the seventeenth-century poet.[18]

Like the supernatural, love had its problems. Instead of treating love episodes as the sweetening of the bitter moral pill,[19] instead of having to choose whether or not to have his hero fall in love, and if so, whether this was to be condoned or condemned, Desmarets linked the establishment of Christianity in France to Clovis's union with Clotilde, thus combining from the start two themes which might have conflicted. Instead of distracting the hero, love became the main motive for the action. Le Moyne certainly, and perhaps even Tasso, foundered on this problem. In the *Gerusalemme* and *Saint Louis* the love interest always conflicted with the inflexible chastity of Goffredo or Saint Louis. To Tasso and Le Moyne love was a moral dilemma and a structural excrescence; for Desmarets it was the force which led his hero to his true destiny.

Fifteen years after the first edition Desmarets brought out a revised version of *Clovis* of whose novelty he boasted to the king: 'Ce Poëme paroistra aussi tout nouveau par les augmentations & par les changemens que j'y ai faits, & par vne soigneuse application à le fortifier, à le polir, & à le mettre au point où il est . . .'[20] The 'new' *Clovis* had only twenty books instead of twenty-six. This gave the appearance of abridgement, but Desmarets had omitted little of what he wrote in 1657. He merely rearranged the numbering of the books by compressing the first twenty-three books of 1657 into seventeen in 1673, and allowing the last three books to remain virtually unchanged.

The additions to which Desmarets hoped the king's attention would be specially drawn occur in the prophetic parts of the poem. In each case the poet, profiting from the progress of Louis XIV's reign, inserted more extensive passages of praise of the king than was possible in the early years of the reign, when the poem was first published and the king had done little. In two places Desmarets omitted some of the praise devoted to Richelieu and substituted more for Louis XIV.[21] No poet needed fear the absurd provided he praised the king. That the prophecies of Daniel should be accomplished in the person of Louis XIV was a conceit from which Desmarets did not shrink; indeed he believed he was witnessing the culmination of history:

C'est l'Empire dernier promis par le Prophete
C'est l'Empire où tout ame à Dieu sera sujete.[22]

Other alterations affected style, usually only slightly. There were some cuts. Seven lines at the end of the poem[23] describing the intervention in the duel between Clovis and Alaric of their respective seconds disappeared in 1673. Doubtless Desmarets felt that at the climax of the poem the hero should perform his task unaided.[24]

Garnier, Le Moyne, and Saint Louis

The same motives which had inspired Sébastien Garnier's *Henriade*[25] influenced his choice of Saint Louis as an epic hero. Eager to justify Henry's claim to the throne, he glorified the particular ancestor from whom both Valois and Bourbon descended. Like Delbene, d'Urfé, and Schelandre, Garnier used epic for the glorification of ancestors, but with the difference that while the former glorified patron and ancestor in the same poem, Garnier devoted two separate epics to patron and ancestor respectively.

Three books of the *Loyssée* appeared in 1593. With the *Henriade* it received a second edition in 1770, the spelling being modified and the marginal notes omitted. Despite hints that Garnier had planned or written much more than the beginning of the poem only three books survive.[26] Book i describes Louis's departure for Egypt; Book ii his skirmish with Megapenthe on landing in Cyprus, followed by his reconciliation with Guy de Lusignan, the king of the island; Book iii relates Louis's delay in Cyprus to administer justice and convert the infidel.

Little time need be spent on Garnier's *Loyssée*. It displays more strikingly the stylistic defects that mar the *Henriade*. Sentences, meandering from one co-ordinating conjunction to another, sprouting accumulations of relative clauses on the way, abound. Just as Garnier's first epic was rescued from oblivion to be compared with Voltaire's *Henriade*, so his *Loyssée* survives mainly for the comparison it affords with Le Moyne's *Saint Louis*. To Le Moyne's epic, first published complete in 1658, we shall return presently, after showing in what respects it differs from the *Loyssée*.

The plots of the two poems do not overlap, since the action

of *Saint Louis* begins after the capture of Damietta, and the hero's early career is only mentioned in the description of the tapestries in his tent. Even here there is little that is common to Garnier and Le Moyne. One point of comparison is Louis's illness, on which Garnier had dwelt at some length:

> . . . il tomba comme mort
> Sur terre esvanoui: ses membres immobiles,
> Demourans quelque temps, tant ils estoient débiles,
> Son esprit transporté, sans parole, & sans voix,
> Ne restant que le nom du Monarque François,
> Son corps ja prest à mettre en un cercueil enserre,
> Pour après le porter dessouz la tombe en terre.[27]

Le Moyne, who showed Louis's illness on one of his tapestries, was much briefer:

> D'autre part où l'on voit Louys malade au Louure,
> D'vne triste pasleur son visage se couure:
> Deux Reynes, de sa fiévre ont l'esprit agité,
> Leur vie auec la sienne est à l'extremité.[28]

Another tapestry showed the vision which spurred Louis to embark on the crusade. Here the essential difference between the poets is plain. In the *Loyssée* Garnier used the familiar device of God rebuking Louis for his idleness and then sending him on his way. In *Saint Louis* the king sees an angel offering him a crown of thorns. Garnier's epic followed the sequence of events in the histories; he adorned that narrative with epic devices. Le Moyne on the other hand, set his hero a fictitious task, the quest for the crown of thorns, and used the historical narrative as the basis on which to erect a complex poetic structure far removed from even the most extravagant accounts of Louis's career. In the transformation of the hero Le Moyne's imagination was also at work. Garnier accepted the historical accounts of Louis's troubles in Cyprus and devoted a whole book to them, introducing them thus:

> Et ne leur restoit plus qu'à mettre pied à terre,
> Quand ils virent venir infinis gents de guerre,
> Hardis & valeureux, à les voir à leur port,
> Qui vouloient empescher qu'ils ne vinssent à bord.[29]

These difficulties were completely dismissed by Le Moyne:

La Flotte sur la fin s'auance vers le bord,
Pour la mettre à l'abry, la Chipre ouure son port :
Le Prince du Pays que son Peuple enuironne,
Met aux pieds de Louys son Sceptre & sa Couronne . . .[30]

Garnier tried to make an epic out of whatever history offered him; whatever history offered him that did not fit his poetic interpretation was omitted by Le Moyne.

This poetic interpretation did not shape Le Moyne's epic right from the start. Indeed the process by which he gradually moved further away from the historical accounts can be traced in the two versions of the poem. Some time between 1645 and 1650 he began work on an epic with Saint Louis as his hero.[31] After 1650 he was resident in the Jesuit house in the rue Saint-Antoine where paintings by Simon Vouet of the life of Saint Louis doubtless fed his imagination as he worked on the epic. Even as early as 1651 printed copies of the first seven books may have been in circulation, but no edition bearing that date had been found.[32] In 1653 the poem was published in a folio edition with the title *Saint Louis ou le héros chrétien*[33] and pirated editions reproducing the same text appeared in 1656.[34] This version was still in only seven books. In the registers of the Society of Jesus for the year 1655 Le Moyne was described as 'totus in scribendo gallicè';[35] soon the results were published. In 1658 the complete poem appeared with a new title *Saint Louis ou la sainte couronne reconquise.*[36] There were now eighteen books, but this was not simply a continuation of what had appeared in 1653. The first seven books had been drastically rearranged and the whole conception of the poem entirely changed. In 1661 a second edition had modifications so slight that they have little bearing on the substance of the poem.[37] Finally in *Les Oeuvres poëtiques du P. Le Moyne*, a large folio volume published first in 1671, the year of Le Moyne's death, and reissued in 1672, *Saint Louis* appeared again, with further alterations of little importance.[38] The discussion of *Saint Louis* is based on the text of 1658, except where it is compared with the 1653 text to show Le Moyne's change of plan.

'Une action qui ne brille ni par sa simplicité, ni par son unité . . .'.[39] Few readers of *Saint Louis* would disagree. Le Moyne's plot is loaded with such an abundance of episodes that it scarcely stands the strain. Digressions obscure the main theme at every point. Had the poet put his own precept into practice, all this could have been avoided:

Le troisiesme point necessaire à l'Vnité de la Fable, est la iuste liaison des Episodes. . . . Il se faut souuenir que ces Actions inserées estant à l'Action principale, ce que les membres sont au corps, & ce que les rameaux sont à l'arbre, elles ne ¹a doiuent pas accabler, elles doiuent l'embellir: & si la moderation n'y est pas gardée, bien loin de l'embellir elles l'étouffent.⁴⁰

This sounds like a critic pulling *Saint Louis* to pieces; in fact it is the poet telling the critics how epic should be written. Le Moyne saw the dangers; he failed to avoid them. Though his technique was based on the same theories and models as Scudéry's, though Scudéry was the one to stress the affinity between the 'poème épique' and the 'roman',⁴¹ it was Scudéry who kept his episodes under control and Le Moyne who let them get out of hand. This predilection for episodic embellishment, though fatal to the unity of *Saint Louis*, represented none the less an advance in epic technique that need not in itself have been pernicious. According to Le Moyne the way to avoid stifling the plot was simple: 'On euitera cet inconuenient, si ces pieces naissant du corps de l'Action, par vne suite ou necessaire ou vray-semblable; & si elles vont à la fin de l'Action, par vne descente ou vray-semblable ou necessaire.'⁴² Taken one by one the episodes in *Saint Louis* could probably all be justified on these grounds. The main events of Book i, for example, are Louis's quest for the crown, the Sultan's dismay at the fall of Damietta, and the despatch of two ambassadors bearing the poisoned armour to Louis. Around this simple narrative digressions multiply: the history of the crown, the exploits of Mélédin's family, the history of the poisoned armour, the engravings on the armour, the tapestries in Louis's tent . . . . No doubt Le Moyne would have claimed that these digressions, like the digressions which amplify each book, like books which are in themselves digressions,⁴³ were all justified on the grounds that 'ces pièces naissent du corps de l'Action'. No doubt when Le Moyne wrote of the dangers of too much embellishment and of the means of preserving unity, he believed that he had avoided the former by applying the latter. But what analysis may show to be technically justifiable may to the reader seem diffuse, prolix, and tedious. Each episode individually could perhaps be justified; so many episodes, so much justification destroy all unity.

Pervading this discursive composition at every point is religious enthusiasm and a passion for moralizing. In every event Le Moyne sees the hand of God. It is impossible to distinguish between the divine and human spheres of activity. So close is Louis to God, so close is the magician Mirème to the devil, that there is no need for celestial messengers or infernal councils to keep the action moving. Saint Michael does once conduct Louis to heaven for an interview with Christ, but this in no way advances the action. The *anges intendants* are Le Moyne's innovation; they appear frequently to ensure the fulfilment of divine decrees. One might search the poem in vain for an episode in which the supernatural plays no part. Poisoned armour miraculously melts; an angel helps Archambaud to slay the dragon; another angel exhorts Aimon de Bourbon and gives him a suit of armour.[44] Since angels or demons have a hand in practically everything that happens in the poem, the two levels of action which are usually evident when the *merveilleux* is employed become so confused in *Saint Louis* that it is impossible to separate them. 'Le merveilleux est l'*âme* du *Saint Louis*,'[45] claimed Chérot; once again it is hard to disagree.

That the hero is a saint and the poet a priest may explain the pervasive role of the supernatural. Why love should also pervade the poem is less easily accounted for. The sole motive for the actions of many characters is love. Love inspires Brenne to cajole Archambaud into fetching the holy water; for love Bethune sets out in search of Lisamante; even the fierce Olgan neglects his duty to confess to Alcinde that he loves her.[46] Is Le Moyne demonstrating that love is the root of all human activity? If so why does he devote so much space to depicting the manner in which Archambaud liberates himself from the snares of Almasonte?[47] The question is debated in the pageant of Love during the triumphal games. The pageant of Cold proclaims:

> Nous venons maintenir aux yeux de cette Cour,
> Que la Valeur ne peut s'allier à l'Amour.[48]

To which the pageant of Heat replies:

Nous venons à dessein d'apprendre aux froides Ames,
Que le feu, des grands coeurs est le propre Element;
Et qu'vne mesme ardeur fait le Braue & l'Amant.[49]

Alfonse and Robert defend the first cause, Charles the second, but the joust is inconclusive. Nor does Le Moyne offer in the succeeding jousts,[50] all of the same allegorical intention, any indication of which kind of love he favours. His treatment of Archambaud and Almasonte suggests that love is incompatible with valour, yet so many noble actions in the poem are motivated by love that the final conclusion is probably the same as in *Alaric*, namely that the physical side of love is pernicious, whilst the spiritual side may inspire great deeds.

Only the complete version of *Saint Louis* has so far been considered. It was the one on which Le Moyne's reputation rested, and the author expressly disavowed the earlier version: 'Ie donne icy mon SAINT LOVYS acheué. Ce qu'on en a veu n'estoit qu'vn morceau; & ce morceau n'estoit pas encore bien ébauché, quand il me fut arraché des mains.'[51] The subtitles of the two versions are significant and will be used to distinguish between the seven-book and the eighteen-book *Saint Louis*. In 1653 the subtitle was *le héros chrétien*; in 1658 it was *la sainte couronne reconquise*. When the two versions are compared[52] it is quite clear that Le Moyne did not decide upon the theme of the finished epic until after he had written the first seven books. It was Louis's mission which underwent a complete change. In *le héros chrétien* his mission was simply victory over the infidel, as the proposition made clear:

Ie chante les combats, ie chante les victoires,
D'vn Saint regnant au Ciel, regnant dans les Histoires,
Qui sur les bords du Nil fumant de ses explois,
Fit des Croissans brisez un trophée à la Croix.[53]

In 1658 Le Moyne had a new theme:

Ie chante vn saint Guerrier, & la Guerre entreprise
Pour oster aux Sultans, & pour rendre à l'Eglise,
Le Diademe saint, que l'Homme-Dieu porta,
Quand pour vaincre la Mort, sur la Croix il monta.[54]

Although none of the material of *le héros chrétien* was sacrificed, it was considerably rearranged when incorporated into the new poem, and whilst long passages of the two poems remained identical, it was natural that whenever Louis's mission was mentioned, there should have been some alteration.[55]

The crown of thorns was not absent from the earlier version. In *le héros chrétien* Louis was transported to heaven, there to choose between three crowns of purely symbolic significance. He chose the crown of thorns. In *la sainte couronne*, the symbolic crown became the physical object, without however losing its symbolic significance entirely. The earlier version stressed the sufferings of Louis—a convenient way to account for his many misfortunes on this crusade—and these sufferings gave him a taste of Christ's passion. When the idea came to Le Moyne of making the actual crown of thorns the object of Louis's expedition, the parallel between the hero's suffering and those of Christ was hinted at by retaining the episode of the choice of crowns in heaven, but the hero was made a practical example of a Christian Prince rather than a vehicle for exploring the significance of his sufferings. The shift from the spiritual atmosphere of the earlier version to the more practical achievements of the later was exactly reversed by Courtin when he wrote his two epics on Charlemagne.

Le Laboureur, Courtin, and Charlemagne

Charlemagne attracted two poets, who both wrote shortly after the great wave of epic production in the 1650s. Louis Le Laboureur published Books i—iii of his *Charlemagne* in 1664, and Books i—vi in 1666. In the preface to the 1666 edition he declared: 'Ie feray bien tost succeder à ces six premiers liures vne suite de six autres,' but there is no trace of the remainder.[56] Also in 1666 Nicolas Courtin published *Charlemagne ou le rétablissement de l'empire romain* complete in six books; and in 1687 appeared his *Charlemagne pénitent*.[57] Courtin's first *Charlemagne* did not overlap in subject with Le Laboureur's. Le Laboureur was to have dealt with the restoration of Pope Leo, but his six books deal mainly with the Saxon wars culminating in the conversion of Widukind in 785; Courtin dealt with the battle of Pavia and the defeat of Desiderius in 774, by which Charles was deemed to have restored the Roman Empire. Courtin's second epic devoted to Charlemagne showed a complete change of approach. From the misfortunes and disillusionment of Charlemagne he drew a picture of the Christian hero suffering in adversity, exactly as Le Moyne had started to do in the 1653 version of *Saint Louis*. Courtin proceeded from practical achievements to spiritual symbolism; Le Moyne proceeded from spiritual symbolism to practical achievements.

Since the publication of the 1658 version of *Saint Louis* no new epic had appeared. Le Laboureur, the first to try to supply the deficiency, was conscious that his predecessors had thoroughly exploited the epic genre and felt that he was at something of a disadvantage:

Tous ces illustres Concurrens qui m'ont precedé ont ietté, pour parler ainsi, leur faulx dans ma moisson, & ne m'ont rien laissé presque à recueillir apres eux. Ils ont entierement dépoüillé le champ de l'Epopée; ils en ont enleué tous les beaux épics d'or dont il étoit couuert, & n'ont laissé pour ma recolte que la nille & le mauuais grain. Toutes ces belles descriptions, les Tournois, les reueuës d'Armées, les riches Palais, les superbes galeries peintes par les plus sçauans Maistres, les tempestes, les naufrages, & toutes ces merueilleuses images des Cieux & du Paradis; enfin je ne sçay combien de semblables choses dont la Poësie heroïque fait ses plus beaux & ses plus frequens ornemens, m'ont esté prises par tous ces fameux Precurseurs . . .[58]

This is an important piece of evidence, showing how the epic genre appeared to a poet in 1664. The emphasis on externals is still there. We notice too the enduring popularity of storms and shipwrecks ('les tempestes, les naufrages'). To Le Laboureur, however, it appeared that there was nothing left to exploit. How then did he succeed in adorning his epic?

il n'est rien de plus pesamment, de plus irrémissiblement ennuyeux.[59]

. . . nous aurions déjà jeté loin de nous ce livre médiocre, s'il n'était pas utile de savoir ce qu'était devenue la légende de Charlemagne à une époque où l'on témoignait d'un si profond dédain pour notre ancienne poésie.[60]

To refute these criticisms would be idle. The six books of *Charlemagne* straggle on in an ever deepening labyrinth of recitals and digressions, through which characters without personality wander without motive. Of the subject of the epic, the restoration of Pope Leo, there is scarcely a hint. The Saxon

wars are irrelevant to the main theme; the episodes and adornments are irrelevant to the Saxon wars. Patient search might
reveal a plot beneath the accumulation of episodes in *Saint
Louis: Charlemagne* reveals no trace of a plot even to the
closest inspection.

Yet Le Laboureur was sincere in his desire to break new
ground. He did not avail himself of the epic devices he listed
in the preface, though he does overwork the use of recitals
and amorous discussions. He was anxious to give a faithful
representation of the court of Charlemagne and the customs of
the infidel.[61] To this end he concentrated the *merveilleux* in
the person of Hirmensul, a Saxon idol who plays the part of
the devil without actually being identified with him. The poet
also raised important philosophical questions. At the end of
Saint Michael's discourse Charlemagne asks:

> Mais à nous autres Rois ce point est d'importance :
> C'est de connoistre l'homme & de voir ce qu'il pense.
> Fay-moy comme par tout penetrer dans son coeur
> Et ioins à tant de biens ce supréme bonheur.

The portrayal of the perfect prince was an epic commonplace;
the nature of man was a new theme. Saint Michael's reply,
however, did not solve the problem:

> Ta priere ô Mortel ne peut estre exaucée
> Ton desir est trop grand, trop exquis sont ces dons.
> Homme, tu veux sçauoir que ignorons![62]

Elsewhere Le Laboureur raised other unexpected questions.
The conversion of the pagan was another commonplace.
Usually the catechumen listened humbly to a versified exposi-
tion of the Christian faith: not so Widukind. Charles offered
him wealth and power if he would accept Christianity, but
Widukind had a sharp eye for paradox:

> Mais toy-méme crois-tu de semblables chimeres?
> Cet Homme-Dieu viuant dans vn ignoble corps
> Et du haut d'vne croix tombant parmy les morts,
> Qui n'enseigna qu'affronts & que bassesse extréme?
> Pourquoy, si tu le crois, ne vis tu pas de méme?[63]

The problem of reconciling Christian humility with the traditional temperament of the epic hero had long been an em-

barrassment to Christian poets. No one had yet put the question so bluntly. Le Laboureur had an answer—God's magnificence is reflected in Christian kings:

> C'est luy qui fait les Roys; & sa toute-Puissance
> Se peint comme en petit dans leur magnificence;
> Leur éclat qui te blesse est vn rayon du sien . . .[64]

With this Widukind seemed satisfied and was duly converted. For all its faults Le Laboureur's *Charlemagne* showed that the epic tradition was developing. Some of the traditional devices were being rejected as outworn; new ways were being found to inject life into others.

Dismay was Courtin's first reaction when he discovered that Le Laboureur had published a *Charlemagne* before him. Only on showing his manuscript to some friends had he become aware of the coincidence: '. . . [mes Amis] n'eurent pas plustost jetté les yeux sur le nom de Charlemagne, qu'ils me parurent surpris, & me dirent que M. le Laboureur auoit trauaillé sur le mesme sujet, & qu'il y auoit là-dessus à prendre, ou du moins à garder quelques mesures.'[65] Off he hurried to the Palais to consult his rival's poem. To his relief he discovered that Le Laboureur had taken Charles's final exploits as his theme whereas he had chosen his earliest victories so that the actions of their two poems did not overlap. Their use of episodes and fictions is also entirely different. Whereas Le Laboureur's poem is merely a mass of digressions, Courtin's goes straight to the point.[66] His central event is the siege of Pavia and the defeat of Desiderius. Some love affairs are sketched, visions are employed, allegories suggested; but the six books move swiftly towards their conclusion and the epic is complete. Courtin's originality lay in severely limiting the use of epic embellishments. As might be expected in such circumstances, the *merveilleux* plays a relatively small part. Neither God nor his angels make any direct intervention; their influence is merely implied. Arons, the magician, who is more forcefully portrayed than any other character, does indeed have at his disposal hordes of demons whom he continually throws into the struggle against Charlemagne, but his activities belong more to the realm of magic than to the supernatural, and there is no real opposition between God and the devil. The religious enthusiasm that marked the epics of the 1650s was now definitely subdued.

Like Le Laboureur, Courtin gave a new twist to some of the traditional devices. D'Urfé had used a mirror to recount the rise of the house of Savoy.[67] Courtin also uses a mirror, but to disguise the future not to reveal it. Desiderius, with the help of Arons, sees in a magic mirror the rout of a French army outside Pavia. He naturally takes this to be his own army routing that of Charlemagne; hence his stubborn resistance throughout the poem. What in fact he saw in the mirror was the defeat of Francis I by the forces of Charles V, another episode in another century.[68] Courtin was a professor of rhetoric, so his use of a wide range of historical authorities need not surprise us. Whereas others sought their epic embellishments from the epics of Antiquity or of Italy, he frequently adorned his poem with titbits of information from the history books. Claude Fauchet, Paolo Emilio, François de Mézeray, Cesar Baronius, and Paulus Diaconus contributed many details, and their assistance is acknowledged in footnotes.[69]

The epic starts and ends with Arons and Desiderius, who are more vividly drawn than the Charlemagne and his Christians. Much of Book i is taken up with a powerful description of magic rituals, but in Book vi the Lombard king and his magician realize that all their plans have been futile:

> Mais de tout son grand Art l'inutile pouuoir
> Laisse Arons sans effet, & Didier sans espoir.
> Ce miserable Roy déchû de son attente,
> Voit du Sorcier pour luy la magie impuissante,
> Le voit seul échaper aprés tant de forfaits,
> Et rauir à ses yeux dans vn nuage épais . . .

Thus Arons betrays his own master and departs to make war on the French elsewhere. Desiderius makes a humiliating submission to Charles:

> Prosterné maintenant aux pieds de ce grand Homme,
> Le Soustien de l'Eglise & le Salut de Rome,
> N'est plus que lâcheté, que bassesse, qu'effroy,
> Et l'on ne voit en luy rien de digne d'vn Roy.

Charles just brings himself to spare Desiderius's life:

Il fait signe à ces mots qu'on l'oste de ses yeux,
Et commence par-là de regner en ces lieux.[70]

Charlemagne pénitent[71] begins where most other poems usually end: at the height of the hero's career. Charles has brought all his campaigns to a successful conclusion; his life has been distinguished by his encouragement of the arts and benefactions to the Church. How is the devil to bring him down? This is the theme of *Charlemagne pénitent*. The devil disguises himself as an angel and promises the Emperor greater glory than that of Theodosius or Constantine if only he will persevere in his good works. Provided that the motive for piety can be perverted, the devil will succeed. God, however, observes Charles's peril and despatches Saint James of Compostella to save him. Charlemagne's spiritual smugness is shattered by the saint's arrival:

> Et Charlemagne seul en un profond silence
> Jettoit sur ses vertus un oeil de complaisance,
> En pesoit le merite, en contemploit le prix,
> Quand le glorieux saint s'offre à ses yeux surpris.[72]

James warns Charles that heaven cannot be won without trials and self-violence. The rest of the poem shows how Charles's new life as a penitent influences his public actions, and how events around him produce further torment in his soul. This theme permits Courtin to transform the *merveilleux*, so long merely an adornment or device in epic, into the very substance of his poem. God and Satan now become principle actors, and Charles's soul the scene of their struggle. Charles discovers that his son has plotted against him; he pardons his son. He hears the news of the successive deaths of three sons and a daughter; his virtue triumphs.[73] Courtin introduces a twist of irony. Charles's entourage whisper that he must have been particularly wicked to deserve such misfortune; the calumny is hard to bear, but Charles succeeds.[74] Similar trials and victories occupy the last two books. The devil's supreme effort to win Charles's soul before his death fails, and the final victory of the hero over himself is won.

The structure of *Charlemagne pénitent* thus brought a solution to the problem that had perplexed Christian poets. Instead of a conflict between worldly success and Christian humility, victory over self was placed firmly above victory in battle, territorial expansion, and power over other men. 'Quelle action plus difficile que de vaincre la volupté qui a vaincu les plus grands vainqueurs?' asked Courtin in his preface to this the last historical epic of the seventeenth century. Amidst the religious zeal that characterized the latter years of Louis XIV, the Christian hero forsook the battlefield where temporal glory was to be won, and struggled to achieve mastery over the warring elements of his own soul.

NOTES TO CHAPTER IX

1. On *Clovis* see Petit, 'Etude sur le *Clovis* de Desmarets', *Bull. Soc. Sarthe*, 11 (1867–8), 698–719; Rigault, *Querelle*, p. 90; Toinet, i. 179–83; Duchesne, pp. 101–35; Marni, *Allegory*, pp. 166–8; Edelman, *Attitudes*, pp. 207–11; Cioranescu, *L'Arioste*, ii. 47–8; Beall, *Fortune du Tasse*, pp. 94–7; Cottaz, *Influence*, pp. 42–5; Canivet, *Illustration*, no. 93; Adam, *Histoire*, ii. 63, 66; Hall, 'Three illustrated works of Desmarets', *Yale Univ. Lib. Gazette*, 33 (1958), 23–5. On the controversies surrounding *Clovis* see Chapelain, *Observations sur le Clovis de Saint-Sorlin* in *Opuscules critiques*, pp. 321–31; Desmarets's reply to Boileau in *Deffense du poëme heroïque*, pp. 90–105; and in general Bornemann, *Boileau im Urtheile seines Zeitgenossen Desmarets* (Heilbronn, 1883). Picard, *Poésie française 1640–1680*, gives useful extracts: pp. 41–2 ('Avis'), pp. 197–212 (*Clovis*, iii. 324–62, iv. 34–129, vii. 383–416, xv. 199–320). For Desmarets's other works see Cioranescu, *XVIIe*.

2. 'Au Roy', sig. **l^{r}.

3. Though he does mention the most prominent (viii, pp. 141–2; ix, pp. 155–7) and also praises Richelieu (iv, p. 66).

4. e.g. The sack of Troy (Ronsard, *Franciade*, Book i); the adventures of Beroldo (d'Urfé, *Savoysiade*, Book vi); the adventures of Lisamante (Le Moyne, *Saint Louis*, Book iii).

5. Duchesne praised Desmarets for 'la brillante variété, la noblesse ou la grâce du style' (p. 118), but not everyone, of course, has shared his opinion: 'il est, du premier au dernier vers illisible; on n'a jamais poussé plus loin la platitude prétentieuse' (Toinet, i. 183).

6. ix, p. 153 to xi, p. 191.

7. e.g. Lisois's love for Yoland (xii, pp. 200–7); Alphéide's recital describing her adventures with Argyric (xvii, pp. 284–6); the contest between Aurèle and Arismond for the hand of Agilane (xxii, pp. 370–3).

8. xvi, p. 275.

9. pp. 377–86.

10. He wrote comedies and tragedies between 1636 and 1643.

11. xv, pp. 251 ff.

12. ii, § 29, *MGH*, i. 74.

13. xvi, p. 278.

14. ii, § 29, *MGH*, i. 74.

15. v, p. 81.

16. ii, § 30, *MGH*, i. 75.

17. xx, p. 337.

18. For the development of such episodes as the vase of Soissons, the marriage between Clotilde and Clovis, or Clovis's conversion and baptism, all to be found in the chronicles and histories, see Duchesne, pp. 101–7, and Edelman, *Attitudes*, p. 208.

19. Così a l'egro fanciul porgiamo aspersi/di soavi licor gli orli del vaso . . .' (Tasso, *Gerusalemme*, i. 3).

20. 'Epître au Roy' (1673), a3r-v.

21. Compare iv, pp. 67–8 (1657) with iii, pp. 53–5 (1673); and viii, p. 144 (1657) with vii, p. 133–7 (1673).

22. vii, p. 133 (1673).

23. xxvi, p. 464 (1657).

24. xx, p. 413 (1673).

25. See above, pp. 55–9.

26. e.g. 'Allusion a la cheute de S. Loys en la mer, liu. 9' (Marginal note, 1593 edition, p. 23).

27. i, p. 270.

28. i, p. 30.

29. ii, p. 299.

30. i, p. 31.

31. Chérot, *Vie et oeuvres du P. Le Moyne*, pp. 25–7. Chérot's is the best work on Le Moyne and *Saint Louis*. See also Delmont, *Le Meilleur Poète épique du XVIIe siècle* (Arras, 1901); Sommervogel, *Bibliothèque*, v. 1356–71; Toinet, i. 146–52; Duchesne, pp. 137–51; Beall, *Fortune du Tasse*, pp. 96–8; Cottaz, *Influence*, pp. 45–50; Marni, *Allegory*, pp. 163–6; Edelman, *Attitudes*, pp. 236–45; Cioranescu, *L'Arioste*, ii. 46–7; Canivet, *Illustration*, nos. 95 and 116.

32. The question is fully discussed by Chérot, *Le Moyne*, pp. 527–9.

33. Chérot, pp. 527–30, XXI, no. I.

34. From Grenoble and Rouen; Chérot, p. 530, XXI, nos. II and III.

35. Chérot, p. 462.

36. Chérot, p. 530, XXI, no. IV.

37. Chérot lists the principal variants, pp. 531–2, XXI, no V.

38. Chérot, pp. 540–1, XL. In this edition the title of the 'Traité du poème héroïque', which had preceded the poem in 1658, was changed to 'Dissertation du poème héroïque', and some minor alterations to the text were introduced.

39. Chérot, *Le Moyne*, p. 269. There is a good summary of the poem

on pp. 270–90. Duchesne, whilst praising Le Moyne's rhetoric, condemns his undisciplined imagination (p. 151).

40. 'Traité', i4^{r-v}; 'Dissertation', i2^r.

41. 'Comme le Poëme Epique a beaucoup de raport, quant à la constitution, avec ces ingenieuses Fables, que nous apellons des Romans . . .' (Preface to *Alaric*, A6^r).

42. 'Traité', i4^v; 'Dissertation', i2^r.

43. e.g. Book xi, occupied entirely by Archambaud's rejection of Almasonte.

44. x, p. 292; xii, pp. 357–61; x, p. 300–1.

45. *Le Moyne*, p. 295.

46. xvi, pp. 490 ff.; xiii, p. 400; iii, p. 87.

47. Book xi.

48. iv, p. 97.

49. iv, p. 100.

50. Later Colligny represents 'l'ardent inextinguible' and Bethune 'l' ardent imperceptible' (iv, p. 115).

51. 'Traité', a3^r; this, the opening sentence of the 'Traité', was replaced in the 'Dissertation' of 1671 by: 'Aprés trois editions de mon SAINT LOUIS, je le donne plus correct en celle-cy . . .' (elr).

52. The pirated edition of 1656 reproduced the text of the 1653 edition. Reference here is to the 1653 edition.

53. i, p. 1.

54. i, p. 1.

55. For example, when describing the situation after the capture of Damietta, Le Moyne first wrote:

> Le Prince conquerant, poursuiuant sa conqueste,
> De l'Egypte ébranlée alloit choquer la teste (i, p. 3).

The corresponding verses in the new version were:

> Louys qui n'aspiroit, qu'à se voir sur la teste,
> L'adorable Couronne offerte à sa conqueste (i, p. 3).

Similarly Louis first protested to the Sultan's ambassadors:

> Non, non, l'vnique but où tend mon entreprise,
> Est de vous amener au saint joug de l'Eglise (i, p. 21).

But in the new poem he had changed his mind:

> Tous mes desseins ne vont qu'à la Couronne Sainte,
> Qui du Sang precieux de mon Sauueur fut teinte (i, p. 19).

56. The poem was to have been in twelve books, but as Le Laboureur describes the contents of the remainder in vague terms, they were

probably never written: 'Les six derniers Liures contiennent des auantures tout à fait propres au sujet & toutes nouuelles, qui ouuriront
assûrement vn beau champ aux passions, & à tout ce qui peut faire
dire de douces & de grandes choses' (Preface to *Charlemagne,* i2ʳ). On
Charlemagne see Toinet, i. 210–13; Duchesne, pp. 244–6 (very inaccurate on bibliography; he speaks of a 1687 edition, probably con-
fusing Le Laboureur with Courtin); Bergounioux, *Dominici,* pp. 440–1;
Gautier, *Epopées françaises,* ii. 631–3 (also inaccurate on bibliography);
Marni, *Allegory,* p. 169; Edelman, *Attitudes,* pp. 215–36; Simpson, *Le
Tasse,* p. 117 (ignores the 1666 edition); Cottaz, *Influence,* pp. 50–2. For
Le Laboureur's other works see Cioranescu, *XVIIe.*

57. For Courtin's epics, see Toinet, i. 221–6; Edelman, *Attitudes,* pp.
215–36; Cioranescu, *L'Arioste,* ii. 48–9; Marni, *Allegory,* pp. 180–3,
187–8. For his other works, see Cioranescu, *XVIIe.*

58. Preface to *Charlemagne,* a7ʳ⁻ᵛ.

59. Toinet, i. 211.

60. Gautier, ii. 653.

61 'I'ay tâché sur toutes choses à bien donner l'idée du siecle & de la
Cour de mon Heros; à bien marquer les differentes moeurs de ses
Paladins & de ses Ennemis' (Preface to *Charlemagne,* a8ʳ).

62. iii, p. 80 (1664); p. 75 (1666).

63. vi, p. 178 (1666).

64. vi, p. 179 (1666).

65. 'Avertissement', a5ᵛ.

66. Courtin is rather indulgent towards Le Laboureur's abundance of
episodes and recitals: '. . . si vous n'y trouuez pas toutes les *beautez*
qui sont dans l'autre, vous y trouuerez du moins la grace de la
nouueauté, comme dans le premier' ('Avertissement', a6r—my italics).
Note also the desire for 'nouveauté'; cf. the quotation from Le
Laboureur p. 127 above.

67. *Savoysiade,* iv, fol. 133–5.

68. i, pp. 9–10.

69. See pp. 12, 18, 19, 61, 87, 93, and 111.

70. vi, pp. 152–3.

71. In five books, published with other spiritual works in 1687, in a
volume entitled *Poésies chrétiennes.*

72. i, p. 13.

73. iii, p. 67.

74. iii, p. 69.

X

JOAN OF ARC

Epic treatment of the Christian kings showed a certain ambivalence of attitude. True, the kings were eminently suitable as heroes if poets were seeking both an illustration of Christian virtues and a focus for national pride; but the temptations of romanesque development, which was in theory intended to embellish the themes of religion and patriotism, in fact obscured the underlying seriousness of purpose and brought the genre into discredit. The ambivalence is displayed on a grander scale in the epic whose preparation, publication, and reception dominated the epic scene during the seventeenth century: Chapelain's *La Pucelle ou la France délivrée.* The recovery of France at the lowest point of her fortunes during the Hundred Years' War, the miraculous nature of that recovery, the paradox of the recovery being effected by a woman, the further paradox of her inglorious death—all these were subjects which national enthusiasm and Christian dialectic could work upon with relevance and profit. In previous chapters the experiments of Chapelain's predecessors were analysed, and the aspirations of Chapelain's contemporaries appreciated; against this background we can better understand how appropriate was the subject of *La Pucelle* to the epic genre in the seventeenth century. How Chapelain responded to the challenge posed by the religious and national implications of his subject will be examined presently. First we must turn back to the start of the sixteenth century and see how the story of Joan of Arc was treated by a poet writing less than a hundred years after her death.

Valerand de Varanne and Saint Joan

First published in 1516 under the title *De gestis Joannae virginis,* reproduced by Ravisius Textor in 1521, edited again with an abundant commentary by Prarond in 1889,[1] Valerand de Varanne's poem on Joan of Arc followed the historical structure we have become familiar with when considering the

Latin epics of the early sixteenth century. Yet the poem was no mere chronicle; Varanne had definite convictions about the significance of Joan's career. His poem moved swiftly from her entry into public life to her vindication as a saint. Joan's sanctity was his theme; his epic is the epic of Saint Joan.

According to Varanne Joan, launched on her career by divine intervention, was assured by God that her mission to save France, announced by an angel, accorded with his will. Joan persuaded Baudricourt to send her to Charles; Charles sent her to Poitiers for examination. Her faith was tested by doctors of theology; her virginity established by the Queen of Sicily. The first task was the relief of Orleans. Successful there, successful against Talbot at Patay, Joan led Charles to be crowned at Rheims. Unsuccessful in the attack on Paris, she hung up her armour. Compiègne asked her help; there the Burgundians captured her. Sold to Bedford, condemned by the ecclesiastical court for magic practices, burned at Rouen, Joan, on the instance of her mother, supported by Charles VII, was finally proclaimed innocent by Pope Calistus III. The final book dwells at length on the corruption of her judges and the falsity of the charges.

These are the main episodes of Joan's career, presented straightforwardly by Varanne, embellished for the most part with speeches, with few subordinate episodes attached to the main plot. Varanne, like Chapelain later, worried because Joan was a woman. Joan poses the problem herself to the angel who summons her to save France; the angel assures her that no distinctions of sex are valid before God.[2] The question crops up again in the examination at Poitiers, particularly in the misogynistic diatribe of the third speaker.[3] The reports of Joan's trials[4] were Varanne's chief sources. From them he constructed a narrative and adorned it with Biblical allusions. The Latin writers of Antiquity—Virgil, Ovid, Horace, Valerius Flaccus—furnished further allusions, words, and phrases.[5] The following extract shows how Varanne handled Virgil. Intercalated between consecutive lines from *De gestis Joannae* are phrases from the *Aeneid*, preceded by their references, with correspondences italicized:

Vallicori *praeses* tum Baudrecurtus agebat
Cui *praestans animi virtus*: & multa gerendi
   xii. 19: o *praestans animi* iuvenis
   viii. 548: *praestantis virtute* legit
   v. 363: si cui *virtus animus*que in pectore praesens
Dexteritas belli. Patruo comitata puella
Tendit eo *gressum*, & tales *dat pectore voces*:
   i. 410: *gressum* ad moenia *tendit*
   v. 409: referebat *pectore voces*
   iii. 246: rumpit hanc *pectore vocem*
   xi. 377: *dat* gemitum rumpitque has imo *pectore voces*
Huc ego *prodigiis caelestibus acta* venire
Cogor . . .[6]
   vi. 379: *prodigiis acti caelestibus*

    To compare Varanne's treatment of Joan with that of Chapelain clarifies the motives of both poets and helps avoid the irrelevancies of critics[7] who accuse Varanne of distorting the saviour of France, and Chapelain of misrepresenting the simplicity of the peasant girl. Varanne knew the transcripts of the trials and from them selected what served his purpose, namely the vindication of the saint. He adorned his narrative with speeches, because he liked rhetoric, and because his readers liked rhetoric. If he played down the French victories, it was because, unlike his critics, he was concerned with other things. He wanted to vindicate Joan's character; the title of the poem stresses her virginity—so does the episode of the Queen of Sicily. Of course Varanne distorted the sources: he was not producing a critical edition of the documents concerned with Joan's career. Chapelain's aims were quite different. His subtitle, *la France délivrée*, shows it. So Joan underwent a different transformation. Her humble origins, her name,[8] the homely details of her entry into public life, were not suitable for Chapelain's predominantly aristocratic audience, for whom he was celebrating the nation's deliverance and allegorizing the triumph of free will over corrupt influences.

    Each stage of the story illustrates the diverse aims of the two poets. Both start with divine intervention. Varanne has Charlemagne pray to Mary to save France; Mary passes the message on to Christ; an angel appears abruptly to Joan. Chapelain begins more cohesively: Charles prays in despair for the fall of Orleans to be averted, the sequence of messages is repeated, and the relief of Orleans follows naturally. The assistance rendered by Baudricourt and Poulengy is omitted by Chapelain, and Charles accepts Joan without question. All this is the logical consequence of Chapelain's interest in France's recovery. Since, however, Varanne is interested in establishing the authenticity of Joan's divine inspiration, he naturally stresses the steps by which she is accepted, and uses the conversation with Baudricourt to reply to objections which might also be in his readers' minds. The testing by the doctors of Poitiers and by the Queen also allay suspicions that Joan may be in league with the devil or have dabbled in witchcraft.

Quite naturally the patriotic Chapelain expanded on the battle of Patay and dwelt on the campaigns that followed. Quite naturally the hagiographically inclined Varanne dealt summarily with the battles, and paid little attention to Joan until after her capture, when her reputation most needed to be vindicated. The capture was, of course, something of an embarrassment to Chapelain, and he took great pains to motivate it convincingly. Amaury becomes jealous of Joan, betrays the French army at the siege of Paris, and is killed in the rout by a stray arrow from Joan. Charles, doubly incensed at the death of his favourite and at the defeat of his army, for which he blames Joan, dismisses his saviour, who then retires to Compiègne. The inhabitants of Compiègne welcome her; she therefore helps them in defence against the Burgundians, and thus is captured. Varanne does not explain the Compiègne incident so well.

The trial, death, and vindication of Joan were Varanne's real interest; to Chapelain, they were another problem, which he solved ingeniously, but which he needlessly complicated. Chapelain starts promisingly enough. An attempt to rescue Joan fails, betrayed by Bedford's son Edward, disguised as Joan's brother, Rodolphe. To forestall other attempts the English needed to dispose of their captive. Thus the motive for burning Joan was clearly established. Here, however, the romanesque took over. Books xvi to xxi of *La Pucelle* are a mass of episodes, only tenuously linked to each other and to the main story. Once again, as has been observed in previous epics, the patriotic and religious theme risked being obscured by the embellishments. From a hagiographical point of view Chapelain completely distorted the trial and burning, but for his own purpose it was an ingenious manipulation of events. The French in Joan's absence lose the advantages she has won for them, and slide towards disaster again. Charles makes a pilgrimage; God pities him, and allows Joan to be sacrificed to atone for the sins of France. The details of the trial and the stake therefore held little interest for Chapelain, who concentrated all his attention on the triumphal entry into Paris: thus France was delivered. Varanne, on the other hand, depicted the trial in detail to expose the corruption of the judges. Joan's vindication by Calistus III, which Chapelain omitted because it clashed with his interpretation of Joan's death and was superfluous to the deliverance of France, is in Varanne's epic the triumphant conclusion of Joan's career.

Chapelain and the saviour of France

Chapelain first conceived La Pucelle[9] when epic poets were still looking back to Ronsard's Franciade as a model for epic poetry. He worked on it for fifty years until his death in 1674. This lengthy period of composition may be compared to that which preceded the Franciade; and, in other respects, Ronsard and Chapelain, as epic poets, had much in common. Both were leading literary figures of their day. Chapelain had established his reputation as a critic with his preface to Marino's Adone in 1623; in 1633 his Ode à Richelieu established him as a lyric poet, the undisputed successor of Malherbe.[10] He was a founder-member of the Académie Française; corresponded with men of letters all over Europe;[11] Racine was to seek his opinion on the Nymphe de la Seine; Colbert was to ask his advice when pensions were to be distributed to writers who would serve the king. Chapelain's prestige was enormous, and guaranteed his epic a vast amount of advance publicity. But just as the public had been obliged to wait from 1550 until 1572 before they could judge the Franciade, so they had to wait from 1625 until 1656 before La Pucelle appeared in print. On one point there is an important difference between the poems: La Pucelle was eventually completed, the Franciade was not.

The first edition of La Pucelle in 1656 contained only twelve books, and so did all subsequent editions in the seventeenth century.[12] Chapelain had completed Books xiii to xxiv by 1670,

but, fearing a repetition of the acrimonious controversy which
had greeted the first twelve, he did not publish any more, and
contented himself with revising the whole poem until his death
in 1674.[13] The last twelve books were not published until 1882
and therefore most discussion of *La Pucelle* has concentrated
on the first half.[14] The epic represents the work of a lifetime.
Conceived by a man of thirty, *La Pucelle* received its finishing
touches from a man of eighty. Its great length was not due to
the prolixity of a poet to whom verses came easily. Chapelain
spent five years composing a version in prose and the rest of
his life versifying it. *La Pucelle* was the fruit of years of medi-
tation and years of labour.

Once published, the epic was the target of admiration and
abuse. It was unreservedly praised by Mambrun;[15] it enjoyed
the flattering attentions of Paulet and Montaigu, both of whom
embarked independently on translations of the poem into Latin
hexameters.[16] The average reader found the epic hard going,
but blamed himself: 'Quand on bâillait, on s'en prenait à soi, on
s'en voulait de son ignorance et de sa frivolité.'[17] The hostile
reactions ranged from the epigrams of Linière which were hard
to refute,[18] to the erudite criticism of the *Lettre du sieur du
Rivage*, with which Chapelain, better than anyone else, was
equipped to deal.[19] When the controversy had died down,
Boileau entered the lists against *La Pucelle*, and continued to
heap every sarcasm on the poem until its author died. What
inspired Boileau's unrelenting animosity?

. . . Chapelain était l'auteur de *la Pucelle* et le représentant le plus
qualifié de tout ce qu'il [Boileau] voulait abattre Il a frappé
fort parce que le livre était de ceux qu'un Boileau ne lit pas sans
colère; parce qu'il avait résisté à l'épreuve de l'impression, où tant
d'autres avaient sombré, qui valaient mieux; parce que l'homme
qui s'était rendu coupable d'un tel crime contre l'art et la poésie
dominait sans partage l'Académie et les salons, faisait la loi au
Parnasse et disposait de la faveur du Roi.[20]

Posterity has accepted the view of the critic who had a vested
interest in denigrating the author of *La Pucelle,* and the poem
has remained unread. Perhaps Boileau was right. None the less,
it is still profitable to examine *La Pucelle* against the background of the heroic tradition so far described and to compare

Chapelain's approach to the problems of epic with that of his predecessors or contemporaries.

Chapelain's poem is above all the triumph of regular epic. He more than any other poet put into practice the theories that had been elaborated during the period from 1620 to 1650. Le Moyne's 'Traité du poème héroïque' was remarkable for its good sense and wise observations; yet when Le Moyne composed *Saint Louis*, he abandoned almost every precept and principle that he had propounded. To Chapelain the precepts and principles governing literary composition were sacred. If they had been correctly reasoned, to flout them was to act against reason, and to invite disaster. On this basis he conceived epic as the greatest genre in literature, embracing human passions in all their variety, divine providence in all its mystery, and the natural world in all its complexity, unified by a single theme that should illustrate the truths of the Christian religion and the grandeur of the French nation.

Such a conception demanded a fitting style. In his modest fashion, Chapelain acknowledged Le Moyne's sparkling inventiveness, Scudéry's pomp and abundance, Desmarets's delicacy and variety.[21] But were such styles really appropriate to epic? Surely if the epics of Antiquity were to be equalled or surpassed in French, sobriety and dignity were essential. Evidently Chapelain believed this to be so, for the main characteristics of his style show his desire to avoid the extravagance, however dazzling, that characterized Le Moyne, and the naivety, however endearing, that characterized Desmarets. But the pursuit of sobriety and dignity led Chapelain over thorny paths. Sobriety could degenerate into monotony. From Boileau onwards critics collected the cacophonies, the platitudes, the improprieties, the repetitions, and the harsh inversions which abound in the poem.[22] These faults suggest that Chapelain had little ear for the sound of his own language; yet they result from his groping for a style suitable for epic. He conceived this style mainly in terms of the arrangement of appropriate words according to the manifold convolutions of rhetorical precept. A mechanical preoccupation with the handling of language is evident in his often abrupt transition from one style to another, according to the matter in hand. Be it a speech, a narrative, a simile, or the description of natural phenomena, of supernatural intervention, of the appearance of characters, of their inner feelings, the style changes, signalling the change of subject. The whole poem thus breaks up all too easily into passages that fall under one or another of the above headings. The very quest for variety, through the juxtaposition of different styles, became an irritating mannerism, and the pursuit of sobriety led to a devastating banality of vocabulary.

Yet *La Pucelle* embraced an extraordinary range of subjects. Most epic narratives offered a place for descriptions of land-scapes, war, love, humans, animals, angels, seasons, arts and crafts; *La Pucelle* has its share. In addition Chapelain used the simile to include material that lent itself less readily to the epic theme: a penitent drunkard, a caged lion, a bulldog fighting two wolves, the emotions of a murderer awaiting a pardon.[23] Patiently Chapelain surveyed the universe, observed its work-ings, and chronicled the result in his epic. On every page there is evidence of his meticulous eye for detail: the manner in which the circle of vision extends as night recedes,[24] the decep-tive movement of the town of Chinon as Roger glides down the Loire,[25] Talbot's plunge into the filthy river bed when the bridge at Orleans collapses,[26] the sensation of boiling oil enter-ing the wounds of those attacking Paris,[27] the patches of moss on the sun-baked rock where Joan rests after her dismissal,[28] the celebrated piling of log upon log in the construction of Joan's bonfire.[29] Chapelain did not lack the capacity to observe the physical world and describe it in Alexandrines. He studied objects and events with clinical detachment. Dramatists were analysing human emotions and the values which governed their lives; Chapelain subjected the material world to the same scrutiny. When he applied this process to human psychology, and the minds of his characters underwent the same pains-taking analysis, the results were less fortunate. Chapelain ex-celled in the minute cataloguing of sensorial impressions, but lacked the power of synthesis to portray the complexity of the human mind.

Yet he was interested in character and his powers of charac-terization were not negligible. It was above all his handling of a small group of characters that gave *La Pucelle* its unity. He did not, like Scudéry, ruthlessly simplify his plot; he did not, like Desmarets, increase the pace of his narrative. Instead he brought together his chief characters—Charles, Joan, Dunois, Marie, Agnes, Bedford, Edward, and Philip of Burgundy— and his minor characters—Amaury, Gillon, Talbot, Roger, Rodolphe, Tanneguy, Yolande, and Henry of England—in a series of situations which reveal their reactions to one another and to the course of events. He abandoned the technique of recitals as a means of expanding the story; his fictitious charac- ters always fit plausibly with the historical ones; the interest that each character has in the destinies of the others gives co- hesion to the poem. It was a novel approach to the problem of unity and one which set Chapelain apart from the other practitioners of the genre.[30]

Using the characters to link episodes Chapelain used the Iliadic structure to give overall unity to his poem. Misunder- standing of this has led to unjustified criticism of Joan's absence from the greater part of the second half.[31] It is precisely Joan's absence which influences the course of events. It is shown how fatal her dismissal was to the French, just as Achilles's was to the Greeks, and Rinaldo's to the crusaders. On the other hand Joan's imprisonment is kept constantly in mind, either through her friends' plots to rescue her,[32] or Causson's plots to have her burned.[33] Edward's impersonation of Joan's brother Rodolphe may be an unhistorical embellishment, but could not have succeeded without Joan's absence. The whole episode of Agnes's death is devoted to convincing Charles of the evil he has done in abandoning Joan. Marie's escape from Bedford and the defeat of the French fleet indicate how English affairs prospered in Joan's absence. Her martyrdom ultimately saved France because God accepted it to atone for the sins of the French king and people. With considerable ingenunity Chape- lain thus turned the disadvantage of Joan's unfortunate end into a means of giving unity to the poem, and at the same time adapted the historical event to an epic structure exemplified in the *Iliad* and the *Gerusalemme*. He also made a familiar epic topos, the review of armies, serve the same purpose. The reviews of the French army in Book vi, and the English army in Book xviii, contribute to a comprehensive picture of two nations at war. Though Chapelain himself assumed his readers would skip them, his great litany on the provinces of France and his panoramic inventory of the English countryside[34] were wholly consistent with his interpretation of Joan's martyrdom. The national and patriotic theme of the expulsion of the English from French soil was thus embellished to arouse emotion in a way that Saint Louis's crusade in far off Egypt, Clovis's amorous adventures with Clotilda, and Charlemagne's campaigns against Widukind or Desiderius could never do.

As unified as *Alaric*, but wider in scope; more dignified and more credible than *Saint Louis* or *Clovis*; of more immediate interest than the *Franciade*; combining respect for history with a flair for invention; ingenious in circumventing the problems of a heroine who ended at the stake; technically superior in so many respects to its rivals—why should *La Pucelle*, with so much to its credit, be the most ridiculed and least read poem of the seventeenth century? Circumstances did not favour Chapelain: the length of the poem demanded excessive goodwill from the reader; it was never published complete; its author's peculiar eminence in literary circles could only excite his critics' envy. These factors may explain the attitude of critics at the time; they do not help in assessing the poem. The reason for *La Pucelle*'s failure was that Chapelain, with infinite care, produced only a corpse. He meticulously fulfilled every requirement of epic theory, but failed to impart the mysterious touch of life. The touch of life requires that conception and execution should be excellent, and that excellence should be manifest in the whole, in the parts, and in the details. In literature, detail is style, and Chapelain lacked the genius of words. To illustrate his merits, one must quote him; to quote him is to reveal his verbal impotence. Once must give him credit for all that he attempted and achieved in *La Pucelle* and regret that one failing should inevitably invalidate so much labour and so many merits.

NOTES TO CHAPTER X

1. Prarond's edition has been reprinted by Slatkine 1969. His introduction gives the best account of Varanne's life. See also Cougny, *Jeanne Darc, épopée latine du XVIe siècle* (Paris, 1874); Murarasu, *Poésie néo-latine,* pp. 63–9; van Tieghem, *Littérature latine,* p. 128.

2. i, a8^v—b1^r.

3. i, b8^v—c2^r.

4. For the documents, see Quicherat, *Procès de condamnation et de réhabilitation de Jeanne d'Arc* (Paris, 1841–9). He gives a brief account of Varanne (v. 83–9).

5. See Prarond's commentary for details.

6. i, b2^r.

7. Cougny, pp. 4–6; Murarasu, pp. 66–7. The former is unjust to Chapelain, the latter to Varanne.

8. She is always referred to as 'la Pucelle' never as 'Jeanne'. Chapelain justified his choice of a woman as heroine by explaining that women were as capable of heroism as men. Timidly, he added another excuse: '. . . je ne l'ay pas tant regardée, comme le principal Heros du Poëme, qui, a proprement parler, est le CONTE DE DVNOIS' (Preface, sig. c2^v). This merely covers a supposed blemish with a real fault since the unity of the epic cannot profit from rival heroes.

9. On *La Pucelle* see Tallemant, *Historiettes,* ed. Adam, i. 574–6; Sayce, 'Marolles' *Traité* annoté par Richelet', p. 362; Southey, 'Analysis of *La Pucelle*' preceding his poem *Joan of Arc;* Toinet, i. 174–9; Duchesne, pp. 155–215; Kerviler, 'Etude sur le poème de *La Pucelle*', in Herluison's edition of the last twelve books, pp. xv–lxxx; Molènes's introduction to his abridged edition of the first twelve books, i. i–xxxii; Beall, *Fortune du Tasse,* pp. 91–4; Marni, *Allegory,* pp. 147–62; Delaporte, *Du Merveilleux,* pp. 359–61; Edelman, *Attitudes,* pp. 245–74; Cottaz, *Influence,* pp. 38–42; Collas, *Chapelain,* pp. 205–92; Adam, *Histoire,* ii. 57–60. On the engravings see Duportal, *Livres à figures,* pp. 273–5, and Canivet, *Illustration,* no. 90. On the composition of the poem see especially *77 lettres à Heinsius,* ed. Bray, letters lix, lx, lxi, lxviii, and Bray's notes, pp. 341–2, nn. 6–7, p. 345, n. 8, pp. 348–9, n. 12, p. 382, n. 10. For extracts from the poem see Picard, *Poésie française 1640–1680,* pp. 36–40 (Preface); pp. 187–96 (ii. 49–108; ix. 478–664). For other works on Chapelain see Cioranescu, *XVIIe,* and Collas's bibliography, pp. 479–522.

10. '. . . l'auteur en fut en son temps à peu près unanimement salué pour l'héritier de Malherbe' (Collas, p. 114).

11. See especially the published selections of letters by Tamizey de Larroque, 2 vols (1880–3), Ciureanu (1964), and Bray (1966). Further

collections listed in Cioranescu, *XVIIe,* nos. 18499–510, and Collas pp. 479–83.

12. The authorized editions do not show substantial textual changes. The most important were those from Courbé in 1656 (folio and 12mo) and 1657. For the pirated editions, see *Lettres,* ed. Bray, p. 382 n. 10.

13. For full details see Collas, pp. 205–13, for Books i–xii, and pp. 277–92, for Books xiii–xxiv.

14. With unfortunate results: 'Ayant lu les douze premiers livres, je ne me suis pas senti le courage de lire les derniers,' says Beall (p. 91 n. 46). He then goes on to affirm, 'c'est surtout dans les premiers livres qu'on rencontre des réminiscences du Tasse' (p. 92): hardly surprising if they are the only books he has read. Marni likewise says: 'We shall not discuss them [the last 12 books] because they add nothing to our treatment of Chapelain and they are not an integral part of the allegory of the *Pucelle*' (p. 148). But the allegory can hardly be fulfilled before Joan's mission has been accomplished.

15. See Collas, p. 271; Chérot, *Le Moyne,* p. 248.

16. See Chapelain's preface to the last twelve books (ed. Herluison, p. xviii) and Collas, pp. 275–7.

17. Collas, p. 258.

18. Collas, pp. 260–4.

19. Collas, pp. 264–70.

20. Collas, p. 446. Chapelain was very sensitive about his position: 'Quant à ce que vous souhaités de sçavoir de mes affaires du Parnasse, il s'est élevé ou plustost resveillé une faction de poetastres contre moy. Ils ne veulent pas que ma versification soit poëtique, et deschirent par des satyres et des libelles furieux dans l'esperance de rüiner mon crédit à la Cour et ma reputation dans le monde.' (Letter to Graziani, 12 November 1668; ed. Ciureanu, p. 165.) See also Fabre, *Ennemis,* pp. 642–96.

21. Preface to *La Pucelle* (1656), d2ʳ.

22.   Maudit soit l'auteur dur, dont l'âpre & rude verve,
           Son cerveau tenaillant, rima malgré Minerve;
           Et, de son lourd marteau martelant le Bon-sens,
           A fait de méchans Vers douze fois cens.
              (Boileau, *Epigramme* viii, 'Vers en stile de Chapelain').
       For examples see Collas, pp. 244–55.

23. xxii, p. 275; xvii, p. 139; xvi, p. 116; i, p. 25.

24. iii, p. 89.

25. v, p. 187.

26. iii, p. 120.

27. xi, p. 455.

28. xii, pp. 504–5.

29. xxiii, pp. 304–5.

30. That Chapelain was familiar with the characters of medieval romance, and saw them as exemplars of medieval chivalry, emerges from his dialogue *De la Lecture des vieux romans.* In some respects his own characters are exemplars of seventeenth-century *galanterie*; cf. Jacoubet, *Le genre troubadour*, pp. 21–4. However, in summing up Chapelain's characters, Collas sums up the merits and demerits of the whole poem: 'A ces personnages bien compris et sagement conduits il manque l'essentiel, la vie' (p. 240).

31. 'Car enfin quoiqu'on ne perde pas les but de vue, il faut bien avouer qu'après le XIIe chant la Pucelle est à peu près oubliée jusqu'au XXIIe' (Collas, p. 238).

32. xvi, pp. 97–108.

33. xvii, pp. 125–9.

34. Derived from Camden's *Britannia,* of which he had a copy in his library (see above, p. 49 n. 24). The review is full of scholarly detail such as the political divisions of England, Scotland, and Ireland (p. 159); Plymouth harbour (p. 160); the distinction between Thames and Isis at Oxford (p. 170). Ascoli does not credit Chapelain with much understanding of the English character (*Grande Bretagne*, i. 492).

XI

ROMANESQUE EPIC

HEROES were the means by which poets gave sometimes tenuous unity to the epics we have so far considered. The romanesque epics differ from the heroic epics in not being unified by a single hero; their relation to history was often slight; and their fictions so numerous that they became almost entirely works of the imagination. The poems of Boyssières and Ennetières were intended to illustrate the chivalric code; those of Montreux, Deimier, and Carel de Sainte-Garde to entertain. Obviously the distinction between romanesque and heroic epic cannot be pressed too far. There were plenty of romanesque features in the previous epics; there might be some justification for calling *Clovis* and *Saint Louis* romances rather than epics. On the other hand Ennetières's *Chevalier* has a single hero and follows historical events very closely. His theme, however, is medieval chivalry. The distinctions must therefore only be used in so far as they are useful, and the utility in this case is to group four poems, which have no hero comparable to those considered so far, and whose structure is extremely loose.

To list the chief characters of these romanesque epics is sufficient to show that the tone is quite different. Who, one might ask, were Jacques de Lalain, Franc Gautier, or Childebrand, beside the mighty figures of Charlemagne, Saint Louis, or even Francus? The scope for invention around such obscure characters was clearly much greater than in the case of the better-known heroes. The poets took advantage of this freedom. Around the character, whose name might figure in the title, were grouped a host of other characters, whose recitals and adventures were the fabric of the poem. Any suggestion of a single theme was submerged beneath a mass of digressions. In the absence of structural unity the poet could only succeed if he was continually entertaining. The results showed that the imitators of Ariostos were in a more precarious position than the imitators of Tasso. Having set out to be entertaining, they risked more spectacular failure. By a curious coincidence, a complete inability to entertain was just what most of these poets had in common. The romanesque epics thus furnish some of the gloomiest pages in the whole field of historical epic.

Boyssières: La Croisade

The earliest of these poems, *La Croisade*[1], is the most faithful imitation of Ariosto, though the subject is the same as that of the *Gerusalemme*, namely the First Crusade. The activities of the different characters—Godefroi de Bouillon, Franc Gautier, Pierre l'Hermite, and Clerambaud de Vandeuil—are described in separate episodes, often interrupted at their climax, like Ariosto's, with a promise to return to the subject later. Similarly, moralizing digressions at the start of Book i on peace and war, and at the start of Book ii on love and friendship, are typical of the *Orlando furioso*. Boyssières refers to Jocondo and Medoro;[2] to Brandimard, Fiordiligi, and Roland.[3] In the introductory letter to Anne d'Este, Boyssières named Ariosto alongside Virgil and Homer, as a poet driven to distraction by the burden of composing epic.[4] Boyssières also translated and imitated the *Furioso*. Thus only twelve years after the publication of the *Franciade* Boyssières showed that Ronsard had not turned French epic decisively in the direction of Virgilian epic, but that the romanesque tradition was capable of new life.

La Croisade, in Alexandrines, contains only three books and is incomplete.[5] Book i immediately displays the fragmentation that is typical of romanesque epic. The Papal Nuncio approaches Godefroi for help; Godefroi refuses because his orders have not been obeyed, and the poet then goes back to explain the events which led to this situation. Of the three land expeditions to the Holy Land, the first was led by Franc Gautier, who was delayed by opposition in Hungary; the second by Pierre l'Hermite, who became involved in quarrels between Germans and Hungarians; the third by Clerambaud, who returned to check whether rumours that his mistress was being unfaithful to him were true. As he is returning he meets her lover. At this critical moment the books ends.

Much of Book ii is taken up with the duel between Clerambaud and the supposed lover, who turns out to be his mistress's

cousin. Having cleared up the misunderstanding, they both
continue back to Verdun where Clerambaud's mistress has
heard a report of Clerambaud's death. Just as he bursts in on
her the scene changes to Hungary, where the adventures of
Gautier are recounted at length and with some confusion. A
complicated recital is interrupted at the end of Book ii while
Gautier receives a message. The recital is briefly resumed in
Book iii, but here the poem is cut short.

Even this fragment shows quite a different approach to epic
from that of the heroic poets. Desmarets, whose rapid narrative
and profusion of incident come closest to Ariosto in style,
never goes so far as to break off in the middle of an episode in
order to create suspense. Although the *Croisade* was very much
a tribute to Ariosto, Boyssières was certainly familiar with the
work of Ronsard and Tasso. He regretted Ronsard's failure to
complete the *Franciade*,[6] and evidently considered himself one
of Ronsard's successors. His use of pagan mythology, especially at the start of the poem shows that some of Ronsard's
characteristics had rubbed off. The invocation, however, was
closely modelled on Tasso's opening stanzas, particularly in
the simile of the child and the medicine.[7] The rest, however, is
entirely in the style of Ariosto. It is a pity that Boyssières went
no further. He was clearly determined to keep the reader in
constant suspense, a technique which other poets could have
used to advantage. A complete romanesque epic composed so
soon after Ronsard's attempt to revive ancient epic would be
of the greatest interest. Moreover, alone of the poets of this
group, Boyssières not only set out to entertain his reader, but
also showed some aptitude in doing so.

Montreux: L'Espagne conquise

In 1597 Nicolas de Montreux published under the pseudo-
nym Ollenix du Mont-Sacré an enormous poem which
achieved that complete imitation of Ariosto which had eluded
Boyssières. Though nominally devoted to the exploits of
Charlemagne, the poem, like Ariosto's, relies for its appeal on
a proliferation of romanesque episodes which drive the historical characters entirely into the background. Unfortunately, the
prolixity of Montreux's romanesque imagination was not

accompanied by the stylistic virtuosity which carries the reader
through the *Orlando furioso*:

L'Espagne conquise est le seul essai que nous connaissions, d'adop-
ter intégralement à la poésie française la conception et la manière
de l'Arioste. La tâche était au-dessus des forces de ce poète médiocre . . . Il aime trop les longueurs, et son style n'atteint pas à la
variété qu'il recherche par ses épisodes; dans les mille pages de son
poème, on aurait de la peine à découvrir quelques vers bien frappés.[8]

Not only is Charlemagne a shadowy figure, but even the
familiar characters of the *Furioso*—Orlando, Rinaldo, Ruggiero, Bradamante—are reduced to secondary roles by Montreux. The reason is the dedication of the poem to Philippe-
Emmanuel de Lorraine, Duke of Mercoeur; great pro-
minence is therefore given to Ferry, Duke of Lorraine, and the
pagan Favente, from whose union the Lorraine family, catalogued in a magic mirror in Book i, *chant* 22, are to spring.
Ferry and Favente thus resemble those other couples who
appeared in the epics devoted to the glorification of ancestors,
and whose prototypes were Ruggiero and Bradamante, the
ancestors of the Este family.

No summary could possibly convey any idea of the structure
of *L'Espagne conquise*: it has none. The main difference between the poems of Ariosto and Montreux, apart from the
abyss that separates their style, is that Montreux allows the
supernatural a greater importance and is fonder than Ariosto
of allegory.

Deimier: L'Austriade *and* La Néréide

Ariosto was also the main influence on the *Néréide*, which
represented the final stage of Deimier's epic projects. The
gradual elaboration of this epic was a complex affair, and really
began with a poem by James VI of Scotland on the battle of
Lepanto, written as an exhortation to the persecuted Protestants of France. This poem was translated into French by du
Bartas,[9] whose command of language and grasp of the wider
implications of a historical event might have enriched the field
of historical epic if he had not turned his talents to other kinds
of epic. To search for these qualities in Deimier's *Austriade*[10]
is a hopeless task. He too sang of the battle of Lepanto, and
confidently assumed he was producing an epic, but even du

Bartas's modest translation is more epic than Deimier's sprawl-
ing narrative. Comparison between the poems shows that at
this stage Deimier owed nothing to du Bartas despite their common theme. Deimier started not with a debate in heaven but by
narrating the historical background.[11] When God despatched
help to the Christians, Deimier made Saint Michael his messenger, not the angel Gabriel.[12] In episodes common to the two
poems[13] there is no trace of Deimier's being influenced by du
Bartas. Not until Deimier produced the second version of his
epic, with the title *La Néréide*, did he show signs of having
read *La Lépanthe*. However, before dealing with the *Néréide*,
which besides showing du Bartas's influence, also illustrates
Deimier's complete acceptance of Ariosto as a model, we must
look briefly at the *Austriade*.

The theme of the *Austriade* is confused. Deimier could not
decide whether Don John was his hero or whether he was producing a versified account of the battle of Lepanto. The fact
that the poem is in two books is no guarantee of brevity, for
the two books contain more than 5,000 lines. To gain some
impression of its overwhelming monotony, it is only necessary
to imagine a poem equal in length to half the *Aeneid* in which,
after brief preparations, the poet settles down to an interminable catalogue of duels and deaths. Not that in itself Deimier's
style is monotonous; here and there a striking phrase shines
forth, and the fighting is often described dramatically. Usually
Deimier distinguishes the warriors by describing their country
of origin, their handling of their weapons, the nature of their
wounds, their manner of falling and dying, and the fate of their
souls. But there is a limit to the amount of pleasure to be
derived from the endless repetition of such devices. They may
perhaps render a battle scene more vivid when the battle scene
is but one type of episode out of many; they are not sufficient
to grip the reader's attention when the poem contains little
else. Occasionally, it is true, other devices are employed. God
sends Saint Michael to ensure victory for the Christians; Don
John's armour is described in detail; Nereids are disturbed by
cannon-balls. Obviously Deimier was aware that the epic poet
had other resources at his disposal. Yet he devoted nine-tenths
of his poem to innumerable descriptions of hand-to-hand
combat. Could such leaden repetition really be called epic?

Even Deimier must have had doubts about the assaults and combats which he had inflicted remorselessly upon his readers, and soon after publishing the *Austriade*, having realized that it was susceptible of improvement, he tried to improve it.

The result was the *Néréide*. The new poem was a new kind of epic, if nothing else. Don John was relegated to the background and the battle of Lepanto became the framework for the unrelated and entirely imaginary story of the loves of Cléophile and Néréclie. Despite Bosco's claim that Deimier owed nothing to his predecessors, his debt to the *Furioso* was now plain. The story was set in Cathay, and Néréclie was descended from Angelica. Deimier's new inspiration did nothing to diminish the confusion which had characterized the *Austriade*. He had accumulated rather than absorbed the new ideas which had come to him in the interval, and a multiplicity of themes now jostled for attention. Although Don Juan had slipped into the background in the poem, he still occupied, by oversight, a prominent place in the proposition, whilst the real subject of the poem, the love story, was tacked on as an afterthought.[14] Deimier started the poem with a portrait of Mars, weary of peace and promising victory to the French if they would go to war. Then Deimier had the unhappy idea of giving a general description of the battle, before starting on the detailed narrative of it. When eventually he reached the preliminaries of the battle, he followed the sequence of events in the *Austriade*, with slight modifications inspired by du Bartas. The descriptions of the combats, which contributed so powerfully to the tedium of the *Austriade*, were somewhat reduced, but retain enough of their monotony. In the middle of Book iv, at the height of the battle, Deimier introduced his romance.

Contarini captures Jaffer and Dorothée, and sends them from battle in a ship, along with some Christians wounded in the fight.[15] At the request of Alfonso of Ferrara, Cliador diverts the tranquil inactivity of the erstwhile combatants, by unfolding the tale of Néréclie and Cléophile. The battle of Lepanto, the tedious versifying of duels and deaths, is abandoned, and Deimier produces (relatively) far more entertainment in the recitals of amorous adventures. Néréclie is a beautiful woman, indifferent to all her suitors; Cléophile is a handsome youth, addicted to hunting, and indifferent to women. Love resolves to change these unnatural tastes. Prince Pharidor issues a challenge to fight for the hand of Néréclie, to which Cléophile responds, whilst Néréclie foregoes her seclusion. The setting is ostensibly oriental, but the full pageantry of medieval jousting is nonchalantly introduced. Amidst the chivalric display the poem ends incomplete. Deimier doubtless preferred the freedom of imaginary situations to the discipline of historical events; or he felt that the public wanted romance not epic. In his *Art poétique* he indicated where his tastes lay: '. . . le stile de l'Arioste est plus dous & intelligible que celuy du Tasse: Les inuentions, les sentences & les auantures y sont plus amples, plus belles, plus esgayantes & plus variees de notables accidens & de merueilles . . .'[16] This opinion, and Deimier's practice in the *Néréide*, would have appealed to Le Moyne, whose *Saint Louis* may be compared to the *Néréide* both for its recitals and its chivalric pageantry.

Du Bartas's reputation, like Ronsard's, stood high among the epic poets of the early seventeenth century. When passages from the *Austriade* diverge from the corresponding ones in the *Néréide*, the influence of du Bartas can often be detected. Describing the sound of drums before battle, Deimier first wrote:

> S'aprochans de plus pres le battant des tambours,
> Que Mars en s'esbatant nomme ses chants d'amours,
> Le clair son allarmeux des courbées trompettes . . .[17]

Then in the *Lépanthe* he read:

> On oit bruire à l'entour cent bouches salpetreuses,
> Et leur ton ton-tonant erre, et prompt, rompt le rond
> Du plancher estoillé.[18]

He therefore tried his hand as onomatopoeia in the *Néréide*:

> S'approchans de plus pres pour les plus durs estours,
> Le tant tant batatant des rebatans tambours,
> Le clair son allarmeux des tonnantes trompettes . . .[19]

The striving for verbal effects is reminiscent of Navières who was writing his *Henriade* at exactly the same time. This example illustrates Deimier's care in adapting du Bartas's contributions rather than merely plagiarizing them.[20]

Ennetières: Le Chevalier sans reproche

In the comforting world of chivalrous romance, Jean d'Ennetières also sought refuge. Carrying on the tradition of romanesque epic started by Boyssières and Deimier, he published the
sixteen books of *Le Chevalier sans reproche, Jacques de Lalain*
in 1633. [21] The theme of his poem is contained in his lamenta-
tions for the good times past:

> O temps d'alors! qui rend nos fronts couuerts de honte,
> De tels gens maintenant on ne fait plus de compte;
> On ne chaume tels saints, & pour trancher le mot,
> Celuy seul est sçauant qui sçait faire le sot. [22]

To illustrate the virtues which he found lacking in his own
times, Ennetières chose the person of Jacques de Lalain, a
Flemish knight who died in 1453. The details of the career of
this exemplar of medieval chivalry were contained in the *Histoire de Jacques de Lalain* by Georges Chastellain, [23] and further
information could be found in the *Mémoires* of Olivier de la
Marche who frequently mentions Lalain in his accounts of the
campaigns of Philip, Duke of Burgundy. Ennetières's narrative
closely followed the events described in these sources, and consequently his poem falls into two parts. First, Books i to xi
describe Lalain's visits to foreign courts in search of opportunities to prove his valour and virtue; in every case he was
welcomed in the best traditions of courtly hospitality, with
hunting, banquets, and dancing. He jousted, and defeated all
his opponents with magnanimity and courtesy. His relations
with his social superiors, and his attitude to women, were
marked by due respect and reverence. As he journeyed from
Paris to Navarre, from Navarre to Valladolid, on to Portugal,
back to Valladolid, back to Navarre, thence to his home, only
to depart at once for Scotland, then England, then back to
Flanders, and on to Italy, visiting Rome, Naples, and Milan,
the same sequence of welcomes and jousts and banquets and
hunting and polite departures was repeated again and again.
Like Deimier, Ennetières had a strange faith in the power of
repetition. The same pattern of episodes is used for nearly three-
quarters of the poem. The expeditions are indeed narrated
briskly; the style is more vigorous than Deimier's insipidity; but
the choice of subject matter cannot be called adventurous. In

Books xii to xvi, however, the tone does change. Instead of chivalry it is war. The revolt of Ghent is crushed mercilessly by the Duke of Burgundy. In the campaign Lalain, along with other captains, distingushes himself. At the siege of Poucques a stray cannon-ball puts a sudden end to the hero's life and brings the poem to its conclusion.

What emerges from Ennetières's portrayal of Lalain's travels is not a deepening of character, but a code of manners. Whereas the heroic epics generally illustrated moral qualities, Ennetières's *Chevalier* is a text-book of behaviour at court and in the lists. The hero is no warring king or suffering saint, merely a noble knight whose conduct is held up for the admiration of the poet's early seventeenth-century audience. There is no proliferation of character nor variety of episode; the model for this romanesque epic seems to be not Ariosto's *Furioso* but Castiglione's *Cortegiano*. There are several evocations of leisurely and aristocratic conversations, which are strongly reminiscent of the placid discussions at the court of Ferrara. Yet Ennetières is nowhere moved to question the discrepancy between these elegant frivolities and the brutal war in Ghent in which fugitives were murdered in churches:

> Deux cents de ces villains entrent dans vne Eglise,
> Des mieux emmuraillée, & de tres-bonne assise;
> Pour se pouuoir sauuer. . . .
> Chacun d'eux à qui mieux tache de se cacher,
> Qui dessous les autels, qui dedans le clocher,
> Mais las! ils voyent tous leur attente trompée,
> Tout passe par le fer, & au fil de l'espée.[24]

In Books i to xi Ennetières wallows in sentimental admiration for the trappings of chivalry; in Books xii to xvi he recounts the horrors of war with no trace of compassion. He manages to destroy the unity of his poem whilst preserving the monotony of his narrative.

Carel de Sainte-Garde: Charles Martel

Romanesque elements continued to be popular in the epics of the 1650s and reasserted themselves in 1667 with Carel's *Charles Martel*, the final flowering of the tradition of Ariosto. It was not a conscious imitation unfortunately—that might have been some prop for Carel to lean on—but a typical example of history being used merely as a framework for a tissue of inventions. There has been little doubt amongst critics that *Charles Martel* cannot be called an epic:

Je n'ose même pas dire qu'elle soit mauvaise; elle n'existe point, et elle échappe à toute analyse, à toute appréciation.[25]

. . . un énorme entassement de digressions, labeur d'une imagination puérile et d'une érudition indigeste . . .[26]

. . . le *Charles Martel* de Carel de Sainte-Garde ne présente aucune unité d'action, mais seulement un certain nombre d'épisodes, dont la liaison n'est pas toujours nécessaire.[27]

. . . Sainte-Garde a une passion malheureuse pour les descriptions, les digressions et les épisodes, qui le pousse à couper incessamment, de la façon la plus fatigante, le fil de son récit et de son action principale.[28]

. . . his work . . . in reality, is not a regular epic but a romance of chivalry.[29]

These are fair comments; yet, by a curious paradox, *Charles Martel* also reflects the most obscure details of a controversy that involved the most learned historians and antiquaries of the mid-seventeenth century.[30] Consequently in the same poem can be found, side by side, romanesque embellishment pushed to extreme limits and evidence of acquaintance with the latest developments of historical research.

A proper appreciation of Carel's poem, already perplexing enough by virtue of this paradox at its heart, is rendered even more difficult by the confusion concerning its title. Goujet described the first edition as follows:

Childebrand, ou les Sarrasins chassés de France, Poëme héroïque, par Jacques CAREL, sieur de SAINTE-GARDE, Paris, 1666, in-12.[31]

He also suggested that the poem met with no success, not only because Childebrand was a barbaric name but also 'par le fond même du poëme & par la versification. Une preuve, ce semble, de cette vérité, c'est que le sieur de Sainte-Garde ayant fait réimprimer son poëme en 1668, & y ayant substitué le nom de *Charles Martel* à celui de *Childebrand*, ce poëme n'en fut pas plus applaudi.'[32] Lelong also described a volume entitled 'Childebrand':

16125. Childebrand, ou les Sarrazins chassés de France, Poëme héroïque; par DE SAINTE-GARDE, Aumônier du Roi, Paris, 1666, in-12. . . . le Poëme suivant [i.e. no. 16126, *Charles Martel*, Paris, 1680] n'est qu'une nouvelle Edition, où l'on a un peu changé le titre.[33]

However, outside the work of the bibliographers, I have nowhere been able to find an edition of 1666, nor one bearing the title 'Childebrand'. But even if we leave aside 'Childebrand' as a title, there remain two other possibilities. The *privilège* of October 1666 and an edition of 1667 have the title *Les Sarrazins chassez de France*,[34] whilst editions of 1668 bear the title *Charle Martel ou les Sarrazins chassez de France*.[35] What then is the date and title of the first edition of Carel's poem? Edelman places his faith in the bibliographers and believes in a 'Childebrand' of 1666.[36] Bergounioux dismisses this as a fiction and believes the original title to have been *Les Sarrazins chassés de France*.[37] Toinet follows Goujet and Lelong, and gives a 'Childebrand' for 1666 and 1667, and a *Charles Martel* for 1667 and 1668.[38] Until a volume bearing the title 'Childebrand' has been unearthed,[39] it seems safest to conclude that the first four books were published in 1667 with the title *Les Sarrazins chassez de France*. This title indeed would best suit the poem, for it is not a heroic epic about either Childebrand or Charles Martel, but a romanesque epic based upon their campaigns against the Saracens.

The remainder of the poem came out in 1679 in two parts with the title *Charles Martel*.[40] Books i to iv were included as they appeared in the 1667 and 1668 editions, without alteration, and Books v to xvi were added to them. The whole was divided into *chants*, of which there were 151 in all. Carel carefully explained why he had thus divided his poem: 'Cette mesme crainte, que j'ay eûë de t'ennuier trop, a fait que j'ay divisé chaque livre par chans; afinque ton oeil ne s'estonnast pas dans ces vastes campagnes d'écriture, comme dans des péis perdus.'[41] No other epic poet of the seventeenth century dared to describe with such candour the fatigue that might assail the reader of epic. The division into *chants* certainly made *Charles Martel* more digestible, but could not completely disguise Carel's ineptitude as an epic poet.

The tedium generated by the poem may be due in part to the circumstances in which it was composed. Carel was secretary to Georges d'Aubusson de la Feuillade, who was French ambassador in Madrid from 1661 to 1667.[42] It was a period of strained relations between France and Spain, and the ambassador lived in a atmosphere of hostility and suspicion, cut off from the normal contacts of everyday life. His secretary, condemned like his master to enforced solitude, consoled himself by writing verse.[43] This may have alleviated the writer's own boredom but there was no guarantee that his readers would relish the fruits of his labours.

The object of Carel's poem was to show that the Capetians were descended from Childebrand, the half-brother of Charles Martel. This linked the reigning house of France with Charlemagne, and even with Clovis. Controversy on this subject had raged between 1645 and 1659, and several historians and polemicists had fed the flames.[44] The theory of the descent of the Capetians from Childebrand was, however, eventually discarded, and Boileau may have called Carel 'ignorant' because he had chosen the losing side in the controversy.[45]

Although Carel was obviously in touch with the detailed researches into the origins of the Capetians, history played only a small part in his poem, which is almost entirely taken up with recitals by a multitude of minor characters. The only mitigation of this tedious accumulation of episodes is the division into *chants*, which rarely exceed 100 lines in length. Yet though the reader may thus be spared the 'vastes campagnes d'écriture', he is swamped by a torrent of episodes. Arduous search amidst this mass of episodes may reveal the remnants of a story, but Carel does not assist the investigator anxious to discover what his poem is about, by adorning his title page with the name of Charles Martel, and then proceeding to show him in as bad a light as possible. Charles starts off by receiving Athin's envoys, who make a pretence of submission. He therefore believes that his ascendancy over the Saracens will enable him to outshine his half-brother, Childebrand. In fact he does nothing of the sort. Labouring under the disadvantage of having laid sacrilegious hands on relics in Orléans,[46] Charles becomes the constant victim of the ruses of the devil, against which God offers him no protection, since he is determined to punish Charles for his sacrilege. Having got his eponymous hero off to a bad start, Carel then turns his attention to Childebrand. Childebrand comes to the rescue of the beleaguered Christians.[47] Childebrand's long recital occupies Books vii to ix. To Childebrand, Charles Martel is finally compelled to relinquish the command after his appalling defeat at the hands of the Saracens.[48] Childebrand finally overcomes Athin in a duel, even though the Saracen uses an enchanted lance.[49] This threadbare story only makes its appearance occasionally amidst the accumulation of digressions.

If *Charles Martel* fails through lack of unity, its very variety might have given it different merits. Unfortunately, despite the far-flung settings of the various episodes, their themes are banal and their pattern repetitive. The overthrow of tyrants, the oppression of innocence, and the triumph of chivalry are illustrated over and over again. Love is the principal motive: little happens in the poem that is not inspired by it. The result is a compendium of romanesque themes, remarkable only for the fact that Carel manages to introduce nearly every one without betraying any hint of originality.

For all its faults *Charles Martel* has a few passages of interest. The description of the bull-fight may have been inspired by direct observation during the poet's stay in Spain.[50] A climax of horror is reached when Philo meditates which torture to use on Imundar.[51] Interesting details are supplied on the use of elephants for military purposes.[52] The account of Childebrand's single combat with an elephant is full of ingenuity if not of suspense.[53] If Carel lacked the genius of the sublime, he had a robust talent for the ridiculous. The giant Orambox addresses Childebrand thus:

> Mortel, qui que tu sois, admire tes destins
> Tu repais d'Orambox les nobles intestins . . .[54]

Such verses are the only consolation for the reader of *Charles Martel*.[55] Carel de Saint-Garde, and the other writers of romanesque epic, having exhausted themselves in the battle to entertain, could only lapse into unimaginable monotony.

NOTES TO CHAPTER XI

1. Jean de Boyssières (1555–*c.* 1585), from Montferrand, possibly studied in Italy. He gave up law to devote himself to poetry. He experimented with phonetic spelling. See Lachèvre, 'J. de Boyssières et J. Morel', *Bulletin du Bibliophile* (1926), pp. 298–310, 345–50 (detailed bibliography of Boyssières, pp. 300–5); Picot, *Français italianisants*, ii. 187–91; Beall, *Fortune du Tasse*, p. 17; Simpson, *Le Tasse*, p. 75; Cioranescu, *L'Arioste*, i. 190–2; Fleuret & Perceau, *Satires du XVIe*, i. 244–5.

2. *Croisade*, fol. 28^r (for 29^r, see below, note 5); fol. 34^v.

3. Fol. 37^v.

4. Sig. A3^v.

5. I have seen two copies dated 1584. One, in the Bibliothèque Mazarine, is dedicated to Monsieur Gobellin and published by Robert le Fizelier; the other, in the Bibliothèque de l'Arsenal, is dedicated to Monsieur Berterand and is published by Pierre Sevestre. The only differences between these editions are the title pages, and some spellings in the liminary verses. Both editions reproduce the same text even down to errors in foliation. From fol. 28 the sequence of numbers is 28, *28* [=29], 30, 3[1], 32, *25* [=33], 34, *27* [=35], *28* [=36], 37, *30* [=38], 39, *39* [=40]. The incorrect numbers are here italicized and the correct foliation may easily be restituted.

6. *Croisade*, 'Epître à Anne d'Este', A4^r.

7. See Beall, 'The first French imitation of Tasso's invocation', *MLN*, 53 (1938), 531–2, and *Fortune du Tasse*, p. 17.

8. Cioranescu, *L'Arioste*, i. 200. The first 24 *chants* were published in 1597, and another 22 *chants* were added in 1598.

9. James's *Lepanto* was published in *His Maiesties poeticall exercises at vacant houres* (Edinburgh, 1582). James makes it clear in his preface that, though the hero of the battle is Don John, he has no intention of praising 'a forraine Papist bastard' (sig. G4^r). James's poem, in 1068 lines, is followed, after a false title 'Edinburgh, 1591', by du Bartas's translation *La Lépanthe*. References to James's *Lepanto* are to the Edinburgh edition; references to du Bartas's *Lépanthe* are to the *Works of du Bartas*, ed. Holmes and others, iii. 506–26.

10. Pierre de Deimier was born at Avignon about 1580. He published the *Austriade* in 1601, the *Néréide* in 1605 and the *Académie de l'art poétique* in 1610. He frequented the circle of Marguerite de Valois, and fell under the influence of Malherbe. He probably died around 1615. On Deimier, see Colotte, *P. de Deimier, sa carrière provençale* (Marseilles, 1952), . . . *sa carrière à Paris* (Gap, 1953), and Gay, 'Sources of

the *Académie de l'Art Poétique'*, *PMLA*, 27 (1912), 398–418. On his epics, see Toinet, i. 1–6, ii, 105; Marni, *Allegory*, pp. 67, 109, 111; Beall, *Fortune du Tasse*, pp. 48–9, 80; Simpson, *Le Tasse*, p. 72; Cioranescu, *L'Arioste*, i. 195–7. The *Néréide* had a preface by A. Bosco.

11. Compare *Lépanthe*, 31–85 with *Austriade*, i. pp. 2–3.

12. *Lépanthe*, 80; *Austriade*, i, pp. 10–11.

13. e.g. Rumour spreading information about the Christian fleet (*Lépanthe*, 231–42; *Austriade*, p. 4); the exhortations of the two leaders (*Lépanthe*, 325–68; *Austriade*, pp. 14–21; the exchange of cannon fire (*Lépanthe*, 369 ff; *Austriade*, p. 21).

14. *Néréide*, i, pp. 4–5.

15. iv, pp. 145–7.

16. p. 242.

17. *Austriade*, i, p. 25.

18. Lines 414–16. In a marginal note du Bartas says: 'J'ay voulu icy imiter l'Onomatopoee de l'autheur.' James had written:

> The Fishes were astonisht all
>   To heare such hideous sound,
> The Azur Skie was dim'd with Smoke,
>   The dinne that did abound,
> Like thunder rearding rumling raue
>   With roares the highest Heauen,
> And pearst with pith the glistering vaults
>   Of all the planets seauen . . .
>   (lines 616–23)

19. *Néréide*, ii, p. 56.

20. In his *Art poétique* he was particularly harsh on plagiarists: 'C'est aussi en ceste façon qu'il faut s'approprier en la Poësie les inuentions & les sentences des estrangers; mais d'en vser ainsi enuers ceux de sa nation: c'est vn vice que les Muses ne sçauroyent assez mespriser & punir' (p. 214). Other examples from *La Lépanthe* and the *Néréide*: a speech before battle is given by du Bartas to Ascaigne de la Corne (lines 155–190) and by Deimier to Colonna (p. 20); Satan sows discord among the Christians (*Lépanthe*, 225–30; *Néréide*, p. 19); from du Bartas's debate between Love and Justice (lines 259–81) Deimier may have derived the idea of his debate between Saint Michael and the guardian angel of the Turks (pp. 33–4), and perhaps also the vision of Astrée, Carithée, and Philide (pp. 36–7); when God decides the issue of the battle by weighing the sins of the Christians against those of the Turks, Deimier places the emphasis on the Turks going down (p. 38), du Bartas on the Christians going up (lines 275–8).

21. Ennetières (1585–1650) was born and died at Tournai. He was a prolific writer much inclined to philosophy, moralizing, and mysticism. See Toinet, ii. 106–10; Marni, *Allegory*, p. 114; Edelman, *Attitudes*, pp. 206–7.

22. *Chevalier*, vii, p. 168. Elsewhere he proclaims his intentions in a marginal note: 'Exclamation pour le bon temps passé, & le pauure du iourd'huy' (p. 5). The marginal notes, many of the same moralizing tendency, are collected into an alphabetical index at the end.

23. Edited in 1634, a year after Ennetières's poem, by Jules Chifflet.

24. xiv, pp. 344–5.

25. Toinet, i. 229.

26. Duchesne, pp. 243–4.

27. Cioranescu, *L'Arioste*, ii. 49.

28. La Borderie, 'Le Poème de *Childebrand*', *R. Bretagne*, 7 (1865), 344.

29. Marni, *Allegory*, p. 187.

30. For a detailed account see Bergounioux, *Marc-Antoine Dominici*, pp. 455–511.

31. *Bibliothèque françoise*, xviii. 462.

32. xviii. 171.

33. ii. 94.

34. Two copies in the Bibliothèque de l'Arsenal bear this title: BL 15, 465 and BL 15, 466.

35. e.g. ARS: 8° BL 15, 468; BM: 1073. f. 43; BN: Rés. Ye. 2177.

36. *Attitudes*, p. 212.

37. *Dominici*, p. 443.

38. i. 226–8.

39. Those who claim that a 'Childebrand' exists tend to be inaccurate on other points. Lelong seems unaware that the later *Charles Martel* contains sixteen books and is much longer than earlier versions (ii. 94). Goujet is unaware of the very existence of the longer version (xviii. 169), and La Borderie, who had gone to much trouble to procure an edition, which he describes as a *Childebrand* without giving further information except that it contained only four books, claimed: 'les trois dernières parties du *Childebrand* [i.e. Books v–xvi] restèrent enfouies à jamais dans l'ombre du manuscrit.' ('Le Poème de *Childebrand*', p. 317). Prévost (*DBF*, vii. 1137) does not give a 'Childebrand'.

40. Another edition bears the date 1680 but is simply a reissue.

41. *Charles Martel* (1667), 'Au lecteur', but not in the 1679 edition.

42. An account of La Feuillade's embassy may be found in Morel-Fatio, *Recueil des instructions données aux ambassadeurs*, vol. 11, t.1, pp. 161–72.

43. Bergounioux, *Dominici*, p. 446.

44. See above, note 30.

45.   O le plaisant projet d'un Poëte ignorant,
             Qui de tant de Heros va choisir Childebrand!
             D'un seul nom quelquefois le son dur ou bizarre
             Rend un Poëme entier, ou burlesque ou barbare.
                                        (*Art poétique*, iii. 241–4)

Chronology is important here. In 1667 Carel's poem was called *Les Sarrazins chassez*; in 1668 it was changed to *Charles Martel*. Boileau's *Art poétique* was composed in 1672 and published in 1674. Those *Epîtres* in which Boileau mocks Carel were published after that date. Boileau's published criticisms cannot have affected Carel's choice of title, as suggested by some commentators on the above verses (e.g. Boudhors, p. 291).

46. i, pp. 7–8.

47. iv, p. 122.

48. xv, p. 187.

49. xvi, *chants* 8–10.

50. ii, *chant* 10.

51. vi, *chant* 7.

52. xiv, *chant* 8.

53. xvi, *chant* 5.

54. ix, p. 32.

55. Another poet, Pierre de Boissat (1603–62), seems to have been attracted to Charles Martel, but his epic has only survived in a mutilated state, and presents thorny problems. The volume inscribed *Petri de Boissat opuscula latina* (BN: Rés. Z. 348), which lacks title-page and any indication of date or printer, contains six books of a poem, entitled *Martellus, poëma heroicum*, on pp. 17–144 (second pagination), but the text starts abruptly in the middle of Book i. Each book is preceded by an 'Argumentum' and concludes with an 'Allegoria'. According to Pintard, 'Autour de *Cinna*', *RHLF*, 64 (1964), 380, the same six books are to be found in the Bibliothèque Municipale de Lyon (105. 503, in-4°), whilst MS. 314 of the Bibliothèque de la Ville de Vienne, (MS. H. 64 of the Archives de l'Hôpital de Vienne) contains twelve books and about 8,506 lines. I have been unable to compare these versions. BN: Rés. Z. 348, which has about 4,000 lines, seems to be a complete poem (apart from the lacuna at the beginning). Until the printed version has been compared in detail with the manuscripts it would be rash to speculate on the relationship between them. There is a summary of *Martellus* in Latreille, *De P. Boessatio*, p. 57.

XII

ANNALISTIC EPIC

FROM THE frivolities and fantasies of romanesque epic we turn to annalistic epic, in which the links between history and epic were closest. Annalistic epic usually amounted to little more than versification of the rise of a dynasty or a nation, though there were various means by which this theme was rendered more or less poetic. The device of prophecy, whereby in a poem like Ronsard's *Franciade* a line of ancestors or descendants could be described, was a strong link between heroic and annalistic epic. This device was employed in three of the annalistic poems which we shall presently consider. Other features of the epic tradition were also employed. The encyclopedic tendency could easily be combined with the exposition of a country's history. Palma Cayet went far in this direction. The portrait of a perfect prince, or his opposite, could be built up from the poet's judgements on a series of kings, just as it could from the portrayal of different characters in heroic epic. The workings of divine providence could also be demonstrated, not necessarily by supernatural machinery, but by the poet's own reflections on God's will at work in human affairs. To a large extent, however, there was little to distinguish annalistic epic from a prose chronicle except the verse.

Beaujeu: La Suisse

The first annalistic epic of which anything survives[1] was *La Suisse* published by Christophe de Beaujeu in 1589. The author was a soldier by profession, who incurred the displeasure of Henry III, spent ten years in exile, first in Italy, then, for the last three years, in Switzerland, where he became acquainted with the country whose history he celebrated in verse. On his return to France he published the poems which he had composed in exile. Amongst sonnets, elegies, and odes, appeared the first book of his epic, whose remaining eleven books were promised but never published.[2] The incompleteness of the work necessitates some speculation about Beaujeu's intentions.

In his 'Epître au lecteur' Beaujeu contradicted the popular prejudice that the Swiss were a race of cruel barbarous peasants addicted to drunkenness and ignorant of the arts. In his experience the Swiss nation was 'douce & gracieuse autant que nulle autre de la Chrestienté'. So that he should not waste time in exile, he tells us, 'ie mis la main à la plume, pour faire vne Suisse à l'imitation de la Franciade, que ce tant docte Ronsard a commencee . . .'[3] Clearly he desired to write epic, but the only surviving book of *La Suisse* is so different from the *Franciade*, and the indications given by Beaujeu of his intentions are so ambiguous, that it is hard to determine in what sense he believed himself to be imitating Ronsard. The question is not made easier by the poet's revelation that the first book is rather different from the others.[4]

The first book, in Alexandrines, contains scenes from early Swiss history, a description of the Emperor Albert Habsburg, and the conflict between William Tell and the imperial governor, Gessler.[5] Tell was naturally an important figure for anyone dealing with the origins of Swiss independence, though Beaujeu never actually refers to him by name. Did Beaujeu intend *La Suisse* to be a verse history of Switzerland, or William Tell to be his hero? The proposition of his epic does little to resolve the problem.[6] On the one hand Beaujeu's theme seems to be Swiss history: he wishes to sing of 'le loz de ma belle Suisse'. On the other hand he seems to attach special importance to 'le premier qui sema des Suisses la race' and 'le vieil Pere & les braues enfans'. But Tell could hardly be Beaujeu's hero as Francus was Ronsard's. He emphasizes Griseler's downfall rather than Tell's heroism. Tell indeed is depicted as a somewhat timid character, sustained only by God's help. Moreover Tell's career, including its climax, the murder of Griseler, are all recounted in a few pages, leaving little material for the rest of the poem, if he was to have been its hero. True, the possibility of recitals to fill in the earlier events such as the pact of Grüttli cannot be excluded, and, according to Beaujeu himself, there were battle scenes to come later.[7] These might have included the battle of Morgarten or other episodes in which Tell appeared as a warrior. But the small part he plays in the first book, together with Beaujeu's fondness for moralizing, which is so typical of the annalistic poets, makes it more probable that he intended to celebrate the whole of Swiss history in verse.[8]

The poem opens with the Muse recounting to Beaujeu in person how the first Swiss were defeated by the Romans and took refuge in the alpine valleys. After further discourse, she abandons the poet who finds himself in the path of a huge army led by Albert Habsburg, whose claim to the Swiss cantons provoked their desire for independence. The poet eventually ends up by a lake where a nymph summons three demons, one of whom narrates the story of Griseler and Tell. After the allegorical scenes of the earlier part of the book, Beaujeu resumes the pace of normal historical narrative, and recounts the incident of the apple as far as Tell's escape and Griseler's murder. The differences between Beaujeu and Ronsard are obvious. Ronsard never intrudes personally into the *Franciade*, nor does he use the nymphs, demons, and monsters to be found in Beaujeu's poem. Clearly Beaujeu's statement that he was imitating Ronsard must be treated with some caution. In the case of Guillot and Geuffrin, the claim to be imitating Ronsard could refer simply to the annalistic parts of Book iv of the *Franciade*. Beaujeu, however, has no list of kings, and his epic technique is everywhere quite dissimilar to Ronsard's. Yet he does introduce his historical narrative by means of a vision, even if in the first book the amplification of this framework rather overwhelms the history. The incompleteness of the poem obscures its plan. Had it been completed, the proportions would have been clearer, and it would probably be seen to resemble the poems of Geuffrin or Cayet more closely.

Because Beaujeu did not follow well-trodden paths, and because his style lacks the facile intelligibility of more prolific poets, *La Suisse* does not make easy reading. To follow the unexpected detours of the story demands unremitting attention, and on the basis of a single book, the significance of the allegories and the drift of his intentions is not always easy to grasp. Nevertheless his admiration for the Swiss and appreciation for their country are unmistakable.[9] The poem is a grateful tribute to the nation which sheltered the poet in exile, and if it is lacking in polish, Beaujeu was the first to admit that his military career had left him little time for learning.[10]

Palma Cayet: L'Heptaméron de la Navarride

This immense poem was, according to Cayet,[11] composed in Latin and French verse about the year 1584, and was presented to Henry IV after his victory at Coutras.[12] It was not published until 1602.[13] The title needs some explanation. *Heptaméron* means that the poem is divided into seven books, corresponding to seven days; each book is divided further into varying numbers of *chants. Navarride* is not an imitation of the title *Enéide,* but designates the nymph or sybil of Navarre. Thus the history of Navarre is presented as a prophecy in the mouth of the Navarride, and the title means 'the seven days of the sybil of Navarre'.

Cayet was a professor of oriental languages at the Collège de Navarre. The *Heptaméron* is what one might expect from such a man. From start to finish it is an instructive and edifying lecture on the history of Navarre, preceded by liminary verses not only in Latin and French, but also in Syriac, Arabic, Chaldaic, Hebrew, and Greek. The narrative is interrupted by lengthy digressions on the origins of peoples, places, and persons. The author pauses here and there to reply to imaginary objections. He imparts a vast amount of information, pervaded throughout by moral judgements.[14] There are few poetic fictions to render the lesson more palatable. The only reason why the work cannot be called prose is that the natural word order has been tortured into verses of ten syllables. At the beginning, Cayet invokes the Muse; at the end he explains that his prophetic framework is imitated from Virgil; in between he turns his back completely on poetic ornament, and devotes himself to a display of erudition. For all this the sybil of Navarre is responsible. She is the granddaughter of Noah and, by virtue of her gift of prophecy, she is numbered among the sybils. Leaving Palestine, she wanders over the world, noting the iniquities by which mankind has forfeited the happiness of the Golden Age. Finally she settles near the Pyrenees, knowing that one day the Messiah, Henry IV, will descend there.[15] But the inhabitants of this land, the Navarrese, are idolators; the Navarride entreats God to convert them, and so doing she is permitted to ascend to heaven where God grants her a vision of the creation of the world. The rest of the poem is, as the title proclaims: *Histoire entière du Royaume de Navarre, depuis le commencement du monde, tirée de l'Espagnol de Dom-Charles, Infant de Navarre.* The revelation of Cayet's source prompts the question: is the *Heptaméron* simply a verse translation of the medieval Spanish chronicle?[16] A comparison between the two shows that whilst Cayet generally followed Don Carlos quite closely, he drew on other sources besides the chronicle, and also used his own imagination.

To start with Don Carlos made no mention of a sybil. In his first chapter he enumerated very briefly the rulers of Spain down to the conversion of Pamplona, whereas Cayet started not only with the wanderings of the Navarride mentioned above, but also with the history of Abraham, Moses, and the kings of Israel, contained in the Old Testament, as well as a hundred other details, such as a description of heaven, the foundation of Rome, and the exploits of Hercules. It is true that Don Carlos also enriched his chronicle with extraneous matter, as he explained at the beginning of his third chapter: 'Bien será que agora digamos, por mas reinchir é decorar la presente crónica, quales é quantos emperadores é papas regnaron en la militante eglesia de Dios, despues de Sant Pedro, en Roma.'[17] His enrichment consisted of an enumeration of all the emperors and popes down to the ninth century, and in the next chapter he treated the kings of France down to Charlemagne in a similar fashion. Cayet's erudition, however, went far beyond this. It is the most substantial part of his poem, not merely confined to digressive chapters.

The conversion of Pamplona is the first event, described by both Cayet and Carlos, to provide a useful basis for comparison.[18] The most striking difference between the two is the incoherence of Cayet's narrative, a feature which remains constant throughout the *Heptaméron*. Here, as later in the case of the battle of Roncevaux,[19] anyone unacquainted with the original version would find it hard to reconstruct a plausible sequence of events. Instead of describing Saint Peter's arrival in Rome, and his preaching before the tyrant Nero, Cayet simply has Saint Peter residing 'en ville' and preaching the gospel to the Senate. Carlos had plainly said of Saint Peter 'ordenó los descipulos ir á predicar à diversas partes é regiones'. Cayet less plainly states, 'et envoya ses disciples,' without any mention of the reason. Similarly, whilst Carlos explained that the purpose

of Saint Cernin's mission was to convert the idolatrous Spanish,
Cayet contents himself with a gnomic utterance about mission-
aries receiving divine grace, and by omitting to mention the
Spaniards he fails to provide the link between Saint Cernin's
conversion of Toulouse and Honestus's errand to Navarre, as
the first step in Saint Cernin's conversion of that country. On
the other hand Saint Cernin's instructions to Honestus not to
shrink from martyrdom do not occur in the chronicle. When
Honestus arrives at Pamplona, Carlos has him make contact
only with three senators, Firmus, Fortunatus, and Faustinus.
Cayet rather improbably makes the whole people welcome
Honestus, and adds that when he departed to fetch Saint Cernin, Firmus's son Firminus was 'ordonné sacriste'. The progress
of conversion was not at all so rapid, according to Carlos. He
had implied, more plausibly, that Honestus's mission only interested the three senators, and that not until Saint Cernin's
arrival and preaching were they and the whole people converted.

Cayet's rude syntax, his battle with versification, the rapidity
of his narrative, his lapses into incoherence, are unchanging
features of the 24,000 lines of his poem. Don Carlos's simple
chronicle was amplified, expanded, and confused in the course
of Cayet's erratic progress from Moses to Henry IV, via the
Goths, Ostrogoths, and Visigoths, the kings of Navarre, Saint
Louis, Philip II, du Guesclin, Francis I, Charles V, Guise, Cal-
vin, Bèze, and Condé, to indicate only a few stepping stones in
the mighty torrent. The author had a strong encyclopedic bent,
and viewed history as an accumulation of facts rather than as a
series of connected events. He had no sense of the drama that
Beaujeu displayed in the tale of Tell, nor any clear moral lesson
such as in Geuffrin's *Franciade*. 'Neither history nor epic poetry
is the author's forte,' wrote Edelman;[20] one cannot disagree.
None the less the sheer bulk of the *Heptaméron de la Navarride*
permits an extensive appreciation of the use made by a would-
be poet of the historical material at his disposal.

Geuffrin: La Franciade

Geuffrin in his *Franciade* simply took up the story of Ronsard's *Franciade* where his predecessor had left off.[21] Yet, whilst
claiming to be carrying out Ronsard's plan,[22] his real object was

to describe all the kings of France for the benefit of Louis XIII. Fiction, which for Ronsard was the essential part of epic, was considered by Geuffrin to be a useless addition to the catalogue of Francus's historical descendants, and he casually dismisses the whole plot and conception of Ronsard's epic:

> Mais sans m'embarasser sur mille vaines fables,
> Qui voilent à nos yeux les choses veritables,
> Ie diray que le sort fauorisant Francus,
> Amenant auec luy ces Troyens inuaincus,
> Apres auoir couru de riuage en riuage,
> Au haure du Danube arresta son voyage.[23]

Geuffrin's real object was therefore the portrait of an ideal prince, drawn from the series of French kings between Pharamond and Louis XIII. This is exactly what he achieved in his *Franciade*.

His method of dealing with the successive dynasties was to narrate the events of each reign, and to add his own comments where a useful lesson for Louis XIII could be drawn.[24] The poem is not entirely impersonal; he laments the death of his own father during the troubles under Henry IV. At the beginning of the first three books, he gives his views on more general questions relating to politics and poetry. The poem is therefore less tedious than its full title suggests.[25] Geuffrin never delays too long on one point. Though his syntax can be involved, his language is sober. He vividly sketches some dramatic moments in French history. There is passion in his didactic digressions. His concept of a king's duty is clear and precise. Some flashes of acute observation occur in the similes.

The ideal prince is depicted in Geuffrin's comments on the events he is describing, or in direct recommendations to the king. Saint Louis on his deathbed gives a picture of the ideal monarch;[26] the opposite picture is conveyed in the accounts of rulers who were detested, notably Chilperic I,[27] Chilperic II,[28] and Henry III.[29] Other kings furnish examples of particular faults and failings. Of these the worst is a passion for women. For this Chilperic I stands condemned:

> Les grands de son Estat faschez de son ordure,
> Et de luy voir rauir dans le sein des parens
> Les plus rares beautez de quatorze à quinze ans,

> Volupté qui versoit vne douleur amere,
> Dans le coeur adueillé du pere & de la mere.[30]

Philip I is severely censured for his many adulterous affairs;[31] according to Geuffrin, John II returned to England to rejoin a mistress;[32] even Aumale and Henry IV do not escape condemnation.[33] The next worst evil is inattention to affairs of state. Naturally the *rois fainéants* provide the prime example of this.[34] Louis III is blamed for letting things slide;[35] John II for his half-hearted victories over the English;[36] Charles VI[37] and Henry III[38] epitomize the evils of feeble government:

> Vn Royaume à tous maux se voit abandonné,
> Quand par vn Prince mol il se voit gouuerné.[39]

Other kings are held up as models for their wise and vigorous conduct of affairs. Hugh Capet forestalls rival claimants to the throne by allowing his son to share in government.[40] Saint Louis merits special praise for speedily crushing rebellious barons:

> Conseil vrayment prudent vtil à vn grand Prince,
> De ne laisser former de ligue en sa prouince.[41]

Geuffrin greatly admires Louis XI for rejecting violence and achieving his ends by diplomacy and bribery,[42] but he will not tolerate a king who breaks his word.[43] Likewise the fate of the Comte de Saint-Pol is a warning to soldiers not to try to serve two masters.[44] If Louis XIII follows Geuffrin's advice, he will be rewarded by the affection of his subjects:

> Vertu digne d'vn Roy, sa richesse plus grande,
> De voir le peuple aysé sur lequel il commande,
> Vn Monarque chery est tousiours riche assez,
> Les coeurs sont des thresors par milliers amassez.[45]

Zealous subjects had showered their rulers with similar advice from time immemorial. If the rulers read such exhortations from end to end, then their patience and tolerance deserve credit.

On the subject of Church and religion, Geuffrin becomes most passionate. The mention of Saint Bernard in the reign of Louis VII moves him to a scathing comparison between the austere life of the saint and the corrupt clergy of his own day.[46]

His special targets for denunciation are lack of charity in religious orders, benefices granted to the unworthy, extravagant, avaricious, and pleasure-loving prelates. Not only the Church, but society as well need reform. Convinced of the effectiveness of moral legislation, Geuffrin begs Louis to take measures against adultery, blasphemy, and the Protestants.[47] Prejudiced against the reformers, Geuffrin is not blind to the abuses of the established Church. Distinctions of dogma do not interest him much; the quality of the clergy does. He paints a detailed picture of the ideal religious life, with study of the scriptures and literature as the main pursuit.[48] The distribution of benefices would encourage learning.[49] Doubtless he had himself in mind.

Geuffrin's *Franciade* is a commentary on history not a dramatization of it. In this he differed from Ronsard and Delaudun. Yet he also shared some of their preoccupations. Charles IX had after all insisted that every one of his ancestors should be included in the earlier *Franciade* so that he might learn from good and bad alike. Ronsard had accepted this commission; Geuffrin merely developed it to the exclusion of all the rest. Geuffrin also shared his moralizing bent with Cayet, but gave his poem greater coherence of form, and clarity of expression than the poet of Navarre. With his interest in the history of France, and his application of Christian morality to affairs of state, Geuffrin adumbrated two themes which were to be the hall-mark of the epics of the 1650s. 1623 was the date when Geuffrin could still look back to Ronsard's *Franciade* as a model and inspiration. It was also the date when Chapelain published his preface to the *Adone,* which laid the basis for a new approach to epic.

Bérigny: Abrégé de l'histoire de France

When the epics based on Tasso's example had run their course, all of them making abundant use of fictions, yet all being at least nominally unified by a single hero, one poet turned again to annalistic epic, and produced a bald account in Alexandrines of the kings of France from Pharamond to Louis XIV. Bérigny[50] made no attempt to set the kings within any framework, nor did he use the supernatural except occasionally to explain French successes or reverses as the result of divine providence. In his preface he excused his lack of talent and his provincial origins. He also apologized to any nobles whose families he might have slighted by omitting their ancestors, and proclaimed that he would willingly repeat, for their benefit, what he had accomplished in the *Abrégé* for the kings of France. In the absence of any other recorded works by Bérigny of this nature, it must be assumed that no one felt slighted, and no one called on his services.

In his preface Bérigny speaks of the *Abrégé* as a 'coup d'essay'. He might therefore still have been young in 1679; he may have been born as late as 1660. If so, he had known only peace within the frontiers of France. Unlike Geuffrin, who had grown up among the horrors of Condé's brutal campaigns in the south-west, and who had lost his father at the siege of Montauban, Bérigny would have known only the War of Devolution and the Dutch War, both of which were glorious wars of expansion. This doubtless coloured his presentation of the kings of France. He was full of admiration for the warlike ones, and had none of Geuffrin's understandable enthusiasm for those who made law and order their first concern. Recounting the career of Pharamond, Bérigny praised an aggressive foreign policy:

> Pendant qu'on est en guerre, & qu'on a des Rivaux,
> On ne songe qu'à vaincre, & qu'aux nobles travaux.
> Mais si-tost que la Paix a suspendu les armes,
> On méprise la gloire, elle n'a plus de charmes,
> Le plus fier Conquerant languit dans le repos,
> Et la tranquillité détruit tous les Heros.[51]

This would hardly have appealed to some one who had lived through the last decades of the sixteenth century. It was appropriate enough in the year after the Treaty of Nijmegen, which had shown to what pinnacle of prestige military success could raise the French king.

Apart from praise of war and admiration for conquerors, the picture of the ideal monarch that emerges from Bérigny's reflections is pale and conventional. The main events of each reign are narrated briefly, elegantly, and dispassionately. Pharamond is represented as the liberator of Gaul from decadent Roman rule; Clodion as a great but unfortunate monarch; Merovius as the king who established his capital in Paris, and repelled Attila with the help of Aëtius. Childeric's notorious effeminacy is noted, but without censure:

> Des Belles cependant il adore l'empire,
> Il n'est point de ruelle où son coeur ne soûpire.[52]

It would be tedious to follow Bérigny's leisurely progress through Merovingians, Carolingians, Capetians, Valois, and Bourbons. The pace becomes even more leisurely when Bérigny reaches Louis le Juste,[53] whilst the 'Abrégé des conquestes de Louis le Grand, depuis sa naissance jusques à la Paix de 1678' occupies nearly a sixth of the whole poem,[54] and returns to the tone of grovelling obsequiousness which characterizes the 'Epître au Roi' at the beginning of the work.

Toinet is very severe on Bérigny: 'Je ne puis en effet compter parmi ces épopées, dont d'ailleurs il ne porte pas le nom, le détestable ouvrage du sieur de Bérigny, indigeste compilation de neuf mille vers, dont pas un seul n'est lisible.'[55] This is hardly fair on what is a concise, intelligible, and often elegant summary of French history. The progress in style from Cayet's *Heptaméron* is enormous, though, as the language becomes more sober, so too does the poet efface himself. Bérigny displays none of Cayet's unbridled erudition, nor again does he display Geuffirin's passionate hatred of war and ecclesiastical degeneracy. Yet even the most impersonal narrative allows glimpses of the time at which it was written. The poet spoke cheerfully of war and aggression as befitted a man who had neither experienced the one nor been the victim of the other.

If historical epic can be described as the embellishment of history, then romanesque epic may be said to represent embellishment pushed to the extreme, whilst annalistic epic emphasized the historical content. Heroic epic lies somewhere in between. This division has served as a convenient framework within which to examine the surviving epics, but the analysis itself has shown that such a division is an oversimplification. Epic embraces all the features that have come to light during the course of the investigation. These features are like the fibres that make up a thread. Not every strand runs the whole length of the thread, but bound together they effect a continuity.

NOTES TO CHAPTER XII

1. For evidence of earlier annalistic epic, see above, pp. 14–15 nn. 20, 21, 23.

2. On Beaujeu (c. 1550–1636) see Goujet, xiii. 297–303; d'Amat, *DBF*, v. 1098; Cioranescu, *XVIe*. He is one of the interlocutors in d'Aubigné's *Avantures du Baron de Faeneste*, ed. Weber, pp. 772–830. *Le premier livre de la Suisse* is contained in *Les Amours de Christofle de Beaujeu* (1589), fol. 271–288. For an account of Switzerland, see Loritus, *Descriptio de situ Helvetiae* (1519) and Simler, *De republica Helvetiorum* (1576).

3. Fol. 271^r.

4. '. . . il y a douze liures, dont celuy-cy est le moindre en beauté, d'autant que toutes les belles batailles, & autres telles choses qui decorent vne Histoire, sont aux derniers liures . . . Pour doncques sonder le gué, i'ay mis en lumiere seulement ce premier liure, qui n'est pas de telle estoffe que les autres. . .' (fol. 272^r).

5. Or Griseler, as Beaujeu calls him.

6. Fol. 273^r.

7. See above, note 4.

8. This is Goujet's conjecture: 'Ce poëme fort honorable pour les Suisses étoit en douze chants dont les quatres derniers ne rouloient que sur les guerres où la nation Helvétique avoit acquis de la gloire' (xiii. 303).

9. Fol. 273^v.

10. Fol. 272^{r-v}.

11. Pierre Victor Palma Cayet (c. 1525–1610) was a prolific pamphleteer on religious matters (see Cioranescu, *XVIe*). He studied philosophy and theology at Paris, became a Calvinist, and served the Bourbons of Navarre. In 1595 he abjured Calvinism, was pensioned by Henry of Navarre, and made professor of oriental languages at the Collège de Navarre. See Toinet, i. 33–43; Marni, *Allegory*, pp. 109–110; Edelman, *Attitudes*, pp. 206, 224–5; Dubarat, 'Une curiosité bibliographique: L'Heptaméron de la Navarride', *Bull. Soc. Pau*, 46 (1923), 230–2; d'Amat, *DBF*, vii, 1515–16.

12. *Heptaméron*, 'Epître au Roy', sig.)(2^r–3^r.

13. It was reissued in 1618 with a different title-page.

14. This intention is advertised from the start. See the liminary stanza by Cayet, facing p. 1.

15.   Elle comprint qu'vn iour le Messias,
      Pour le salut descendroit icy bas.   (p. 9)

16. Written about 1454. For a modern edition see *Crónica de los reyes de Navarra, escrita por D. Cárlos príncipe de Viana*, ed. D. José Yanguas y Mirandola (Pamplona, 1843).

17. *Crónica*, ed. Yanguas y Mirandola, p. 13.

18. Compare *Crónica*, p. 7 with *Heptaméron*, pp. 46–7.

19. Compare *Crónica*, pp. 36–7 with *Heptaméron*, pp. 161–73.

20. *Attitudes*, p. 206.

21. Little is known of Geuffrin. See Goujet, xv. 126–7; Toinet, i. 106–9, ii. 86–90; Marni, *Allegory*, p. 110; Edelman, *Attitudes*, p. 205; Le Blanc, *Paraphrases*, pp. 142–3; Cioranescu, *XVIIe*.

22. *Franciade*, 'Aux lecteurs', a4ʳ.

23. *Franciade*, p. 3.

24. The contents of the books are as follows: i, Pharamond to Pepin; ii, Charlemagne to Louis V; iii, Hugh Capet to Louis VIII; iv, Louis IX to Charles IX; v, Henry III; vi, Henry IV and Louis XIII.

25. *La Franciade ou histoire générale des rois de France depuis Pharamond jusques à Louys le juste . . . mise en vers françois par le sieur Geuffrin.*

26. iv, pp. 81–2.

27. i, pp. 5–6.

28. i, p. 11.

29. v, pp. 130 ff.

30. i, pp. 5–6. The father of Clovis is called Chilperic by Geuffrin and Childeric by Bérigny. See below, p. 180 n. 52.

31. iii, pp. 58–9.

32. iii, p. 95. Geuffrin calls him 'Jean premier', not recognizing the posthumous son of Louis X.

33. vi, pp. 148–9, 151.

34. i, pp. 16–17.

35. ii, p. 39.

36. iv, p. 96.

37. iv, p. 103.

38. v, pp. 131, 137, 140.

39. iv, p. 103.

40. iii, p. 52.

41. iv, p. 75.

42. iv, p 112.

43. Like the Emperor Charles V (iv, p. 120).

44. iv, p. 110.

45. ii, p. 30.

46. iii, pp. 63 ff.

47. Philip II's laws against blasphemy were held up as the model (iii, p. 68).

48. iii, pp. 65–6.

49. iv, p. 79.

50. Godard de Bérigny is very obscure. See Toinet, i. 107–8; Cioranescu, *XVIIe*.

51. p. 4.

52. p. 21. See above, p. 179 n. 30.

53. pp. 319–35.

54. pp. 339–405.

55. i, pp. 107–8.

PART III
THE GENRE

XIII

EPIC THEMES

IN THE preceding chapters an attempt has been made to assess the historical epics as poems in their own right. This approach has for the most part been denied them previously, because their common features have attracted more attention. These common features, being necessarily repetitive, have done little to enhance the reputation of the epics, but they cannot be ignored. In the remaining three chapters I shall examine these common features, starting with the general themes of heroism, the supernatural, and love, proceeding to an analysis of different kinds of epic structure, and ending with a discussion of style. This will enable us to grasp the wider implications of the epic poets' attitudes to their common problems.

Heroism

If the epic poets had read Homer as often as they mentioned his name, they would have discovered that one type of heroism portrayed in the *Iliad* is the ability to kill large numbers of one's enemies. The slaughter is carried out with considerable excitement by the victorious warriors, but is described with curious detachment by the poet of the *Iliad*, who neither exults in nor sympathizes with the horrors which he recounts.[1] The French poets also relate scenes of repetitive slaughter, though to compose them they did not need the intimate acquaintance with the *Iliad* to which they laid claim. In Deimier's *Austriade*, Dragan-Bey kills Barthelemy, Doria kills Giaffer Aga-bey, Cardonne kills Baialban and Selim-Raix.[2] There are many battles in Le Moyne's *Saint Louis*; in one of them the deaths of Elmonerer, of Berenger, of Gorazel, and of Olgan are narrated in quick succession.[3] Such scenes could be multiplied indefinitely. But if they are compared to those to be found in the *Iliad*, a difference emerges. In the *Iliad* it is the chief characters, Diomedes, Achilles, or Menelaus, who carry out the killing. In the French poems such activities are not usually the chief glory of the hero or of the leading characters. Indeed it is often the leading characters who are the victims of slaughter rather than the perpetrators of it. The reader is more likely to remember the deaths of Athalaric and Radagaise, Alaric's captains,[4] or the death of Robert of Artois, Saint Louis's brother,[5] than any of the victims of Alaric or Saint Louis themselves. If the hero does kill, it is in a dignified single combat rather than in the indiscriminate slaughter of battle. Here then are signs of a discrepancy between the arrogant, brutal, bloodthirsty traditional heroes, and the characters to be found in the French epics.

The French poets were not the first to feel that the attributes of a successful warrior could be an embarrassment rather than an inspiration. Virgil had shown that a hero needed to be ruthless, and that hesitation was weakness; but that did not prevent compassion for an abandoned lover or a slaughtered opponent. The French poets, in addition, were usually Christians writing for a Christian audience about Christian heroes. This was a further curb on the full-blooded celebration of military prowess. It is true that Ronsard could have made Francus savage and bloodthirsty, and simply shrugged him off as a pagan barbarian. But when the hero was a revered figure like Clovis or Charlemagne, a saint like Louis IX or Joan of Arc, or a contemporary like Henry IV, such characteristics were unthinkable. Consequently, according to the personality of the hero and the setting of the poem, the poets experimented with ways of modifying the traditional qualities and ambitions of the hero.

Some poets, like Beaujeu, d'Urfé, or Schelandre, had served as soldiers and seen war at first hand. They were clearly interested in war, and felt that it was essential to epic, but even so, they showed either distaste for it or a desire to raise it to a higher level. D'Urfé's Beroldo gives Humbert a long lecture on the laws of chivalry and urges him to conduct himself according to its ideals.[6] The brutality of war was thus sublimated into a code of manners. Garnier found Henry IV's campaigns the ideal epic subject, but his hero's real grandeur lay in establishing peace. To less gifted poets these contradictions do not seem to have occurred. Deimier's poems are full of bloodshed, but he is as indifferent to it, as he is to holding his reader's attention. Ennetières spent much of his poem on the ritual observances of chivalry, but paid no attention to the horrific and unchivalrous behaviour of the armies during the suppression of the revolt of

Ghent. The annalistic poets, by means of advice and precept, painted a clearer picture. Geuffrin's message was the same as that of the more thoughtful heroic poets. He strongly advocated clemency and magnanimity in the ideal ruler, and the subordination of war and aggression to peace and justice.

All these examples show some disquiet concerning the true nature of heroism. Gradually the hero's role was transformed. His participation in war was played down. Milder virtues were brought to the fore. If the objectives of the hero's mission were emphasized, the means need not be discussed. This was a convenient device by which the poet could lay responsibility for war and slaughter at God's door. Battles were not a way to glory for the Christian hero, they were a regrettable part of a grander design. This is why Christian heroes were so careful to say prayers of thanksgiving after the enemy had been defeated:

> C'est à Dieu, dit le Roy, qu'en est dû tout l'honneur;
> Ses graces sont pour nous des sources de bon-heur . . .[7]

Usually they forbade sack and pillage after their victory:

> Or ce clement Vainqueur n'aymant que cette gloire,
> Pour n'ensanglanter pas son illustre Victoire,
> Satisfait du Laurier qu'il cherche en combatant
> Empesche le pillage, & sauve l'Habitant.[8]

Thus any taint involved in the sad necessity of war was washed away by complete submission to God's will, and the hero's way to glory lay in the exercise of Christian virtues. This new code of conduct is vividly illustrated in *Alaric, Saint Louis*, and *Clovis*. In each case the hero is given a specifically Christian task: the overthrow of pagan Rome, the crusade against Egypt, and the establishment of Christianity in France. Even when a hero, like Alaric, was not a Christian, he could be given a Christian mission. These pious objectives obviously helped to justify any atrocities that might have to be committed, and any taint of savagery or brutality was kept well away from the gallant Alaric, the virtuous Saint Louis, or the amorous Clovis.

Although this change of emphasis mitigated the warlike aspects of these Christian heroes, they remained none the less successful and victorious warriors. The most thought-provoking question was the exact nature of heroism when the hero suffered defeat and imprisonment, like Louis IX, or trial and martyrdom, like Joan of Arc. The choice of unfortunate heroes really did introduce a new element into epic. The case of Saint Louis, however, admitted of an easy solution. The king's captivity was given a typically Christian slant, and became a trial from which the hero would finally emerge triumphant. No such solution was possible for Chapelain. Joan's death could not be ignored, nor the fact that she was not a man and not even of noble birth. How Chapelain replied to these objections, and how he made Joan's martyrdom the pivot of French salvation has been demonstrated above.[9] What emerges from comparing Chapelain's treatment of his heroine with that of other poets, is that instead of whitewashing the traditional hero, or tampering with history to make it fit a preconceived notion of heroism, he tried to extract a new concept of heroism from what at first sight appeared a very unheroic situation. Joan's heroism consisted not in conforming to a set of precepts, but in submitting to the destiny which God had ordained for her and for France. Courtin also rejected the traditional hero. His penitent Charlemagne was no longer the victorious hero of the earlier poems, but the victim of misfortune after misfortune. His heroism lay not in pride but in submission. His victories were not over others but over himself.

The celebration of war always poses a problem. The problem is particularly acute in a Christian context. The epic poets tried to reconcile two sets of values that were fundamentally opposed. The Christian ethic began by undermining the traditional heroic virtues and ended by triumphing over them. If one compares Courtin's meek and docile Charlemagne with the heroes of the *Iliad* or the *Roland*, the contrast is striking. Heroism in the sixteenth- and seventeenth-century epics was not portrayed through the lifeless repetition of outmoded patterns, but was a concept sufficiently flexible to be adapted to the changing values of the times.

The supernatural

On the representation of the supernatural[10] in the epic Christianity wrought the same changes as it had on the concept of heroism. The conflict here was between the gods of Olympus to be found in the epics of Antiquity, and the supernatural

figures associated with the Christian religion. Since the epic
hero was not just any man, but a man in whose destiny the
gods were interested, it was part of the epic poet's task to show
the relationship between the natural and the supernatural
worlds. But how was the supernatural to be portrayed? In the
Latin epics of the early sixteenth century, the Christian supernatural was at work, but only in so far as the characters were
Christian or the theme religious. The supernatural was evoked
in these poems largely by means of prayers, or the occasional
appearance of Christian mythology, such as the infernal council in Pillard's *Rusticiad*.[11] The full apparatus of pagan mythological machinery did not make its appearance until the *Franciade*, in which Ronsard, faithful to his ancient models, made
Jupiter, Juno, Mars, Mercury, Neptune, Venus, Cupid, Cybele,
and Iris, together with allegorical personifications such as
Fama, Aquilo, or Invidia, important characters in his epic.
These pagan representations of the supernatural were accepted
by his continuator Claude Garnier, who made numerous references to their activities in Ronsard's first four books, but did
not actually introduce them as characters in his own Book v.
The only other poets to employ unadulterated pagan mythology
were Delaudun and Schelandre. The former made use of the
same deities as Ronsard, but deliberately reversed their loyalties, so as to distinguish his epic from the first *Franciade*.[12] The
abortive brevity of Schelandre's poem meant that only two
Olympians made their appearance—Neptune[13] and Mars.[14] But
Cupid and Proteus, and an assortment of Nereids and Tritons,
were much in evidence. There is no undisguised case of the
infiltration of Christian mythology, but one sign that Schlandre
did not feel polytheism to be entirely suitable for French epic
was his subjection of all these deities to an omnipotent force
controlling the destinies of men and gods alike.[15]

It is not surprising that the poets should have felt some mis-
giving about portraying the supernatural by means of pagan
mythology. If convincing, this poetic device was unacceptable
from a religious point of view. With less gifted poets these mis-
givings manifested themselves through inconsistencies. They
did not have the courage to throw the ancient traditions over-
board, but their own religious beliefs appeared so patently beneath the surface, that the pagan mythology was convincing

only as a disguise for the Christian supernatural. Guillot's Jupiter presided rather curiously over the destinies of Christian kings.[16] Ennetières made a personification of Flanders descend to the underworld to consult Megaera about preparing the rebellion of Ghent,[17] even though in the same poem the hero had made a vow of chastity to Notre-Dame de Montserrat.[18] This use of pagan mythology as a kind of Christian symbolism, side by side with references to obviously Christian practices, may be described as an adulterated form of the pagan supernatural.

The remedy for these inconsistencies was clearly to substitute Christian mythology for pagan mythology. Just as the Romans had identified their own gods with those of the Greeks, so the Christian poets could identify their mythological figures with those of the ancients. There was no difficulty in equating God with Jupiter and surrounding him with the Virgin, angels, and saints. The picture could be varied by depicting God the Son rather than God the Father, or by including personifications of Justice, Peace, and Clemency among the inhabitants of heaven. Satan and his minions were clearly the appropriate substitutes for those pagan deities who opposed the hero. Once these substitutions had been made, the poets had on their hands not only a new set of characters, but also a new framework which completely changed the relationships between the natural and the supernatural. The gods of Olympus had been colleagues whose internal rivalries dictated whether they should support the hero or not. God and Satan, however, were irreconcilably opposed; they operated from different dimensions, and their activities immediately evoked a moral judgement. Whereas the party which Jupiter or Neptune favoured or opposed did not thereby become good or bad, it is clear that with the Christian supernatural whoever God favoured was automatically good and whoever Satan favoured was automatically bad. If God tampered with the laws of nature the results were hailed as miracles. If Satan did the same, the effects were condemned as magic.[19] This then was the basis of Christian supernatural. It is important to remember that it came into being as a substitute for pagan mythology. This explains why, just as the last poets to use the pagan supernatural were embarrassed by its unorthodox implications, so the first poets to attempt the

Christian supernatural did not immediately free themselves from the overpowering influence of the ancient pagan tradition.

The earlier examples of the Christian supernatural were therefore contaminated with vestiges of pagan mythology. In both of Garnier's epics God set the plot in motion: in the *Henriade* by sending Saint Michael to protect Henry IV, in the *Loyssée* by sending a vision to Louis IX. But the *Henriade* turns out to have a distinctly polytheistic atmosphere—Jupiter tips the scales of battle,[20] Mars and Minerva participate in the fighting,[21] and the nymph Hydromonde personifies the river Eure.[22] The *Loyssée* is rather more consistent. God directs the action single-handed and no Olympians appear; but there are still Tritons and Nereids[23] around, as well as plenty of mythological periphrasis.[24] The same inconsistencies can be found in Deimier's two poems. In both *Austriade* and *Néréide* God sends Saint Michael to ensure a Christian victory,[25] but in the earlier poem Apollo is introduced marvelling at the glittering sea[26] and Nereids are startled by cannon-balls.[27] In the *Néréide* intrusive Olympians are even more in evidence: Mars stirs up the French with an inflammatory speech,[28] Jupiter watches the battle, and Neptune takes fright thinking that Jupiter is making war on him.[29] The supernatural element in *La Suisse* is also a strange mixture, though of a different sort. Beaujeu introduces both himself and the Muse as characters in his poem, and employs abundant allegories. At the same time he admitted the hand of God in the episode of Tell.[30] The beginnings of the Christian supernatural in the late sixteenth century were therefore hesitant and inconsistent.

The unadulterated form of the Christian supernatural was used in two ways. Sometimes God, Satan, the Virgin, Saint Michael, and other figures of Christian mythology were introduced as well-defined characters, talking and debating like human beings. This may be called a 'mechanical' use of the supernatural. A slightly different approach was a wholehearted acceptance of the supernatural, which resulted in hardly any event in the poem happening without divine or diabolical inspiration. This use of the supernatural may be called 'pervasive'. The mechanical system could usually be explained rationally, as an extension of human psychology. The pervasive system constantly interrupted natural laws and made no distinction between miracles and facts. Although the prevailing attitude to the supernatural in the late sixteenth century was towards a mixture of pagan and Christian, Delbene and d'Urfé used an unadulterated form of Christian supernatural. Only in the 1650s did the Christian supernatural triumph over the mixed forms. The chief exponents of the mechanical manipulation of Christian mythology were Chapelain and Scudéry. Whenever they introduced the supernatural, they used some device to show that the natural order was being suspended. The most frequent devices were scenes in heaven or hell, or the apparition of angels. These devices were of course also used by those who favoured the pervasive supernatural,[31] but poets like Desmarets or Le Moyne took it so much for granted that God inspired good actions and Satan evil ones, that they did not usually go to the lengths of scenes in heaven or hell to confirm it. This trend was continued by Le Laboureur, Carel, and Courtin; the only difference was that in the later poems the intervention of the supernatural was accepted without exciting much enthusiasm. Le Laboureur was more interested in love, and Carel in romance. Only in Courtin's *Charlemagne pénitent* was the Christian supernatural employed with the same religious zeal as in the earlier epics, and in this poem God and Satan became the major characters.

One may thus distinguish five approaches to the supernatural: unadulterated pagan mythology, pagan mythology bearing a Christian interpretation, Christian mythology mixed with traces of paganism, pure Christian mythology working mechanically, and the Christian supernatural pervading the whole poem. Ronsard was the main exponent of the first kind. His predecessors and most of his successors used the mixed kinds. After 1650 only the pure Christian supernatural was used. Desmarets alone succeeded in reconciling pagan and Christian mythology in a manner that was both artistically and logically satisfying.[32] As is the case of heroism, the concept of the supernatural underwent profound changes. Just as the traditional concepts of heroism were undermined and replaced by Christian values, so too the traditional ways of representing the interaction of the natural and supernatural were infiltrated and taken over by Christian mythology.

It is against this background that the question of allegory in epic must be considered. Marni has given a convincing account of allegory in the seventeenth century epic, and I accept his conclusions.[33] Naturally the chronological limits of his survey exclude the epics of the sixteenth century, though he does allude briefly to Ronsard, du Bartas, and d'Aubigné. According to Marni, the essence of allegory is a double meaning intended by the author: 'It is the author who must give a twofold meaning to his words, one literal and the other figurative, as it is, also, upon him that falls the responsibility of making the figurative meaning so transparent that the reader does not fail to perceive it almost unconsciously.'[34] Scudéry, Chapelain, and also the writers of biblical epic, Saint-Amant and Coras, left clear indications that they had composed their poems with both figurative and literal meanings, but their sincerity was questioned by Duchesne and other critics: 'aucune de ces chimères n'a réellement présidé au travail de ces écrivains . . . .'[35] Marni, however, asked pertinently: 'Were such critics as La Harpe, Guizot, Duchesne, and Reumann justified in discrediting the good faith of the written statements of Saint-Amant, Scudéry, Chapelain and Coras?'[36] He concluded that they were not justified, and demonstrated how much real allegory there was in the heroic poems of the seventeenth century.

Marni shows how strong were the allegorical tendencies in the early seventeenth century, arising from the combination of the widespread belief that literature should edify, and from the influence of critics who had already interpreted the allegories, real and imaginary, in the ancient and Italian epics. He then analyses all the allegories in the seventeenth-century epics, and shows how Ronsard's successors generally followed Ronsard's practice in including allegorical personifications, but stopped short of the wholesale allegory that characterized later poems. He then discusses in detail the allegories of *Alaric* and *La Pucelle*, and offers a plausible explanation why *Saint Louis* and *Clovis* were not allegorical: 'A poem [*Saint Louis*] inspired by such direct missionary spirit would not need an allegorical meaning to justify its existence before the eyes of the world, or to teach its moral. . . . Desmarets considered the subject of the *Clovis* of sufficient moral and religious importance as it

was.'[37] This distinction between *Alaric* and *La Pucelle* on the
one hand, and *Saint Louis* and *Clovis* on the other, has already
been noticed in the discussion of the mechanical *merveilleux* of
the former and the pervasive *merveilleux* of the latter.[38]
Marni's conclusions thus bear out a distinction that is more
easily felt than proved. He then deals with all the epics of the
latter part of the seventeenth century, and gives due weight to
the originality of Courtin's *Charlemagne pénitent.*

It is clear that the widespread acceptance of allegory made
it an important factor in interpreting the poet's representations
of the supernatural. There is no violation of plausibility in
seeking in allegory the explanation of certain vestiges of pagan
mythology which might otherwise appear perverse or in conflict with the poets' religious beliefs.[39] If Deimier says that
Apollo watched the glittering array of armour, it is only another way of saying that the polished steel reflected the sun.
If Guillot described Mars and Minerva assisting at Condé's
birth, he was only flattering the martial prowess and sagacity of
his patron. But this same process, commonplace enough in the
literature of the time, could also be applied to the Christian
supernatural. The constant and sometimes irritating intervention of angels in *La Pucelle* is better seen, not as an epic device
worked to death, but as the expression of Chapelain's belief
that God constantly guided the destinies of the characters, and
moulded the course of French history, during the Hundred
Years' War.

We must distinguish between the allegorical significance attached
to a whole work and the occasional appearance of abstractions in
human form. In the first we pass from the human to the superhuman, in the second the order is reversed – both are facets of the
desire to join heaven and earth.[40]

Allegory was therefore an integral part of the *merveilleux.*

The epic world was thus based on an elaborate hierarchy of
relationships between the natural and supernatural orders. Had
pagan mythology been a useless poetic device it could have
been discarded along with its unorthodox implications. As it
was, the epic poets of the seventeenth century seized eagerly
upon these implications, and did their best to translate them
into the more acceptable apparatus of Christian mythology.

Their attempts may not always have been rewarding by literary standards, but the fact that they grappled so energetically with the problem showed that the epic poet could not turn his back upon the mysteries of the universe.

Love

Christianity, which had such a profound effect on transforming the heroic ideal and the concept of the supernatural, also influenced the depiction of love in the epic, though, as love was a theme common to other genres, these changes were not confined to epic. As an adornment love was almost indispensible. Though absent from the Latin epics of the early sixteenth century, it played a large part even in Ronsard's abortive *Franciade*, and thereafter made steady progress, so that little would be left of the epics published after 1650 if the love episodes were removed. The tradition of courtly love, the speculations of the Neoplatonists, and Christian morality distinguished two kinds of love: licit and illicit, ennobling and degrading, lawful and lustful. All these nuances are found in the epics. The basic Christian distinction was between love within marriage and love outside marriage. The scope for the portrayal in epic of love within marriage was naturally limited. Only Delaudun, who gave his poem a domestic flavour, depicted legitimate sex. The occasion was the wedding night of Clogio and Mantis:

> . . . Mantis fust mise au giste,
> Clogion sans delay s'y mit à la poursuitte.
> L'on tire les rideaux, chacun se tire à part,
> Bref ils ne sont qu'eux deux comme en vn lieu d'escart,
> Ils ne craignent plus rien: plusieurs fois ils se baisent,
> Se chatouillent tous deux, & enfin se rebaisent:
> Ils ont quelques propos, puis d'vn & d'autre bras
> S'entre-lassent ensemble, & prennent leurs esbats,
> Mais auant que leurs yeux soient charmés par le somme
> Ce mariage sainct se faict, & se consomme.[41]

This, together with the occasional devoted wife, was the full extent of the epic portrayal of married life. It was much more usual for the heroes to meet women to whom they were not married. In these cases any kind of physical attraction was condemned, so much so that the women were often replaced by a misleading vision, or a symbol of lust, to emphasize diabolical inspiration.[42] Alternatively the reverse procedure was employed. Chapelain made Charles VII fall under the spell of a real woman, Agnès Sorel, but explained in his preface that this was an allegory of man's concupiscence. Thus physical attraction between man and woman outside marriage was invariably represented as an obstacle to be overcome. The same theme appeared in the annalistic poems, when poets condemned kings who neglected affairs of state for their mistresses.[43]

But there was a traditional method for turning aside Christian disapproval of love outside marriage. Love, without sex, could be sublimated into an ennobling passion. The desire for a woman could be the inspiration for noble deeds. This was the justification for Alaric's pursuit of Amalasonthe, once he had realized the degrading nature of physical attraction, represented by the enchanted island. This was the justification for Clovis's pursuit of Clotilde, for it led him to Christianity. The concept was carried to the very brink of ridicule in Desmarets's brigade of lovers.[44] Love as an embellishment was thus invariably of a Platonic or courtly nature.

Love episodes were usually presented in human situations, with amorous recriminations, meditations, and debates, but the cumbrous apparatus of Cupid and his darts, functioning as a representation of the supernatural, made occasional appearances.[45] As love was only admitted into epic as an entertaining fiction, one wonders exactly what aspects of it were intended to appeal to the reader. It could hardly have been the predictable machinations of Cupid, or the symbolism of Venus' girdle; nor would a reader who turned to epic for erotic titillation find the slightest satisfaction. It was doubtless the rhetorical developments of the love affairs, the monologues of distracted lovers or their stormy interviews, which provided the entertainment. The lover who pursued a legitimate passion provided the poet with an outlet for sentimentality, whilst the hero who tried to escape from an unwholesome and illicit attachment generated a certain amount of drama and excitement, when the rejected mistress sought to retain his affections. Sometimes the love episode, instead of providing the opportunity for rhetoric, took the shape of a narrative, and the ruses of a lover to gain access to his mistress could add a note of comedy. The two Roman nobles in *Alaric* who contended for the hand of Probé tried to contact her in various disguises. Valère donned the garb of a slave, approached Probé, and confessed his love. A woman who overheard the conversation interrupted. She raised her veil and Tiburse revealed himself in a woman's disguise. Probé indignantly abandoned both of them, and they reproached each other sheepishly:

> Quoy Valère, dit-il, luy que l'on croit si brave,
> A-t-il comme l'habit, pris le coeur d'un Esclave?
> Quoy Tiburse (luy dis-je, emporté de despit)
> Est-il devenu Femme en empruntant l'habit?[46]

Unlike heroism, which was thoughtfully developed, unlike the supernatural which was inexhaustible in its implications, love in the epic remained static and sentimental, justified by the mechanical repetition of courtly or platonic conventions. Corneille's heroes and the speculations of philosophers were echoed in the epic; Racine's lovers were not.

1. See *Iliad*, Book v, for example.

2. i, pp. 41–7.

3. vii, pp. 199–203.

4. *Alaric*, vii, pp. 201–2, 212–3.

5. *Saint Louis*, xiv, p. 441.

6. *Savoysiade*, i, fol. 75ʳ.

7. *Saint Louis*, iii, p. 91.

8. *Alaric*, vii, p. 204.

9. See above, pp. 145–6.

10. On this subject, see especially Delaporte, *Du Merveilleux*, pp. 246–78, 357–72; Buffum, *Les Tragiques*, pp. 55–65; and in general Williams, *The Merveilleux* (Paris, 1925).

11. At the beginning of Books i and iii, and at the end of Book iv.

12. He also gave Apollo a much more important part (v, p. 174) and introduced Vulcan (iv, p. 146).

13. i, pp. 39–44, 54–5.

14. ii, pp. 106 ff.

15. Schelandre apologized for using 'les Dieux & les fables des Payens', but justified the practice on two grounds: (i) they contribute to the 'majesté des poëmes anciens, qui sont enrichis & comme animés de ces plaisantes inuentions, les vrays nerfs de la poësie'; (ii) the gods portrayed (Neptune, Mars, Proteus) are to be considered as 'mauuais Demons, lesquels trauersent la vie des amis du ciel: mais le Tout-puissant (qui allegoriquement est figuré par les Parques, & par vn Iupiter souuerain) rompt & dissipe d'vn seul souffle toutes les machinations de ces ennemis de la vertu' ('Argument', p. 34). There is some inconsistency, because in the poem he introduces 'Dyname, Allegorie de la Toute-puissance' (p. 61), but his general meaning is clear.

16. *Franciade* 6, B3ᵛ, and Dlᵛ.

17. *Chevalier*, xii, pp. 287–9.

18. vii, p. 185. Cf. *Savoysiade*, i, fol. 73ʳ, for a similar prayer.

19. It is curious that whilst the hero was usually in direct contact with God, his enemies generally relied on the intercession of a magician to draw on Satan's resources. Magicians were of much greater importance as Satan's ministers than priests and bishops as God's. This was doubtless partly due to the popularity of Tasso's Ismeno, but it may also reflect a certain lack of confidence in priestly communication with the Almighty.

20. xiv, p. 185.

21. xiii, p. 180.

22. xiv, pp. 189–91.

23. i, p. 293.

24. e.g. Doris, Amphitrite (i, p. 286).

25. *Austriade*, i, pp. 10–11; *Néréide*, i, pp. 31–2.

26. i, p. 24.

27. i, p. 26.

28. i, pp. 1–4.

29. ii, p. 61.

30. Fol. 283^v–285^v.

31. e.g. St. Louis's visit to heaven (*Saint Louis*, Book viii) and Clotilde's visit (*Clovis*, iv, pp. 57–68).

32. By depicting conversion from paganism to Christianity as a conflict between the gods on both sides (*Clovis*, xv, pp. 251 ff).

33. *Allegory in the French heroic poem of the seventeeth century* (Princeton, 1936).

34. *Allegory*, p. 9.

35. Duchesne, p. 270, n. 3.

36. *Allegory*, p. 190.

37. pp. 166, 167.

38. See above p. 188.

39. This could be used on a wider scale. In the preface to Conti's *Mythologie*, a popular mythological handbook, the compiler explains that the fables of Antiquity need explanation, since they were used as a vehicle for philosophy: '. . . attendu que tous les enseignemens & preceptes de Philosophie estoyent pour-lors contenus sous icelles Fables, & que peu deuant les temps d'Aristote, de Platon & autres leurs deuanciers, l'on n'enseignoit pas la Philosophie ouuertement, ains en termes obscurs sous certaines enuelopes & couuertures.' (Baudouin's translation, p. 1.)

40. Sayce, p. 32.

41. *Franciade*, vi, p. 229.

42. e.g. the false Amalasonthe and her island (*Alaric*, iii, pp. 77 ff.) or the enchanted palace in Le Laboureur's *Charlemagne*, ii, pp. 37 ff. (1664), pp. 35 ff. (1666).

43. e.g. Childeric I.

44. *Clovis*, iii, p. 45.

45. e.g. Ronsard, *Franciade*, ii. 744–852.

46. *Alaric*, vii, p. 224.

XIV

EPIC STRUCTURE

THE themes discussed in the preceding chapter can be found in other genres and were not, of course, peculiar to epic. What gives epic its particular identity is its structure, and, to a lesser extent, its style. The epics have so far been classified as annalistic, heroic, and romanesque. These divisions refer to the poets' basic approach to their material, and it has been stressed that the divisions overlap. In analysing the manner in which poets constructed their poems, I propose to consider four kinds of epic structure: historical, Virgilian, Iliadic, and episodic. These divisions are rather more clear-cut than the division into annalistic, heroic, and romanesque epic, since they refer to the fashion in which the poets arranged the elements which made up their poems; but, like all aids to analysis, they must not be considered as a final description. The relationships between types of epic poem and types of epic structure are as follows: annalistic epic is necessarily historical in structure; heroic epic may be constructed on any of the four patterns mentioned above; romanesque epic is necessarily episodic in structure.

Historical structure

What then is the difference between annalistic and heroic epic with a historical structure? The essence of historical structure is that the narrative follows the sequence of historical events. In annalistic epic, the events are spread over a long period of time, with occasional embellishments in the shape of moralizing digressions or poetic fictions. A heroic epic constructed on these lines differs in having a shorter time-span, usually limited to the hero's conduct of a single campaign, and in allowing greater freedom for fictitious embellishment. The main examples of heroic epic with historical structure are Blarru's *Nanceid*, Pillard's *Rusticiad*, and Garnier's *Henriade*. Garnier's poem, which seems to be an odd exception to the general trend in French epic in the late sixteenth century, is better understood when compared with the Latin epics of the earlier part of the century. It is their historical structure which makes them comparable. In each of the three poems, the hero is confronted with a war—either invasion, revolt, or civil discord—which he fights and wins. In each case the epics start with a crisis and move chronologically towards its solution. The circumstances differ for each hero; so too does the poet's interpretation and embellishment of events; but the underlying structure is the same.

The bringing together of poems with a common structure is a convenient way of throwing differences of embellishment and interpretation into sharper relief. Blarru adopts the unusual procedure of making his villain more prominent than his hero. Instead of placing the emphasis on the good prince in his depiction of René of Lorraine, he portrays the decline and fall of a bad prince in the shape of Charles of Burgundy. Charles's failings are highlighted at every turn—his restless passion for self-aggrandisement, his disregard for the laws of chivalry, his oppresive rule over the territory he has conquered. When Blarru departs from the description of historical events, he introduces moralizing digression rather than poetic fictions. The *Nanceid* is clearly a moral poem; the structure serves the purpose of emphasizing Charles's progress from aggression to his ignominious end in a small pond. The structure of the *Rusticiad*, though also chronological, is less coherent. Again the story is one of an aggressor meeting his downfall, but this time the aggressors are Lutheran peasants, and the focus of attention is thus dissipated. Amongst the embellishments, the supernatural makes its appearance: the speeches are not moralizing digressions but prayers, and the leaders of the revolt can only talk of their dealings with the devil. Pillard's poem is therefore primarily religious in intent. His interpretation of history is narrowly orthodox, and its lack of subtlety likely to appeal only to his own partisans. Garnier, whose narrative follows Henry IV's military career in pursuit of his throne, uses speeches to justify Henry's claim to the throne and digressions to castigate his opponents. The *Henriade* is therefore basically a political poem. The historical structure could thus serve as a vehicle for moral, religious, and political ends.

Of the different types of epic structure, clearly historical structure had more in common with history than the other types. There was some danger of history and epic being confused. In order to avoid this, the epic poet had to do what the practitioner of any genre has to do in order to establish his own identity, namely he emphasizes what is most characteristic of his genre. This led to the elaboration of poetic fictions, arranged in a recognizable sequence, imposed on the historical narrative. We shall look at some examples.

Virgilian structure

The Storm–Shipwreck–Recital structure was used by Ronsard, Delbene, Schelandre, and d'Urfé to produce quite a different kind of epic from those which were based on the historical structure outlined above. This structure was derived from Books i to iii of the *Aeneid*, in which Aeneas is driven by a storm to Carthage, and there relates his adventures to Dido. To demonstrate the manner in which poets imposed this structure on their historical material, there follows a series of questions about their narratives. The questions are of the same nature as those which critics raised when discussing the plausibility of the epics, and to which the poets themselves replied when defending themselves. They represent an attempt to analyse the structure of the epics in terms that would have been familiar to the poets who composed them.

Why is the hero at sea?

Aeneid   Aeneas sails from Sicily to seek Latium.

Franciade   Francus is urged by divine messenger to leave Epirus and found Paris.

Amédéide   Amadeus sails to rescue John Paleologus, who has been deposed by Andronicus.

Savoysiade   God chooses Beroldo to rescue Boson of Burgundy. Beroldo sails from Barcelona.

Stuartide   Fleance believes his father is in Scotland and sails from the island of the Parcae to find him.

The common feature here is the journey by sea, the necessary setting for storm and shipwreck. For Delbene and d'Urfé there was some kind of historical justification for the sea journey: it was the natural way for Amadeus or Beroldo to reach their destinations. Neither Ronsard nor Schelandre was obliged to introduce a sea journey, except in so far as each chose it as a poetic fiction.

Why is the hero threatened?

Aeneid Juno has heard that Trojans will destroy her beloved Carthage, so she tries to prevent Aeneas landing there.

Franciade Neptune, still angry at Laomedon's treachery, resolves to destroy the Trojan fleet. He has no special grievance about Francus's mission.

Amédéide God, to punish the Greeks for their schism, decides to leave them to their fate. Amadeus is therefore to be diverted from rescuing the legitimate Greek emperor.

Savoysiade D'Urfé varies the structure here: Beroldo hears of Boson's predicament in a sea-battle and joins in.

Stuartide Neptune has heard that if Fleance reaches Scotland, James, who is to be Fleance's successor, will oust Neptune from command of the sea.

In each case, except for d'Urfé, the threatening agent is supernatural and has no historical justification. For Ronsard and Schelandre the deity is pagan, for Delbene Christian. Only Schelandre tries to relate the divine hostility to historical events, by making James a contender with Neptune for mastery of the sea. Ronsard adheres passively to the Virgilian structure, though reversing Neptune's role. In the *Aeneid* it is Neptune who calms the storm summoned by Juno; in the *Franciade* Neptune invites Juno to participate with him against Francus. Delbene also uses the structure passively, and God's actions do not seem to be directed specifically against Amadeus. D'Urfé strikes out on his own and replaces the storm by the historically justified sea-battle.

How is the storm brought about?

Aeneid Juno begs Aeolus to raise winds.

Franciade Neptune and Juno concert a storm against the Trojans.

Amédéide The elements rise up spontaneously when God says he wishes the Greek empire to perish.

Savoysiade A sea-battle replaces the storm. Beroldo and his son Humbert engage in the fighting but become separated.

Stuartide After Neptune's vain efforts to sink Fleance's magic boat, a sea-nymph suggests making Fleance land somewhere else, so that love may divert him.

Ronsard, though reversing the role of Neptune, is clearly intent on using the structure to introduce a storm in the

Virgilian manner as a set piece. Delbene varies the structure
to accord with his use of the Christian supernatural but does
not linger on the incident. Schelandre creates a more light-
hearted atmosphere, and crowds in more incident. D'Urfé
continues with his own variation.

How does the hero reach land?

Aeneid Neptune indignantly calms the waves and dismisses
Aeolus. The calm allows the Trojans to reach land.

Franciade As both Neptune and Juno are pitted against
Francus, the hero only reaches land of his own accord after a
terrible struggle.

Amédéide Amadeus prays to Mary, reminding her that his
mission to replace the usurper Andronicus by John Paleologus
is just. Mary intercedes with God, who calms the storm and
allows Amadeus to reach Patras.

Savoysiade As the sea battle concludes, Humbert pursues
Spinola to Ventimiglia, and Beroldo is led by divine means to
the same spot.

Stuartide Neptune sends a whale to blow Fleance off course.
Fleance lands in Lewis instead of Scotland.

Francus's special difficulties are the logical result of having
both Neptune and Juno pitted against him. Delbene, to rescue
Amadeus, has to resort to the cumbersome intervention of
Mary, since God is already hostile to Amadeus's mission.
Schelandre continues to multiply his semi-humorous episodes,
and d'Urfé adds to the interest of his variation by dividing
attention between two characters. Humbert's landing follows
naturally out of the sea-battle, but divine intervention is needed
to get Beroldo to Ventimiglia. In all cases the heroes have
landed somewhere unexpected.

How does the hero reach his rescuer?

Aeneid Venus directs Aeneas to Carthage where Dido, prepared by Mercury to be well-disposed towards the Trojans,
has already welcomed his companions. Aeneas reveals himself to Dido while she is holding court.

Franciade Cybele and Sleep induce Dicæe to go hunting and
find Francus.

Amédéide Orytie has recognized Amadeus's fleet and is aware
of his mission to destroy Andronicus, who is her enemy as
well. She sends a knight to invite Amadeus to her palace.

Savoysiade Adelis and her mother, Anne Lascaris, descend from their palace to inspect the newcomers.

Stuartide A band of Hebrideans welcome Fleance after learning who he is from his scouting party. They invite him to Gothrede's castle.

Ronsard follows Virgil most closely by using divine machinery to bring hero and rescuer together. The others prefer more natural methods, though Delbene, like d'Urfé, who has now returned to the basic structure, introduces an element of predestination. Schelandre, though the landing in Lewis is fictitious, draws on historical sources for the description of Gothrede's men. Having multiplied the divine and magical elements at the storm stage he now anchors his plot firmly in historical material.

What purpose does the hero's landing serve?

Aeneid Aeneas, by the very storm which Juno hoped would save Carthage, lands in Carthage. The Dido episode explains the later conflict between Rome and Carthage.

Franciade In Crete Francus hears Hyante's prophecy of his descendants, presumably to encourage him in his mission.

Amédéide The Patras episode would doubtless be Amadeus's first blow against Andronicus. It also provides the opportunity to discourse on the history of Savoy through the engravings.

Savoysiade Humbert is to marry Adelis and from them Charles Emmanuel will descend. Beroldo also sees portraits of his ancestors.

Stuartide Apart from bringing Fleance near Scotland, it is not quite clear how this episode would fit in with the rest of the story.

At this point one may ask how well the poets have integrated the storm and shipwreck topos with the historical material at their disposal. Their common objective seems to be the preparation for a prophecy but in no case does the structure seem particularly relevant to the historical events. Only d'Urfé's Adelis has a significant role to play, the other rescuers are merely episodic characters. It suggests that on the whole the structure was followed for its own sake. The situation the poets had now reached allowed them the choice of two recitals: that of the hero explaining how he came to be there, and that of his rescuer whose story could introduce a new element. The recitals

are a pause in the action, which has so far progressed continu-
ously since the beginning of the poem. The pause is the first
opportunity to counteract the effects of beginning *in medias
res*, and allows some background to be filled in. The purpose
of the rescuers' recitals is not always clear, as the poems are all
incomplete.

What is the substance and purpose of the recitals?

Aeneid Aeneas' companions recount part of their adventures.
Dido requests help against her unruly neighbours. It suits
Aeneas to oblige her further request to hear his own tale.

Franciade Francus tells his own story briefly at his first meeting with Dicæe. At the feast Dicæe's sadness attracts Francus's
attention and Dicæe recounts the story of Phovère.

Amédéide Amadeus's own story is not mentioned, but Orytie,
like Dicæe, is sad at the feast and tells her troubles.

Savoysiade Anne tells the story of her husband being captured by a giant. Later at a feast Beroldo begins his own
recital.

Stuartide Fleance gives little of his own story to Gothrede but
Gothrede's recital fills in the historical background with the
story of Macbeth.

Ronsard, Delbene, and Schelandre lay more emphasis on the
rescuer's plight and less on the hero's previous history. They
thus develop the episodic nature of their poems and do not
fully exploit the opportunity to integrate the background.
D'Urfé does both: Anne Lascaris prepares for a future episode,
which would doubtless solve her problems, and then Beroldo,
exactly like Aeneas, fills a whole book with his adventures.

The conclusions to be drawn from these comparisons are
that the Storm–Shipwreck–Recital structure was used without
much concern for its application to the historical background.
Even when used for its own sake, the structure tended to be
employed passively; that is to say, the poets did not give cohesion even to the fictions which they themselves introduced
into the poem. Nevertheless the poets did not use this structure
passively all the time. D'Urfé was outstanding for his large-
scale variations, and Schelandre for his lesser variations,
coupled with the desire to integrate the structure with at least
some of the historical setting. Not surprisingly history made its
appearance mainly in the recitals, where it could be more easily

accommodated. Delbene's poem seems to be the least well thought out; he does little to harmonize structure and history. Ronsard appears to use the structure most passively, but his structure does not jar with the history, because there is no history for it to jar with.

Iliadic structure

The Virgilian structure affected only the beginning of the poem, but since all the poems that exhibit it are incomplete, this structure embraces all that survives of them. We now turn to the structure that may be called Iliadic. The basic elements of the model are the quarrel between Achilles and Agamemnon, Achilles' retirement from battle, the reconciliation between Achilles and Agamemnon, and Achilles' return to battle. The essential theme is absence and return; it could embrace the whole of a poem and give the reader some guide through the mass of incident. Although its use by Chapelain and Scudéry is evidently the result of Tasso's influence, we cannot exclude the possibility of the *Iliad* playing its part, especially as the *Iliad* was commonly presented in the terms outlined above. Setting the structural elements of the *Iliad* and *Gerusalemme Liberata* beside the French poems demonstrates the difficulty of assigning sources with certainty.

How is the hero's absence brought about?

Iliad   Agamemnon and Achilles quarrel over the allotment of women. Achilles retires to his tent and refuses to fight.

Gerusalemme   Rinaldo and Gernando quarrel. Rinaldo leaves camp, and is later ensnared by Armida.

Alaric   Amalasonthe, the jilted lover, plots with Rigilde, who leads Alaric to an enchanted palace, where a magic ring and the beguilements of Amalasonthe make him forget his mission.

Pucelle   After being disgraced, Joan is captured when Philip attacks Compiègne.

Tasso follows the Iliadic pattern closely, reproducing the conflict between leader and right-hand man. Scudéry gives Alaric no right-hand man so cannot have such a quarrel. Instead he uses the magical element with which Tasso expanded the Iliadic quarrel. Joan's capture was for Chapelain a fact of history; it is one of the rare cases where history fitted neatly into epic structure.

What are the consequences of the absence?

Iliad   The Greeks suffer reverses.

Gerusalemme   The effects of Rinaldo's absence are not at first very obvious, but suspicion falls on the French of having killed him and this causes mutiny. The Crusaders' fortunes reach a low point.

Alaric   Confusion among Alaric's captains. Alaric on the enchanted island becomes a prey to corrupting love.

Pucelle   Charles is beguiled by Agnès, and Edward is enabled to impersonate Rodolphe. French reverses.

Because Scudéry gives Alaric a preponderant role, there is not much scope for developing the action in his absence. The confusion of his captains is predictable, nor is it surprising that Scudéry, having embarked on the abduction incident in imitation of Tasso, should make the most of its amorous implications. Chapelain again follows history in his treatment of Charles and Agnès, but also uses Joan's absence for further poetic development—the episode of Rodolphe's impersonation. This is reminiscent of Tasso's technique. Instead of following his model passively, he uses it as the starting-point for further poetic developments. For example, Rinaldo does not merely stay in his tent like Achilles; the situation is pushed a stage further by the adbuction episode. This active use of an epic structure by Tasso was a lesson from which his imitators sometimes profited.

How is the absentee made to return?

Iliad   Patroclus fights in Achilles' armour and is killed by Hector. Achilles, grief-stricken, resolves to avenge him.

Gerusalemme   Immediately after the low point in the Crusaders' fortunes, measures are taken to rescue Rinaldo. Carlo and Ubaldo use a magic book, rod, and shield to break Armida's spell. Rinaldo returns.

Alaric   An angel leads Upsala to Alaric. Upsala removes the magic ring and Rigilde's spells are broken.

Pucelle   God in answer to Charles's prayer decrees that Joan's death will atone for Charles's faults.

Tasso has little that is comparable to the human drama which brings Achilles inexorably back to the fight. Having developed the absence with magic episodes, Tasso needs magic again to restore the situation, though the attempts to rescue Rinaldo follow appropriately after the disasters described in

Book xiii. Scudéry follows Tasso passively, and does not invest Alaric's return with any special significance. Chapelain does not bring Joan back : history did not permit it. But God's decision meant that Joan was once again responsible for French successes, so that her absence had the same effect as if she had returned. Chapelain's new interpretation of history shows how a poet might resist the temptation to substitute fiction for history. Had Joan's story been less well known, Chapelain might have altered it and brought her back to the French army.

What does the absentee achieve on return?

Iliad Achilles helps recover the body of Patroclus, inflicts losses on the Trojans, and kills Hector.

Gerusalemme Rinaldo, after noble deeds, plants a cross on the wall, and the Crusaders enter Jerusalem. Tancredi resumes his interrupted duel with Argante, in circumstances now made more favourable by the return of Rinaldo. Rinaldo kills Solimano and Tisaferno.

Alaric The hero's character is purified by the abduction experience. He now overcomes all obstacles and leads the expedition to a successful conclusion.

Pucelle Joan's death at the stake puts new heart into Charles, who proceeds to capture Paris.

As the poems are now nearing their conclusion, it is not surprising that the hero's return is a prelude to victory in each case. Scudéry develops his abduction episode by making it the instrument of Alaric's purification. Chapelain's conclusion is essential for the understanding of his epic interpretation of Joan of Arc : it is not her fate as such that interests him, but 'La France délivrée', the subtitle of his poem.

The Iliadic structure was fully exploited by Tasso. Scudéry on the whole followed Tasso passively, whilst Chapelain showed how the epic structure could be used not to replace history but to give it a new interpretation. One naturally asks whether Tasso's other imitators, Desmarets and Le Moyne, also employed the Iliadic structure. They did not. Their only guiding thread was the achievement of the hero's particular goal : the marriage and conversion of Clovis, and the recon- of incident, which defies classification, sugests a different and quest of the crown of thorns by Saint Louis. Yet this very mass equally legitimate structure, the episodic.

Episodic structure

The dividing line between heroic and romanesque epic, as we have defined them, is not a sharp one. It depends on how one interprets the balance between fiction and history. The justification for including *Saint Louis* and *Clovis* among the heroic epics is that their fictions, though numerous, were still in some way based on the historical situation. In the *Néréide* and *Charles Martel*, which we have called romanesque epics, the fictions seem to be mainly applied from outside.

Episodic structure is characterized by recitals and episodes. Episodes are narrations by the poet of incidents arising out of the main narrative. Recitals are the narrations of episodes by a character in the epic; they require greater vigilance on the part of the poet to ensure that they are structurally integrated and do not violate plausibility. The effect of accumulated recitals is a continuous recession of perspective, and when they are placed within one another they become a series of pictures within pictures. The effect of accumulated episodes is to increase the pace of the narrative.

Amplification by recitals can be observed in the second and third books of *Saint Louis*. Bethune is sent by Alfonse to Louis's camp, where he begins a recital of Alfonse's adventures between leaving Cyprus and reaching Damietta. Framed in this recital is another recital, that of Lisamante, who recounts her own fairy-tale adventures. Bethune finishes the story of Lisamante, and returns to Alfonse, and at the end of his recital brings the reader back to Louis and the present. As soon as Alfonse arrives at the camp in person, Coucy, the bard, starts to sing stories from the Old Testament, and then, at Alfonse's request, he recounts Louis's adventures between his departure from Cyprus and his investment of Damietta. Coucy's recital in turn encloses another, that of Léonin, which describes events within Damietta. All this mass of material hangs on only one incident proper to the main narrative: Alfonse's arrival at Louis's camp.

The first three books of *Saint Louis* taken together reveal LeMoyne's considerable ingenuity in presenting the historical background within a complex structure of recitals. In Book i we hear the Sultan Mélédin's story, and Louis's tent is covered with tapestries depicting his career up to the sailing from

Cyprus. Then we hear separately of the activities of Louis and Alfonse between Cyprus and Damietta. Léonin's recital gives the Christian view of events inside the besieged city of Damietta. The interlude on Old Testament subjects, which show the infidel defeated by God's chosen leaders, emphasizes the poem's wider significance. All this is set in a symmetrical system of recitals: Bethune's encloses Lisamante's, Coucy's encloses Léonin's. It is the recital structure which gives coherence to the mass of incident.

Le Moyne's efforts to order his romanesque and historical material by recitals exchanged between the main characters indicates a striving for unity. This unity becomes more elusive when the scene shifts episodically from character to character, which is Desmarets's technique in *Clovis*. To be sure he does use recitals, but for the most part the poet unfolds his story by switching backwards and forwards between Clovis, Aurèle, Auberon, Clotilde, Gondebaud, Yoland, or Albione. The links are discernible, and, with an effort, one can follow the story of any one character through his encounters with the others. In this respect the structure of the *Clovis* resembled that of the *Orlando Furioso*, but neither structure was specifically epic: the structure could equally be that of a novel. Indeed Desmarets seemed deliberately to reject the ancient models, and attempted a new structure which he doubtless believed to be appropriate to modern Christian epic. The result, if not specifically epic, was at least readable.

The types of epic structure that have been discussed do not exhaust the patterns of epic, nor are they mutually exclusive. Examples of poets following the sequence of historical events, introducing recitals or episodes, depicting storms, shipwrecks, quarrels, or reconciliations, are clearly to be found elsewhere than in the specific cases we have discussed. What we have looked for is the repetition of certain combinations of these elements, which suggest that the poet had a definite structure in mind. The comparisons, which such an approach permits, enable us to judge how far repeated features were used actively or passively, and how far a preconceived epic structure might influence the portrayal of historical events.

XV

EPIC STYLE

HAVING EXAMINED combinations of topoi as structural elements, we now turn to topoi which do not, by virtue of their combination with other topoi, have a structural function, but which poets used to display their rhetorical virtuosity. The field is vast.[1] Its very magnitude permits numerous comparisons to be made, which are not possible in genres poorer in techniques susceptible of repetition. Such comparisons are invited by the poets themselves, who indicated their sources in marginal notes, or listed their topoi in indexes.[2] That this abundant repetition is a constant feature of epic, not even the most casual reader will need convincing; but some precision about its exact nature is desirable. First we shall consider a number of topoi in general terms, and then the storm topos in detail. The object of bringing comparable passages together is to throw into relief the stylistic peculiarities of individual poets. Obviously, since epic displays many stylistic features common to other genres, it could also furnish material for a general discussion of literary style in these two centuries, but that is not our purpose. The question which is relevant, and which will be posed in the final section, is how writers used the stylistic resources available to any poet for the specific purposes of epic.

Topoi

The number of topoi repeated in the epics of these two centuries is so large, that to discuss them exhaustively is impossible. I have therefore selected a few topoi, partly by way of example, and partly to illustrate the style of certain poets. First, since war was the chief theme of epic, there are some topoi connected with war; then topoi connected with travel, which had wide-ranging implications; then descriptive topoi, which were essential to the narrative requirements of epic; and, finally, some reminiscences of ancient epic, which acquired the status of topoi by virtue of their frequent repetition.

For the description of war several topoi were used, which helped the poet to set a battle in motion, but which do not readily fall into a structural pattern. The council of war occurred frequently. It might merely provide an enumeration of the hero's chief lieutenants,[3] but could also be used for rhetorical set pieces analysing the causes of the war. Scudéry's councils tended to be a mechanical succession of speeches expressing different points of view, with little attempt to match the speech to the character.[4] Chapelain, on the other hand, used the council of war with more subtlety to individualize the chief characters and penetrate their motives. The council at Chinon is the setting for Joan's entry into the action. In it Chapelain contrasted her confidence with the King's timidity, and sketched the covert hostility of Gillon and Amaury, a theme that runs through the whole poem.[5] In a later council these same characters, together with Dunois and Tanneguy, are brought into a conflict of character and motive.[6] Whilst Scudéry treated this topos as a rhetorical exercise, Chapelain invested it with some drama.

The speech before battle was another method of analysing the causes of war, and was a device common to historians and poets. The speech of one general was often followed by another from his opponent,[7] but the opportunity to enlarge on the hero's character or give point to the ensuing battle was not everywhere exploited. Mere vilification of the enemy was more frequent:

> Vous tremperez vos bras, & vos mains homicides,
> Se souilleront du sang de ces peuples perfides.[8]

Such exhortations could be applied to any army. Sometimes a particular case called for particular persuasion, as when Beroldo had to persuade his men to slaughter a sleeping enemy.[9] D'Urfé's successive versions of an earlier speech by Beroldo show the care that could be lavished on speeches of this type.[10]

The review of armies or fleets was another essential preliminary to war.[11] It could be a tedious list of minor captains and their contingents, or could be used, as Chapelain used it, to give a panorama of nations at war.[12] Scudéry's ingenuity might be taxed to fit awkward names into his verse:

> Les gens de Midelphar, & ceux d'Angermanie;
> Les Habitans d'Upsale, & ceux de Nicopie;
> De Narve, de Castrolme, & de mille autres lieux . . .[13]

but this exercise satisfied the encyclopedic tendencies of epic. Le Moyne enlivened his review with observations on the origins of the leaders or their ancestral lands.[14] The catalogue of ships in Book ii of the *Iliad* furnished examples both for Chapelain's panoramic approach and for Le Moyne's individual characterization.

To grip the reader, the battle required, but did not always receive, careful composition. Wiser poets, following Tasso's example, gave it coherence by focusing attention on characters known to the reader, and by linking the duels in a logical sequence. D'Urfé illustrated this best,[15] but Tasso's other imitators did not exploit this procedure to such an extent. Desmarets and Chapelain concentrated on the movement of squadrons rather than on individual duels.[16] Le Moyne attended particularly to ingenious deaths. Those who had seen action as soldiers themselves were not necessarily the best at describing battles. One of the most concise and interesting accounts of a complex battle was that of Courtin, a professor of rhetoric.[17] Scudéry, however, put his military experience to good advantage, and made each battle a different type of action: ambush, siege, sea-battle, landing.[18]

The movements of the hero by land and sea gave occasion for lists of places visited on the journey.[19] Like the reviews, such journeys, rich in proper names, familiar and unfamiliar, satisfied the encyclopedic spirit. They could be developed into descriptions of particular localities.[20] The eulogy of a country was a long-established topos of epic[21] and many epic-type poems in the sixteenth century were devoted exclusively to this subject.[22] The sources of such descriptions could be personal observation or historical works.[23]

Travel and foreign places were usually associated with education, perhaps in part under the influence of the opening of the *Odyssey* and the character of Odysseus.[24] Beroldo admitted to Anne Lascaris that he had gained much from travel.[25] Half Ennetières's epic was taken up with the hero's travels over Europe, all with the object of self-improvement. For self-improvement Delaudun's Francus sent Clogio abroad,[26] and Helenin despatched Ronsard's Francus for the same reason.[27]

Descriptive topoi were popular: temples, palaces, forests, armour, or shields. They were the poet's pride and Scudéry indexed his. Three dissimilar poets described the Alps. For Beaujeu they represented the Swiss countryside:

> Venez à la fenestre, & voyons les montagnes
> Qui seruent de remparts à ces vertes campagnes,
> Aux lacs cernez de rochs, afin que puissiez voir
> Le peuple & le pays qui me fait esmouuoir.[28]

Beaujeu conveys their attraction in concrete terms (*seruent de remparts, lacs, cernez de rochs*) and also tries to involve the reader directly, whilst at the same time introducing a personal note (*venez à la fenestre & voyons, qui me fait esmouuoir*). Scudéry, too, tried to involve the reader by affective description, but his terms are abstract and general. After enumerating the hazards—ice, snow, darkness—he continued:

> Des Cimes des Rochers les figures cornuës,
> En lassant les regards se perdent dans les Nuës :
> Et de tous les costez en ces lieux peu feconds,
> Des Antres tenebreux s'enfoncent sous ces Monts.
> Des chemins escarpez bordez de precipices;
> Qui pour le desespoir sont seulement propices,
> Font trembler de frayeur les plus hardis Soldats
> Car la mort ou la vie y depend d'un faux pas. . . .
> Lieux deserts, lieux maudits, où va ce vaillant Roy;
> Et dont le triste aspect imprime de l'effroy.[29]

The emotions are impersonal: *lassant les regards, pour le desespoir, imprime de l'effroy*. Even the more personal *font trembler de frayeur les plus hardis Soldats* does not make it clear whether Alaric's soldiers in particular or the bravest soldiers in general are meant.

Le Laboureur took up Beaujeu's theme of ramparts, and evoked the dangers of avalanche:

> Ces Rochers, que la Terre extrait de ses entrailles,
> Sont d'horribles remparts & d'affreuses murailles,
> Que la Nature semble auoir fait autrefois
> En faueur des Romains contre les fiers Gaulois.
> Vn sentier âpre & creux, de cent pieges capable,
> Rompoit de ces hauts Monts la chaîne formidable;
> Non si bien neanmoins que leurs rocs menaçants
> Ne fissent peur en l'air d'écrazer les passants.

Sous leur cime courbée, à tomber toûiours preste,
On ne marche qu'en crainte & qu'en baissant la teste :
L'Echo qui s'y retire augmente la terreur,
On croit qu'vn Roc se brise & l'on fremit d'horreur.[30]

He revels in colourless exaggeration: *horribles remparts, affreuses murailles, cent pieges, chaîne formidable* but the dangers of avalanche are exactly and succinctly described. The affective element, as with Scudéry, is impersonal: *l'on fremit d'horreur.*

Reminiscences of well-known phrases from ancient epic also recur as topoi, perhaps not always consciously. It was not a procedure peculiar to epic, but naturally epic favoured it. Du Bellay employed the *ter quaterque* formula.[31] Epic poets favoured the *ter conatus*, which was usually applied to embracing a shade[32] but fitted almost any activity.[33]

Virgil had established India as the extremity of the world.[34] Later poets, if they wished to convey the idea that a reputation spread over the whole world, described it as reaching as far as India or Thule or both.[35] Blarru did this, using the Ganges for India :

> Immortale mihi partum per secula nomen :
> Ad regnum Athlantis stellati a Gange refusum est.[36]

D'Urfé combined Ganges and Thule :

> & auxquels il dorroit tant d'heureuses victoires
> que du Gange on orroit iusqu'au Tyle lointin
> de leur bras invincus le bien heureux destin.[37]

To express the same idea, Ronsard drew on another Virgilian passage :

> . . . l'empire de ce Roy
> Qui florira comme une chose ferme
> En son entier, sans limite & sans terme.[38]

Dawn, saffron or rosy-fingered,[39] was an indispensable ornament for the passage of time :

> Ronsard
> Incontinent que l'Aube ensaffrannée
> Eut du beau jour la clarté ramenée . . .[40]

S. Garnier

Attant que le courrier à la perruque blonde
Eust ramané çà-bas la lumiere du monde.[41]

Scudéry

Or durant qu'Alaric restablit toutes choses,
L'Aurore peint le Ciel de la couleur des Roses . . .[42]

Le Laboureur

L'Aurore à coups de traits d'vne rouge lumiere
Commençoit à chasser la nuit de sa carriere . . .[43]

Examples of this could be multiplied almost indefinitely;[44] the variations were purely verbal.

Fama was equally popular. Virgil's well-known description[45] had wide application and satisfied the allegorizing tendency:

Ronsard

En-cependant la pronte Renommée
Au front de vierge, à l'echine emplumée . . .[46]

D'Urfé

Il dict & cependant la prompte renommee
de ce meurtre par tout la nouvelle a semee.[47]

Ennetières

Tandis d'vn petit bruit, s'en vient la renommée
A la teste d'airain, à la hanche emplumée . . .[48]

Scudéry

Mais pendant qu'il travaille à former son Armée,
Par tout de son dessein vole la Renommée . . .[49]

Chapelain

De toutes parts alors l'errante Renommée,
Comme si la Cité venoit d'estre abysmée . . .[50]

Desmarets

Desia de toutes parts la prompte Renommée
Répandoit les exploits de la vaillante armée . . .[51]

Virgil's distinction between true and false news was gradually lost and the topos became a simple allegorical personification conveying merely 'news was spread.'[52]

The storm

The selection of topoi discussed in the preceding section gives some idea of the possibilities of comparison between different poets writing on the same subject. In order to have some specific, though necessarily limited, texts on which to base suggestions about the nature of epic style, it will be profitable to examine one topos in detail. The advantage of choosing the storm topos is that it has already been discussed as part of the Virgilian structure. Some of the examples below will illustrate the style of the poets whose use of this topos as a structural element has been analysed, whilst the other examples will illustrate how other poets used the topos merely as an opportunity for stylistic display.

Ronsard used the storm as part of his structure. It was the means by which Francus lost his fleet and was driven to Crete. After the preliminaries, in which Neptune's alliance with Juno is described, there are four movements: (i) the gathering of the storm (125-62);[53] (ii) the plight of the sailors (163-224); (iii) the fate of the ships (225-310); (iv) Francus's landing (311-70). Ronsard draws heavily on mythology to produce the storm. No sooner has Iris recounted Neptune's grievance to Juno than clouds assemble of their own accord (125). Two similes dominate the passage: the clouds are likened to sheep flocking to a shepherd (127-31), and Juno's fashioning of the clouds into varied shapes to a bowman casting arrow-heads of lead (138-41). One might question the wisdom of doubly emphasizing the rather absurd picture of Juno manipulating the clouds, and indeed the second simile was removed from the editions between 1578 and 1587. Neither simile is as effective as that which was added in 1573 to describe Iris at Juno's feet like a dog awaiting instructions from its master. This serves to characterize Iris, and to establish her relationship with Juno. To attempt the same for Juno's relationship with the clouds was to attempt the impossible. In his description of the storm, Ronsard deployed the following vocabulary to convey size, movement, colour, and noise:

SIZE: *corps moien, petit & grand, cornuës, grosses ou menuës* (132–3), *quarrée, rond, long* (140–1).
MOVEMENT: *pesle mesle* (126), *flot dessus flot* (152), *ranversant*

(153), *s'elevant à grands monceaux* (155–6), *branle sur branle &
onde dessus onde* (157), *coup dessus coup* (159 and 160).
COLOUR : *foudres pers de scintile* (146), *blafarde, noiratre* (148),
azur (149).
NOISE : *bruiant* (147),[54] *siflant, bruiant, grondant* (155).

The choice of parts of speech accorded with his purpose : epithets, naturally, for size and colour; participles for noise; ad-
verbial phrases, compounded of repeated nouns and preposi-
tions, for movement. The semi-personification of the winds was
conveyed more successfully than in the similes by the choice of
emotional epithets : *importune, outrageuse* (154), *mutine rage*
(161). Both the similes applied to the clouds, and the epithets
applied to the winds show Ronsard's desire to invest the storm
with drama by giving some kind of human personality to the
elements.

Delbene introduced his storm immediately after God's
tirade against the Greeks for their impiety. God resolves to
annihilate the Greek empire; as soon as he has finished speaking, Delbene continues :

Ces propos acheves, les bien heureux espris   57
Furent attains soudain d'une effroiable crainte,
Et d'un juste courroux justement ennaigris :
Les cieux, les elemens qui ont senti la plainte   60
De leur moteur puissant, de fraieur furent epris,
Flechissant soubz le joug de la volonté saincte.
   Dans les cieux azurez les astres flamboians
Leur plus malin aspet ont jetté sur la terre
Et sur neptune aussy, & ses flots ondoians,   65
L'air et le feu esmeus leur ont dressé la guerre,
Leurs vapoureux enfans horribles tornoians,
Et jupiter dardant son rugissant tonnerre.
   Par le vuide de l'air, Austre le pluvieux
Galloppe librement, de mesme l'accompaigne   70
Le Tracien, Circie & Eure furieux :
D'autrepart Aquilon, Euronote qui baigne
Et l'horrible Afriquain s'efforcent à qui mieux mieux
Troublera le plus creux de l'humide campaigne,
   Flot dessus flot faisant ces ondes escumer,   75
Et les daulphins courbés presaige de tempeste,
Avecque les vaisseaux sautiloient sur la mer :

Ils esgallent aux cieux leur chancellante teste,
Puis soudain on les voit es gouffres abismer,
Aux yeux rien n'aparoist que la fureur celeste.   80
    Et le ciel rugissant d'eclairs brillans reluit,
Obscursissant son jour de l'espesseur des nues,
Qui change aux matelots en une obscure nuict.
Il creve aussy de gresles & de pluies menues,
Menassant les nochers de son horrible bruit,   85
De les ensevelir dans les vagues tortues.
    Le genereux Amé qui voit devant ses yeux
Le péril eminent, lors fut saisy de crainte,
Et oultré de douleur levant ses mains aux cieux,
Disoit Royne du ciel oy ma juste complainte,   90
Tornant sur nous chetis tes beaux yeux gracieux,
Sy jamais aresté de vray pitié attainte.
    Je veux en ton honneur ung bel ordre sacrer
De nobles chevaliers, valeureus & preudhommes,
Et nos armes & vie a ton nom consacrer,   95
Sy tu fais que ma flotte, advocate des hommes,
A ton ayde, et secours puisse a bon port ancrer,
Nous tirant du danger, & peril ou nous sommes.
    Tandis qu'il fait ses voeux, euronote Aquillon
Donne au travers la voille & faict cracquer l'antene,   100
Piroetant les flots d'un roüant tourbillon:
Du saige nautonnier la science certaine
Se sert contre l'orage outrageux, et selon,
Il fuit de son pouvoir les rochers & l'areine:
    L'Affriquain violant escarte les vaysseaux   105
En plaine, & haute mer, & le pillotte sage
Calle la voille au vent, l'un au plus creux des eaux
Est engouffré soudain, trois fois dessus l'orage
On le voit eslevé, puis les rompus morceaux
Flotter dessus les flots, tesmoignant son naufrage.[55]   110

Delbene makes the storm start spontaneously as soon as God
has expressed his displeasure. Like Ronsard he describes the
sky first and then the winds, but his picture is much less clear.
The winds are a mere catalogue of names—Austre, le Tracien,
Circie, Eure, Aquilon, Euronote, l'Afriquain (69-73)—to which
the epithets *pluvieux, furieux, horrible,* add little. If we look at
the manner in which Delbene conveyed size, movement, colour,
and noise, we observe the following:

SIZE: *gouffres* (79), *pluies menues* (84).

MOVEMENT: *ondoians* (65), *tornoians* (67), *galopper* (70), *troublera* (74), *flot dessus flot faisant ces ondes escumer* (75),[56] *sautiloient* (77), *chancellante* (78), *abisiner* (79), *tortues* (86),[57] *dauphins courbés* (76), *piroetant* (101), *roüant tourbillon* (101).

COLOUR: *flamboians* (63), *eclairs brillans, reluit* (81), *obscursissant son jour* (82), *obscure nuict* (83).

NOISE: *rugissant tonnerre* (68), *ciel rugissant* (81), *horrible bruit* (85), *craquer* (100).

Comparing this with Ronsard's methods of enlivening his description, we note that words suggestive of movement predominate. Delbene's vocabulary of colour is less precise than Ronsard's whilst the words which convey noise are vague and repetitive. Size is left mainly to the imagination. Delbene's choice of epithets is neither varied nor arresting: *enfans* **horribles** (67) **horrible** *Afriquain* (73) **horrible** *bruit* (85); **furieux** (71), **fureur** (80), **saige** *nautonnier* (102), *pillote* **sage** (106). Like Ronsard he describes the storm as *outrageux*,[58] but there is little else to dramatize the conflict, which is speedily resolved by Amadeus's prayer to Mary and her intercession with God.

Beaujeu's storm is briefly narrated, but prepared at length in God's speech. It serves a dramatic purpose because it is the means of Tell's escape from Griseler, but it clearly is not used as a part of the Storm-Shipwreck-Recital structure. Just as Delbene's God inveighed against the Greeks, so Beaujeu's God inveighs against tyrants, concluding that he can no longer tolerate the evil-doers. Beaujeu then continues:

> A ce mot le reflus
> Du lac mesme, estonné d'ouyr tant de menaces,
> S'enfle, saulte, bondit, dans les longues espaces
> Des grands flots enragez, la barque va nageant
> En laquelle chacun se monstre diligent   5
> A resister aux flots qui laissent deux campagnes
> Chacun derriere soy esleuez en montagnes,
> L'vn de l'autre irritez ils se heurtent de front,
> Et plus de deux cens pas en arriere il reffont.
>
>   Lors le fier Tyran meurt en sa mane chargee,   10
> Enclose en cent perils sur ceste onde enragee,
> N'esperant iamais plus autre grace des Cieux
> Qu'abismer sans secours dans les flots furieux,

Vn flot outrecuidé vient passer sur la prouë
Qui fait tourner la Nef plus viste qu'vne rouë,   15
Du chariot vollant dont les astrez cheuaux
Surpassent à courir les plus vistes oiseaux,
Cest barque fait eau, cependant qu'on l'estouppe
Vn flot froisse le mas, vient innonder la pouppe,
Vn autre par le flanc luy donne vn si grand heurt   20
Que le Tyran surpris d'estonnement se meurt
Il se laisse ia vaincre à la peur qui l'emporte,
Et demeure confus en la tourmente forte.[59]

In this description Beaujeu concentrates mainly on the movement of the water, appropriately enough, since he is talking
about Lake Geneva not the sea, and Neptune would be out of
place. The sense of movement is conveyed by verbs: *s'enfle,
saute, bondit* (3); and the picture of the vast rolling waves is
spoilt only by the precision of *plus de deux cens pas* at the end
(9). The drama is heightened by a quick shift to the characters
involved (10-23), and by the expressions which personalize the
elements: *estonné d'ouyr* (2), *l'vn de l'autre irritez* (8), *flot
outrecuidé* (14).[60] Delbene was guilty of the repetition of vague
epithets: Beaujeu committed the same fault with *enragé* (4
and 11).

Garnier's storm in the *Loyssée* is very brief, and lacks the
elaborate preparation of his predecessors:

Or depuis que Loys eut pris port au rivage
De la terre de Cypre, il fist un tel orage,
Et vents si furieux de toutes parts sur mer,
Qu'il sembloit proprement à la voir escumer,
Que nous feussions au bout de la fin de ce monde,
Tant fort le ciel, le vent, se faisoient guerre, & l'onde.[61]

There is just enough space for Garnier to include the tritest
commonplaces—furious winds, foaming sea, and warring elements. Ever ready to spot a Biblical parallel, Garnier likens the
scene to the end of the world. The desperate expedient to get
a rhyme at the end of the last line speaks for itself.

With Schelandre's storm we have an obvious attempt to seek
originality at all costs. There is little that is directly comparable
to the other passages, and clichés are resolutely avoided:

Tandis, desia soubs le beccu nauire
Le fils de Rhee auoit tout refrongné
Son triple fer à deux mains empongné,
Bandant les reins en posture pareille
Au Salernois qui membru s'appareille,   5
Sur le portail de son Seigneur aymé,
Contre l'effort d'vn aggresseur armé :
Le garde-corps sur ses iambes se campe
Vn pied deuant, couche la grosse hampe
Pres de sa cuisse &, le corps de costé,   10
Mesure vn coup, coup qui roide ietté
Romproit du Grec la targue sept fois forte ;
La main senestre est celle qui supporte
Tout le fardeau, la dextre tout le chocq,
L'vne glissant l'autre auançant l'estocq.   15
Ainsi le Roy de la plaine escumeuze
Alla frapper la carene odieuze
Du mesme outil qui souuent met à fonds
Le cher trauail des digues & des ponts,
Pour desmembrer les Zelandoïzes villes   20
Parmi les flots & les sables mobiles.
Mais l'escrimeur qui, sans fraude croyant
Son champion, sent que l'acier ployant
Est repoussé d'vne iacque traistresse,
Perd bien le coeur du rebut qui le blesse   25
Son propre effort luy estonnant le bras ;
Ainsi, trouuants ce qu'ils ne pensoyent pas,
L'esprit s'esmeût & les doigts s'escorcherent
Quand du baston les langues reboucherent
Comme de plom, sur vn chesne fatal   30
Sans faire marque & moins effect de mal :
Le chastelet quitte l'onde chenuë
Pris bien à point, & va fendre la nuë
En la façon qu'vn balon Milannois
Battu d'vn bras tout dentelé de bois   35
Saulte auec bruit enuiron demy-stade,
Où retombant il bondit en balsade
De plus en moins, tant qu'il roulle amorti
Bien loin du lieu dont il estoit party.
    Qu'est-il de faire ô Monarque des ondes ?   40
La barque est droitte, & ses toiles my-rondes
Toutes au large empaument le bon vent,
Elle s'eslongne & tu la vas suiuant
Comme vn marchant destroussé qui en plainte

Suit le voleur, mais tousiours auec crainte: 45
Vray que le flus en ta faueur armé
Chocque sa proüe, & l'orage animé
Par ton instinct, sans que le ciel s'en mesle,
Trouble sa route & retarde son aisle,
Desia Triton prompt à ta volonté   50
Fait retentir son cornet argenté
Creux de nature à tortis de limasse,
La plaine large en fricassant amasse
Mille monceaux, le blanc dessus le bleu
Roulle à randons: balançant peu à peu   55
Le bransle croist, comme aux bouches de fonte
Des saintes tours le batail tombe & monte
Pendant dedans, tandis du dancement
Redonde vn ton bourdonnant sourdement:
Les monts de sel qui en pointes se léuent   60
Entrechocqués en escume se créuent,
Puis, refendus, soubs vn affreux vallon
Vont estaler au courant Apollon
Les cabinets de la grande Amphitrite,
Le barquerot qui là se precipite   65
Frappe la gréue & souuent mis à fonds
Donne la chasse aux nageurs plus profonds,
Puis reguindé vers la voulte solaire
Frize du mast la lampe chaude-claire,
AEthon s'ombrage, & dans l'eau reniflant   70
La mesle au feu que son nez va soufflant,
Troublé de voir au milieu de sa traitte
Le mesme bain qu'il trouue à sa retraitte:
Mais quoy Neptun? tousiours comme vn plongeon
Demeure sec ce mobile dongeon,   75
Si lentement, toutesfois il chemine;
Rien ne le sappe & ton despit te mine.[62]

Neptune to life. The storm is portrayed not as a downpour, but device than Ronsard's to breathe life into a pagan deity. The simile of the watchful guard is vigorous, and evokes a clear picture of Neptune poised to strike (5-15). The image of the dykes of Zetland is further suggestion of the reality of Neptune's threat (18-21), whilst the expressions *bandant les reins* (4) and *les doigts s'escorcherent* (28) are colourful touches which bring Neptune to life. The storm is portrayed not as a downpour, but as the upheaval of an angry sea; this is made clear by *sans que le ciel s'en mesle* (48). Instead of the trite *onde dessus onde* and *flot dessus flot* of Ronsard and Delbene, Schelandre has the vivid *le blanc dessus le bleu* (54), and instead of the impersonal *faire escumer* of his predecessors he has the more lively *en escume se créuent* (61). Such touches render the hyperbole of lines 65-9 unnecessary, but even in exaggeration he avoids the colourless cliché.

At first reading Scudéry's description of his storm has an elegance and fluidity that set it above the preceding passages:

Ce fut là que Rigilde encor plus irrité,   115
Ces cruels Prisonniers vint mettre en liberté:
Et que les delivrant pour exercer leur rage,
Il trouua ses plaisirs dans l'horreur d'un Orage.
D'abord un bruit confus murmure sourdement,
Et parmy le Cordage on l'entend foiblement: 120
D'abord les Flots troublez perdent leur Couleur verte;
De Poissons bondissans cette Mer est couverte;
Et le Ciel tenebreux en ramenant la nuit,
Mesle au bruit de ces Flots un effroyable bruit.
Le Tonnerre & la Vague à l'instant se respondent;   125
Tout le Ciel retentit de leurs bruits qu'ils confondent;
Et la pluye, & la gresle, & les flâmes, & l'eau,
Tombent confusément sur plus d'un grand Vaisseau.
D'un costé l'Aquilon vient heurter un Navire;
Et de l'autre Vulturne y vient soufler son ire: 130
Tous les Vents deschainez, changeans & furieux,
Semblent vouloir mesler la Mer avec les Cieux.
L'un heurte les Vaisseaux, & les jette en arriere;
Et l'autre les repousse à leur place premiere:
Tout l'Art des Mariniers ne leur sert plus de rien;   135
Ils vont à droit; à gauche; & ne vont jamais bien.
Eure les piroüette, & les tourne en furie;
Eure ce Tourbillon si plein de barbarie:
Et donnant de la crainte aux plus fiers Matelots,
Ils font trembler la Terre, & souslevent les Flots.   140
Ils renversent la Mer jusques dans ses Abysmes;
Ils cachent des Rochers les plus superbes cimes;
Et le Vent Afriquain, terrible en ses efforts,
Pousse Vague sur Vague, & franchit tous les bords.
De cét humide Vent le soufle impitoyable;   145
Fait voir que le Deluge est possible & croyable;
Car joignant Flot à Flot, il y verse tant d'eaux,

Qu'il met entre deux Mers ces malheureux Vaisseaux.
Les cris des Mariniers, & le bruit du Cordage;
La rumeur de ces Vents qui souslevent l'Orage;   150
Le Tonnerre qui roule, & gronde horriblement;
L'obscure & prompte nuit qui tombe en un moment;
Le feu de mille éclairs qui brille en ces tenebres;
Monstrant & puis cachant tous ces objets funebres;
Monstrant & puis cachant les périlleux Rochers;   155
Font trembler de frayeur les plus hardis Nochers.
Ils sont transis d'effroy par la Vague aboyante,
Où tombe en boüillonnant la Foudre flamboyante :
Et leurs tristes Vaisseaux heurtez & fracassez,
Gemissent sous les coups dont on les sent froissez.   160
L'on s'abandonne au Vent; l'on ameine les Voiles;
Et le Pilote au Ciel cherche en vain des Estoiles :
Car lors que les Esclairs espouvente[n]t ses sens,
Il voit le Ciel tout noir, & les Flots blanchissans.
Tantost la Mer le cache en ses vastes Abysmes,   165
Tantost des plus hauts Monts il surpasse les Cimes;
Et l'Onde se fendant monstre en ces tristes lieux,
Le plus affreux objet qui tombe sous les yeux.
Dans ce Gouffre entr'ouvert par le feu du Tonnerre,
Au milieu de la Mer il aperçoit la Terre :   170
Mais cette horrible veuë augmente sa terreur,
Car il la voit si bas qu'elle luy fait horreur.
Une nuit de trois jours comme celle d'Alcmene,
Luy rend l'heure douteuse, & la route incertaine :
Il ne sçait s'il est jour; il ne sçait s'il est nuit;   175
Et ce Pilote ignore où le Sort le conduit.
En cent lieux differens la Flote dispersée,
Erre au gré de ces Vents dont elle est traversée :
Sans pouvoir descouvrir ny suivre l'Amiral,
Car le Vaisseau du Roy n'avoit plus de Fanal.   180
Ce malheureux Vaisseau, sans Mast & sans Cordage,
Et tout brisé qu'il est par les coups de l'Orage;
Reçoit l'eau dans son ventre; & par ce Flot amer,
S'enfonce trop chargé presque tout dans la Mer.
Alors pour se sauver l'on jette tout aux Ondes;   185
L'Ocean reçoit tout dans ses Vagues profondes;
Et la Mer en fureur roule parmy ses Flots,
Des Casques, des Boucliers, des Tables & des Pots.
L'Onde paroist tousjours plus superbe & plus fiere;
Haut; bas : à droit; à gauche; en avant; en arriere;   190
Comme un Balon bondit d'un & d'autre costé,

Ainsi le grand Navire alors est balotté.
A longs Serpents de feu le Tonnerre qui tombe,
Leur fait voir de ces Flots l'affreuse & noire Tombe:
Et succombant enfin dans un si long travail,   195
Le Pilote effrayé quitte le Gouvernail.[63]

Here, listed in the same manner as for Ronsard and Delbene, is
the vocabulary which Scudéry employed to render his description more striking:

SIZE: *gouffre* (169), *abysmes* (141), *vagues profondes* (186) *longs
serpents de feu* (193).
MOVEMENT: *flots troublez* (121), *poissons bondissans* (122)
tombent confusément (128), *heurter* (129), *vents deschainez,
changeans* (131), *mesler* (132), *heurte, jette* (133), *repousse* (134),
ils vont à droit etc. (136), *piroüette, tourne* (137), *tourbillon* (138),
trembler, souslevent (140), *renversent* (141), *pousse* (144), *verse*
(147), *heurtez, fracassez* (159).
COLOUR: *couleur verte* (121), *ciel tenebreux, nuit* (123) *l'obscure
nuit* (152), *feu, éclairs, brille, tenebres* (153), *flots blanchissans* (164).
NOISE: *bruit confus murmure sourdement* (119), *foiblement* (120),
bruit, effroyable bruit (124), *tonnerre* (125), *retentit, bruits* (126),
soufler (130), *bruit, cris* (149), *rumeur* (150), *tonnerre, gronde* (151),
vague aboyante (157).

From such a list it emerges that Scudéry employed more verbs
to convey movement, colour, and noise than did Ronsard or
Delbene. It also emerges that he has a tendency to let his description drift on in a succession of repetitive and unimaginative
formulae. *Heurter* is used three times; *bruit* five times. There
are variations on *horreur* (118 and 172), *horrible* (171), and
horriblement (151). There are hackneyed couplings: *vents
furieux* (131) *superbes cimes* (142), *l'onde superbe & fiere* (189),
affreux objet (168), *affreuse & noire tombe* (194). All these are
signs of hasty and careless composition; yet, as so often in epic,
the careless was combined with the careful. The premonitions of
the storm, the changing green of the sea, and the leaping fishes
are all convincingly portrayed (119-22). Scudéry, like Garnier,
brings in a Biblical allusion—the Deluge (146)—but his choice
of image is far more apt and its expression far crisper than
Garnier's. There are other vivid strokes—the two seas (148),
and the barking waves (157)—but they are few in comparison
with the signs of pedestrian verse-filling catalogued above.

Other passages might show Scudéry to better advantage, but this is a fair specimen of how good intentions remained half-executed.

It was with these faults that Chapelain was most frequently reproached. From the point of view of structure he compared favourably with other poets. How does he stand up to comparison on the topos that we are considering?

> L'Océan nous reçoit, et paisible d'abord
> Avant la fin du jour nous devoit rendre au port,
> Quand, non loin du milieu de l'orageuse Manche,
> Un bruyant tourbillon sur l'eau calme s'espanche;
> L'eau va chercher la nüe, et l'ombre qui la suit
> Sur le front du soleil fait parestre la nuict.
> Aux foudres redoublés, la céleste machine
> Semble esbranler sa vouste et tomber en ruïne,
> Et la terre à l'envy semble de tous costés
> S'entr'ouvrir à l'aboy des flots entre-heurtés.
> Nos voiles, que bientost met en pièces l'orage,
> Roulent autour des mâts, sous la grondante rage.
> Câbles, ancres, timons, tout cède à son effort,[64]
> Et tout offre à nos yeux l'image de la mort.
> Sous plus d'un choq puissant les navires gémissent;
> Les vagues en leur sein par mille endroits se glissent.
> Nous en sommes dontés, et nos soins assidus
> Pour en vuider nos bords demeurent tous perdus.
> Du souffle impétueux la fureur la plus forte
> Presque tousjours unis à son gré les emporte;
> Elle les pousse enfin contre le mesme escueil,
> Et les plonge brisés dans le mesme cercueil.
> Ainsi tous abysmés au moite sein des ondes,
> Nous tombons au plus bas de leurs grottes profondes,
> Et ton fils,[65] comme tous enseveli dans l'eau,
> Fut le seul dont la mer ne fut pas le tombeau.[66]

It is a style whose virtues are mainly negative. There are clichés, but not in excess. The tone is stately and dignified, without being unduly tedious. The structure of the episode is simple, without being striking. It exhibits neither Chapelain's abuse of inversion nor his talent for observation.

Desmarets's storm at the beginning of *Clovis* takes place on land, not at sea. In a sense it is a miniature version of the Virgilian structure. The storm is aroused by supernatural agency; it drives Clovis and Clotilde to Auberon's palace, which is the source of all their troubles. The storm therefore has a structural function, but, in keeping with Desmarets's tendency to pass rapidly from one episode to another, the sequence of events is quickly narrated, and does not form the framework for further developments.

Le Ciel estoit serain; & la voûte azurée
Blanchissant de l'ardeur d'vne flamme épurée,
N'avoit vn seul nuage en sa vaste grandeur,
Qui cachast du Soleil la brillante splendeur;
Quand vn grand voile obscur s'épandit sur leurs testes;   5
Sans entendre les vents, presages des tempestes;
Et sans voir dans les airs de ces vistes oyseaux
Qui rasent de leur aile & les champs & les eaux.
La Terre s'embrunit d'vne horreur impreveuë;
Et le Ciel à regret se dérobe à la veuë.   10
Clotilde s'estonnant de ce calme trompeur,
Sent à sa peur se joindre vne plus grande peur.
Vn vent impetueux tout à coup se réveille.
Les éclairs frapent l'oeil, & les foudres l'oreille.
Le nuage se creve; & l'onde à gros boüillons   15
Dé-ja couvre la terre, & court par les sillons.
Alors sur les Amans semblent estre versées
Les humides vapeurs dés long-temps amassées.
Sur leurs riches habits coulent de longs ruisseaux.
Clotilde enfin cedant aux importunes eaux,   20
Sous le manteau du Roy s'en deffend, & se cache;
Et d'vn pudique bras à son Prince s'attache.
Cependant des costaux tombent de gros torrens,
Qui roulant aux vallons par des chemins errans.
De là commence à naistre vn danger qui les presse.   25
Sous le pied des chevaux l'onde s'enfle sans cesse.
Le fleuve rompt ses bords; l'eau s'espand des estangs;
Et dé-ja les assiege, & leur gagne les flancs.
La tempeste redouble, & la pluye, & la gresle.
De la Terre & du Ciel les sources pesle-mesle,   30
Font vne large mer, dont la prompte fureur
Renverse en vn moment l'espoir du laboureur.
Ainsi quand des humains l'outrageuse insolence
Eût irrité de Dieu la longue patience,
Et les Cieux & les mers firent vn juste accord,   35
Pour punir tant d'horreurs par vne égale mort,
Les humides amas des airs & des abysmes,

De la race mortelle esteignirent les crimes;
Les villes & les monts de flots furent couverts;
Et l'element liquide engloutit l'Vnivers.   40
Clovis qui de torrens void la terre couverte,
Croid que le Ciel de mesme a conspiré leur perte.
Il gagne vn lieu plus haut. Le fleuve qui le suit,
S'enfle, & semble orgueilleux de ce qu'un Roy le fuit.
Enfin il cede aux eaux; & va sur la montagne,   45
Vient offrir au Roy Franc sa maison secourable.[67]

In spite of many of the now familiar clichés—*vaste grandeur* (3), *brillante splendeur* (4), *vent impetueux* (13 and 64), *prompte fureur* (31)—there are also several telling details: the absence of swooping swallows (7-8), the dripping clothes (19), Clotilde hiding beneath Clovis's cloak (21-2), and the emphatic caesura of line 43, suggesting a pause during which Clovis believes himself safe. What is striking about Desmarets's narration of this episode is the intricate interweaving of the description of the storm with the reactions of the characters concerned, which contrasts with the practice of Ronsard or Delbene, who segregated more rigidly the descriptive and emotive aspects. The steps of Desmarets's narrative are as follows: Clotilde is frightened at the darkening of the sky (11); the lovers' clothes

Découvrir le deluge épars dans la campagne.
Il arrive au sommet; & ses yeux sont surpris
De voir d'vn grand Palais le superbe pourpris.
Aurele s'en approche, & curieux regarde
Que la pompeuse porte est ouverte & sans garde.   50
Ils admirent ce lieu, de forests enfermé,
Et de telle structure, & si peu renommé.
Ils entrent dans la court, où cent torses colonnes,
Dont les chapiteaux d'or sont les riches couronnes:
Separoient cent Heros, que le ciseau sçavant   55
Sembloit avoir changez en vn marbre vivant.
Le beau couple d'Amans sous des voutes se range.
Ma Reyne, dit Clovis, quelle avanture estrange!
Quel sejour admirable icy s'offre à nos yeux?
Aurele, suis-je en terre: ou suis-je dans les Cieux? 60
Mais ces cruelles eaux, & ces coups de tonnerre,
Font voir qu'encore icy le Ciel combat la Terre.
Alors l'orage cesse; & le Ciel s'éclaircit.
Des vents impetueux l'haleine s'adoucit.
Et le Prince enchanteur, en robbe venerable,   65

are drenched (19); Clotilde puts an arm round Clovis (21); the horses' hooves trample the rising water (26); Clovis looks round for higher ground (41); they reach the top of a hill (47); they see a palace (48). In each case the description of the storm is tied to the reactions or movements of the couple. This is even done for the simile of the Deluge (33-42), which is presented as a comparison that might have occurred to Clovis himself.[68] Presumably the reader is expected to think of the Biblical Deluge, whilst, if it was in Clovis's mind, it must have been the flood of the pagan Deucalion; or it may have been inconsistency on Desmarets's part. It is clear that Desmarets was anxious to avoid the segregation of styles which threatened to dissolve Chapelain's poem into a collection of rhetorical set pieces.

The application of rhetorical ornaments to banal conceptions characterizes Courtin's treatment of this topos. His storm serves a different purpose from that of his predecessors. It is on land; it is accompanied by an earthquake; and it has a prophetic significance.

> Le Roy pendant huit jours sans cesse reïtere,
> Et les mêmes souhaits, & la même priere;
> Et le neuviéme jour au moite sein des airs,
> Un violent Orage accompagné d'éclairs,
> Par la fureur des Vents & des coups de la foudre,   5
> Menace en un instant de tout reduire en poudre.
>   Le Soleil obscurcy s'éclipse en un moment,
> La Terre jusqu'au centre est dans le tremblement,
> Et les feux vagabonds de la foudre qui gronde,
> Semblent tracer dans l'air la ruine du monde.   10
> Des Temples & des tours les fronts audacieux,
> Sous ces éclats frequens disparoissent aux yeux;
> Les plus fermes rochers sentent même secousse,
> Et plus l'obstacle est grand, plus le Ciel se courouce.
>   Cet Orage contraire aux loix de la saison,   15
> Des plus judicieux étonne la raison;
> Et ce prodige a droit d'épouvanter la Terre,
> Qui joint au Verseur d'eau les flames du Tonnerre.
>   La Ville intimidée aussi bien que la Cour,
> Dans ce jour de terreur croit voir son dernier jour,   20
> Et chacun croit perir par la même avanture,
> Qui doit estre fatal à toute la Nature.
>   Ces Spectres odieux, ces tenebreux Esprits,

D'un Orage si grand sont eux-mêmes surpris;
Et n'ayant point de part à ce fracas terrible,   25
N'en conçoivent pour eux qu'un malheur infaillible,
Pendant que l'Empereur toûjours égal à soy,
Voit cet affreux debris sans trouble & sans effroy,
Et que malgré les coups qui menacent sa teste,
A peine écoute-t'il le bruit de la tempeste.   30
    Enfin l'Orage cesse, & les Foudres grondans,
N'embrasent plus le Ciel de leurs Quarreaux ardens;
Les Vents prennent la fuite, & laissent en leur place,
Le silence, la paix, le calme, & la bonace.
L'air reprend sa beauté, le Soleil sa splendeur,   35
L'assurance renaist, & dissipe la peur.
    Cependant chacun voit l'effroyable ravage,
Causé par la fureur de ce terrible Orage;
Mais parmy le fracas que la foudre a causé,
On voit du Temple saint le grand comble brisé,   40
La façade emportée, & d'un grand coup de foudre,
Le nom de *Charlemagne*, & ses titres en poundre.[69]

This is an elegant arrangement of the familiar clichés: *violent orage* (4), *fureur des vents* (5), *soleil obscurcy* (7), *foudre qui gronde* (9). The attempt at personification in line 14 gives a glimmer of life. Other figures of speech are deployed judiciously: polysyndeton and *compar* combine to convey the repetitive nature of the king's prayer (1-2); hyperbaton is associated with tumbling buildings (11 and 40); the antithesis between the *ville intimidée and the empereur toûjours égal à soy* (19-30) is mechanical. One can hardly applaud a style which cannot be praised for anything more striking than this.

From the analysis and comparison of these passages, some of the weaknesses of the style of the epic poets become evident. It would indeed be possible to select passages that would show each poet to better advantage, but the comparison of their performance on a single topos is instructive and illuminating. From them we may grasp some of the dominant characteristics of the poets quoted; an accumulation of further examples would add nuances to the picture but would not radically alter it. Ronsard, even when handling mythology clumsily, rarely used words carelessly. Delbene, Garnier, and Beaujeu illustrate the pedestrian versifying of the late sixteenth century. Schelandre emerges well from the comparison, characterized by his avoidance of cliché, his rich vocabulary, and his lightness of touch: not a straightforward style, but a rewarding one. The best that Chapelain could do, was to avoid spoiling the sobriety and dignity of which he was capable, with the vices for which he was notorious. Scudéry and Desmarets achieved so nice a balance between well-conceived ideas and slipshod writing that they cannot be admired or detested wholeheartedly. When Courtin took refuge in the banal, he disguised it with clarity and elegance, thus contriving an apt vehicle for that pleasurable solemnity at which the epic poets of the later seventeenth century aimed.

Epic and Rhetoric

To what extent did the poets use for the specific ends of epic the linguistic resources and the rhetorical devices at their disposal? Clearly a large part of their writing followed conventions common to other literary genres, and cannot therefore be properly assessed within the narrow context of epic alone. On the other hand the epic poet had certain objectives in mind and these objectives shaped his approach to the problem of style.

Illustriousness was the chief characteristic of epic, and it found expression in a variety of ways. High-sounding words were a natural choice. In the descriptions of the storm, itself a grandiose theme, we noted a recurrence of words like *grandeur*, *splendeur, élevé, celeste, gloire, prince, ciel*; and also words expressive of violence and vigour, such as *violent, furieux, terrible, impétueux, outrageux, outrecuidé, généreux*. However evocative of illustriousness these words were, their effect was severely diminished if they were overworked; and this was usually the case.[70] The quest for a noble vocabulary not only implied the choice of noble words, but also the omission of everyday words. This was generally the policy of the poets of the seventeenth century, but in the sixteenth the position was more complex. Ronsard and Schelandre deliberately included commonplace words, partly as a result of attempts to enrich the French literary language, but also perhaps in an endeavour to imitate the Homeric style, which appeared to achieve greater dignity by not disdaining the details of everyday life. Delaudun frankly adopted an unelevated style in order to appeal to a public that was 'moins docte', and, if Sébastien Garnier admitted unheroic words, it was because he was less concerned with the nobility of epic than with polemic, which, to be successful, needed popular appeal. Even in the seventeenth century, everyday words got in by the back door, so to speak, when poets were satisfying their encyclopedic tendencies. Many a word which would have seemed out of place in the narration of an episode involving a ship, gained free admittance in a passage describing the shipwright's trade. Fondness for technical words, a legacy from the Pléiade, continued to play its part in epic, by virtue of the encyclopedic spirit, even when the doctrines of the Pléiade no longer commanded respect. The simile also permitted a wider range of vocabulary than was possible in the main narrative, and Chapelain took most advantage of the opportunities the simile offered. None the less illustrious language remained the hall-mark of epic.

All literature had some moral purpose; but epic had a stronger moral purpose than most other genres. Certain figures of speech were particularly appropriate to moralizing. *Communicatio* and apostrophe highlighted the relationship between the poet and his reader, or the poet and a character in the epic. Beaujeu employed *communicatio* after the storm to point the moral to the reader:

> Lecteur voila comment iamais Dieu ne delaisse
> Ceux qui croyent en luy, sont tirez de l'oppresse.
> Vous, mal-heureux humains qui desplaisez voz Rois,
> Et qui tant offensez leur grandeur & leurs lois,
> N'auez vous point de peur que Dieu ne se courousse . . .[71]

Blarru apostrophized Charles of Burgundy in order to contrast the Duke's ambitions with his father's mildness:

> Viuere vis? regnare diu? securus amari?
> Laudibus et clarum transcendere queris olimpum?
> In patrem totus conuertere.[72]

Sententiae, vital to moralizing, were usually indicated in the text by quotation marks or marginal notes, and were most common in the sixteenth century. The discipline of the *sententia*, which compressed a universal truth into one or two verses—more would dissipate the sententious quality—doubtless encouraged concision even in non-sententious verses, though the favour enjoyed by the epigram, and the taste for antithesis and paradox played their part as well. *Exempla* too, drawn from the Bible, from pagan mythology, or from ancient history, were a perennial stand-by of the moralizing tradition. They were frequent and very obvious in the Latin epic of the early sixteenth century. When noise was mentioned, Cyclops, Echo, and Narcissus followed.[73] If mercy was the theme, Scipio and Pyrrhus were cited.[74] If it was a question of divine punishment on iniquitous towns, then Sodom, Gomorrah, Seboim, and Adama sprang to mind.[75] *Exempla* often masqueraded as similes. Did Guillaume de Pot's horse carry him to safety before expiring? Garnier reminds us of Alexander's Bucephalus.[76] Was Henry IV startled by the appearance of an angel? We are told that Moses and Gideon did likewise, when confronted by God's messengers.[77] The *exemplum* was a reassuring way of hinting at the universality of human experience, and of thus rendering the reader receptive to moral persuasion.

The epic was a narration. The poet stood outside his characters, and recounted their activities as if he were watching them. When he described a succession of events the narrative was dynamic, and usually contributed to the forward motion of the story. When he described inanimate objects, or animate objects that were stationary, the narrative became static, and, without great skill on the poet's part, could degenerate into a potent source of tedium from which Boileau begged to be delivered.[78] The distinction between these types of narrative, and the dangers inherent in the abuse of static description, were recognized by those poets who attempted to combine dynamic and static narrative. A storm, for example could be enlivened, either by giving it a personality, as did Scudéry, or by describing it, like Desmarets, in terms of the reaction of the characters to it. In contradiction of the requirement that epic should be the narration as opposed to the representation of an action, direct speech played a large part in epic, almost to the exclusion of indirect speech. The normal way of reporting a speech was to reproduce it verbatim, even to the unlikely lengths of enclosing one long recital within another, as did Le Moyne. Though contrary to the theory of epic, this procedure was sanctioned by the practice of the ancients. Most speeches were elaborate, and usually ran to at least four verses. Only Desmarets exploited rapid repartee. Speech could also be used for purposes other than debate, exhortation, or conversation. The monologue was the normal means of describing the state of mind of a character. Psychology was presented as a discussion with oneself of dilemmas or emotions. The varieties of narration were familiar to the poets, and were reinforced by the recommendations of the rhetoricians. The danger of too sharp a distinction between them is evident in *La Pucelle*, but was avoided in *Clovis*. Diversity of technique was admirable if judiciously blended, but pernicious if it fragmented the narrative.

Despite many exceptions, due to different conceptions of epic and to personal idiosyncrasy, the linguistic and rhetorical features most commonly to be met with in epic, are those which emphasized its illustrious nature, its moralizing tendencies, and its essential narrative quality. Elevated vocabulary, apostrophe, *communicatio, sententia, exemplum*, and description, were the most characteristic devices of the rhetoric of epic. They served the main purpose of the epic genre, which was the narration of the illustrious actions of illustrious characters in an illustrious style.

NOTES TO CHAPTER XV

1. For a list of the topoi in Italian epic of the same period, see Belloni, *Epigoni*, pp. 471–3.

2. e.g. Blarru, S. Garnier, Ennetières, Chapelain, and Scudéry.

3. e.g. d'Urfé, *Savoysiade*, iv, fol. 136ᵛ.

4. *Alaric*, i, pp. 12 ff.

5. *Pucelle*, i, pp. 30–41.

6. x, pp. 408–16.

7. e.g. Don John's followed by Aly Pasha's (Deimier, *Austriade*, i, pp. 14 ff.) or Saint Louis's followed by Mélédin's (Le Moyne, *S. Louis*, vii, pp. 195 ff.).

8. Delaudun, *Franciade*, ii, p. 43.

9. D'Urfé, *Savoysiade*, vi, fol. 176ᵛ.

10. i, fol. 80ʳ.

11. e.g. Blarru, *Nanceid*, vi, p. 194; Pillard, *Rusticiad*, iii, p. 298; Garnier, *Loyssée*, i, pp. 279–80; Desmarets, *Clovis*, iii, pp. 42–50, xiii, pp. 216–9, xix, pp. 312–6, xxv, pp. 430–3.

12. *Pucelle*, vi, pp. 230–41 (France) and xviii, pp. 165–80 (England).

13. *Alaric*, ii, p. 47.

14. *S. Louis*, v, pp. 125–41.

15. *Savoysiade*, Books ii and iii.

16. *Clovis*, xix, pp. 323 ff.; *Pucelle*, iii, pp. 91 ff.

17. *Charlemagne*, ii, pp. 36 ff; vi, pp. 133 ff.

18. *Alaric*, vii, pp. 211–17; ix, p. 264; vi, pp. 191–5; vii, p. 199.

19. Paris to Marseilles and Marseilles to Cyprus (S. Garnier, *Loyssée*, i, pp. 283 and 294–5); Lalain past England (Ennetières, *Chevalier*, viii, pp. 202–5); Alaric through Italy (Scudéry, *Alaric*, viii, p. 238). Francus's itinerary from Buthrotum to Paris (Ronsard, *Franciade*, i, 1095 ff.); from the island of the Parcae to Scotland (Schelandre, *Stuartide*, i, pp. 70–81); from the Baltic sea to Spain (Scudéry, *Alaric*, iii, p. 75; vi, p. 188).

20. Paris (Ronsard, *Franciade*, i. 204–14); Switzerland (Beaujeu, *Suisse*, fol. 273ʳ); Rhodes and Cyprus (S. Garnier, *Loyssée*, ii, pp. 298–9); Ventimiglia and Scythia (d'Urfé, *Savoysiade*, iii, fol. 123ʳ⁻ᵛ and fol. 132ʳ); island of Lewis (Schelandre, *Stuartide*, i, p. 88); Rueil (Desmarets, *Clovis*, viii, pp. 143–6).

21. See Curtius, *European literature*, p. 158 on *laudes*; Sayce, pp. 199–200 on *descriptio loci*; Griffin, *Coronation*, p. 152 on encomium; Gor-

don, *Ronsard et la Rhétorique*, pp. 49–72, on the eulogy in general, and as illustrated by Ronsard.

22. e.g. Germain Audebert on Venice, Naples, and Rome.

23. Blarru and Pillard described their own localities in Lorraine; Schelandre used the Scottish historians Boethius and Buchanan.

24. 'He saw the cities of many men, and learned how their minds worked' (*Odyssey* i. 3).

25. D'Urfé, *Savoysiade*, vi, fol. 169^{r-v}.

26. *Franciade*, iii, p. 108.

27. *Franciade*, i. 719–22.

28. *Suisse*, fol. 273^v.

29. *Alaric*, vii, p. 210.

30. *Charlemagne*, vi, p. 186.

31. 'Certain verse fragments from Virgil are integrated into the *Regrets* and recur, just like specific rhetorical tropes, to establish unity and thematic progression' (Griffin, *Coronation*, p. 152).

32. *Aeneid* ii. 792–4 and vi. 700–2 was the source; *Alaric*, vi, pp. 184–5, a typical derivation. Embracing a shade was a common topos without *ter conatus*: e.g. S. Garnier, *Loyssée*, i, p. 288; *Henriade*, i, p. 23; d'Urfé, *Savoysiade*, vi, fol. 180^r; Garnier, *Franciade 5*, p. 32; Ronsard, *Franciade*, i. 671 ff.

33. *Aeneid* iv. 690–1; Ronsard, *Franciade*, iii. 1501–3; Le Moyne, *S. Louis*, vi, p. 166.

34. *Georgics* ii. 122; *Aeneid* vi. 794.

35. See Curtius, *European literature*, pp. 160–1 for examples from Fortunatus and *Aymeri de Narbonne*.

36. *Nanceid*, v, p. 132.

37. *Savoysiade*, i, fol. 67^v.

38. *Franciade*, i. 268–70; cf. *Aeneid* i. 279: 'Imperium sine fine dedi . . .'

39. *Iliad* i. 477, xxiv. 788; *Aeneid* iv. 585, ix. 460, vii. 26.

40. *Franciade*, i. 677–8; cf. i. 655, 1153 and ii. 1097.

41. *Loyssée*, ii, p. 315; cf. i, p. 284, iii, p. 317.

42. *Alaric*, iii, p. 65.

43. *Charlemagne*, i, p. 10 (1664), p. 9 (1666).

44. e.g. Pillard, *Rusticiad*, i, p. 152, ii, p. 212, iii, p. 296, iv, p. 72, v, p. 80; Deimier, *Austriade*, i. p. 6; Delaudun, *Franciade*, ix, p. 313; Chapelain, *Pucelle*, iii, p. 89, xiii, p. 3.

45. *Aeneid* iv. 173–97; cf. Valerius Flaccus, *Argonautica* ii. 115–25 and Statius, *Thebaid*, ii. 205–13, iii. 425–31.

46. *Franciade*, i. 453–4.

47. *Savoysiade*, vi, fol. 173ᵛ.

48. *Chevalier*, vi, p. 155.

49. *Alaric*, i, p. 20.

50. *Pucelle*, i, p. 28; cf. xiii, p. 5.

51. *Clovis*, xxii, p. 365; cf. vii, p. 126, xi, p. 186, xiii, p. 220.

52. e.g. Blarru, *Nanceid*, v, pp. 70–2 and 116; Pillard, *Rusticiad*, i, p. 122, iv, p. 4, vi, p. 146; S. Garnier, *Loyssée*, i, p. 278, *Henriade*, ix, p. 97; Deimier, *Austriade*, i, p. 4; Le Moyne, *S. Louis*, vi, p. 159, x, p. 282, xi, p. 323, xvii, p. 514; Courtin, *Charlemagne Pénitent*, iv, pp. 84–5.

53. References are to the lines of Book ii of the *Franciade* in Laumonier's edition, which is readily available. The passages from the other, less accessible, epics are given in full. The line-numbering is either that of the edition referred to, or, if more convenient, the extract has been numbered independently.

54. Omitted in editions between 1578 and 1587, thus removing the repetition in lines 147 and 155.

55. *Amédéide*, ed. Dufour, tercets 19–36.

56. Cf. Ronsard, 'flot dessus flot la faisoient écumer' (152).

57. Cf. Ronsard, 'pluies tortuës' (169).

58. Delbene, line 103; Ronsard, line 154.

59. *Suisse*, fol. 284ʳ⁻ᵛ.

60. Cf. the 'outrageux' of Ronsard and Delbene. See above p. 217.

61. iii, p. 327.

62. *Stuartide*, pp. 54–6.

63. *Alaric*, pp. 131–4.

64. Cf. Scudéry's list in the passage above (line 188). Chapelain is much more dignified.

65. Edward, Bedford's son, is recounting to his father how he escaped from the shipwreck, and here refers to himself in the third person.

66. *Pucelle*, xiv, p. 40.

67. *Clovis*, i, pp. 9–11.

68. Cf. Scudery's mention of the Deluge in the passage above (line 146); a good example of how a trite comparison could be rendered more striking in two completely different ways.

69. *Charlemagne pénitent*, v, pp. 118–9.

70. Of the repetition of epithets in tragedy P. France claims: 'Epithets such as *funeste, déplorable, fatal* recur throughout [Racine's] tragedies,

creating the right impression of noble calamity whether they are immediately necessary to the nouns which they accompany or not. In the same way in some of Corneille's plays *grand, généreux, beau, glorieux* and similar adjectives form a halo round the characters.' (*Racine's Rhetoric*, p. 98.) Clearly the epic poets were also aiming at this 'halo' effect; but what might succeed in a tragedy of 1,500 lines could fail in an epic of 15,000 lines. Epic, as the longest of the poetic genres, posed stylistic problems of corresponding magnitude.

71. *Suisse*, fol. 285ᵛ.

72. *Nanceid*, i, p. 70.

73. *Nanceid*, iii, p. 172.

74. Pillard, *Rusticiad*, v, p. 130.

75. *Rusticiad*, v, p. 140.

76. *Henriade*, xiii, p. 182.

77. *Henriade*, x, p. 109.

78.   Un Auteur quelquefois trop plein de son objet
        Jamais sans l'épuiser n'abandonne un sujet. . . .
        Fuyez de ces Auteurs l'abondance sterile,
        Et ne vous chargez point d'un détail inutile.

(*Art Poétique*, i. 49–60)

LIST OF HISTORICAL EPICS

1516	Varanne	*De gestis Joannae*	5H*
1518	Blarru	*Nanceid*	6H*
1541	Pillard	*Rusticiad*	5H*
1572	Ronsard	*Franciade*	4D
1584	Boyssières	*Croisade*	3A
1586	Delbene	*Amédéide*	1A
1589	Beaujeu	*La Suisse*	1A
1593	S. Garnier	*Loyssée*	3A
1593–4	S. Garnier	*Henriade*	10A
1597	Montreux	*Espagne conquise*	46A*
1599–1606	d'Urfé	*Savoysiade* MS.	9A
1601	Deimier	*Austriade*	2A
1602	Cayet	*Heptaméron*	7D*
1603	Delaudun	*Franciade*	9A
1604	C. Garnier	*Franciade 5*	1D
1605	Deimier	*Néréide*	5A
1606–10	Navières	*Henriade*	12?A
1611	Schelandre	*Stuartide*	2D
1615	Guillot	*Franciade 6*	1D
1617	Thomas I	*Lutetiad*	5H*
1623	Geuffrin	*Franciade*	6A
1630	Thomas II	*Rupellaid*	6H*
1633	Ennetières	*Chevalier*	16A*
1650?	Boissat	*Martellus*	12?H
1654	Scudéry	*Alaric*	10A*
1656	Chapelain	*La Pucelle*	12A
1657	Desmarets	*Clovis*	26A*
1658	Le Moyne	*Saint Louis*	18A*
1658	Mambrun	*Constantinus*	12H*
1666	Le Laboureur	*Charlemagne*	6A
1666	Courtin	*Charlemagne*	6A*
1671	Desmarets	*Regulus*	5A*
1679	Carel	*Charles Martel*	16A*
1679	Bérigny	*Abrégé*	1A*
1687	Courtin	*Charlemagne pénitent*	5A*

Dates given are those of the most complete version published, or, in the case of manuscripts, the approximate dates of composition. The numbers and letters indicate the number of books and the metre (A=alexandrine; D=decasyllable; H=hexameter). An asterisk indicates that the epic was complete.

BIBLIOGRAPHY

The purpose of this bibliography is to give as full a list as possible of the manuscripts and editions of the historical epics, and also of the critical works directly relevant to the epics. Critical works of a more general nature, and standard bibliographical works, such as Brunet, Klapp, Cabeen, *Index Aureliensis* etc., have not been listed, except when they have been cited in the text (e.g. Lelong, Goujet, Toinet, Cioranescu).

In section B1, under the name of each poet, are listed first his epics, then any treatises by him which make reference to epic theory. Where more than one edition of a work is listed, an asterisk indicates the edition to which reference is made. In this section, the absence of a BN or BM shelf-mark indicates that the work is not to be found in those libraries; certain other shelf-marks have been given for rare works.

In section B2 library shelf-marks are given for any work published before 1700. This section also contains the historical works which were, or which might have been, used by the epic poets.

A. MANUSCRIPTS

BLARRU, Pierre de, *La Nanciade tournée du latin de Piere de Blaru Parisien, prestre en son viuant Chanoine de Sainct Dié par noble N. Romain docteur éz droictz Conseillier de Monseigneur de Vauldemont . . . ou La Guerre de Nancy*. 159 fol., 6 books ARS: 3108.

—— *La Nanceiade composee en latin par Maistre Pierre de Blaru . . . et mise en françois par Nicolas Romain*. 34 fol., first book only. BN: fonds français 12419.

CHAPELAIN, Jean, *Disposition du poeme de la pucelle et la diuision de ses matieres et de son ordre par liures*, 27 pp. (prose sketch of all 24 books of *La Pucelle*).

—— *Response du sieur de la Montagne à sr. du Riuage où ses observations sont examinées sur le Poëme de la Pucelle*, 173 pp. (reply to LA MESNARDIERE, q.v.).

—— *Ordre du dessein du poeme de la pucelle*, 36 fol. (plan of the poem starting after the coronation). These three works (see Collas, p. 485) are contained in BN: fonds français 15005.

—— *La Pucelle*, 'Preface' (fol. 1^r–14^r) and Books xiii–xxiv (fol. 15^r–278^v). See Collas, p. 484. BN: fonds français 15002.

—— *La Pucelle*, 'Preface' (fol. 1^r–41^r) and Books xiii–xxiv (pp. 1–582). See Collas, p. 484. BN: fonds français 15003.

—— *La Pucelle*, 'Preface' (fol. 1^r–14^r) and Books xiii–xxiv (fol. 15^r–275^v). On fol. 1^r is written 'De la propre main de M. Chapelain', which applies to the 'Preface'. The poem is not in Chapelain's writing, but the corrections are. See Collas, pp. 484–5. BN: fonds français 15004.

SCHELANDRE, Jean de, *Le Modelle de la Stuartide* BM : Reg.16.E. xxxiii.

*URFE, Honoré d', *La Béroldide, Bérol*, or *La Savoye*, 6 books dated between 1599 and 1605. BN: fonds français 12486, fol. 67–182.

—— *La Savoysiade*, 9 books dated 1606, with dedicatory letter dated 1615. TUR : Storia della Real Casa, Categoria 2a, Storie generali, Mazzo 7.

—— *La Savoysiade*, 9 books dated 1606. ARS: 2959.

VINTIMILLE, Jacques de, *De bello rhodio*, 3 books, in *Carmina*, fol. 2ʳ–61ᵛ. BN: fonds latin 6069.

B. PRINTED BOOKS

1. Primary sources

BEAUJEU, Christophe de, *Les Amours de Christofle de Beaujeu . . . ensemble le premier livre de la Suisse*, Paris, D. Millot, 1589. BN: Rés. Ye.531, ARS: 4°BL.2878.

BERIGNY, Godard de, *Abrégé de l'histoire de France en vers par le Sr. de Bérigny*, Paris, E. Loyson, 1679. BN: L.40.5.

BLARRU, Pierre de, *Petri de Blarrorivo parhisiani insigne Nanceidos opus de bello nanceiano. Hac primum exaratura nuperrime in lucem emissum*, Saint Nicolas-de-Port, P. Jacob, 1518. BN: Rés.g.Yc. 7, 8 and 9, BM : 77.g.12.

*—— *La Nancéide ou la guerre de Nancy poëme latin de Pierre de Blarru avec la traduction française . . . par M. Ferdinand Schütz*, 2 vols., Nancy, Grimblot, 1840. BN: Yc.9979–9980, BM : 1461.i.1.

BOISSAT, Pierre de, BN: Réz.Z.348, lacking any indication of date or printer. A title-page in manuscript has been added: *Petri de Boissat opuscula latina*. After 530 pp. of Latin works, there begins *Martellus, poëma heroïcum*, with separate pagination, pp. 17–144.

BOYSSIERES, Jean de, *Croisade de I. de Boissieres escuyer, sieur de la Boissiere. A Monsieur Gobellin Conseiller du Roy, Tresorier de l'extraordinaire des Guerres*, Paris, R. le Fizelier, 1584. MAZ: 22009.

—— *La Croisade de Iean de Boissieres Escuyer, Sieur de la Boissiere en Auvergne. A Monsieur Berterand, Conseiller & Advocat General du Roy*, Paris, P. Sevestre, 1584. ARS: 8° BL.15691.

CAREL DE SAINTE-GARDE, Jacques, *Les Sarrazins chassez de France. Poëme Heroïque par le sieur de Sainte Garde*, Paris, C. Barbin, 1667, 130 pp., Books i–iv. ARS: 8° BL.15465 and 8° BL.15466.

—— *Charle [sic] Martel ou les Sarrazins chassez de France. Poëme Heroïque par le Sieur de S.G.*, Paris, T. Jolly, 1668, 130 pp., Books i–iv. ARS: 8° BL.15468, BN: Rés.Ye.2177, BM : 1073.f.43.

*——*Charle-Martel ou les Sarrazins chassez de France, Poëme Heroïque par M. de Sainte-Garde. Premiere partie*, Paris, J. Langlois, 1679, 10 unnumbered leaves + 129 pp., Books i–viii. Second title-page identical with the first, except that *Seconde partie* is substituted for *Premiere partie*, 2 unnumbered leaves + 248 pp., Books ix–xvi. ARS: 8° BL.15467, BN: Ye.7983, BM: 11482.aaa.36.

—— *Charle Martel ou les Sarrazins chassez de France. Poëme Heroïque par M. de Sainte-Garde. Premiere partie*, Paris, J. Langlois, 1680, 10 unnumbered leaves + 129 pp., Books i–viii only. ARS: 8°BL.15469[1].

—— *Réflexions académiques sur les orateurs et sur les poètes*, Paris, C. Rémy, 1676. BN: Z.12749. 'La deffense d'Homère et de Virgile ou la belle manière de composer un Poëme Héroïque', pp. 137–209.

*CAYET, Pierre-Victor Palma, *L'Heptaméron de la Navarride ou histoire entière du Royaume de Navarre, depuis le commencement du monde, tirée de l'Espagnol de Dom-Charles, Infant de Navarre, continuée de l'histoire de Pampelonne de N . . ., l'evesque, iusques au Roy Henri d'Albret et depuis par l'histoire de France, iusqu'au Roy très chrétien Henri IIII, Roy de France et de Navarre; le tout fait et traduit (en vers) par le sieur de la Palme, lecteur du Roy*, Paris, P. Portier, 1602, 869 pp. BN: Rés.Ye.2049. A defective copy, ARS: 8°BL.15638, breaks off at p. 550.

—— *Histoire du Royaume de Navarre depuis le commencement du monde, continuée de l'histoire de Pampelonne* [rest of the title as above], Paris, N. Rousset, 1618, 869 pp. ARS: 8°BL.15640. A reissue of the 1602 edition, lacking the liminary verses in the oriental languages.

*CHAPELAIN, Jean, *La Pucelle ou la France délivrée, poème héroïque H. HERLUISON, précédes d'une préface de l'auteur et d'une étude* 81.1.2, BN: Ye.56 (and three other copies). 'Preface' (a1r–d4r).

—— *La Pucelle ou la France délivrée . . . seconde édition revue & retouchée*, Paris, A. Courbé, 1656, 12mo, Books i–xii. ENS: LF.p.236. 12°.

—— *La Pucelle ou la France délivrée . . . dernière édition, suivant la copie imprimée à Paris*, [Amsterdam, Elzevir], 1656, 12mo, Books i–xii. CHA: XIc29.

—— *La Pucelle ou la France délivrée . . . troisième édition revue & retouchée*, Paris, A. Courbé, 1657, 12mo, Books i–xii. BM: 1073.e.28, BN: Ye.8029.

*—— *Les douze derniers chants du poème de la Pucelle, publiés pour la première fois sur les manuscrits de la Bibliothèque Nationale par H. HERLUISON, précédes d'un préface de l'auteur et d'une étude sur le poème de la Pucelle par R. KERVILER, Orléans*, H. Herluison, 1882, Books xiii–xxiv. BM: 11483.bbb.5, BN: 8°Ye.121.

—— *La Pucelle ou la France délivrée poème héroïque en douze chants par Jean Chapelain . . . ouvrage en français moderne, revu et annoté par EMILE DE MOLENES*, 2 vols., Paris, Flammarion, [1892], Books i–xii. BM: 11475.d.49, BN: 8°Y.175. An appendix, pp. 303–22, contains 'les courts fragments qui ont été supprimés dans le poème, tantôt pour en alléger la marche, tantôt pour lui éviter la monotonie de comparaisons trop souvent répétées'.

—— *Lettre ou discours de M. Chapelain à M. Favereau . . . portant son opinion sur le poème d'Adonis du cavalier Marin* in Marino, *Adone*, 1623 (see section B2. s.v. MARINO).

—— *Opuscules critiques*, ed. A. C. Hunter, Paris, 1936.

—— *Lettres*, ed. P. Tamizey de Larroque, 2 vols., Paris, 1880–3.

—— *De la lecture des vieux romans*, ed. A. Feillet, Paris, 1870.

—— *Lettere inedite a corrispondenti italiani*, ed. P. Ciureanu, Genoa, 1964.

—— *Soixante-dix-sept lettres inédites à Nicolas Heinsius (1649–1658) publiées d'après le manuscrit de Leyde*, ed. B. Bray, The Hague, 1966.

COURTIN, Nicolas, *Charlemagne ou le rétablissement de l'empire romain, poëme héroïque*, Paris, T. Jolly, 1666, Books i–vi. BN: 8°Ye.4753, MAZ: 44076. 'Avertissement' (a5^v-6^v).

—— *Charlemagne pénitent* in *Poësies chrétiennes*, Paris, C. de Sercy, 1687. BN: Ye.8126, MAZ: 45876.

—— *Sur la nouvelle conquête de la Franche Comté*, Paris, T. Girard and C. Osmont, 1674. BN: Ye.1391, MAZ: A.15386, 15e pièce.

DEIMIER, Pierre de, *L'Austriade du Sieur de Deimier*, Lyon, T. Ancelin, 1601, Books i–ii. BN: Rés.p.Ye.376, ARS: 8°BL.15674, TAY: UNS. 157.b.16.

—— *La Néréide ou victoire navale ensemble les destins héroïques de Cléophile & de Néréclie par Pierre de Deimier*, Paris, P. Mettayer, 1605, Books i–v. BN: Rés.Ye.2060, ARS: 8°BL.15675 and 8°BL. 15676.

—— *L'Académie de l'art poétique*, Paris, J. de Bordeaux, 1610. BN: Rés. Ye.1218, BM: 11840.bb.22.

DELAUDUN D'AIGALIERS, Pierre, *La Franciade de Pierre Delaudun, sieur d'Aigaliers, divisée en neuf livres*, Paris. A. du Brueil, 1603, Books i–ix. BN: Rés.Ye.2013. Reissued with same title, dated 1604. BM: 11475.a.23, ARS: 8°BL.15437 and 8°BL.15438.

—— *L'Art poétique françois de Pierre Delaudun Daigaliers divisée en cinq livres*, Paris, A. du Brueil, 1597. BN: Rés.Ye.4283, BM: 11795. a.15.

DELBENE, Alphonse, *Le premier livre de l'Amédéide à . . . Charles Emmanuel, Duc de Savoye, par A.D.A.D.H.* [i.e. Alphonse Delbene Abbé D'Hautecombe], Chambéry, C. Pomar, 1586. ARS: 8°BL. 15432.

*—— 'Le premier livre de l'*Amédéide* par Alphonse Delbene . . ., publié pour la première fois par AUGUSTE DUFOUR', *Mémoires et documents publiés par la société savoysienne d'histoire et d'archéologie*, Chambéry, 8 (1864), 209–53. BN: 8°Lc^{10}55.

*DESMARETS DE SAINT-SORLIN, Jean, *Clovis ou la France chrestienne, poëme héroïque par I. Desmarests*, Paris, A. Courbé, 1657, 4to, Books i–xxvi. BN: Ye.1395 and Rés.Ye.677, BM: 84.h.11. Contains 'Au Roy' (sig. *1^r-**2^r); 'Avis' (e1^r-o2^v).

—— *Clovis ou la France chrestienne*, Leyden, Elzevirs, 1657, 12mo, Books i–xxvi. BN: Ye. 8040, BM: 11475.a.14, TAY: Vet.Fr.I.A.52.

—— *Clovis ou la France chrestienne . . . sur l'imprimé*, Leyden, 1658, 12mo, Books i–xxvi. TAY: UNS.103.E.11.

—— *Clovis ou la France chrestienne . . . enrichy de plusieurs figures*, Paris, F. Lambert, 1661, 4to, Books i–xxvi. BN: Ye.1396 (second edition).

—— *Clovis ou la France chrestienne . . . enrichy de plusieurs figures*, Paris, M. Bobin and N. Le Gras, 1666, 8vo, Books i–xxvi. The only copy I have found of this edition, which appears to be in most respects similar to the second edition of 1661, is in the private collection of R. J. Hayhurst, Esq., to whom I am most grateful for supplying the above details.

—— *Clovis ou la France chrestienne, poeme reveu exactement & augmenté d'inventions, & des actions merveilleuses du Roi. Dedié a sa Majesté pour la seconde fois . . . Troisiesme édition*, Paris, C. Cramoisy, 1673, 8vo, Books i–xx. BN: Ye.8041–8042. Contains 'Epître au roy' (a2r-elv); 'Discours pour prouver que les sujets chrétiens sont les seuls propres à la poésie héroïque' (e2r-i8r); 'Traité pour juger des poètes, grecs, latins, et françois' separately paginated at end, pp. 1–102. This 'Traité' corresponds to the first part of the *Comparaison* of 1670 (pp. 1–105), for which see below.

—— *Regulus ou le vray généreux, poëme héroïque dédié à M. de Bartillat*, Paris, L. Rondet, 1671. BN: Ye.1398. The dedicatory letter is signed J.D.M.

——*Esther*, Paris, P. le Petit, 1670. BN: Ye.1352–1353, BM: 11475.g.9. Contains 'L'Excellence et les plaintes de la poësie héroïque', pp. 1–16.

—— *La Comparaison de la langue et de la poësie françoise avec la grecque & la latine . . .*, Paris, T. Jolly, 1670. BN: X.19888. The first part of this work (pp. 1–105) was reproduced in *Clovis* of 1673 (see above); the second part (pp. 108–266) contains some extracts from *Clovis*, notably the storm, pp. 217–18.

—— *La deffense du poëme héroïque, avec quelques remarques sur les oeuvres satyriques du Sieur D***. Dialogues en vers & en prose*, Paris, J. le Gras, 1674, 4to, 136 pp. (BN: Ye.1353, bound with *Esther* (1670), see above).

*—— *Le deffense du poëme héroïque . . .*, Paris, J. le Gras, 1675, 12mo, 142 pp. BN: Ye.7248, BM: 240.e.11, TAY: UNS.157.b.11.

ENNETIÈRES, Jean d', *Le chevalier sans reproche, Jacques de Lalain*, Tournai, A. Quinqué, 1633, Books i–xvi. BN: Ye.7710, BM: 1464.a.6, MAZ: 45223.

GARNIER, Claude, *Livre de la Franciade à la suite de celle de Ronsard*, s.l., 1604. BN: Ye.7561, MAZ: 58355, 10°p.

GARNIER, Sébastien, *Les premiers livres de la Loysee contenans le voyage de Sainct Loys Roy de France pour aller en Ægypte contre les Sarrazins, son embarquement & son arrivée en l'Isle de Cypre & advantures survenue*, Blois, veuve Gomet, 1593, Books i–iii. BM: 1073.i.6(2), ARS: 8°BL.15476.

—— *Les huict premiers livres de la Henriade contenant les faicts admirables de Henry Roy de France & de Navarre quatriesme de ce nom,*

depuis son advenement à la Couronne iusques à la bataille d'Ivry,
Blois, veuve Gomet, 1594, Book i–ii only. ARS: 4°BL.3938.

—— *Les huict derniers livres de la Henriade contenant les faicts merveilleux de Henry . . . & des Princes & Seigneurs françois qui l'ont accompagné à la poursuicte des Espagnols & autres ennemys conjurez de son estat*, Blois, veuve Gomet, 1593, Books viii–xvi. (ARS: 4°BL. 3938, bound with the *Premiers livres* above), BN: Rés.p.Ye.254.

*—— *La Henriade et la Loyssée de Sebastian Garnier . . . seconde édition sur la copie imprimée à Blois chez la veuve Gomet en 1594 & 1593*, Paris, J. B. G. Musier et fils, 1770, Books i–ii, viii–xvi of *Henriade*, Books i–iii of *Loyssée*. BN: Ye.7460, BM: 86.c.23, ARS: 8°L⁴⁰2, ARS: 8°BL.15439, 8°BL.15440.

GEUFFRIN, Nicolas, *La Franciade ou histoire générale des roys de France depuis Pharamond jusques à Louys le juste . . . mise en vers françois par le sieur Geuffrin*, Paris, A. de Sommaville, 1623, Books i–vi. BN: 8°BL.15518, 8°BL.15519, 8°BL.15520.

GUILLOT, Jacques, *La suite de la Franciade de Pierre de Ronsard . . . livre sixiesme, par Messire Jacques Guillot P. Chanoine en l'eglise de Bourges*, Bourges, M. Levez, 1615. ARS: 8°BL.8813.Rés., CHA: IV.C.5.

LE LABOUREUR, Louis, *Charlemagne, poëme héroïque*, Paris, L. Billaine, 1664, Books i–iii. BN: Ye.7971. 'Preface' (a2ʳ-i2ʳ).

—— *Charlemagne, poëme héroïque*, Paris, L. Billaine, 1666, Books i–vi. BN: Ye.7972, BM: 11482.aa.23. 'Preface' (a6ʳ-i2ʳ).
References are given for both editions.

—— *Les avantages de la langue françoise sur la langue latine*, Paris F. Lambert, 1667. BN: X.2370, BM: 626.f.26 (attributed to Jean Le Laboureur). Contains a quotation from *Charlemagne* on p. 16.

LE MOYNE, Pierre, *Saint Louys ou le héros chrétien, poëme héroïque par le P. Pierre Le Moyne de la compagnie de Iesus*, Paris, C. du Mesnil, 1653, folio, Books i–vii. BN: Ye.53, ARS: Fol.BL.845.

—— *Saint Louys ou le héros chrétien, poëme héroïque, jouxte la copie imprimée*, Paris, C. du Mesnil, 1656, 12mo, Books i–vii. BN: Ye.8013, ARS: 8°BL.15479.

*—— *Saint Louys ou la sainte couronne reconquise, poëme héroïque*, Paris, A. Courbé, 1658, 12mo, Books i–xviii. BN: Ye.8012, ARS: 8°BL.15481, BM: 1065.c.10. Contains 'Traité du poème héroïque' (a3ʳ-u7ᵛ).

—— *Saint Louys ou la sainte couronne reconquise, poëme héroïque*, Paris, T. Jolly, 1666, 12mo, Books i–xviii. BM: 11475.de.5, ARS: 8°BL.15482, 8°BL.15483 (BN: Ye.8014 has Louis Billaine instead of Jolly). Contains 'Traité du poème héroïque' (a3ʳ-o3ᵛ).

—— *Saint Louis*, Books i–xviii, in *Les oeuvres poétiques du P. Le Moyne*, Paris, L. Billaine, 1671, pp. 1–235. BN: Ye.257, BM: 82.l.12. Also contains 'Dissertation du poème héroïque' (e1ʳ-o3ᵛ).

—— *Saint Louis*, Books i–xviii, in *Les oeuvres poétiques du P. Le Moyne, enrichies de tres-belles figures en taille-douce*, Paris, T. Jolly, 1672, BN: Ye.52, BM: 82.l.11. Contains *Saint Louis* and 'Dissertation' with same pagination as the *Oeuvres* of 1671.

MAMBRUN, Pierre, *Constantinus sive idololatria debellata authore Petro Mambruno è societate Iesu*, Paris, D. Bechet and L. Billaine, 1658, Books i–xii. BN: Yc.1512, BM: 887.k.12.

—— *Dissertatio peripatetica de epico carmine*, Paris, S. and G. Cramoisy, 1652. BN: Y.123, BM: 836.k.14.

*—— In *Petri Mambruni . . . Opera Poetica*, Angers, G. Laboe, 1661, *Idololatria debellata sive Constantinus*, pp. 101–323, and *De epico carmine dissertatio peripatetica*, pp. 325–483. BN: Yc.162, BM: 586.k.11.

MONTREUX, Nicolas, *L'Espagne conquise par Charles le Grand, Roy de France, premiere partie . . . par OLLENIX DU MONT-SACRE*, Nantes, P. Doriou, 1597. BN: Rés.Ye.2012, ARS: 8°BL.15687(1) (24 'chants', first part only).

—— *L'Espagne conquise . . . seconde partie*, Paris, Abraham Saugrain, 1598 (colophon: Imprimé à Nantes par François Faverye, 1598). ARS: 8°BL.15687(2) (22 'chants', second part, completing the poem in 46 'chants').

NAVIERES, Charles de, *La Henriade*, extracts in the following works (the number in brackets indicates the number of lines in the extract; the book number indicates the place of the extract in the *Henriade*):

—— *Vers et musique de Navières au baptesme de Monseigneur le Dauphin*, Paris, G. Lombard, 1606. BN: Ye.28461. Book i (92), pp. 19–21; Book v or vi (8), p. 4.

—— *Memorial du feu . . . Henry de Bourbon, Duc de Montpensier*, Paris, C. Chappelain, 1608. BN: 28452. Liminary verse by Jean Morel alludes to the *Henriade*, p. 2.

—— *Actions de grace solemnelles a pareil iour 22 mars que Henry le Grand . . . entra pacifiquement en sa bonne ville de Paris . . . l'an 1594*, Paris, C. Chappelain, 1608. BN: L³⁵b.551. Book ? (10), p. 5.

—— *Alegresse et resiouissance publique pour la nativité de Mgr. le Duc d'Anjou*, Paris, C. Chappelain, 1608. BN: Ye.28446. Reference to 50,000 verses of *Henriade*, p. 15; Book ? (39), pp. 16–17.

—— *Trépas du grand duc de Florence*, Paris, D. Ramier, 1609. BN: Ye.28459. Reference to 30,000 verses of *Henriade*, p. 5.

—— *L'heureuse entrée au ciel du feu Roy Henry le Grand*, Paris, P. Mettayer, 1610. BN: L³⁵b947. Reference to 30,000 verses of *Henriade*, p. 64; Book iv (1–4), p. 21; Book vi (678), pp. 23–49; Book vii (12), pp. 10–11; Book xi (97), pp. 65–8; Books ? (4+4+6), p. 5, (3), p. 11, (180, on the apotheosis of Henry), pp. 19–20.

—— *Avant-chants alaigres . . . sur les alliances royales*, Paris, F. Bourriquant, [1612]. BN: Ye.14578. Request to Louis XIII to encourage the *Henriade*, p. 4.

—— *Trépas et mémorial de la . . . Royne Marguerite et la ressemblance conforme d'elle au grand roy François son ayeul. Extraicte de la cinquante neufiesme colonne Royale de la heroique Henriade*, Paris, F. Bourriquant, 1615, 8pp. BN: Ye.28460. Apparently an extract from some episode glorifying the predecessors of Henry IV.

PILLARD, Laurent, *Laurentii Pilladii . . . Rusticiados libri sex* in CALMET, *Histoire de Lorraine, nouvelle edition*, Nancy, 1751, vol. iv (reissued separately with the title *Bibliothèque lorraine*, Nancy, 1751). BN: Ln²⁰73, BM: 186.h.9. I have not seen the edition of Metz, 1548, on which Calmet's edition is based.

*—— *La Rusticiade ou la guerre des paysans en Lorraine*, ed. F.-R. Dupeux, 2 vols., Nancy, 1876, BN: Yc.11936–11937, BM: 11403.b.5. Text and translation.

RONSARD, Pierre de, *Les quatre premiers livre* [sic] *de la Franciade*, Paris, Gabriel Buon, 1572. BN: Rés.Ye.506, BM: C.39.f.22.

—— *Les quatre premiers livres de la Franciade . . . reveue, corrigée et augmentée*, Paris, G. Buon, 1573. BN: Rés.Ye.1111.

—— *Les quatre premiers livres de la Franciade . . . reveue, & corrigée de nouveau*, Turin, Jean-François Pico, 1574. BN: Rés.Ye.4763. (BM: 11475.a.40 has the same title arranged slightly differently, and no date.)

*—— *La Franciade* in *Oeuvres complètes*, ed. P. Laumonier, vol. xvi, 2 pts., Paris, 1950–2.

—— *L'Abrégé de l'art poétique françois*, in *Oeuvres complètes*, ed. P. Laumonier, vol. xiv, Paris, 1949.

SCHELANDRE, Jean de, *Les deux premiers livres de la Stuartide en l'honneur de la Très-Illustre maison des Stuarts*, Paris, F. Bourriquant, 1611. BM: C.59.g.30. 'Argument de la Stuartide', pp. 27–34.

SCUDERY, Georges de, *Alaric ou Rome vaincuë, poëme héroïque*, Paris, A. Courbé, 1654, folio, Books i–x, as in all later editions. BN: Rés.Ye. 69, BM: 82.l.1.

—— *Alaric*, Leyden, J. Sambix, 1654, 8vo. BN: Ye.7976.

—— *Alaric . . . jouxte la copie*, Paris, A. Courbé, 1655, 8vo. BN: Rés. p.Ye.619, BM: 11474.aa.42.

—— *Alaric . . . jouxte la copie*, Paris, A. Courbé, 1656, 12mo. ENS: LF.p.213.12°.

—— *Alaric . . . imprimé à Rouen et se vend à Paris*, A. Courbé, 1659, 12mo. BM: 1065.c.11.

*—— *Alaric . . . suivant la copie de Paris*, The Hague, J. van Ellinkhuysen, 1685, 12mo. BN: Ye.7977, BM: 1161.c.42.

——*Discours de la France à Monseigneur le Cardinal de Richelieu après son retour de Nancy*, Paris, F. Targa, 1634. BN: Ye.1334. Contains reference to *Robert le Grand*, p. 13.

*THOMAS I, Paul, *Lutetias*, Books i–v, in *Pauli Thomae Engolismensis Poemata partim nunc primum, partim olim edita*, Paris, C. Morel, 1617, pp. 1–121. BN: Yc.8698, BM: 1213.f.12.

—— *Lutetias*, Books i–v, in *Pauli Thomae Engolismensis Poemata ab authore aucta & recognita, tertia editio*, Angoulême, C. Rèze, 1640, pp. 1–138. BM: 11405.b.35.

THOMAS II, Paul (sieur des Maisonnettes), *Pauli Thomae Engolismensis Rupellaidos sive de rebus gestis Ludovici XIII Franc. & Navarr. regis invictissimi libri VI*, Paris, C. Morel, 1630. BN: Yc.1743, BM: 837.g.25.

URFE, Honoré d', extracts from the *Savoysiade* in the following (see above, p. 000, n. 0):
—— *Nouveau recueil des plus beaux vers de ce temps*, Paris, Toussainct du Bray, 1609, supplement, pp. 1–22. BN: Ye.11434. (BN: Ye.11433 and Ye.11442 do not contain the supplement with the extracts.)
—— *Les Délices de la poésie françoise ou recueil des plus beaux vers de ce temps*, Paris, T. du Bray, 1615, pp. 493–514. ARS: Rés.8°BL. 9961(1).
—— *Les Délices de la poésie françoise ou recueil des plus beaux vers de ce temps . . . recueilly par F. de Rosset*, Paris, T. du Bray, 1618, pp. 551–72. BN: Ye.11443.
—— Benedetto, L. F. 'Una redazione inedita della leggenda degli infanti di Lara', *Studi medievali*, 4 (1912–13), 253–70.

*VARANNE, Valerand de, *Valerandi Varanii de gestis Ioannae virginis France egregie bellatricis libri quattuor*, Paris, J. de la Porte, 1516. BM: G.9961. BN: Rés.m.Yc.851(1).
—— *Valerandi Varanii de gestis Ioannae . . . libri quattuor* in *De memorabilibus et claris mulieribus aliquot scriptorum opera*, ed. J. Ravisius Textor, Paris, S. de Colines, 1521, fol. 199r-214r. BN: Rés.G.436, BM: 1329.l.8.
—— *Valerandi Varanii de gestis Ioannae . . . Poème de 1516*, ed. E. Prarond, 2 vols., Paris, A. Picard, 1889 BN: 8°Yc.278, BM: 11409.f. 39. Text and notes.

2. *Secondary sources*

ADAM, A., *Théophile de Viau et la libre pensée française en 1620*, Paris, 1935.
—— *Histoire de la littérature française*, 5 vols., Paris, 1948–56.

ADAMS, H. M., *Catalogue of books printed on the continent of Europe (1501–1600) in Cambridge libraries*, 2 vols., Cambridge, 1967.

ALLAIS, G., *De Franciadis epica fabula in posteriore XVI saeculi parte*, Paris, 1891.

ARIOSTO, L., *Orlando Furioso*, ed. L. Caretti, Milan–Naples, 1954.

ARISTOTLE, *De arte poetica*, ed. R. Kassel, Oxford, 1965.

ASCOLI, G., *La Grande-Bretagne devant l'opinion française au XVIIe Siècle*, 2 vols., Paris, 1930.

ASSELINEAU, C., *Jean de Schelandre*, Paris, 1854.

AUBIGNE, A. d', *Oeuvres,* ed. H. Weber, J. Bailbé, A. Soulié, Paris, 1969 (Pléiade).

BABINOT, A., *La Christiade*, Poitiers, Pierre and Jean Moines, 1559. ARS: 8°BL.10387 Rés.

BANDELLO, M., *Tutte le opere*, ed. F. Flora, 2 vols., Verona, 1943.

BARBIER, O., and BILLARD, R., *Dictionnaire des ouvrages anonymes*, 4 vols., Paris, 1872–9.

BEALL, C. B., 'The first French imitation of Tasso's invocation to the Muse', *MLN*, 53 (1938), 531–2.
—— *La Fortune du Tasse en France*, Oregon, 1942.

BELLEFOREST, F. de, see GILLES.

BELLONI, A., *Gli epigoni della Gerusalemme Liberata*, Padua, 1893.

BENEDETTO, L. F., 'Una redazione inedita della leggenda degli infanti di Lara,' *Studi medievali*, 4 (1912–13), 231–70.

BERGOUNIOUX, L. A., *L'Esprit de polémique et les querelles savantes vers le milieu du XVIIe siècle. Marc-Antoine Dominici*, Paris, 1936.

BERNARD, A., *Les d'Urfé*, Paris, 1839.

BERNADET, E., *Un Abbé d'Hautecombe ami de Ronsard: Alphonse Delbene*, Grenoble, 1937.

BERTHIER, A.-F., *Oeuvres*, ed. E. Minoret, 2 vols., 1889–90.

BILLAUT, A., *Le Vilebrequin*, Paris, G. de Luyne, 1663. BM: 11481.a.6.

BINET, C., *La Vie de P. de Ronsard*, ed. P. Laumonier, Paris, 1910.

BODIN, J., *Methodus ad facilem historiarum cognitionem*, Paris, M. Le Jeune, 1566. BM: 580.g.2.
——*Method for the easy comprehension of history*, translated by B. Reynolds, New York, 1945.

BOETHIUS, H., *Scotorum historiae a prima gentis origine*, Paris, Josse Bade, 1526. BM: 600.gg.12.

BOILEAU-DESPREAUX, N., *Oeuvres*, 2 vols., Amsterdam, 1718.
——*Epîtres, Art Poétique, Lutrin*, ed. C.-H. Boudhors, 1952.

BONAFOUS, N., *Etudes sur 'L Astrée' et sur Honoré d'Urfé*, Paris, 1846.

BORNEMANN, W., *Boileau-Despréaux im Urtheile seines Zeitgenossen Jean Desmarets de Saint-Sorlin*, Heilbronn, 1883.

BORZELLI, A., *Storia della vita e delle opere di Giovan Battista Marino,* Naples, 1927.

BOUCHET, J., *Les Anciennes et Modernes Généalogies des rois de France,* Paris, 1536. BN: Rés. 8°L37.2.B.

BRICE, G., *Herveus sive Chordigerae navis conflagratio*, Strasburg, M. Schürer, 1514. BM: 11403.b.37.

—— *Herveus* in Ranutius Gherus, *Deliciae C. poetarum Gallorum*, [Frankfurt], 1609, pp. 755–63. BM: 1213.a.3.

——*Herveus*, ed. Grandpont, in *Nouvelles annales de la marine et des colonies*, Paris, 13 (1855), 216–28.

BUCHANAN, G., *Rerum scoticarum historia*, Edinburgh, A. Arbuthnot, 1582. BM: 186.c.16.

BUFFUM, I., *Agrippa d'Aubigné's 'Les Tragiques': a study of the Baroque style in poetry*, New Haven, 1951.

CABEEN, C. W., *L'Influence de Giambattista Marino sur la littérature française dans la première moitié du XVIIe siècle*, Grenoble, 1904.

CALMET, A., *Histoire de Lorraine, nouvelle édition*, 7 vols., Nancy, 1745–57. Vol. iv (also reissued separately with the title *Bibliothèque lorraine*, Nancy, 1751) contains Pillard's *Rusticiad*; vol. vii contains the *Chronique de Lorraine* (cols. lxxx–cxxxviii) and Chrétien's *Vraye declaration* (cols. cli–clx).

CAMDEN, W., *Britannia*, London, 1607. BM: 576.m.7.

CAMERON, A., *The influence of Ariosto's epic and lyric poetry on Ronsard and his group*, Baltimore, 1930.

CAMERON, K., 'Ronsard and Book iv of the *Franciade*: a study of Ronsard's changes to the tableau of the Kings of France', *BHR*, 32 (1970), 395–406.

CANIVET, D., *L'Illustration de la poésie et du roman français au XVIIe siècle*, Paris, 1957.

CARLOS, Prince of Viana, *Crónica de los reyes de Navarra*, ed. J. Yanguas y Miranda, Pamplona, 1843.

Catalogue de l'histoire de France, Paris, 1855–95.

CESARE, M. di, *Vida's 'Christiad' and Vergilian epic*, Columbia, 1964.

CHAMARD, H., *Histoire de la Pléide*, 4 vols., Paris, 1939–40.

CHAPPUYS, G., See GILLES.

CHASTELLAIN, G., *Histoire du bon chevalier Messire Jacques de Lalain*, ed. J. Chifflet, Brussels, 1634. BM: 277.i.31.

CHEROT, H., *Etude sur la vie et les oeuvres du P. Le Moyne (1602–1671)*, Paris, 1887.

CHIABRERA, G., *Amedeida*, Genoa, 1620. BM: 1063.i.4.

CHIARADIA, E. N., *L'imitazione omerica nella 'Gerusalemme Liberata'*, Naples, 1903.

CHRETIEN, *La Vraye Declaration du fait & conduite de la bataille de Nancy ... en 1476 dressé par Chrétien ... donée à Maître Pierre de Blaru ... qui a composé le livre appellé les Nanceydes*, see CALMET.

La Chronique de Lorraine depuis l'an 1350 ou environ, jusqu'à l'an 1544, see CALMET.

CIORANESCU, A., *L'Arioste en France des origines à la fin du XVIIIe siècle*, 2 vols., Paris, 1939.
—— *Bibliographie de la littérature française du seizième siècle*, Paris 1959.
—— *Bibliographie de la littérature française du dix-septième siècle*, 3 vols., Paris, 1965–6.
—— 'La Pléiade et le poème épique', in *Lumières de la Pléiade (Neuvième stage international d'études humanistes, Tours, 1965)*, Paris, 1966, pp. 75–86.
Codices manuscripti bibliothecae regii Taurinensis . . . pars altera, Turin, 1749.

COHEN, G., *Ecrivains français en Hollande dans la première moitié du XVIIe siècle*, Paris, 1920.

COLLAS, G., *Jean Chapelain (1595–1674). étude historique et littéraire d'après des documents inédits*, Paris, 1912.

COLLIGNON, A., *De Nanceide Petri de Blaro Rivo*, Nancy, 1892.
—— 'De quelques imitations dans la *Rusticiade*', *Annales de l'Est*, 7 (1893), 594–601.
—— 'Etude sur la *Rusticiade* de Laurent Pillard', *Mémoires de l'Académie de Stanislas*, 6e série, 15 (1918), 230–58; 16 (1919), 108–44.

COLOTTE, P., *Le Poète Pierre de Deimier: sa carrière provençale*, Marseilles, 1952.
—— *Pierre de Deimier, poète et théoricien de la poésie . . . sa carrière à Paris et ses relations avec Malherbe*, Gap, 1953.

COMPARETTI, D., *Vergil in the Middle Ages*, translated by E. Benecke, 2nd edition, London, 1908.

CONSTANS, A., 'Georges de Scudéry's lost epic', *MLN*, 37 (1922), 212–5.

CONTI, N., *Mythologiae sive explicationum fabularum libri decem*, Venice, 1568. BM: 704.d.7.
—— *Mythologie ou explication des fables*, translated and edited by J. Baudouin, Paris, 1627. BM: 82.l.15.

CORBIN, J., *La Sainte Franciade contenant la vie, gestes & miracles du bienheureux Saint François*, Paris, 1632. BN: Ye.7734.

COTTAZ, J., *Le Tasse et la conception épique*, Paris, 1942.
—— *L'Influence des théories du Tasse sur l'épopée en France*, Paris, 1942.

COUDERC, C., 'Oeuvres inédites de Pierre de Blarru d'après un manuscrit récemment acquis par la Bibliothèque Nationale', *Le Bibliographe Moderne*, 4 (1900), 86–112.

COUGNY, E., *Jeanne Darc, épopée latine du XVIe siècle*, Paris, 1874 (extrait du 10e volume des Mémoires de la Société des Sciences Morales, Lettres, et Arts de Seine-et-Oise).

COURTEAULT, P., *Geoffroy de Malvyn, magistrat et humaniste bordelais (1545?–1617). Etude biographique et littéraire*, Paris, 1907.

COX, E. L., *The Green Count of Savoy: Amadeus VI and Transalpine Savoy in the fourteenth century*, Princeton, 1967.

CURTIUS, E. R., *European literature and the Latin Middle Ages*, translated by W. Trask, London, 1953.

DAMIANI, G. F., *Sopra la poesia del cavalier Marino*, Turin, 1899.

DEDEYAN, C., 'Henri II, la *Franciade* et les *Hymnes* de 1555–1556', *BHR*, 9 (1947), 114–28.

DELAPORTE, P. V., *Du Merveilleux dans la littérature française sous le règne de Louis XIV*, Paris, 1891.

DELMONT, T., *Le Meilleur Poète épique du XVIIe siècle*, Arras, [1901] (extrait de la *Revue de Lille*, décembre 1900).

DESCALLIS, F., *La Lydiade divisee en sept livres*, Tournon, 1602. ARS: 8°BL.9010.

DESREY, P., see GAGUIN.

Dictionnaire de biographie française, 11 vols., Paris, 1933–67, as far as DUGUET only.

DOLET, E., *Francisci Valesii Gallorum Regis fata*, Lyon, 1539. BM: G.9713(3).

DUBARAT, V., 'Une Curiosité bibliographique: L'"Heptaméron de la Navarride" du sieur de la Palme—Paris, Portier, 1602', *Bulletin de la Société des Sciences, Lettres et Arts de Pau*, 2e série, 46 (1923), 230–2.

DU BARTAS, G., *The works of G. de Salluste, sieur Du Bartas*, ed. U. Holmes, J. Lyons, R. Linker, 3 vols., Chapel Hill, 1935–40.
—— *La Lépanthe*, Edinburgh, 1591, see JAMES I.

DU BELLAY, J., *La Deffence et illustration de la langue francoyse*, ed. H. Chamard, Paris, 1904.

DU BRAY, Toussainct, see section B1, URFE.

DUCHESNE, J., *Histoire des poëmes épiques français du XVIIe siècle*, Paris, 1870.

DUFOUR, A., see section B1, DELBENE.

DU HAILLAN, B., *Promesse et desseing de l'histoire de France*, Paris, P. L'Huillier, 1571. Reproduced by P. Bonnefon, 'L'historien du Haillan', *RHLF*, 22 (1915), 457–71.
—— *L'Histoire de France*, Paris, P. L'Huillier, 1576. BM: 186.e.4.

DUPARC, P., 'La *Savoysiade* d'Honoré d'Urfé', *Revue Savoysienne*, 86 (1945), 60–4.

DUPLEIX, S., *Histoire générale de France*, 3 vols., Paris, L., Sonnius, 1621–8. BN: Rés.L35.80.A.

DUPORTAL, J., *Etude sur les livres à figures édités en France de 1601 à 1660*, Paris, 1914.

DUPRE, A., 'Observations sur la famille et les fonctions judiciaires de Sébastien Garnier', *Mémoires de la société des sciences et des lettres du Loir-et-Cher*, 4 (1852), 506–11.

DU RIVAGE, sieur de, see LA MESNARDIERE.

DU VERDIER, see LA CROIX DU MAINE.

EDELMAN, N., *Attitudes of seventeenth century France to the Middle Ages*, New York, 1946.

EGGER, E., *L'Hellénisme en France, Leçons sur l'influence des études Grecques dans le développement de la langue et de la littérature françaises*, 2 vols., Paris, 1869.
—— *Mémoires de littérature ancienne*, Paris, 1882.

ELTON, G. R., *The practice of history*, London, 1969 (Fontana).

EMILIO, P., *Pauli Aemilii . . . de rebus gestis Francorum libri IIII*, Paris, J. Bade, [1517]. BN: Rés. L.35.22.
—— *De rebus gestis Francorum . . . libri decem*, Paris, M. Vascosan, 1539. BN: Rés. L.35.23α.

ERASMUS, D., *Adagiorum opus*, Lyon, S. Gryphius, 1541. BM: 1476.d.21.

EVANS, W. H., *L'Historien Mézeray et la conception de l'histoire en France au XVIIe siècle*, Paris, 1930.

FABRE, A., *Les Ennemis de Chapelain*, Paris, 1888.

FARAL, E., 'Sur deux manuscrits du livre II de la *Franciade* (Bibl. Nat. fr. 19141 et Nlles. acq. 10695)', *RHLF*, 17 (1910), 685–708.
—— 'Les Manuscrits du livre II de la *Franciade*', *RHLF*, 20 (1913), 672–4.
—— *La Légende arthurienne: études et documents*, 3 vols., Paris, 1929.

FINSLER, G., *Homer in der Neuzeit von Dante bis Goethe*, Leipzig and Berlin, 1912.

FLEURET, F., and PERCEAU, L., *Les Satires françaises du XVIe siècle*, 2 vols., Paris, 1922.
—— *Les Satires françaises du XVIIe siècle*, 2 vols., Paris, 1923.

FREDEGAR, *Chronicarum quae dicuntur Fredegarii scholastici libri iv*, ed. B. Krusch, in *Monumenta Germaniae Historica: scriptores rerum merovingicarum*, vol. ii, Hanover, 1888.

FRANCE, P., *Racine's rhetoric*, Oxford, 1965.

GAGUIN, R., *Roberti Gaguini compendium de origine et gestis Francorum*, Paris, D. Gerlier, 1497. BN: Rés.L.35.10.
—— *Les Grandes Croniques . . . composées en latin par . . . Robert Gaguin . . . translatées à la lettre de latin en nostre vulgaire françoys* [by Pierre Desrey], Paris, G. du Pré, 1514. BN: Rés.L.35.15.
—— *Epistolae et orationes*, ed. L. Thuasne, 2 vols., Paris, 1903.

GANDAR, E., *Ronsard considéré comme imitateur d'Homere & de Pindare*, Metz, 1854.

GAUTIER, L., *Les Epopées françaises . . . seconde édition, entièrement refondue*, 4 vols., Paris, 1878–92.

GAY, L. M., 'Sources of the *Académie de l'Art Poétique* of Pierre de Deimier: Peletier du Mans', *PMLA*, 27 (1912), 398–418.

GILLES, N., *Les très élégantes, très véridiques et copieuses Annales des très preux, très nobles, très chrestiens et très excellens modérateurs des belliqueuses Gaules . . . compilées par Nicole Gilles*, Paris, G. du Pré, 1525. BN: Rés. L35.37.

—— *Annales et chroniques de France, depuis la destruction de Troye iusques au temps du roy Loys XI, iadis composées par feu maistre Nicole Gilles . . . depuis additionnées selon les modernes hystoriens, iusques en l'an 1549 . . . reveu & corrigé . . . par Denis SAUVAGE de Fontenailles en Brie*, Paris, G. du Pré, 1549. BOD: G.S.14.Art.

—— *Les Chroniques et annales de France, des l'origine des Francoys et leur venue es Gaules. Faictes iadis briefvement par Nicole Gilles . . . & depuis continuees par Denis Sauvage . . . a present reveues, corrigees & augmentees . . . jusqu'au roy Charles neufième . . . par François de BELLEFOREST*, Paris, G. Buon, 1573. BM: 595.k.12.

—— *Les Chroniques et annales de France . . . augmentées et continuées . . . jusqu'au roy Henri III . . . par Guillaume CHAPPUYS*, Paris, J. Cavellat, 1585. BN: Rés. L35.45.

—— *Les Chroniques et annales de France . . . avec la suite et continuation jusques au roy . . . Louys XIII . . . par M. Jean SAVARON*, Paris, P. Chevalier, 1621. BN: Fol. L35.46.

GILLOT, H., *La Querelle des anciens et des modernes en France*, Paris, 1914.

GODARD, J., *L'Oracle ou chant de Protée . . . auec les commentaires de Claude Le Brun*, Lyon, T. Ancelin, 1594. BM: 85.d.2.

—— *Les Oeuvres de Iean Godard*, 2 vols., Lyon, P. Landry, 1594. BN: Rés.Ye.2109.

—— *Meslanges poetiques, tragiques, comiques et autres diverses*, Lyon, A. Travers, 1624 (pirated edition of vol. ii of the *Oeuvres* of 1594). BM: 11475.dd.3.

GODEAU, A., *Oeuvres chrétiennes*, Paris, J. Camusat, 1633. BN: Ye.8019.

—— *Saint Paul poeme chrestien*, Paris, P. Le Petit, 1654. BM: 1065.b.18.

GORDON, A., *Ronsard et la Rhétorique*, Geneva, 1970.

GOUJET, C. P., *Bibliothèque françoise*, 18 vols., Paris, 1741–56.

Les Grandes Chroniques de France, 10 vols., ed. J. Viard, Paris, 1920–53; 3 vols., ed. R. Delachenel, Paris, 1910–19 (Société de l'Histoire de France).

GRANDI, A., *Tancredi*, Lecce, 1636. BM: 1063.b.18.

GREENE, T., *The descent from heaven: a study in epic continuity*, Yale, 1963.

GREGORY OF TOURS, *Gregorii Turonensis episcopi historiae Francorum libri decem*, ed. L. Bochel, Paris, N. du Fossé, 1610. BN: 8°La5.5.

*—— *Decem libri historiarum*, ed. B. Krusch and W. Levison, in *Monumenta Germaniae Historica: scriptores rerum merovingicarum*, vol. i, part 1, second edition, Hanover, 1951.

GRIFFIN, R., *The coronation of the poet: du Bellay's debt to the trivium*, California, 1969.

GUY, H., 'Les Sources françaises de Ronsard', *RHLF*, 9 (1902), 217–56.

HAGIWARA, M. P., *French epic poetry in the sixteenth century: theory and practice*, The Hague, 1972. This work was published too late for me to use. There is a chapter on epic theory in the sixteenth century and another on Ronsard's *Franciade*.

HALL, H. G., 'Three illustrated works of Desmarets de Saint-Sorlin', *Yale University Library Gazette*, 33 (1958), 18–28.

HANKISS, J., 'Schelandre et Shakespeare', *MLN*, 36 (1921), 464–9.

HENNEBERT, F., 'Histoire des traductions françaises d'auteurs grecs et latins pendant le XVIe et le XVIIe siècles', in *Annales des universités de Belgique, années 1858 et 1859*, Brussels, 1861.

HEPP, N., 'Homère en France au XVIe siècle', *Atti della Accademia delle scienze di Torino* (II, Classe di scienze morali, storiche, e filologiche), 96 (1961–2), 389–508.

—— *Homère en France au XVIIe siècle*, Paris, 1968.

HEUDON, J., *Les Adventures de la France*, Paris, P. Bonfons, 1602. BM: 11482.a.16.

HOMER, *Iliad*, ed. D. Monro and T. Allen, 3rd edition, 2 vols., Oxford, 1920.

—— *Odyssey*, ed. T. Allen, 2nd edition, 2 vols., Oxford, 1917.

HULUBEI, A. 'Virgile en France au XVIe siècle, '*Revue de Seizième Siècle*, 18 (1931), 1–77.

HUPPERT, G., *The idea of perfect history: historical erudition and historical philosophy in Renaissance France*, Illinois, 1969.

JACOUBET, H., *Le Genre troubadour et les origines françaises du Romantisme*, Paris, 1929.

JAMES I, King of England, *His maiesties poeticall exercises at vacant houres*, Edinburgh, R. Waldegrave, 1582. After James's *Lepanto* comes du Bartas's translation preceded by a false title: *La Lepanthe de Iaques VI Roy d'Escosse faicte françoise par le Sieur du Bartas*, Edinburgh, R. Waldegrave, 1591. BM: C.10.a.17.

JEROME, *Interpretatio chronicae Eusebii Pamphili*, in Migne, *Patrologiae cursus completus, series latina*, Paris, 1866, vol. 27, tom.8.

JOINVILLE, J. de, *L'Histoire & cronique du treschrestien Roy S. Loys IX*, ed. A. P. de Rieux, Poitiers, E. de Marnef, [1561], BM: C.38.f.1.

JOLY, A., *Benoît de Sainte-More et le roman de Troie*, 2 vols., Paris, 1870–71.

KELLEY, D., *The foundations of modern historical scholarship: language, law and history in the French Renaissance*, Columbia, 1970.

KLIPPEL, M., *Die Darstellung der fränkischen Trojanersage in Geschichtsschreibung und Dichtung vom Mittelalter bis zur Renaissance in Frankreich*, Marburg, 1936.

LA BORDERIE, A. de, 'Le Poème de *Childebrand*', *Revue de Bretagne et de Vendée*, 2e série, 7 (1865), 308–20, 337–51.

LACHEVRE, F., *Bibliographie des recueils collectifs de poésies publiés de 1597 à 1700*, 4 vols., Paris, 1901–5.
—— 'Glanes Bibliographiques: Jean de Boyssières de Montferrand et Jean Morel de Reims. Une querelle littéraire . . . ', *Bulletin du Bibliophile* (1926), pp. 298–310, 345–50.

LA CROIX DU MAINE, F. Grudé de, *Les Bibliothèques françoises de la Croix du Maine et de du Verdier*, ed. Rigoley de Juvigny, 6 vols., Paris, 1792–3.

LA MARCHE, O. de, *Les Mémoires de Messire Olivier de la Marche*, ed. Petitot, 2 vols., Paris, 1825 (Collection complète des mémoires relatifs à l'histoire de France, vols. 9 and 10).

LA MESNARDIERE, H.-J. Pilet de, *Lettre du sieur du Rivage contenant quelques observations sur le poème épique et sur le poème de la Pucelle*, Paris, A. de Sommaville, 1656. BM: 836.h.20.

LA MOTTE-MESSEME, F. le Poulchre de, *Les Sept Livres des honnestes loisirs . . . qui est un discours en forme de chronoviologie* [sic] *où sera véritablement discouru des plus notables occurrances de noz guerres civiles, & des divers accidens de l'Autheur*, Paris, Marc Orry, 1587. BN: Ye.7435.

LANGE, P., *Ronsards Franciade und ihr Verhältnis zu Vergils Aeneide*, Wurzen, 1887.

LATREILLE, C., *De Petro Boessatio (1603–1662) ac de conditione litteratorum virorum in Delphinatu eadem aetate*, Vienne, 1899.

LAWTON, H., *Handbook of French Renaissance dramatic theory*, Manchester, 1949.

LEBEGUE, R., *Ronsard: l'homme et l'oeuvre*, Paris, 1950.

LE BLANC, P., *Les Paraphrases françaises des Psaumes à la fin de la période Baroque 1610–1660*, Paris 1960.

LE BOSSU, R., *Traité du poème épique*, 2 vols., Paris, 1675. BM: 75.b.4.

LE FEVRE DE LA BODERIE, G., *La Galliade ou de la Revolution des Arts et Sciences*, Paris, G. Chaudière, 1578. BN: Rés.Ye.519.

LELONG, J., *Bibliothèque historique de la France*, ed. F. de Fontette, 5 vols., Paris, 1768.

LEMAIRE DE BELGES, J., *Oeuvres*, ed. J. Stecher, 4 vols., Louvain, 1882–91.

—— *Liber historiae Francorum*, ed. B. Krusch, in *Monumenta Germaniae historica: scriptores rerum merovingicarum*, vol. ii, Hanover, 1888.

LORITUS, H., *Descriptio de situ Helvetiae et vicinis gentibus*, Basle, 1519. BM: 837.e.2(2).

LUCAN, *Pharsalia*, ed. and translated by J. D. Duff, London, 1928 (Loeb).

MAGENDIE, M., *Du nouveau sur l'Astrée*, Paris, 1927.

MARIE JOSE, Ex-queen of Italy, *La Maison de Savoie: les origines, le Comte Vert, le Comte Rouge*, Paris, 1956.

MARINO, G. B., *L'Adone*, Paris, 1623. BN: Rés. Yd.52. Contains Chapelain's *Lettre ou discours à M. Favereau*.

MARNI, A., *Allegory in the French heroic poem of the seventeenth century*, Princeton, 1936.

MAROLLES, M. de, *Traité du poème épique*, Paris, 1662. BM: 1000.e.17(3).

MAROT, C., *Les Epîtres*, ed. C. Mayer, London, 1958.

MASKELL, D., 'The transformation of history into epic: the *Stuartide* (1611) of Jean de Schelandre', *MLR*, 66 (1971), 53–65.

MEZERAY, F. Eudes de, *Histoire de France*, 3 vols., Paris, M. Guillemot, 1643–51. BN: Fol. L35.94.

—— *Histoire de France ... nouvelle édition*, 3 vols., Paris, D. Thierry, 1685. BM: 704.l.16.

—— *Abrégé chronologique ou extraict de l'histoire de France*, 6 vols., Amsterdam, A. Schelte, 1696. BN: 8°L35.98.I.

La Montmorenciade contenant les exploits héroïques de Mgr. le Duc de Montmorency en ces derniers guerres tant par mer que par terre, [*post* 1628]. CHA: Vd.16.

MONTMORET, H. de, *Bellorum britannicorum a Carolo Francorum rege eo nomine septimo in Henricum anglorum regem ... gestorum prima pars*, Paris, 1512. BM: G.9971.

—— *Fratris Humberti Montismoretani Herveis*, Paris, H. le Fèvre, [1514?]. CUL: F.151.d.4.25.

MORCAY, R., and MULLER, A., *La Renaissance*, Paris, 1960.

MOREL-FATIO, A., *Recueil des instructions données aux ambassadeurs et ministres de France*, vol. 11 (Espagne), Paris, 1894.

MORERI, Louis, *Grand Dictionnaire historique*, 10 vols., Paris, 1759.

MOUFLARD, M.-M., *Robert Garnier (1545–1590), la vie*, La Ferté-Bernard, 1961.

MURARASU, D., *La Poésie néo-latine et la renaissance des lettres antiques en France (1500–1549)*, Paris, 1928.

NOLHAC, P. de, *Ronsard et l'humanisme*, Paris, 1921.

OROSIUS, *Pauli Orosii presbyteri hispani adversus paganos historiarum libri septem*, Mainz, 1615. BM: 799.c.12.

OTIS, B., *Ovid as an epic poet*, Cambridge, 1966.

OVID, *Tristium libri V*, ed. S. G. Owen, Oxford, 1889.
—— *Metamorphoseon libri XV*, ed. H. Magnus, Berlin, 1914.

PARADIN, G., *Chronique de Savoie*, Lyon, J. de Tournes, 1561. BM: 177.i.15.

PARDUCCI, A., 'Le imitazioni ariostee nella *Franciade* del Ronsard', *Archivum Romanicum*, 14 (1930), 361–94.

PASQUIER, E., *Les Oeuvres*, 2 vols., Amsterdam, 1723.

PATTERSON, W. F., *Three centuries of French poetic theory: a critical history of the chief arts of poetry in France (1328–1630)*, 2 vols., Michigan, 1930.

PELETIER DU MANS, J., *L'Art poëtique (1555)*, ed. A. Boulanger, Paris, 1930.

PERRAULT, C., *Saint Paulin evesque de Nole, poëme*, Paris, J. Coignard, 1687. BN: Ye.8111.

PETIT, J.-F., 'Etude sur le *Clovis* de Desmarets', *Bulletin de la société d'agriculture, sciences et arts de la Sarthe*, 2e série, 11 (1867–8), 698–719.

PETRARCA, F., *Rime, trionfi, e poesie latine*, Milan–Naples, 1951. Contains extracts from *Africa*.

PICARD, R., *La Poésie française de 1640 à 1680: poésie religieuse, épopée, lyrisme officiel*, 2e édition, Paris, 1965.

PICOT, E., *Les Français italianisants au XVIe siècle*, 2 vols., Paris, 1906–7.

PINTARD, R., 'Autour de *Cinna* et de *Polyeucte*', *RHLF*, 64 (1964), 377–413.

PREVOST, J., *Apothéose du très chrestien Roy ... Henry IIII*, Poitiers, J. Thoreau, 1613. BM: 241.c.27.

PROCOPIUS, *Historiarum Procopii caesariensis libri VIII*, ed. D. Hoeschel, Augsburg, 1607. BM: 589.i.11.
—— *Procopius*, ed. and translated by D. B. Dewing, 7 vols., London and New York, 1914–40 (Loeb).

PLEE, L., 'Notice sur la première *Henriade* publiée en 1593–1594', *Mémoires de la société des sciences et des lettres du Loir-et-Cher*, 4 (1852), 460–505.

QUERARD, J. M., *Les Supercheries littéraires dévoilées*, 2nd edition, Paris, 1869–70.

QUICHERAT, J., *Procès de condamnation et de réhabilitation de Jeanne d'Arc*, 5 vols., Paris, 1841–9 (Société de l'histoire de France).

RAPIN, R., *Les Réflexions sur la poétique de ce temps et sur les ouvrages des poètes anciens et modernes*, ed. E. Dubois, Geneva, 1970.

RAVISIUS TEXTOR, J., *Epithetorum opus absolutissimum*, Basle, 1573. BM: 1477.b.38.

RAYMOND, M., *L'Influence de Ronsard sur la poésie française (1550–1585)*, 2 vols., Paris, 1927.

REIBETANZ, A., *Jean Desmarets de Saint-Sorlin, sein Leben und seine Werke*, Leipzig, 1910.

REMOND, F. de, *Sacrarum elegiarum deliciae*, Paris, 1648. BN: Yc.7992.

REUMANN, R., *Georges de Scudéry als Epiker*, Coburg, 1911.

REURE, C. O., *La Vie et les oeuvres d'Honoré d'Urfé*, Paris, 1910.

RICCIO, M., *De regibus Hispaniae, Hierusalem, Galliae, utriusque Siciliae et Vngariae historia*, Naples, 1645. BM: 596.e.31.

RICHTER, B., 'Ronsard and Belleforest on the origins of France', *Essays in history and literature presented to Stanley Pargellis*, ed. H. Bluhm, Chicago, 1965, pp. 65–80.

RIGAULT, H., *Histoire de la querelle des anciens et des modernes*, Paris, 1856.

ROUYER, J., 'De Pierre de Blarru et de son poème la *Nancéide* à propos d'un manuscrit de cette oeuvre appartenant au musée historique lorrain', *Mémoires de la société d'archéologie lorraine et du musée historique lorrain*, 3e série, 4 (1876), 360–420.
—— 'Nouvelles Recherches biographiques sur Pierre de Blarru', *Mém. soc. arch. lorraine*, 3e série, 11 (1883), 213–25.
—— 'Le testament de Pierre de Blarru ... suivi de quelques dernières observations sur ce qui a été écrit dans deux notices précédentes au sujet ou à l'occasion de cet ancien poète', *Mém. soc. arch. lorraine*, 3e série, 16 (1887), 173–5.

RUA, G., *L'Epopea savoina alla corte di Carlo Emmanuele I: La Savoysiade di Onorato d'Urfé*, Turin, 1893.

SAINT-AMANT, M.-A. de Gérard de, *Moyse sauvé*, Paris, A. Courbé, 1653. BN: Rés.Ye.648.

SAINTSBURY, G.. *A history of criticism and literary taste in Europe from the earliest texts to the present day*, 3 vols., Edinburgh–London, 1900–4.

SANNAZARO, J., *De partu virginis*, Naples, 1526. BM: G.10031.

SAUVAGE, D., see GILLES.

SAVARON, J., see GILLES.

SAYCE, R. A., 'A copy of Marolles' *Traité du poème épique* annoté par Richelet', *MLR*, (1947), 361–3.

—— *The French Biblical epic in the seventeenth century*, Oxford, 1955. Referred to as 'Sayce'.

—— 'L'Architecture dans l'*Alaric* de Scudéry,' *Mélanges d'histoire littéraire (XVIe–XVIIe siècle) offerts à Raymond Lebègue*, Paris, 1969, pp. 185–93.

SCHELANDRE, J. de, *Tyr et Sidon*, ed. J. Haraszti, Paris, 1908.

SEARLES, C. (ed.), *Catalogue de tous les livres de feu M. Chapelain*, Stanford, 1912.

SEBILLET, T., *Art poétique françoys*, ed. F. Gaiffe, Paris, 1910.

SECRET, F., *Les Kabbalistes chrétiens de la Renaissance*, Paris, 1964.

—— *L'Esotérisme de Guy Le Fèvre de la Boderie*, Geneva, 1969.

SEGRAIS, J.-R. de, *Athys, poème pastoral*, Paris, G. de Luynes, 1653. BN: Ye.1479.

SEZNEC, J., *La Survivance des dieux antiques. Essai sur le rôle de la tradition mythologique dans l'humanisme et dans l'art de la Renaissance*, London, 1940.

SILVER, I., 'Pierre de Ronsard: Panegyrist, Pensioner and Satirist of the French court', *Romanic Review*, 45 (1954), 89–108.

—— 'The birth of the modern French epic: Ronsard's independence of Jean Lemaire's Homeric historiography', *PMLA*, 70 (1955), 1118–32.

—— *Ronsard and the Hellenic Renaissance in France*: vol. 1, *Ronsard and the Greek epic*, Washington, 1961.

SIMLER, J., *De republica Helvetiorum libri duo*, Zurich, 1576. BM: 8073.bb.61.

—— *La République des Suisses*, s.l., 1577. BM: 1193.i.22.

SIMONE, F., *Il rinascimento francese*, Turin, 1961.

SIMPSON, J., *Le Tasse et la littérature et l'art baroques en France*, Paris, 1962.

SOMMERVOGEL, C., *Bibliothèque de la Compagnie de Jésus, nouvelle édition*, 12 vols., Brussels–Paris, 1890–1900.

SOUTHEY, R., *Joan of Arc*, London, 1806.

SPINGARN, J., *A history of literary criticism in the Renaissance*, New York, 1899.

STATIUS, *Silvae, Thebaid, Achilleid*, ed. and translated by J. Mozley, 2 vols., London, 1928 (Loeb).

STORER, W. H., *Virgil and Ronsard*, Paris, 1923.

TALLEMANT DES REAUX, G., *Historiettes*, ed. A. Adam, 2 vols., 1960–1 (Pléiade).

TASSO, T., *Gerusalemme liberata*, Casalmaggiore, 1581. BM.84.c.23.

—— *Opere*, ed. B. T. Sozzi, 2 vols., Turin, 1955–6 (UTET).

—— *Le lettere di T. Tasso*, ed. C. Guasti, 5 vols., Florence, 1852–5.

—— *Le prose diverse di T. Tasso*, ed. C. Guasti, 5 vols., Florence, 1875.

TCHEMERZINE, A., *Bibliographie d'éditions originales et rares d'auteurs français des XVe, XVIe, XVIIe et XVIIIe siècles*, 10 vols., Paris, 1927–33.

TILLEY, A., *Studies in the French Renaissance*, Cambridge, 1922.

TOINET, R., *Quelques Recherches autour des poèmes héroïques–épiques français du dix-septième siecle*, 2 vols., Tulle, 1899–1907.

TRITHEMIUS, J., *Compendium sive breviarium primi voluminis annalium sive historiarum de origine regum et gentis Francorum*, Mainz, 1515. BM: 183.c.1.

VALERIUS FLACCUS, *Argonautica*, ed. and translated by J. Mozley, London, 1934 (Loeb).

VAN TIEGHEM, P., *La Littérature latine de la Renaissance*, Paris, 1944.

VAUQUELIN DE LA FRESNAYE, J., *L'Art poétique*, ed. G. Pellissier, Paris, 1885.

VIDA, M., *Christiados libri sex*, Cremona, 1535. BN: Rés.m.Yc.716.

VILLON, F., *Oeuvres*, ed. L. Thuasne, 3 vols., Paris, 1923.

VIRGIL, *Opera*, ed. R. A. B. Mynors, Oxford, 1969.

VOLCYRE DE SEROUVILLE, N., *L'Histoire et recueil de la triumphante et glorieuse victoire contre les seduyctz et abusez Lutheriens*, Paris, 1526. BM: C.107.e.11.

VOLTAIRE, *La Henriade*, ed. O. Taylor, 2nd edition, Geneva, 1970.

WILLIAMS, R. C., 'Italian influence on Ronsard's theory of the epic', *MLN*, 35 (1920), 161–5.
—— 'Metrical form of the epic as discussed by sixteenth-century critics', *MLN*, 36 (1921), 449–57.
—— 'Two studies in epic theory: I Verisimilitude in the epic; II Plagiarism by Scudéry of Tasso's epic theory', *Modern Philology*, 22 (1924–5), 133–58.
—— *The Merveilleux in the epic*, Paris, 1925.

ZABUGHIN, V., *Vergilio nel Rinascimento italiano da Dante a Torquato Tasso*, 2 vols., Bologna, 1921–3.

INDEX

cision rule d_{ij} has the following properties:

re exists at least one non-empty winning coalition $C_{ij} \subseteq V_{ij}$ ($C_{ij} \neq \phi$) h that if for all $k \in C_{ij}$, $x_i P_k x_j$ is true, "society prefers" x_i to x_j, i.e., x_j.

$C_{ij} \subseteq V_{ij}$ and if $x_i P_g x_j$ for $g \in V_{ij} - C_{ij}$, and if the preferences of all er members of V_{ij} are unchanged, then $C'_{ij} \equiv C_{ij} \cup \{g\}$ is a winng coalition, too, such that $x_i P x_j$.

is obvious that there may be many winning coalitions C_{ij}, C'_{ij}, C''_{ij} or each pair of issues x_i, $x_j \in U$.

no winning coalition for x_i against x_j is present, because there are nough individuals $k \in V_{ij}$ for whom $x_i P_k x_j$ is true, then a blocking tion B_{ji}, for all of whose members $k \in B_{ji}$ $x_j R_k x_i$ holds, does exist. In case we will write for society, $x_j R x_i$. Again, usually several blocking tions $B_{ji}, B'_{ji}, B''_{ji}, \ldots$, exist. On the other hand, if a winning coali- C_{ij} exists, then no blocking coalition B_{ji} can be present. If neither nor $x_j P x_i$ are valid, i.e., if neither a winning coalition for x_i against r for x_j exists, society will be said to be "indifferent" between these omes, $x_i I x_j$. In this case, at least two blocking coalitions B_{ij} and B_{ji} . It is important to realize that, for each pair of outcomes, either tionship P or I must be present, since a V_{ij}, V_{ji}, B_{ij} or B_{ji} exist for any x_i and x_j. Moreover, we use D_{ij} to describe if either a winning or a king coalition for x_i against x_j exists. Note that either D_{ij} or D_{ji} must present, whatever the individual preferences of the members of V_{ij}. ce there may be several winning or blocking coalitions, there may everal $D_{ij}, D'_{ij}, D''_{ij}, \ldots$

inally, we shall denote by a *profile of preference orderings* for the m mbers of society an m-tuple of individual preference orderings, one each member. Obviously there are many such profiles, since indiuals can have quite a number of different preference orderings.

Let us mention that the above definitions allow all kinds of olichic and non-oligarchic decentralized institutional arrangements of iety, including the extremes of dictatorship, "pure liberalism," ere $V_{ij} = \{k_{ij}\}$ (for all $i, j = 1, 2, \ldots, n$; $i \neq j$), and $\bigcap_{\substack{i,j \\ i \neq j}} V_{ij} = \phi$, and

tal direct democracy," where all members of society together have e right to make all the decisions, i.e., $V_{ij} = V$ (for all $i, j = 1, 2, \ldots$, $i \neq j$), by using simple majority voting.

A GENERAL CONSTITUTIONAL POSSIBILITY THEOREM

PETER BERNHOLZ

I INTRODUCTION

The specter of Arrow's General Impossibility Theorem (Arrow, 1963) has haunted social scientists for about thirty years (Sen, 1970; Plott, 1967; McKelvey, 1976; Kramer, 1977; Mueller, 1979; Bernholz, 1980, 1982; Schwartz, 1981). The impossibility of aggregating individual preferences in non-dictatorial societies into a consistent social pattern seems still to disturb many people (Tullock, 1981; Koford, 1982) in spite of the many efforts to escape Arrow's results by weakening his rather plausible assumptions. The situation looks even worse since Sen's theorem about the impossibility of a Paretian Liberal (Sen, 1970) has been found to be valid for all non-oligarchical organizations of society (Bernholz, 1980). Indeed, intransitive or cyclical social preferences possibly containing non-Pareto-optimal outcomes side by side with others within the same cycle are certainly not appealing.

In this paper we propose to look at the consistency problem of non-oligarchic societies from a different perspective than that taken by Arrow and the authors interpreting and enlarging his work by weakening and changing one or the other of his assumptions. First, we are concerned with the possible assignments of the rights to decide among different pairs of outcomes and the decision rules used, i.e., with different organizational settings of non-oligarchic societies. The members of society decide within an institutional framework and this may result in mutually inconsistent decisions and in non-Pareto-optimal outcomes which have not been wanted by anybody. This is the meaning to us of expressions like "intransitive" or "cyclical social preferences" containing non-Pareto-optimal outcomes. The existence of a "social welfare function" or a "social preference ordering" would thus convey the idea that the decisions taken by the members of society lead to a consistent pattern and to Pareto-optimal outcomes, if individuals have complete, weak, and transitive preferences.

Second, Arrow and the literature starting from his theorem mostly take some non-oligarchic assignment of the rights to decide among pairs of outcomes and the decision rules applied explicitly or implicitly as given, and ask whether such an assignment allows, in the presence of certain plausible additional assumptions, a transitive social ordering to be generated for all or some configurations of the possible preference orderings of the members of society. The non-oligarchic assignment of decision rights is thus, in a sense, taken as a parameter, whereas the individual preference orderings are taken as variables. Of course, this does not preclude the validity of the theorems derived for the different parameter values, i.e., for different non-oligarchic assignments of decision rights.

I suggest that this way of looking at the problems of non-oligarchic societies has precluded the discovery of some important results, and that a modified approach may lead to a quite different evaluation of the relevance of the General Impossibility Theorem for such societies. This paper will not take individual preference orderings but, rather, the assignment of decision rights to different subsets of society as a variable, and then start from some configuration of individual preference orderings as a parameter. By proceeding in this fashion, we will be able to prove that there exists for any collection of preference orderings of the members of society some non-oligarchic allocation of decision rights to different subsets of society, implying

1) a transitive social preference ordering;
2) a Pareto-optimal outcome "preferred by society" to all other outcomes, including all other Pareto-optimal outcomes (if not all members of society are indifferent among all Pareto-optimal outcomes).

Result 2) allows, moreover, for any configuration of individual preferences an assignment of rights which lets society "prefer" any Pareto-optimal outcome to all other outcomes, and hence, is "superior" to all other Pareto-optimal outcomes.

Moreover, by taking this different approach, it can be shown that results 1) and 2) can be derived for some purely liberal assignments of rights but that there can be cases in which such an assignment is oligarchic. Results 1) and 2) do not hold, however, for total direct democracy, i.e., an organization of society in which all members have the

right to decide among all pairs of outcomes majority voting.

Some people may argue that these results a or not of much significance. Indeed, one may fe ing that there exists at least one non-oligarchic a any collection of individual preference ordering sitive social preferences. I am not sure, howeve is justified. First, no such constitution may exist all members of society on all pairs of outcomes. constitutions of this kind may be oligarchic. Fin this vein, Arrow's theorem would seem to be would have expected that *one and the same non-* (or assignment of rights to subsets of the membe imply intransitive social preference orderings for a preference orderings, e.g., for those in a medieval Western, or a traditional Islamic, society?

If we accept these judgments, then the results suggest two important questions: First—which se profiles of individual preference orderings allow w constitutions in the sense of excluding intransitivit erence orderings? (or better: which sets prevent the sistent decisions?) Second—which changes of which kind of constitutional reform? It is obvious th tant but difficult problems. But they cannot be dealt article.

II   NOTATION AND DEFINITIONS

We consider a set V of $m \geq 2$ individuals with weak, c and transitive preferences over a finite set U of $n \geq 3$ 1, 2, . . . , n). Further, define $U_1 \equiv U - \{x_1\}$, $U_2 \equiv U - \{$ $U - \{x_1, x_2, . . . , x_k\}$. Moreover, call U^P the set of Par comes in U and U_i^P the set of Pareto-optimal outcomes 3, . . . , n−1).

For each pair of outcomes $x_i, x_j \, \epsilon$ U let there exist a c V of one or more individuals who have the right to d to some non-stochastic decision rule d_{ij} among these x_i, x_j are treated as an unordered pair, we obviously ha all i,j. Note that only one deicsion rule is used to deci pair of outcomes. Otherwise, contradicting results migh

III   PROOF OF THE GENERAL POSSIBILITY THEOREM

We state now—

Theorem 1: For each possible profile of preference orderings of the members of society, there exists a non-oligarchic assignment of the rights to decide among all pairs of outcomes such that no intransitive or cyclical social preferences exist and that the only outcome to which no other outcome is preferred by society is Pareto-optimal.

The subsequent proof of the *Theorem* is arranged as follows. We assume any profile of preference orderings to be given and we show in the first part of the proof that all outcomes can be ordered transitively by society if the rights to decide among the different pairs of outcomes are assigned to adequate subsets V_{ij} of society. Consequently, a transitive preference ordering of society does exist.

In the second part of the proof it remains to be demonstrated that the assignment of rights chosen can be non-oligarchic.

We turn now to the first part of the proof. Consider the set U of all outcomes and select any Pareto-optimal outcome which may be called, without loss of generality, x_1. It is obvious from the definition of Pareto-optimality that at least one such outcome exists, since U is a finite set by assumption. Recall that, according to definition, x_i is Pareto-optimal if no x_j exists such that

$$x_j R_k x_i \text{ for all } k$$

and

$$x_j P_k x_i \text{ for at least one } k.$$

Let us next compare x_1 to any other outcome $x_i \, \varepsilon \, U$. Obviously, this outcome is either Pareto-optimal, too, or it is not. In the first case, if $x_i P_u x_1$ for some u, then $x_1 P_k x_i$ must be true for at least one k from the definition, with k, u ε V. If, however, $x_i P_u x_1$ is not true for any u ε V, then $x_1 I_k x_i$ must hold for all k ε V.

In the second case, x_i is not Pareto-optimal. Thus, $x_1 P_k x_i$ is valid for at least one k ε V.

It follows that in both cases there is at least one individual k ε V for whom $x_1 R_k x_i$ for all $x_i \, \varepsilon \, U$. Assign now the right to decide among x_1 and x_i to a set V_{1i} of one or more individuals k for whom this relationship holds. Then, $x_1 R x_i$ by assumption for all i and the corresponding V_{1i}.

Next select a Pareto-optimal outcome $x_2 \, \varepsilon \, U^p \cap U_1$, if such exists. Otherwise, take any outcome $x_2 \, \varepsilon \, U^p$, which is Pareto-optimal only in

U_1. Obviously, $x_1 R x_2$ with $V_{1i} = V_{12}$ according to the conclusion just derived. Proceeding, consider any other $x_i \, \varepsilon \, U_1$. Form V_{2i}, as before, to get $x_2 R x_i$ for all $i = 3, 4, \ldots, n$.

Repeat the last steps of the proof for U_2 to get $x_2 R x_3$ and $x_3 R x_i$ for all $x_i \, \varepsilon \, U_2$ ($i = 4, 5, \ldots, n$). Note that $x_3 \, \varepsilon \, U^P \cap U_1^P \cap U_2^P$ if such exists, or $x_3 \, \varepsilon \, U_1^P \cap U_2^P$ otherwise, and if there is such x_3, or $x_3 \, \varepsilon \, U_2^P$ if both these sets are empty.

Proceed similarly with x_4, x_5 etc., until $x_n \, \varepsilon \, U_{n-1} = \{x_n\}$ has been reached. Putting the results together we get

(1) $x_i R x_{i+g}$ for all $i = 1, 2, \ldots, n - 1$ and all $g = 1, 2, \ldots, n - i$.

More specifically, (1) implies

(1a) $x_1 R x_2 R x_3 R. \ldots . R x_{n-1} R x_n$.

Note that if some outcomes in set U are not Pareto-optimal, beginning, e.g., with x_{s+1}, then $V_{s,s+g}$ ($1 \leqq g \leqq n - s$) can be formed in a way to include only individuals k for whom $x_s P_k x_{s+g}$ is true, such that $x_s P x_{s+g}$ holds for society.

Let us next move to the second part of the proof to show that a transitive social preference ordering is consistent with a non-oligarchic assignment of rights to decide among the pairs of outcomes. We first define what it would mean if (1) were brought about by an oligarchy. Obviously an oligarchy is a minority of society able to decide between each pair of outcomes at least in such a way that no outcome results which is not wanted by that minority. More formally, (1) results from the decisions of an oligarchy if

(2)
$$\left| \begin{array}{c|c} n-1 & n-i \\ U & (\, U \, D_{i,i+g}) \\ i=1 & g=1 \end{array} \right| < \frac{m}{2}.$$

This definition can be justified as follows: The first part of the proof implied an assignment of rights to subsets of society in such a way that either a winning or a blocking coalition is present for x_i as against x_{i+g} ($i = 1, 2, \ldots, n - 1; g = 1, 2, \ldots, n - i$). For the rights were assigned in such a way that $x_i R_k x_{i+g}$ for all $k \, \varepsilon \, V_{i,i+g}$ and that $x_j P_k x_t$ for all $k \, \varepsilon \, V_{jt}$ ($j = 1, 2, \ldots, s; t = s + 1, s + 2, \ldots, n$). Recall that the latter relationships do hold only if there exist outcomes $x_{s+1}, x_{s+2}, \ldots, x_n$ which are not Pareto-optimal in U.

Now it follows from (2) that $|D_{i,i+g}| < \dfrac{m}{2}$ for all $i = 1, 2, \ldots, n - 1$
and $g = 1, 2, \ldots, n - i$. The decisions for society, between each pair
of outcomes x_i and x_{i+g} in favor of the first, can be blocked by minorities
which together again form a minority according to (2). Consequently
(1) and (1a) are determined by a minority, an oligarchy, at least in the
sense that this oligarchy can block any decision in favor of x_{i+g} as
against x_i for all pairs of outcomes.

It is obvious that this definition of an oligarchy is still rather weak if
a great number of outcomes exist. It would, e.g., not be an oligarchic
system if a minority should be able to block all decisions between all
pairs of outcomes except one. Still, it is rather difficult to think of a
more satisfactory definition. Should we speak of an oligarchy in case a
minority were able to block more than one-half or one-third of all pairs
of outcomes?

We are now able to prove that there exists a non-oligarchic assignment of rights with adequate decision rules such that a transitive social
preference ordering exists. Let us assume that (2) holds. Then two cases
are possible.

The first is given if there exists a $S_{i,i+g} \overset{c}{\subseteq} V$ for at least one i and g
($i = 1, 2, \ldots, n - 1$; $g = 1, 2, \ldots, n - i$), such that

$$x_i R_k x_{i+g} \text{ for all } k \; \varepsilon \; S_{i,i+g}$$

and $|S_{i,i+g}| \geq \dfrac{m}{2}$. If this is true, set $V_{i,i+g} = S_{i,i+g}$ for all these $S_{i,i+g}$
and select a decision rule for each of the corresponding pairs of out-
comes x_i and x_{i+g} such that no $|D_{i,i+g}| < \dfrac{m}{2}$ exists. As a consequence
(2) is no longer true, but (1) holds and is brought about by a non-oligarchic assignment of rights and an adequate selection of decision
rules.

The second case is present if no such $S_{i,i+g} \; c \; V$ exists. If this is true,
then there must be a $W_{i,i+g} \; c \; V$ for all i and g, such that

$$x_{i+g} P_k x_i \text{ for all } k \; \varepsilon \; W_{i,i+g}$$

and with $|W_{i,i+g}| > \dfrac{m}{2}$. But then we can first set $V_{i,i+1} = W_{i,i+1}$ for
all $i = 1, 2, \ldots, n - 1$, and get for any decision rule having the

required properties:

(3a) $$x_nPx_{n-1}P\ldots\ldots Px_2Px_1.$$

Second, note that

$$T_{ig} \equiv W_{i,i+1} \cap W_{i,i+g} \neq 0,$$

since $|W_{i,i+g}| > \dfrac{m}{2}$ for all $i = 1, 2, \ldots, n-1$ and all $g = 2, 3, \ldots,$ $n-i$. But this implies that for at least one $k_i \, \varepsilon \, T_{ig}$, $x_{i+1} \, P_{ki}x_i$ and $x_{i+g} \, P_{ki}x_i$ must be valid. Thus, set $V_{i,i+g} = T_{ig}$ for all i and g to get $x_{i+g} \, P \, x_i$ for society. From this and from (3a) we have

(3) $$x_{i+g}Px_i$$

for all $i = 1, 2, \ldots, n - 1$ and all $g = 1, 2, \ldots, n - i$. By construction, however, (2) does not hold, since for all $V_{i,i+1}$ we have $|V_{i,i+1}| > \dfrac{m}{2}$.

Again we get a transitive social preference ordering in both cases, but this time with no oligarchy present. It is important to realize that the second case can only happen if all outcomes are Pareto-optimal. Recall that $x_1, x_2, \ldots, x_s$ ($s \le n$) are Pareto-optimal (see the construction of the first part of the proof). Now assume that some x_{s+g} were not Pareto-optimal ($g = 1, 2, \ldots, n - s$). Then, there would exist some x_i ($i = 1, 2, \ldots, s$) such that

$$x_iR_kx_{s+g} \text{ for all k and}$$
$$x_iP_kx_{s+g} \text{ for at least one k.}$$

But this is impossible, for (3) implies that

$$x_{s+g}P_kx_i \text{ for at least one k.}$$

It follows that x_{s+g} must be Pareto-optimal.

Next, we state a corollary to *Theorem 1*—

Corollary 1: There exists an assignment of rights to decide among the pairs of outcomes to subsets of society such that society prefers any Pareto-optimal outcome to all other outcomes or is at least indifferent between this outcome and other Pareto-optimal outcomes. The latter can only be true if all members of society are indifferent between the respective pairs of Pareto-optimal outcomes.

The proof of *Corollary 1* follows directly from that of *Theorem 1*. First, we started from any Pareto-optimal outcome, so that each of the Pareto-optimal outcomes could be selected as x_1. Second, if there are one or more members of society k ε V for whom $x_1P_kx_i$, then V_{1i} can be formed out of one or more of these members such that $x_1P_kx_i$. But $x_1P_kx_i$ does not hold only in the case in which $x_1I_kx_i$ for all k ε V. This completes the proof.

Corollary 1 is important since it shows that the validity of (5) has not been bought by what may be considered to be an unfair distribution implied by x_1. For if not all members of society are indifferent among the Pareto-optimal outcomes, then such an outcome x_1 is consistent with *Theorem 1*, which seems to fulfill best some principle of equity.

Finally let us demonstrate the validity of—

Theorem 2: For any possible profile of individual preferences, there exists a purely liberal assignment of the rights to decide among all pairs of outcomes, such that no intransitive or cyclical social preferences exist and that the only outcome to which no other outcome is preferred is Pareto-optimal. The same does not hold, however, if the rights to decide among *all* pairs of outcomes are assigned to *all* members of society (total direct democracy) deciding with simple or qualified majorities.

Theorem 2 says that a liberal constitution can always be found which assigns the rights to decide among all different pairs of outcomes to two or more individuals, and which assures the existence of a transitive social preference order and a Pareto-optimal outcome to which no other Pareto-optimal outcome is preferred by society and which is preferred by society to all other outcomes. By contrast to liberalism, if all members of society have the right to decide among all pairs of outcomes by simple or qualified majorities (total direct democracy), then there are profiles of individual preference orderings for which no transitive social preference order exists and for which there may be non-Pareto-optimal outcomes "preferred by society" to Pareto-optimal outcomes. Together with *Theorem 1*, this does imply that these problems can in certain cases only be removed by decentralizing and thus, by restricting the right of the members of society to participate in all decisions.

The proof of *Theorem 2* is simple. In the argument employed in the proof of *Theorem 1* we have used the fact that there is always at least one individual k ε V for whom $x_iR_kx_{i+g}$ is valid, i = 1, 2, . . . , n − 1; g = 1, 2, . . . , n − i. Then we assigned the right to decide between x_i and x_{i+g} to just this individual or to some of these individuals.

We have thus proved that a transitive social preference ordering (1) can be brought about by limiting the $V_{i,i+g}$ to single individuals.

It is important to realize that we have used only the first part of the proof of *Theorem 1*, which suggests that oligarchy may be present. And indeed, it is quite possible that liberalism is combined with oligarchy as defined above. We can realize this at once if we consider, e.g., a situation with seven members of society and three outcomes, which allow the formation of three pairs of outcomes. Now assign the rights to decide among these pairs to three different individuals. As a consequence, these three people decide everything, whereas the remaining four have no right to participate in any decision. Thus, liberalism and oligarchy prevail at the same time.

The example suggests that it is the more probable that a non-oligarchic purely liberal assignment of decision rights fulfilling *Theorem 2* can be found, the greater the number of outcomes relative to the number of the members of society. With an increasing number of outcomes, it becomes more and more probable that the rights to decide among pairs of outcomes can be assigned to more and more different people such that they together form a majority of society. But then (2) is not fulfilled any longer.

We have just demonstrated that there exists always a liberal assignment of decision rights giving rise to a transitive social preference ordering. To complete the proof of *Theorem 2*, it has still to be shown that the same is not true for simple or qualified majorities of all members of society. But this can easily be done. Turning to the first part of the proof of *Theorem 1*, it is obvious that there may be no sequence of outcomes $x_1, x_2, x_3, . . . , x_n$ such that relationships like (1) and (1a) hold *and* that the required majorities for each pair of outcomes x_i and x_{i+g} exist. But then no reassignment of rights can help since total direct democracy requires that $V_{i,i+g} = V$ for all i = 1, 2, . . . , n − 1; g = 1, 2, . . . , n − i. Of course, with qualified majority voting the decision rule can be weakened until simple majority rule is reached. This would be sufficient to get the results of *Theorem 1*, if at least simple majorities existed, for whose members $x_iR_kx_{i+g}$ were true for all i and g. But if this is not the case then total direct democracy will not be able to solve the problem. The first example of Section Four describes such a case.

IV SOME EXAMPLES

A few examples may help one to grasp the intuitive meaning of the
theorems. Assume the simple case of a society with three members V
$= \{1, 2, 3\}$ which has to consider a set of four outcomes $U = \{x_1, x_2, x_3,$
$x_4\}$. The individuals have the following strong preference orderings:

Table 5.14

1	2	3
x_2	x_1	x_4
x_1	x_3	x_2
x_3	x_4	x_1
x_4	x_2	x_3

Assume first that $V_{ij} = V$ for all $i, j, = 1, 2, 3, 4; i \neq j$. Decisions are
made by simple majorities. Then the social preferences can be represented by Figure 5.14, in which an arrow pointing to one outcome
shows that this outcome is dominated by the outcome at which the
arrow begins. The winning coalitions C_{ij} are given next to the arrows.

One realizes at once that cyclical preferences are present. In fact,
there exist three cycles and all four outcomes are members of cycles,
even x_3, which is worse than x_1 for all members of society and thus,
not Pareto-optimal.

With all members having the right to participate in all decisions

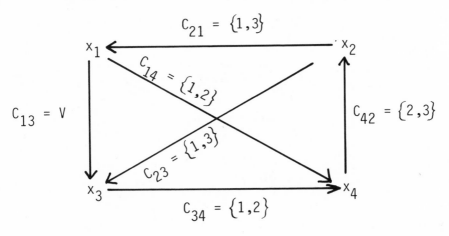

FIG. 5.14

these problems cannot be removed. But the situation changes at once when decision rights are restricted. Let us assume, e.g., that the right to decide between x_2 and x_4 is reassigned to individual 1: $V'_{24} = \{1\}$. Then x_2Px_4 holds, all cycles are removed, and Pareto-optimal outcome x_2 is preferred by society (see Figure 5.15) to all other outcomes. Obviously, these results correspond to *Theorems 1* and *2*.

Now, one could argue that x_2 is not a very good solution since it is the worst outcome for member 2. In our example x_1 is better in this respect. But this argument can be easily taken into account. For *Corollary 1* shows that *each* Pareto-optimal outcome can be brought about as socially preferred to all other outcomes by an adequate reassignment of rights, unless all members of society are indifferent between this and other Pareto-optimal outcomes. But this is not the case according to Table 5.14. Thus, distributional aspects or aspects of justice can be taken into consideration. In our example, let $V'_{12} = \{2\}$ and keep $V'_{24} = \{1\}$. Then, x_1 is the socially most preferred outcome, since x_1Px_2 holds. All social preference cycles are removed.

Let us now analyze an example with pure liberalism, taking again $V = \{1,2,3\}$ and the preferences of Table 5.14 as given. The assignment of rights by the constitution is now as follows: $V_{12} = \{2\}$, $V_{13} = \{3\}$, $V_{14} = \{3\}$, $V_{23} = \{3\}$, $V_{24} = \{1\}$ and $V_{34} = \{2\}$. The social preference relations are represented in Figure 5.16. The winning coalitions are now smaller since they comprise only the individual who has the right to make the decision among the respective pair of outcomes—e.g., $C_{13} = \{3\}$ and $C_{41} = \{3\}$. Again, the problems connected with social preferences with

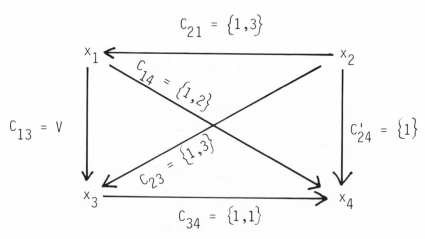

FIG. 5.15

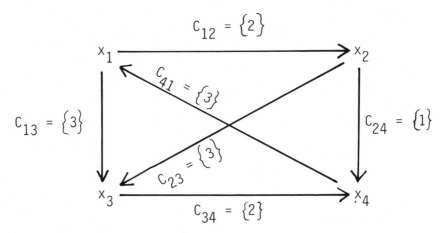

FIG. 5.16

no outcome socially preferred to all other outcomes, and of a non-Pareto-optimal outcome as a member of two cycles, can be solved by a reassignment of decision rights as asserted by *Theorem 1*. Interestingly, we can now do so by centralizing. Replace V_{14} in our last example by $V'_{14} = V$ with majority voting on the respective pair of outcomes and keep all other assignments and the liberal decision rules for the other pairs of outcomes as before. Then we get the social preference relations of Figure 5.17 in which the above problems have vanished.

But according to *Theorem 2*, there should also exist a liberal solution to the problems represented in Figure 5.16. This is in fact the case. Reassign the right to decide between x_1 and x_4 to 1 such that $V''_{14} = \{1\}$. Then $x_1 P x_4$ will hold, all cycles will be removed, and Pareto-optimal outcome x_1 will be socially preferred to all other outcomes. The social preference relations are the same as those in Figure 5.17, but now $C''_{14} = \{1\}$.

Finally, let us look at Sen's (1970) example for the impossibility of a Paretian liberal, in which mother and daughter are concerned with four possible outcomes—whether the daughter alone, x_3, the mother alone, x_2, or both, x_1, or neither daughter nor mother, x_4, read *Lady Chatterly's Lover*. The four outcomes are represented in Table 5.15. Sen neglects outcome x_1, but there is no reason not to include it here. In Table 5.16 the (strong) preference orderings of mother and daughter are given.

With liberalism, each of them has the right to decide whether to read *Lady Chatterly's Lover* or not (at least if the daughter is of age). Thus,

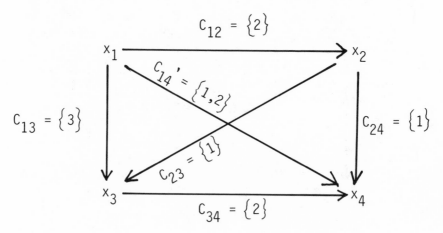

FIG. 5.17

$V_{13} = V_{24} = \{m\}$, $V_{12} = V_{34} = \{d\}$. Sen does not discuss the question of who has the right to decide between x_1 and x_4, and x_2 and x_3. It would, however, correspond to the spirit of liberalism if mother and daughter together had the right to make these decisions unanimously by concluding agreements concerning their reading or not reading the book. This implies that $V_{14} = V_{23} = \{m,d\}$ and the use of the unanimity rule. Such an assumption is, moreover, in tune with Sen's application of the Pareto principle. The resulting social preference relations are given in Figure 5.18.

Table 5.15

	Daughter	
Mother	Reads	Does not read
Reads	x_1	x_2
Does not read	x_3	x_4

Table 5.16

Mother	Daughter
x_4	x_1
x_2	x_2
x_3	x_3
x_1	x_4

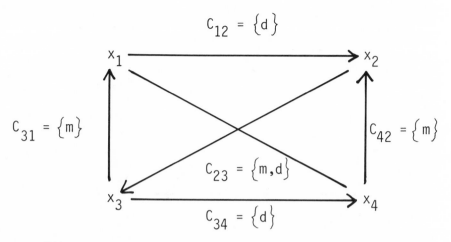

$$C_{12} = \{d\}$$

$$C_{31} = \{m\} \qquad C_{42} = \{m\}$$

$$C_{23} = \{m,d\}$$

$$C_{34} = \{d\}$$

FIG. 5.18

Obviously we have cyclical social preferences with cycles containing non-Pareto-optimal outcome x_3. No winning coalition exists for the decision between x_1 and x_4, $x_1 I x_4$. Sen presents the resulting situation as a contradiction between liberalism and the Pareto principle. For the mother would decide for x_4 as against x_2, and the daughter for x_3 as against x_4. But x_2 is Pareto-superior compared to the resulting outcome x_3 and Sen does not consider the possibility that liberalism could give individuals the right to conclude agreements. It seems, however, that this right is essential to liberalism.

If one accepts this position one would prefer to speak of the presence of cyclical social preferences with a cycle containing a non-Pareto-optimal social outcome, x_3, instead of a contradiction between liberalism and the Pareto-principle. Moreover, *Theorem 2* makes sure that these problems can be removed by reassigning decision rights within a liberal constitution. Let, e.g., $V'_{12} = V'_{34} = \{m\}$ and $V'_{13} = V'_{24} = \{d\}$. Then the social preference relations of Figure 5.19 result. Cyclical social preferences have been removed and a Pareto-optimal outcome, which is the second best outcome for both mother and daughter, will be selected by society within the framework of a liberal constitution.

V CONCLUSION

In this paper two theorems have been derived which seem to suggest a drastically changed judgment concerning the relevance of Arrow's

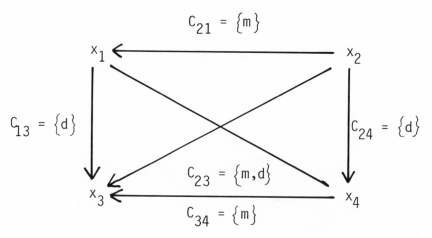

FIG. 5.19

General Impossibility Theorem and of Sen's generalized theorem that outcomes which are not Pareto-optimal may be present in the "social preference" cycles which are possible in all non-oligarchic societies.

Theorem 1 shows that a transitive social preference ordering can always be found for any given profile of individual preferences with a Pareto-optimal outcome most preferred by society, by designing a non-oligarchic constitution with an adequate assignment of decision rights to subsets of society. This means that after such an adequate constitution has once been reached, the problems brought forward by Arrow and Sen can only arise when the preferences of the present members of society change, or when old members leave and new members with different preferences enter it. In these cases, constitutional reforms may become necessary to get rid of the newly-created problems.

Theorem 2 demonstrates that the constitutional reforms necessary to solve the problems mentioned often cannot take place within the framework of a total direct democracy, whereas this is mostly possible with a purely liberal constitution. From this conclusion there seems to follow a certain presumption in favor of decentralized constitutions, not to speak of the greater freedom they offer their members.

If a liberal constitution provides for sanctions in cases of a breach of contracts, the change of the assignment of rights from one subset of society to another may even be brought about by free agreements among the members of society if they have the meta-right to depose of the rights they own and to acquire new ones from others. Such contracts would give all participants the chance to get the rights necessary to move to better outcomes. Moreover, all members of society could avail themselves of the possibility to reach a reassignment of rights more favorable to them. Consequently, abstracting from transaction and information costs a reassignment of rights, allowing Pareto-optimal outcomes to materialize, could perhaps be accomplished within a general liberal constitution which allowed the free transfer of rights and which would punish adequately the violation of contracts. In such a setting, a kind of permanent constitutional reform concerning the assignment of rights would take place within the general liberal constitution. As we have seen, however, a move towards an oligarchy would not be fully excluded under these conditions.

It is probable that these results correspond to a generalization of the Coase Theorem (Coase, 1960), since it has been shown that cyclical social preferences can only exist if negative externalities are present (Bernholz, 1982). But the free exchange of rights between the members of society could, of course, result in the selection of some Pareto-optimal outcome, which might not be too attractive, e.g., from a distributional point of view. Would not such an unfair distribution of wealth (and thus, income) and the danger of an oligarchy, strongly influencing the amount and value of rights individuals and groups could exchange, be a serious objection against the liberal society sketched above? This would indeed be the case if no provisions for redistribution of wealth were contained in the liberal constitution. But this is always possible, e.g., by an adequate hereditary clause in the constitution, which would bring about a quasi-automatic redistribution of property rights.

The results stated in this paper, like those of Arrow and Sen, do not take into account the problems of information and of transaction costs. They have thus to be interpreted with caution. Nothing seems to be more important at the moment for the further discussion of the merits and problems connected with different constitutional settings than to introduce these neglected problems into the analysis to find out how they influence the results derived so far.

NOTES

The author is grateful to Hans-Peter Bauer, Friedrich Breyer, James M. Buchanan and Malte Faber for critical remarks and for helpful suggestions in the preparation of this paper.

REFERENCES

Arrow, Kenneth J., *Social Choice and Individual Values,* New York (1963).

Bernholz, Peter, "A General Social Dilemma: Profitable Exchange and Intransitive Group Preferences," *Zeitschrift fur Nationalokonomie* Vol.40 (1–2), (1980).

———, "Externalities as a Necessary Condition for Cyclical Social Preferences," *Quarterly Journal of Economics* Vol. 47, No. 4 (November, 1982).

Coase, Ronald H., "The Problem of Social Cost," *Journal of Law and Economics* Vol. 3 (Oct., 1960).

Koford, Kenneth, "An Optimistic View of Rational Legislative Decision-Making," *Public Choice* Vol. 38 (1), (1982).

Kramer, Gerald, "On a Class of Equilibrium Conditions for Majority Rule," *Econometrica* (March, 1977).

McKelvey, R. D., "Intransitivities in Multi-dimensional Voting Models and Some Implications for Agenda Control," *Journal of Economic Theory* (1976).

Mueller, Dennis C., *Public Choice,* Cambridge Surveys of Economic Literature, Cambridge University Press: Cambridge, London, New York, Melbourne (1979).

Plott, Charles R., "The Notion of Equilibrium and Its Possibility under Majority Rule," *American Economic Review* (September, 1967).

Schwartz, Thomas, "The Universal-Instability Theorem," *Public Choice* Vol. 37 (3), (1981).

Sen, Amartya K., *Collective Choice and Social Welfare,* Holden-Day, San Francisco (1970).

———, "The Impossibility of a Paretian Liberal," *Journal of Political Economy* Vol. 78 (1970).

Tullock, Gordon, "Why So Much Stability?" *Public Choice* Vol. 37 (2), (1981).

NOTES ON CONTRIBUTORS

LOUIS De ALESSI has been Professor of Economics, University of Miami, Coral Gables, Florida, U.S.A., since 1976; economist, United States Department of State Foreign Aid Mission to the Republic of Korea, 1956–57; Fulbright Scholar, London School of Economics, 1959–60; Associate Professor, Duke University, 1961–68; Professor, George Washington University, 1968–76.

Selected Publications: "The Demand for Money: A Cross-Section Study of British Business Firms," *Economica* (August, 1966) 33:288–302; "The Economics of Property Rights: A Review of the Evidence," *Research in Law anā Economics* (1980) 2:147, "On the Nature and Consequence of Private and Public Enterprises," *Minnesota Law Review* (October, 1982) 67:201–19; "Property Rights, Transaction Costs, and X-Efficiency: An Essay in Economic Theory," *American Economic Review* (March, 1983) 73:64–81—about 60 papers in special journals.

PETER BERNHOLZ has been Professor of Economics (chair for economics with special reference to monetary theory and to public choice), at the University of Basle, Switzerland, since 1971, at the Techmische Universe-faet Berlin from 1966-71; Assistant Professor at the University of Frankfurt, 1962–1966; Rockefeller Fellowship 1963–64 spent at Harvard and Stanford Universities; 1969 Visiting Professor at the Massachusetts Institute of Technology. Since 1974 he has been a member of the Council of Advisors of the Minister of Economics of the Federal Republic of Germany; 1981 Guest Professor at Stanford University.

Among his publications are: *Mehrergiebigkeit längerer Produktionswege und Reine Kapitaltheorie* (Marburg Dissertation, 1955); *Aussenpolitik und Internationale Wirtschaftsbeziehungen* (Klostermann, Frankfurt 1966); *Grundlagen der Politischen Oekonomie*, 3 vols. (Siebeck, Tubingen, 1972–79). 2nd edition, 1 vol., 1984.; *Waehrungskrisen und Waehrungsordnung*, (Hoffmann & Campe, Hamburg 1974); *Flexible Exchange Rates in Historical Perspective* (Princeton Studies in International Finance No. 49, 1982); *The International Game of Power* (Mouton Publishers, 1985).

WALTER BLOCK is Senior Economist at the Fraser Institute in Vancouver, British Columbia, and Director of its Center for the Study of Economics and Religion. A member of the British Columbia Association of Professional Economists, the Canadian Economic Association, the Canadian Association for Business Economists, and an ex-university professor of economics, he has worked in various research capacities for the National Bureau of Economic Research, the Tax Foundation, and *Business Week* magazine.

Dr. Block has published numerous articles on economics. He is editor of The Fraser Institute books: *Zoning: Its Costs and Relevance* (1980), *Rent Control: Myths & Realities* (1981), *Discrimination, Affirmative Action and Equal Opportunity* (1982), *Taxation: An International Perspective* (1984), and is author of *Defending the Undefendable* (1976), *Amending the Combines Investigation Act* (1982), and *Focus on Economics and the Canadian Bishops* (1983).

HIROYUKI CHUMA is Assistant Professor of Economics, at Southern Illinois University at Carbondale.

JAMES S. COLEMAN has been Professor at the Department of Sociology, University of Chicago since 1973; Assistant Professor, University of Chicago, 1956–59; Associate Professor and Professor, Johns Hopkins University, 1959–73.

Among his publications are the following books: *The Adolescent Society* (1961), *Introduction to Mathematical Sociology* (1964), *Equality of Educational Opportunity* (with others) (1966), *Power and the Structure of Society* (1974), *Longitudinal Data Analysis* (1981), *The Asymmetric Society* (1982), *High School Achievement* (with others) (1982).

ISAAC EHRLICH is Melvin H. Baker Professor of American Enterprise and Professor of Economics at the State University of New York at Buffalo. Among his previous affiliations are the University of Chicago, 1970–78, and the National Bureau of Economic Research, where he was a Senior Research Associate.

He has published extensively in the area of the economics of crime and general applications of economic theory. Among his leading publications are: "Market-Insurance, Self-Insurance, and Self-Protection," *JPE* (1972); "The Deterrent Effect of Capital Punishment: A Question of Life and Death," *AER* (1975); "Asset Management, Allocation of Time, and Return to Saving," *Economic Journal* (1976); "On the Usefulness of Controlling Individuals: An Economic Analysis of Rehabilitation, Incapacitations and Deterrence," *AER* (1981); "The Derived Demand for Advertising: A Theoretical and Empirical Investigation," *AER* (1982); and *National Health Policy: What Role for Government* (Stanford: Hoover Press, 1980). He has served as a member of President Reagan's Health Policy Advisory Group and the Transition Team on Health Policy (1980–81) and is included in the first (short) as well as second edition of *Who Is Who in Economics: A Bibliographical Dictionary of Major Economists 1700–1980.*

MICHAEL T. GHISELIN is Professor of Biology and Research Fellow at the California Academy of Sciences in San Francisco. He is a marine evolutionary biologist with broad interests, including the history and philosophy of biology.

His books include *The Triumph of the Darwinian Method* and *The Economy of Nature and the Evolution of Sex.* After completing his doctoral studies at Stanford University, he held postdoctoral fellowships at Harvard University and at the Marine Biological Laboratory, Woods Hole. He has held faculty positions at the University of California at Berkeley and the University of Utah. He has been awarded a Guggenheim Fellowship, the Pfizer Prize of the History of Science Society, and a MacArthur Prize Fellowship. His current research deals mostly with systematic zoology and bioeconomics.

JOHN GRAY has been a Fellow of Jesus College, Oxford, since 1976. Educated at Exeter College, Oxford, where he received his B.A. (Hons.), M.A. and Ph.D. Lecturer in Political Thought in the Department of Government, University of Essex, 1973–76.

Among his publications are: *Mill on Liberty* (Routledge & Kegan Paul, London, 1983); *Hayek on Liberty* (Basil Blackwell, Oxford, 1984).

ANTHONY F. HEATH is a Fellow of Jesus College, Oxford, and Lecturer in Sociology at the University of Oxford.

His book (with J. K. Curtice and R. M. Jowell) *How Britain Votes* was published by Pergamon Press in 1985. It elaborates on the themes dealt with in this volume and compliments the results reported there. His previous publications include: *Rational Choice and Social Exchange* (Cambridge University Press, 1976), *Social Mobility* (Fontana, 1981) and with A. H. Halsey and J. M. Ridge *Origins and Destinations* (Oxford University Press, 1980).

JACK HIRSHLEIFER has been Professor of Economics in the University of California at Los Angeles since 1960. Harvard University, B.A. 1945, M.A. 1948, Ph.D. 1950; U.S. Naval Reserve (active duty), 1943–45; The Rand Corporation, 1949–55; University of Chicago, 1955–60.

His publications include: *Water Supply: Economics, Technology and Policy,* co-authors J. C. DeHaven and J. W. Milliman (University of Chicago Press, 1960); *Investment, Interest and Capital* (Prentice-Hall, Inc., 1970); *Price Theory and Applications* (Prentice-Hall, Inc., 1976; 3rd ed.

1984); "On the Theory of Optimal Investment Decision," *Journal of Political Economy.*, v. 66 (Aug., 1958); "On the Economics of Transfer Pricing," *Journal of Business.*, v. 29 (July, 1956); "The Private and Social Value of Information and the Reward to Inventive Activity," *American Economic Review.*, v. 61 (Sept., 1971); "Economics from a Biological Viewpoint," *Journal of Law & Economy*, v. 20 (April, 1977); "The Analytics of Uncertainty and Information: An Expository Survey," co-author J. G. Riley, *Journal of Economic Literature*, v. 17 (Dec., 1979); "Privacy: Its Origin, Function, and Future," *Journal of Legal Sudies*, v. 9 (Dec., 1980); "Evolutionary Models in Economics and Law: Cooperation versus Conflict Strategies," *Research in Economics and Law*, v. 4 (1982).

HENRY G. MANNE is Dean of the George Mason University School of Law, also founder and director of the GMU Law and Economics Center, Arlington, Virginia. He is a member of the American Bar Association, the Mont Pelerin Society, the American Economic Association, and the Administrative Conference of the United States. Also, Professor Manne is a patron of the Institut Economique de Paris.

He is the author or editor of nine books and over 100 articles. Some major publications are: *Insider Trading and the Stock Market* (The Free Press, New York, 1966); *Wall Street in Transition* (New York University Press, New York, 1974); "Mergers and the Market for Corporate Control" in *Journal of Political Economy* (1965); and "Our Two Corporation Systems: Law and Economics" in *Virginia Law Review* (1967).

ROGER E. MEINERS is Professor of Law and Economics and Director of the Policy Studies Center at Clemson University, Clemson, South Carolina. His Ph.D. in economics is from Virginia Polytechnic Institute and his J.D. (law) is from the University of Miami, where he was a John M. Olin Fellow. After receiving his degrees, Dr. Meiners was a member of the faculty at Texas A&M University, the Law and Economics Center at Emory University, and the Law and Economics Center at the University of Miami. Before moving to Clemson University, he was Director of the Atlanta Regional Office of the Federal Trade Commission.

Dr. Meiners has published several books and numerous articles that reflect his research interest in economic analysis and legal institutions. His major publications include: *The Legal Environment of Business* (1985); "The Contractual Alternatives to Patents" in *International Review of Law and Economics* (1981); and "On the Evaluation of Corporate Contributors" in *Public Choice* (1980).

GERARD RADNITZKY has been Professor of Philosophy of Science at the University of Trier, West Germany, since 1976; Associate Professor of Philosophy of Science at the University of Gothenburg, Sweden, 1968–72; Professor of Philosophy with special reference to philosophy of science and history of science at the Ruhr-Universität Bochum, West Germany, 1973–76; Visiting Professor at the State University of New York at Stony Brook, 1972; Fellow of the Japan Society for the Promotion of Science, 1978. He has been Premier Assesseur of the Académie Internationale de Philosophie des Sciences since 1982.

Among his publications are: *Contemporary Schools of Metascience* (New York: Humanities, 1968, enl. ed. from 1977 Chicago: Gateway Editions); *Preconceptions in Research* (London: Literary Services & Production, 1974); "Méthodologie poppérienne et recherche scientifique," *Archives de Philosophie* (Paris) 42:3–40, 295–325 (1979); "Justifying a Theory vs. Giving Good Reasons for Preferring a Theory," in Radnitzky, G., and G. Andersson (eds.), *The Structure and Development of Science, (Boston Studies in Philosophy of Science,* Vol. 59), Dordrecht: del, 1979, pp. 213–256; "Wertfreiheitsthese: Wissenschaft, Ethik und Politik" in Radnitzky, G., und G. Andersson (Hg.). *Voraussetzungen und Grenzen der Wissenschaft* (Tübingen: J.C.B. Mohr, 1981, pp. 47–126); "Science, Technology, and Political Responsibility," *Minerva* (London), 21:234–264 (1983); "Die ungeplante Gesellschaft," *Hamburger Jahrbuch für Wirtschafts- und Sozialpolitik* 29:9–33 (1984); *L'epistemoligía di Popper e la ricerca scientifica* (Rome: Borla, 1986); "In Defense of Self-applicable Critical Rationalism" in G. Radnitzky and W. W. Bartley, III (eds.), *Evolutionary epistemology, rationality, and the sociology of knowledge* (LaSalle, IL: Open Court 1986, chapter 14).

GORDON TULLOCK is Holbert R. Harris University Professor at the Center for the Study of Public Choice at George Mason University, Fairfax, VA (previously based at the Virginia Polytechnic Institute). He was originally trained in the law, then served for some time in the American Diplomatic Service as China Language Officer. Since 1958 he has been in academic life a professor in International Studies, Political Science, Economics, and most recently, Public Choice. He taught at the Universities of South Carolina, 1959–62, Virginia, 1962–67, and Rice, 1967–68. He is editor of *Public Choice*, and author of numerous works including *The Politics of Bureaucracy, Private Wants, Public Means, The Calculus of Consent* (with James Buchanan), *Logic of the Law*, and most recently, *The Economics of Income Redistribution*, and *The Economics of Wealth and Poverty*.

INDEX OF NAMES

INDEX OF SUBJECTS